Charles Gordelier

The Truth as it is in Jesus

Twenty-four Sermons doctrinal, experimental, and practical, on important and

interesting Subjects

Charles Gordelier

The Truth as it is in Jesus
Twenty-four Sermons doctrinal, experimental, and practical, on important and interesting Subjects

ISBN/EAN: 9783337160678

Printed in Europe, USA, Canada, Australia, Japan

Cover: Foto ©Lupo / pixelio.de

More available books at **www.hansebooks.com**

THE TRUTH AS IT IS IN JESUS.

TWENTY-FOUR SERMONS

DOCTRINAL, EXPERIMENTAL, AND PRACTICAL,

ON

IMPORTANT AND INTERESTING SUBJECTS.

BY

CHARLES GORDELIER.

LONDON:

JOHN GADSBY, GEORGE YARD, BOUVERIE ST., E.C.

1866.

Price 5s. Cloth: or 4s. in Parts, Stitched in Printed Wrappers.

PREFACE.

THESE Sermons were preached, during the course of seven years of my ministry in the City and the East of London, and are arranged chronologically. Their publication was commenced in the hope that, with the Lord's help and blessing, they might prove useful to some of Zion's children, "the living in Jerusalem;" and now being favoured with seeing the volume completed, I desire to dedicate it to those who love the truth as it is in Jesus, and know by heart-felt experience its life, light, and power. As a literary production, I am sensible it contains many defects, but I shall hope not to be made an offender for a word by those who read for spiritual profit. I cannot but express my devout gratitude and unfeigned thanks for the Lord's condescension in owning this feeble effort; for, judging from the numerous intimations which I have received from all parts of the country, during the issue of the work in Parts, the word thus sent forth has been much blessed in edifying, refreshing, and comforting many of his "hidden ones," particularly in congregations destitute of the ministry, and also to invalids, the aged, and others unable to reach the public sanctuary.

The reader will perceive that most of these sermons possess a decided doctrinal tone, as well as that they are experimentally treated. Modern taste, it is true, is quite averse to this old-fashioned mode of preaching; but doctrinal truth is essentially important to the believer in

Jesus; it is the food of living souls, and forms the basis of genuine experience; indeed the lack of it may be considered as the cause of so much of the ignorance, instability, and flimsiness we see in religious professors. I have, therefore, without attempting complete statements of theological topics, unreservedly declared those distinguishing truths which, in our day, are so little mentioned and so much despised. I have not shrunk from avowing my firm belief in the true and proper doctrine of our Lord's Eternal Sonship. I have also strenuously asserted the spiritual nature of real religion, and the necessity of a divine revelation for a true knowledge of Jesus Christ. And, believing that experience is the criterion of truth, I have aimed to set it forth as derived from my own exercises of thought and feeling; being convinced that if a minister of truth wishes to benefit the minds and hearts of others, he must be guided chiefly by that which he finds most beneficial to himself; and if in any measure I have been made useful in the church by means of these sermons, to God be all the praise. To extol the riches of his grace, to exalt Christ, to crown him Lord of all, and to build up believers in the faith, is my one aim and all my desire in attempting to serve the cause of Truth.

CHARLES GORDELIER.

LONDON, 13, STEPNEY GREEN,
October, 1866.

CONTENTS.

SERMON I.
God's Children fed by their Father's hand.   Ps. lxxxi. 10.

SERMON II.
The Believer's Mouth closed by falling into Sin.   Ps. li. 15.

SERMON III.
The Nest destroyed, but the Bird saved.   Deut. xxxii. 11–12.

SERMON IV.
Samson's History a Warning to Backsliders.   Judges xvi. 19–20.

SERMON V.
Jehovah's Throne the Believer's Sanctuary.   Jer. xvii. 12.

SERMON VI.
The Ministration of the Holy Spirit.   John xiv. 26.

SERMON VII.
David greatly distressed but divinely encouraged.   1 Sam. xxx. 6.

SERMON VIII.
The Divine Relationship between Christ and his Church.
John xx. 17.

SERMON IX.
The True Knowledge of Jesus Christ a Divine Revelation.
Matt. xvi. 17.

SERMON X.
Christ's Life the Fountain of the Believer's Life.   John xvi. 19.

SERMON XI.
The Substitutionary Work of the Son of God.   2 Cor. v. 21.

SERMON XII.
The Believer's Delight in the Law of God.   Rom. vii. 22.

SERMON XIII.
The Eternal Sonship of Christ asserted and defended. John v. 23.

SERMON XIV.
The Unsearchable Riches of Christ. 1. *His Person.* Eph. iii. 8.

SERMON XV.
The Unsearchable Riches of Christ. 2. *His Riches.* Eph. iii. 8.

SERMON XVI.
The Unsearchable Riches of Christ. 3. *Their Unsearchableness.*
Eph. iii. 8.

APPENDIX.—On the term " Eternal Generation."

SERMON XVII.
Jesus more Precious than the Golden Wedge of Ophir. Isa. xiii. 12.

SERMON XVIII.
The Kingdom of God entered through much Tribulation.
Acts xiv. 22.

SERMON XIX.
Finding the Pearl of Great Price. Matt. xiii. 46.

SERMON XX.
The Believer's Conflict with Indwelling Sin. Rom. vii. 18–21.

SERMON XXI.
The Appeal of Zelophehad's Five Daughters. Num. xxvii. 1-7.

SERMON XXII.
Jehovah's Power concealed in his Hand. Hab. iii. 4.

SERMON XXIII.
The Divine Engraving of Seven Eyes on One Stone. Zech. iii. 9.

SERMON XXIV.
The Truth as it is in Jesus. Eph. iv. 21.

TRACT.
Grace Triumphant. A Narrative.

ERRATA.

Sermon 18, page 16 of Part 5, in the heading, the date should be
September, not October.

Sermon 19, page 41, top line, read, before *men*.

Sermon 20, page 50, in the heading, the date should be the 17*th*
December.

GOD'S CHILDREN FED BY THEIR FATHER'S HAND.

A SERMON,

BY CHARLES GORDELIER,

PREACHED AT NEW BROAD STREET CHAPEL, LONDON,

On Lord's Day Afternoon, October 14th, 1860.

" Open thy mouth wide, and I will fill it."—Ps. lxxxi. 1.

WHEN a soul has been quickened by divine grace, born again of the Spirit, such an one feels the eyes of his understanding are enlightened,—he sees things in a new light. The Bible, which before was to him a sealed book, he now perceives to be a revelation of the mind of God towards him ; he finds there revealed the way in which a sinner may be saved ; how that God sent his only-begotten Son, Jesus Christ, into this world to take into personal union with himself our nature, in which he made an atonement to God's law and justice for our sins. He gave himself for us ; his sacrifice has been accepted. Sinners of every class and clime may now approach the Divine Majesty at the throne of grace through the exalted Mediator and Redeemer, Jesus Christ, and now mankind is everywhere called upon to repent and to believe the gospel. " He that believeth, and is baptized, shall be saved ;" and the promise is to those who, having been drawn by the Father, leave the world, and have come to Christ for life and salvation, that God will be a Father unto them, and they shall be the sons and daughters of the Lord God Almighty.

Sons and daughters ! What a high and holy privilege is this ; to be adopted into God's family ; to be called God's children ; to call God our Father ; to realise this great and glorious fact by faith in Christ. How unspeak-

No. 1.—Fourth Edition, Revised.

able its blessedness; how unspeakable the love of God whence it flows.

Now this adoption into God's family being ratified by the death of Jesus Christ, it follows that every blessing consequent thereon and connected therewith is everlastingly secured to all who are united to him by a true and living faith. "He that believeth on him hath everlasting life;" he shall never perish. He that believeth on Jesus, as the Scripture hath said, shall never thirst. He that cometh to Jesus as the Bread of Life shall never hunger.

> "The souls once sprinkled with his blood
> Possess a life that never dies."

Eternal life being thus assured to every believer, it follows that this life must be continuously supplied from the great fountain of life, Jesus Christ himself; he is the only fountain of spiritual life—only he who created life, and possesses it in himself, can impart it; he only can sustain it, he only can renew it when the soul is weak and fainting. This is a great fundamental truth in which every believer should be well grounded, and the inquiry is no less important: "Am I a believer in Christ? Am I a child of God? Do I know and do his will? Am I really living by faith on the Son of God? Am I trusting to his atonement for the free and full pardon of all my sins? Am I, day by day, depending upon him for all I need? Am I looking to his righteousness for the clothing of my naked soul?" If so, then the words of the text will help us to understand how this life in Christ, of which I have been speaking, is supplied and continued to the soul, I mean such who have fled to Christ as the only refuge set before them in the gospel—the glorious gospel of the grace of God.

You will perceive that the text and its connection refer to the chosen people of God, the Israelites of old; the Psalmist commences with a solemn exhortation to praise God and to solemnise the Passover. He then introduces God as speaking and expostulating with his people on account of their idolatry, and repeated departures from him as the fountain of living water; yet, notwithstanding, God treats them as a compassionate father,—treats them as hungry, starving children, who have wandered far and wide from him; they are invited to come to him, and he most lovingly calls upon them to look to him for all they want, and says, "Open thy mouth wide, and I will fill it."

The meaning of the text is undoubtedly spiritual, and can only be so understood by those who are spiritually discerned. The words are spoken to us as children, or rather as babes,—babes in Christ. If we are willing to look at ourselves as such, then, let us consider :

I. The exhortation.

II. The promise.

III. The means.

I. The exhortation: "Open thy mouth." The believer is here called to exercise his own faith, that faith which is of the operation of the Holy Ghost. This the believer must exercise, or his faith will neither grow nor be strengthened ; he must feel his own dependence upon God for the supply of all his needs. Like an infant, he must be fed—he cannot feed himself; he must open his mouth—his mental capacity; he must receive his life from the food supplied to him. As it is in nature, so it is in grace ; this the believer will do, because he feels his need. He feels hungry; no food can satisfy him but the living word; the divine life can only be maintained as imparted to him. He may have been filled with the world, its pleasures, its sins, but he has not been satisfied ; sin and the world have taken away his appetite; he has no relish for the gospel; he is growing weaker and fainter, but when he comes to himself he will say: " I will arise and go to my father ; in my father's house there is bread enough and to spare, why should I perish with hunger?" Ah, why? God calls to the poor soul, "Open thy mouth wide, and I will fill it. Come to your father as a hungry child ; I will fill your soul with the bread which cometh down from heaven, which, if a man eat, he will live for ever. Open, then, thy mouth wide, and I will fill it." My hearers, how is it with you? Are you perishing with hunger? Do you want the bread of life, the bread of heaven? Do you feel as a babe, utterly dependent, looking to Christ as your only and all-sufficient good? Do you indeed feel willing to receive food as a helpless infant —to have it supplied as babes are supplied, just when it pleases your heavenly Father, and with the measure he pleases? If so, O bless and praise God for such a condition of mind and heart. The world knows nothing of

this; only God's children hunger and thirst after righteousness. Blessed are they, for they shall be filled.

If, then, you are a babe in Christ, a child of God, you
know what it is to have tasted and handled of the good
word of life, you cannot receive any other; your language
is:

> " Wealth and honour I disdain;
> Earthly comforts, Lord, are vain;
> These can never satisfy;
> Give me Christ, or else I die."

No, poor soul, you desire to be fed with the sincere
milk of the word, that you may grow thereby. (1 Pet. ii.
2.) You want to thrive—to live on Christ, and to grow
in Christ. Open, then, your mouth—open it wide—let
your faith receive a full Christ; let it be an expanded
faith, so that Christ and all his fulness may be received
and enjoyed; so shall you live on Christ now and through
all eternity.

But further, did you ever notice a nest of young birds
—birds just fledged? How piteous and imploring they
look, all of them with open beaks, gasping for food; they
seem to say, "Feed us, feed us, we perish." These poor
birds can neither fly nor walk, they are totally helpless,
but they open their beaks, and open them wide too. See
how they gasp for the food the parent brings. Have you
not seen, too, many times, the infant gasping, as it were,
to receive the breast? Look at its little mouth, it is open
wide. So it is with the soul—it sees that none but Jesus
can do helpless sinners good. Are any of you gasping for
heavenly food, the sincere milk of the word? You shall
have it; Christ has promised to supply it: "The young
lions do lack and suffer hunger, but they that seek the
Lord shall not want any good thing. He will satisfy thy
mouth with good things, so that thy youth shall be renewed like the eagle's."

II. The promise:—" I will fill it." God is the promiser;
he undertakes to fill the soul. Yes, God who has quickened the soul will certainly keep it alive. None can keep
alive his own soul; this is what God himself undertakes,
it is God's work. He has engaged to supply the soul with
all its wants; he that began the good work of divine grace
in the soul will carry it on till the day of Jesus Christ.
"No good thing will he withhold from them who walk

uprightly"—those who are looking to him and depending on him; they shall be filled. These are Christ's own words; 'tis he who restores the fainting soul. If you faint through weariness in his ways, will he plead against you with his great power? No, he will put strength into you; he will fill your mouth with arguments; he will fill your mouth with the heavenly treasure of his word; he will refresh your spirit with suitable provision from his word, with those exceeding great and precious promises which he has so abundantly stored up for every time of need.

Are you troubled, greatly distressed, sunk in the depths of despondency and gloom? yet remember, God will not forsake you. You may not see his hand, still his hand shall supply your every need. What if you are not supplied day by day—from hand to mouth; it may be that God wills it otherwise. Think how Elijah was supplied; in the strength of one meal did he make a journey of six weeks. God knew what Elijah had to do, and so gave him strength for all that time from one single meal. Is anything too hard for the Lord? No. What is there that God cannot do for his people? He will time every blessing for them exactly as they may want it; and he will adapt them according to his infinite wisdom from that fulness which is in Christ Jesus. Yes, every hungry, gasping soul is supplied, not only according to its faith, but according to its actual need. Our heavenly Father takes care of all his children; none fall short of food, all are well provided for. The hungry soul has an open mouth—I mean, an open faith, an expectant faith, a waiting faith; it receives gladly the communications of grace; it lives and thrives upon the truth as it is in Jesus. "Bread of heaven," says the soul, "feed me now and evermore."

Again, God fills the open mouth of the soul with more discoveries of himself as the all-sufficient good; it feels and acknowledges every day:

> " In Christ my treasure's all contain'd;
> By him my feeble soul's sustain'd;
> From him I all things do receive;
> Through him my soul does daily live."

He makes the believer more acquainted with the realities of divine truth, the preciousness of the Redeemer, the sweetness of the promises, the unction of the Holy

Spirit; yea, he fills the hungry soul with good things, but the rich he sends empty away. He fills the seeking soul with all joy and peace in believing, that it may "abound in hope through the power of the Holy Ghost." He fills the soul with the "fruits of righteousness which are by Christ Jesus unto his glory and praise."

I have said God fills the believer's open mouth, (I mean the hungry desire, the hungry faith,) with the preciousness of the Redeemer. Yes, he that lives on Christ lives on a full Christ; with whom there is plenteous redemption; he feeds on Christ all through the way of his pilgrimage to the heavenly Canaan; he feeds on Christ as his Mediator, through whom he approaches his Father God at the throne of grace; his thoughts dwell in delight on this glorious fact; his heart abounds in joy and peace, as he realizes that the Lord Jesus is the Way to the Father, the Truth of the gospel, and the Life of his soul; his desire is to the remembrance of his name; his heart is full of love and adoration of the dear Redeemer; his mouth is filled with praise to him as the God-man, Christ Jesus; his mouth is filled with humble, earnest, and continuous prayer to him as the Christ who is over all, God blessed for evermore. He cannot live a day, no, not an hour, without an experimental knowledge of these great truths; he finds religion to be a reality—it is heart-work, and where there is no heart-work there is no open mouth to God; but the living soul is filled with Christ as the hope of glory. Christ is made unto him wisdom, and righteousness, and sanctification, and redemption. Thus the soul is filled with the preciousness of the Redeemer in all that can be known of his Person, work, and character; it is filled with the fulness of him who filleth all in all.

III. The means. I have spoken to you of what it is to open the mouth, and told you something of what is implied by God filling it; now we are to consider in what way God fills the mouth of him who is spiritually hungry.

1st. By the direct communication of his own Spirit. It is the Spirit that quickeneth; the flesh profiteth nothing. The soul is renewed by the Holy Ghost, is born again, it is a new creation. It is not only quickened, but is sustained by the immediate operations and influences of God the Holy Ghost. Its life is one, I may say, of heavenly inspiration; there is no real peace, consolation, holiness, or joy, with which the soul can be filled but what is the direct result of the Holy Spirit's work.

2nd. God fills the hungry open mouth of the seeking soul with heavenly food from the treasury of his own word —that blessed book which we call the Bible. This book is one of the great means by which God fills his people: "All thy people shall be taught of God." Taught by his word, which is their guide, their rule of life; it is the map of their journey through the wilderness; it is the great magazine of heavenly ammunition, from which they are furnished to fight the great enemy of souls; it is the great store-house of all the promises which God speaks to his people—and tells of the fulness which is in Christ. The Spirit takes of the things of Christ and applies them with unction and power to the soul. The word without the Spirit's application to the heart is but of small value; it may be of some use to the understanding, but if the understanding only is enlightened, the heart is left poor and dry; mere knowledge of God's word is comparatively of little use; we must have something more, we must have power; there must be influence:

" True religion's more than notion,
  Something must be known and felt."

Yes, God's word is only a means, a channel of communication; it is, nevertheless, a choice means; we cannot value it too highly, we cannot know enough of it, but we must look upon it only as a means by which God fills the mouth, the faith, of the believer. He that is hungry will not make too much of the means by which he is fed; he will prize it most highly, but he will rejoice more in the food by which he is fed, and most of all in God his Father, who giveth every good and perfect gift for him richly to enjoy.

3rd. Prayer is also one of the means by which the soul is filled. I said just now the Christian's life was one of inspiration, an infusion of heavenly power and life by which the soul is animated and sustained, a breathing in, a drawing in, of life by the very act. So, also, it is one of breathing out, the soul breathing out to God in prayer is the soul opening its mouth that God may fill it; the soul feels its need of mercy, it prays for it; God gives it. The soul wanders from God, mourns the loss of light, it feels the burden of guilt; it opens its mouth in prayer for restoring grace, it opens its mouth wide for the joy of his salvation to be restored, and it is done; "For as a father pitieth his children, so the Lord pitieth them that fear him." He meets with his returning children, he kills for them the fatted calf, he feeds them with his choicest meat. Prayer, then, becomes a means by which the soul is fed; it shows life within; it is the channel by which the soul receives renewing life from Christ, and he who is not much in prayer cannot be said to have much life; he only exists. Believer, God calls upon you to open your mouth wide; be then much in prayer. Surely, if believers felt their need, and knew how much God would bestow, they never would go on in that crawling life which we too often see. Why are they not more happy in Christ? Why are they not more useful for God? Because there is so little divine animation in them. They are alive and lively for themselves, for their own profit, for their own pleasure, for their own objects; but O, for God, how dull, how slow they are. If there be such an one present, pray for quickening grace; pray earnestly, pray always; open your mouth wide—God is waiting to fill it.

4th. Praise is also another means by which God fills the soul with divine life. He that is much in prayer will also be much in praise. Prayer brings every blessing from above, and the soul returns its praise for the good it receives. Not only so, the believer praises God for his loving-kindness and truth; for the majesty of his glory, his excellences of character and works. He praises God for the redemption provided in Christ, and is filled and strengthened in the contemplation of divine truth, to which praise to God leads the soul. Praising God is a means of divine life.

5th. The ministry of the word is another means which God employs to fill the soul. "That the soul be without knowledge is not good;" no, it would starve. As it is in the earthly life, so it is in the spiritual; we cannot all prepare the food we eat. So God has provided the ministry of his word, by which his children shall be fed. They are to be fed with knowledge and understanding—God's word; his truth is the material the servants of God are to use in dispensing the word of life; but they are only the means by which God fills the soul. Remember this, my hearers; look not for too much from the minister; look to Jesus Christ, expecting, through him, to be supplied. See, the hungry babe is not satisfied with the mere breast; it is the milk which it affords that it seeks; nothing short of that will satisfy its craving appetite. So is it with the child fed with a spoon; the spoon is used for conveying the food, it is true; but if the spoon were gold, it would be of no use to the child without the food; the instrument is nothing of itself. The soul wants food. Ministers are nothing in themselves but empty vessels. This they often feel, and perhaps you sometimes may have found it so in hearing; but blame not the instrument if you are not fed. Perhaps you are looking at the instrument instead of looking higher; look to Christ; pray for your minister, and you shall not be disappointed.

6th. Afflictions and trials are also means of grace to the soul—Hezekiah, David, Job to wit: "O Lord, by these things men live, and in all these things is the life of my spirit; so wilt thou recover me and make me to live." (Isa. xxxviii. 16.) See also Ps. lxxx. 5, where God is said "to feed his people with the bread of tears, and to give them tears to drink in great measure." Look, then, upon difficulties, trials, crosses, losses, poverty, bereavements, as a part of those means through which God will supply your spiritual life. You have been asking him to make you more acquainted with his salvation, to grow more in grace, to know more of Christ, of his love, and this is the method the Lord takes; it may be a rough way, but you will find it to be a right one; the oak thrives none the worse for being shaken with the storm, and you will not be shaken more than you are able to bear, nor longer than is needful for your good; indeed, we have often reason to say,

"Blest is the sorrow, kind the storm,
That drives us nearer home."

It is a good thing that the heart be established in grace, not with divers meats or fancies; afflictions and trials feed and establish the soul in the divine life far more truly, though not so pleasantly, than the sunshine of prosperity.

To conclude, what shall we say to these things? We have attempted to show you that God is a Father; that he has a family of children; that he supplies them with food. He calls them to him that they may be fed—to open their mouth wide and he will fill it. He is no niggardly Father; he is rich in mercy to all who call upon him in truth; he will make all grace to abound towards them in Christ Jesus; he will feed them with the finest of the wheat, and with honey out of the rock will he satisfy them. He is able to do exceeding above all we can ask or think; he is waiting to be gracious. His language is to all and each of his children, "Open thy mouth wide, and I will fill it." "Open it in prayer, open it for food, I will fill it with substance, the bread of God. You shall know more of me as your Father; you shall know more of Jesus Christ; you shall know more of my Spirit's influence; you shall be fat and flourishing in my courts; you shall live for ever in my presence, where there is fulness of joy, and at my right hand, where there are pleasures for evermore."

Now, let me ask myself, and each of you ask yourselves, Am I a child of God? Do I look upon myself as a babe in Christ; as dependent and waiting to be fed; content to be fed as an infant, with just such means as God may choose? Or am I looking too much to means, and not enough to Christ? O, remember, the best of means without the grace of the means, are poor barren things; a dry breast is of no use to an infant; no, nor yet an empty spoon to a child. O, for grace to look at things in their right light; means as only means. Ministers and ordinances are nothing of themselves, but Christ is all; he is all in all. Then let us look to Christ as the fountain-head of all supplies; let us come to his fulness just as we are, empty, hungry, and dependent. He invites us to come; he knows that without him we are starving. Let us, then, come to him just as we are, and open all our case before him, and say,

> " Just as I am, without one plea,
> Save that thy blood was shed for me,
> And that thou bid'st me come to thee,
> O Lamb of God, I come."

[This was the Author's second sermon in public; it was printed in the "Penny Pulpit" at the suggestion of a ministerial friend and the proprietor of that work, who were both present when it was preached. The Author has been credibly informed that this sermon and five others, preached at New Broad Street Chapel, and which appeared in the same publication, have been translated into the Welsh language, and have been read to congregations in the Principality.]

THE BELIEVER'S MOUTH CLOSED BY FALLING INTO SIN.

A SERMON,

BY CHARLES GORDELIER,

PREACHED AT NEW BROAD STREET CHAPEL, LONDON,

On Lord's Day Afternoon, November 11th, 1860.

" O Lord, open thou my lips, and my mouth shall show forth thy praise."—PSALM li. 15.

SOME of you may, perhaps, remember that on this day month I addressed you from the words of the 81st Psalm, 10th verse: " Open thy mouth wide, and I will fill it." I then endeavoured to explain that in calling upon his children to open their mouth wide, God called upon them to exercise and fully expand their faith in him, and receive thereby those blessings he was ready to bestow. This afternoon we have, on the other hand, the believer calling upon God to unfasten his lips, so that with an open mouth he might show forth the praises of God.

To praise God is certainly the duty, the privilege, and the happiness of the believer. Praising God is the blissful employment of all the inhabitants of heaven. Archangels, cherubim, and seraphim are for ever sounding his lofty praise; before him these mysterious, created beings are perpetually veiling their faces and saying, " Holy, holy, holy is the Lord God Almighty; heaven and earth are full of the majesty of thy glory." The spirits of just men made perfect by the righteousness of Christ, now before the throne, are for ever singing the high praises of him who hath redeemed them by his blood. Praise, too, is the business of the saints on earth; the people whom God hath formed for himself, they shall show forth his praise; " Praise waiteth for thee, O God, in Zion." To praise God is both the desire and the aim of all who have been called out of darkness into his marvellous light.

No. 2.—Fourth Edition, Revised.

But what is praise? This is important to know. We read, " All thy works praise thee." This is said by David himself, when speaking of the works of God. Again he says, " It is a good thing to give thanks unto the Lord, and to sing praises unto thy name, O Most High." " Both young men and maidens, old men and children, let them praise the name of the Lord, for his name alone is excellent." And again: " Whoso offereth praise glorifieth me." (Psalms l., xcii., and cxlviii.) Praise is a confession and acknowledgment of the wonderful excellences of God; it is a feeling of admiration in the heart, and gratefully expressing it by the tongue. Praising God is expressing admiration of his works in creation, in providence, and in the manifold operations of his grace in the hearts of his people. The contemplation of God's works, his truth, and his loving-kindness leads the devout soul to find his only happiness in singing to the honour of his name, and in making his praise glorious.

The psalmist, David, king of Israel, was one who well understood the subject of which we have been speaking; his psalms abound with expressions of praise in every conceivable form, and he is well called the sweet psalmist of Israel. How much he enjoyed and valued praise, may easily be known by reading the psalms in which he speaks of being deprived from attending the house of God, either by affliction, distance, or persecution. We know his heart; it was he who said, " I will praise the Lord at all times, his praise shall continually be in my mouth." But ah, poor David, it was not always so; he could not always praise. When his soul was in prison, a spiritual prison, his prayer was: " Bring my soul out of prison, that I may praise thy name;" and, if we are rightly informed as to the occasion of the psalm whence we have taken the text, we can easily perceive *why it is*, *how it is*, and *when it is* that a Christian man cannot praise God.

David appears in the psalm before us as an humble suppliant for that mercy which he had so disregarded and abused; he whose province it was to administer justice, and protect the innocent, forfeited all claim to his character as a man of honour and as a king over that nation who were chosen to be a holy nation, a peculiar people, the people which God had chosen for himself, of whom he said: " They shall show forth my praise," and in which

David, their king, was to take the lead. By the sad occasion, which is but too well known, David not only brought dishonour on himself and dishonour on the nation, but dishonour on the cause of God; not only so, he deeply wounded his own conscience; he lost the light of God's countenance; he wofully felt what an evil and bitter thing it was to depart from the living God; and now, "robed with sackcloth, and crowned with ashes," he entreats for mercy, laments the corruption of his nature, prays for pardoning and cleansing grace, and to be restored to former favour.

In the text before us we have a prayer that the lips may be opened, so that the mouth may be set at liberty; implying, of course, that the lips are closed. Sin, in the regenerate heart, is ever followed by guilt, sorrow, and shame; and if by penitence, with grief. Grief, especially when accompanied by remorse, shuts up the soul in the blackness of its own prison, and deprives it of the power of looking for divine aid. This the quickened soul feels to be a loss more than it can sustain; not to praise God! not able to look up! to feel itself weak, and yet not able to look to the strong for strength. Oh, sin! what hast thou done? Thou hast taken away my hope; my hope, my honour are laid low in the dust. I now no longer can speak the praises of him whose mercies and goodness have followed me all the days of my life. But, as if the soul had all at once come to itself, it resolves and says: " I will yet pray for pardon; I will pray to God as when I first sought his forgiving love; I will pray that he may remove his stroke from me, for, like Cain, I feel my punishment is greater than I can bear.

In the text there is to be observed what is called a metonomy of speech, *i.e.*, the effect is spoken of for the cause; the lips are asked to be opened, meaning the heart, the affections; the fact being, if the heart is open—free—the lips are so too; on the contrary, if the heart—the feelings—are shut up, so are the lips. David, in thus asking for the effect to be produced, and with the best aim, asks also for the cause—namely, his heart to be set at liberty; he has sinned, he wants pardon, peace, joy; and till he has this realised, there can be no song of praise from him. To praise God is his main object in asking for his lips to be unclosed; it has always been his delight; but now his mouth is closed, he feels a guilty man, and like a guilty man he has nothing to say. If ever his mouth is opened again, he feels God must do it; hence his prayer: "O Lord, open thou my lips, and my mouth shall show forth thy praise."

My impression is, from the peculiar language employed, that it is a figure of speech involving an allusion to a mode of punishment which was common in some countries, and most probably in Palestine, (see Ps. xxxix. 1, in the margin;) certainly it was well known in this country, though many years since. The instrument of punishment was called a "brank," literally a bridle or muzzle, made of iron, and employed for keeping closed the mouths of offenders against good morals, especially those who with their tongue had disgraced themselves and annoyed others. At all events, if the "brank" is not here alluded to, the effect in a spiritual point is the same, and I shall look at it in this light. God puts a "brank" upon all who offend against him, and until God removes it, the mouth is not at liberty. God means to punish, but he means to do the offender good notwithstanding; and when he is truly humbled, penitent, and returns with all his heart in earnest prayer, God will then remove the "brank."

Observe, then, I.—*That guilt is a "brank" on the mouth of God's people.*

This I am sure you will not deny; indeed, I am sure you will at once admit it. You know, and I know too, that when we have sinned, we have found it to take away the use of the tongue. Who can praise God with guilt on his conscience? Guilt empties out the heart of all good emotions and feelings. He can't love as he did before, he can't sing as he did before, he can't even pray. O, when a child of God sins, he makes himself a miserable being; he has shut himself out from enjoying the communications of God's favour, his loving-kindness! There is no communion now. Like as when one friend wrongs another, what a shutting up there is of intercourse with each other; there is no freedom of speech, no interchange of kind looks, no hearty greeting of the hand; so it is with the soul and God. It was so with the first man, Adam; before he sinned he was holy, happy, and enjoyed intercourse with God; he loved to hear his voice; and, at God's call, his willing feet ran to meet him in swift obedience; but when he transgressed, O how reversed the scene! God calls, but no answer: "Adam, where art thou?" No

answer. Again: "Adam, where art thou?" No answer. No, his mouth is stopped; Adam is brought
guilty before God; guilt was a "brank" upon his lips,
he could not speak, he had nothing to say, so he went
and hid himself. But was Adam the only man who has
hidden himself when God called to him? when he called
to him in love, called to him in mercy? O no; there are
some of you here, I doubt not, whom God has called and
called again, but you have not answered. You have
striven to hide yourselves; your mouth has been shut up!
Ah! it is sin that has done it. Sin has taken away the
use of your tongue.

It was sin, too, that closed the mouth of Zacharias;
not sin in its grossest form, as in David's case; nor yet in
the form of disobedience, as in Adam's; but it was the sin
of unbelief. He had no faith; he could not "take God at
his word," and so he was struck dumb for a season. O,
my friends, I am afraid there are too many of us who,
like him, have found no liberty for the tongue, because of
unbelief and doubt. Doubt and unbelief prevent many a
soul from praising God. Faith is like a lark—it rises
from the earth, and as it soars higher and higher, it sings
stronger and stronger; but unbelief—base, blind unbelief
—is like a mole, it runs from the light, burrows and
buries itself in the earth, knows nothing of praise, never
looks up. Unbelief never sung a song in its life. Unbelief, like a "brank," keeps the mouth closed.

But further, self-righteousness will keep a man's mouth
shut. Like the man who accepted the invitation to the
wedding, but did not accept the wedding garment, what
could he say for refusing it? Nothing; he was speech-
less; he knew the terms, but he refused to submit. Did
he think he should pass muster and not be noticed?
Vain man! He could talk to his fellow-guests freely
enough; but to the king who came in to see his guests
not a word could he say; the "brank" of guilt and shame
had closed his lips. O how many there are who get into
churches and chapels, and talk with their fellow-members
so as to pass for Christians, but before God have not a
word of praise to utter. They have never submitted to
the righteousness of Christ. They cannot put off the old
man with his deeds; or they think their own doings and
moral worth will save them; they prefer their own method to God's. Alas for them!

" Self-righteous souls on works rely,
And boast their moral dignity ;
But if I lisp a song of praise,
Each note shall echo, grace, free grace."

My hearer, let me ask you if you know anything of the
mouth being stopped before God on account of sin, guilt,
shame, unbelief, self-righteousness ? If you do, you know
something of David's experience ; shut up as in a prison
—put upon " the silent system"—not a word can you
speak ; not a word dare you speak ; but you can feel.
Well, blessed be God for that. Though not lively, yet
you are alive. You well remember, I dare say, when God
quickened your soul. He opened your eyes, your heart,
and your mouth too. But now your tongue is silent,
your mouth is padlocked, you cannot open it. Sin condemns, conscience accuses ; but though the soul is shut
up in the prison of his own guilt, he yet sees a glimmer
of light shining through the chink of his past experience ;
he mourns his lonely state ; he grieves, but he hopes, and
his petition is : " Bring my soul out of prison, that I may
praise thy name."

II. Let us observe, THAT THE RENEWED SOUL DE-
PLORES SIN IN ITSELF.

Nothing can be more sure than that David hated and
deplored the sin into which he fell, and which doubtless
was the melancholy occasion of this and other psalms
being written which bear his name. No man could appeal to the heart-searching God in the way David did if
he were not sincere. To doubt this, would be to take
away the value of testimony altogether. David sinned ;
David mourned ; David repented ; David prayed ; David
was reclaimed ; and, blessed be God, David again praised.
Now, to make a man feel the sinfulness of sin, it must be
obvious that he could not go on in a sinful course and be
in the enjoyment of God's presence at the same time. No
man has ever found it so, nor ever will. It is utterly impossible that it should be so in the very nature of things.
We are called from sin to holiness : " Be ye holy," saith
God, " for I am holy." God hates sin ; so should we. If
we love God, how can we love sin ? Christ hath no fellowship with Belial. Sin is an enemy to God and to the
soul of man. Then to make a man feel the hatefulness of
sin, he must be made to feel its bitterness, its awful consequences ; he must be made to feel that God is of pure

eyes; that he cannot look upon iniquity. But more than this, he must know something of God's character, of his love, of his mercy. If he has tasted something of God's grace, of the preciousness of Christ, and reflected on what his ransom cost the Saviour, he will then feel and know something of the hatefulness of sin. His language will be, not "O, what shall I suffer!" but, "O, what have I done!" Not so much dreading the consequences of sin, but shocked more because of having committed it against God and his own conscience; of having grieved the Spirit, and of its having put him out of the power to enjoy the presence of God till he has been rebuked, chastened, and punished. Neither can there be any restoration of peace, joy, freedom of spirit, or freedom of speech, till God has unlocked his lips, taken the " brank" off his lips; till then he cannot attempt to praise God. His ear must be reassured of God's loving-kindness, his heart must be set at happy liberty, for it is impossible for the regenerate man to speak *of* God, *for* God, or *to* God, if his conscience is upbraiding him. "O, sin," says the soul, "how it has destroyed me ; how it has withered my affections, blighted my hopes, clouded my sun, darkened my prospect! O, sin, thou hast taken away my evidences; I now hate thee with a perfect hatred. O, woe is me; if grace prevent not, I am undone. O, Lord, I am oppressed, undertake for me; I feel I am all wrong, but do thou put me right; my soul has gone astray like a lost sheep, yet will I not forget thy precepts."

III. My third observation is, GOD'S PRAISE MUST COME FROM THE HEART.

God receives nothing from the hypocrite, nor yet from the formalist. Dr. Watts thus expresses it:

> " Their lifted eyes salute the skies,
>   Their bending knees the ground;
> But God abhors the sacrifice
>   Where not the heart is found."

Nor does God receive praise from the thoughtless tongue. Many there are, it is to be feared, who take up the matter of singing the praises of God more to please themselves than to serve God; these persons seldom reflect on the subject they are singing, nor keep in view the Object of praise. It is the tune that occupies their thoughts; and often, it is to be feared, that if the tune is not one to their fancy they will not sing at all, plainly showing that to praise God is not their object, however much they may like psalmody. O, my friends—my young friends in particular—be not more occupied with the tune than with the theme; remember, God's praise must come from the *heart* as well as the tongue.

But let us observe, as it is " with the heart man believeth unto righteousness, and with the mouth confession is made before God," so "out of the abundance of the heart the mouth speaketh." When the heart is full of love to God the lips will be full of praise; if the heart indites good matter, the pen is as in the hands of a ready writer, and it can then speak of things concerning the King.

The truth is, the believer can only praise God with the heart when the heart is filled with joy; filled with joy in the Holy Ghost; filled with all joy and peace in believing; filled with a sense of pardoned sin; filled with gratitude for mercies bestowed, for favours received; filled with an assurance of divine love; filled with the manifestations of divine love; filled with bright views of the Saviour's glorious Person, his work, and character; filled with devotion and adoration in the contemplation of those rich truths which God reveals in his word, whereby his soul rejoices in the fulness of Christ, who is made unto him everything he can possibly want, both for this world and the next. He finds heavenly realities on earth; the very thought that God is his God, his Father, fills his soul with joy; to feel that Christ is his, that Christ died for him, that Christ is his mediator, his advocate, his intercessor; O, those things make him feel full of joy unbounded, unspeakable; it is, indeed, Christ in him the hope of glory. This it is that helps the soul to praise God. It will never be content with anything short of it; hence the prayer of the Psalmist: "O, Lord, open thou my lips, and my mouth shall show forth thy praise."

IV. Let me now observe, in the fourth and last place, THAT PRAYER IS GOD'S KEY TO UNLOCK THE HEART.

I have already explained to you how the heart of the regenerated soul is shut up by sin, unbelief, and so on; that when the heart is thus shut up, the lips are closed, and God cannot be praised. Not to praise God is like death to the renewed, heaven-born soul. This we have already shown. But, you see, *all* I have been putting before you is "*heart-work*." My hearers, TRUE RELIGION

IS ALL HEART WORK; without the heart, there is no religion that will do you or me any good; there is no praising God unless the heart is quite right with God. This
point has been already touched. You have seen the connection between praise and the state of the heart; how
the one is depending on the other. Now we have to
show you how the state of the heart is connected with
and depending on prayer.

Prayer, I have just said, is God's key; that is, it is the
key which God puts for the sinner's use; it is put into
the bosom of every child of God; it is ready, there, for
meeting every difficulty, every trouble, every trying case.
You remember Bunyan's pilgrim, "Hopeful;" how, with
his key of promise, he opened every gate in Giant
Despair's castle. That key Jacob possessed, and with it
opened up God's resources, and obtained what he wanted:
"And thou saidst, I will surely do thee good."

> " Prayer was appointed to convey
> The blessings God designs to give."

Prayer unlocks the heart. When the soul, feeling itself destitute, miserable, helpless, falls back upon God, it
prays for help; prays for grace; prays for strength;
prays for the light of his countenance; prays for the restoration of the joy of his salvation; and in doing so, the
soul gathers strength; faith is invigorated, hope is encouraged. Then the soul is enlivened; and, being thus
restored and enlivened, it is fitted for praise; it has a
feeling sense of God's light, love, and favour within, and
it must praise. It cannot help it, any more than children
can help expressing their joy when pleased and gratified
with their parents' love and gifts. Who has not found
the words of Cowper true?

> " Prayer makes the darken'd cloud withdraw,
> Prayer climbs the ladder Jacob saw;
> Gives exercise to faith and love,
> Brings every blessing from above."

Yes, the believer knows this is true. When faith and
love are in lively exercise, the heart is unlocked; when
the blessings from above have been received, then comes
praise from the heart. Prayer and praise are so closely
connected that whoever finds himself in the mood for
prayer, will soon find himself in the mood for praise.
Prayer is God's key to unlock the heart. Prayer unlocked the heart of Hannah. She sought the Lord, ob-

tained the blessing; and she, whose lips only moved in prayer, which was not heard by mortal ear, soon moved those lips, and with her mouth joyfully expressed her praise and thanksgiving loud enough for every one to hear; so joyful was it, that an inspired historian has recorded it for our comfort and instruction. Look at Zacharias, too, when his mouth was unclosed, how soon praise was uttered; and his song of praise is also recorded. So was it with the people of Israel. They said: "When the Lord turned again the captivity of Zion, we were like them that dream; then was our mouth filled with laughter, and our tongue with singing." Hezekiah, too, was, when restored to health, filled with praise. "The living, the living; he shall praise thee, as I do, this day." David, too, how often he spake the praises of God when his heart was set at happy liberty; in one instance, (see the 39th Psalm,) lest he should sin with his tongue, he resolves to put on the "brank" himself; but in doing so, he exceeded his good intentions. Still we see plainly the whole history of a Christian's case; when obliged to keep silent, how it affected David's heart, and what result followed? "I said, I will take heed to my ways, that I sin not with my tongue; I will keep my mouth with a bridle, while the wicked is before me. I was dumb with silence; I held my peace, even from good; and my sorrow was stirred. My heart was hot within me; while I was musing the fire burned; then spake I with my tongue."

You see, then, from all this, how much prayer has to do with praise. Need I tell you that what begins in prayer on earth ends in praise in heaven. Ah, Christian! think of this; prayer will lead you to praise. Prayer opens the heart; the heart is warmed; and a warm heart makes the silent tongue speak. O, Christian! cultivate the habit of prayer; avoid sin in every shape and form; be not faithless, but believing. If you feel, at any time, your affections chilled, the praises of God silent upon your tongue, remember David's resource, prayer: "O Lord! open thou my lips." Observe his vehemence and earnestness, as indicated in the very language of his prayer: "O Lord, open thou my lips. O take off this 'brank!' Let me speak freely of thy goodness; let me speak freely of thy love and mercy. It is sin that has closed and fastened my lips. I am the offender; but now, O Lord, all my desire is before thee, and my groaning is not hid from thee.

Hear my prayer, O Lord, and give ear to my cry; hold not thy peace at my tears."

Is this the language of any of you? If it is, be assured, then, God will soon remove the "brank." If sin has closed your mouth, and you have been before God as an humble penitent, he will soon open your lips; he will restore peace to you by speaking pardon to your soul; you shall be set at liberty, your tongue shall sing aloud of his righteousness all the day long, and your lips shall greatly rejoice when you sing praises unto him who hath redeemed your precious soul. You will sing praise to the Father for displaying such marvellous and sovereign love in adopting you into his family. You will sing praise to the Son for his unparalleled love in taking your place—suffering instead of you—that he might bring you near to God. You will sing praise to the Spirit for quickening you when dead in trespasses and in sin; for revealing his truth to you; for opening your understanding; for keeping you from the works and ways of the destroyer; and last, but not least, for restoring your soul when fainting in the way, or falling through temptation. May the Lord, in his rich mercy, lead you all to humble, earnest prayer, that he may open your lips to speak his praise.

> " And wilt thou in dead silence lie,
>   When Christ stands waiting for thy prayer?
> My soul, thou hast a Friend on high;
>   Arise, and try thine interest there.
>
> " If pain afflict, or wrongs oppress;
>   If cares distract, or fears dismay;
> If guilt deject, or sin distress,
>   The remedy's before thee—pray!
>
> " 'Tis prayer supports the soul that's weak,
>   Though thought be broken, language lame;
> Pray, if thou canst or canst not speak;
>   But pray with faith in Jesus' name."
>
>   HART.

THE NEST DESTROYED, BUT THE BIRD SAVED.

A SERMON,

BY CHARLES GORDELIER,

PREACHED AT NEW BROAD STREET CHAPEL, LONDON,

On Lord's Day Afternoon, May 12th, 1861.

"As an eagle stirreth up her nest, fluttereth over her young, spreadeth abroad her wings, taketh them, beareth them on her wings: so the Lord alone did lead him, and there was no strange god with him."—DEUT. xxxii. 11, 12.

THE Book of Deuteronomy is so called because it signifies *a second law*, or *the repetition of the law*. It is the last of the five books denominated the Pentateuch. It is a kind of manual of divine instruction, and contains a compendium of such laws as concerned the people generally, as to their civil, military, and religious government, omitting, for the most part, that which related to the priests and Levites. It contains, indeed, a commentary upon the moral law, and is enforced by the strongest and most persuasive exhortations to obedience. It was particularly adapted for the benefit of those who, being born in the wilderness, were not present at the first promulgation of the law. Moses, the great prophet of Israel, was the author of this book. He appears to have written it about a month before his decease. It contains the history of about forty-six days, and he sets forth in an animated manner the amazing wonders of God's love to Israel, as the sole cause of Jacob's seed inheriting the land of promise on which they were about to enter. With the present generation—for the former, with the exception of himself, Caleb, and Joshua, had all died in the wilderness—he entered into a new covenant, which

No. 3.—Fourth Edition, Unabridged.

not only included that previously made at Horeb, but which also renewed and ratified those assurances of spiritual blessings long before imparted to Abraham, to Isaac, and to Jacob; and he bade them commemorate their first entrance into Canaan by engraving upon a plaistered stone wall the precepts of God's holy law, which was to remain as a memorial of Jehovah's love, faithfulness, and power to his people.   I might just mention that the prophecies of Moses increase in number and in clearness towards the close of his writings; those respecting Christ are in this book more explicitly foretold than in the preceding books, and are described as the completion of the Jewish dispensation; and, previous to "the blessing wherewith Moses the man of God blessed the children of Israel before his death," he addressed them in a song which recapitulates their whole history and describes their entire character.   He states his object in the twenty-first verse of the preceding chapter; and in the chapter containing our text they are reminded that the Most High divided to the nations each their inheritance, and that he chose for his own portion Jacob as the lot of his inheritance. Moses then alludes to that point of Jacob's history where God first met with him as a wandering fugitive in the wilderness, near to Luz; how he led him about and instructed him, kept him as the pupil of his eye; and, in the text before us, how "as an eagle stirreth up her nest, fluttereth over her young, spreadeth abroad her wings, taketh them, beareth them on her wings, the Lord alone did lead him, and there was no strange god with him."   In the figure thus employed, the life and experience of Jacob is not only thus set forth, but also that of Israel as a people.   The figure was doubtless well understood by the Israelites; for, as we may suppose in that rocky and dreary region, the habits of the eagle and the eaglet had often been noticed, and especially as God had himself employed the same figure to Moses in the commencement of his journey: "Ye have seen how I bare you on eagle's wings, and brought you unto myself." (Exod. xix. 4.) God lifted up his people right out of the slavery of Egypt and brought them to serve him in the beauty of holiness, a free and independent people.

Just let me observe here, that the people Israel, though long held in bondage and though they had often sighed by reason of their hard bondage, yet they made no attempt to break their yoke; it was not till Moses came and stirred them up to seek their liberty that they attempted it. They would have lived and died slaves in Egypt, if God had not, in his rich mercy, and in the remembrance and the performance of his oath which he sware to Abraham, to Isaac, and to Jacob, sent them a deliverer. So is it with God's spiritual Israel now; and some of us can well remember how contented we were with the world, this spiritual Egypt. We made no attempt to leave it; we felt the hard service of sin, we found no real happiness, no real prosperity, no real gain to the soul. No, the longer we serve in the world the poorer we become. We make no effort for a better state of things; we make no complaints, yet we feel we have no ease. But when Moses is sent home to us, when God's holy law strikes the conscience, stirs us up, shows us our condition by nature in the sight of God, and to what blessedness God will bring us, then we awake to a deep sense of our slavery to sin, our slavery to the world and to the devil. We are then glad to escape from the bondage in which we were born; and the soul is at length led, under the guidance of the heaven-sent Moses, though by a rough and terrible passage, through the Red Sea of repentance, to leave the slavery of Egypt for the freedom of the Church of God in the wilderness.

The people of Israel, let it be observed, while in the wilderness, often rested in it; following the course of Providence, it is true, guided by the pillar of cloud by day and of fire by night, but, in either case, always in connection with the Tabernacle. Whether it was two days, a month, or a year, as the cloud moved, so they journeyed, according to the commandment of the Lord. Doubtless, they liked resting better than travelling; for, though travelling is an onward movement towards the end, yet is it labour and toil; and, such is the indolence of our nature, we are too apt to be taken up with the things about us, instead of forgetting the things that are behind and going forward. While the Israelites rested in the wilderness, and were well supplied and cared for, we hear no complaints; but when travelling, we then hear that " the souls of the people were much discouraged because of the way." Thus is it with us, while we are travelling in this time state. So long as we are not disturbed, we make no complaints, we are disposed to settle where we are and to rest in the things which the wilderness supplies; but God reminds us, that here we have no continuing city. He says to us, "Depart ye, depart ye; this is not your rest, it is polluted." He stirs us up, and bids us seek the better land. He who called us out of Egypt's darkness and misery to take possession of Canaan's fair and happy land, to serve him for ever, will never allow us to stop short in any intermediate state of this temporary life.

But, now, let us come to the figure employed in the text: "As an eagle stirreth up her nest, fluttereth over her young, spreadeth abroad her wings, taketh them, beareth them on her wings, so the Lord alone did lead him."

The eagle, as naturalists tell us, has a strong affection for her young. She displays it by courageously protecting them in a time of danger, her assiduous attention in finding them provision, and in her unwearied efforts in teaching them to fly. We are also told that as soon as the young ones are strong enough to fly and to provide for themselves, the old bird stirs up the nest, takes away the soft, comfortable, and warm inside, tears it to pieces with her claws, chases them from it, and will not permit them to return. Thus they are aroused from their sloth and inactivity, and made to exert their own strength by trying to use their own wings. Sometimes the old bird will take the young one on its back, and soar aloft, and then shake it off into the air; and if too weak to sustain itself, the old one will fly under it, and catch it on her wings to prevent the fall. Thus the eaglet is taught to fly. The nest is destroyed, but not the bird; to save the bird, the eagle destroys the nest, and the young eagle becomes fitted to provide for itself.

Now, in like manner are God's dealings with his people. God stirs up our nest, the place where we feel comfortably settled, the place where we feel most at home. Not only does he *stir up* our nest and take out the comfort of it, but he *breaks* it up, often destroys it altogether; makes us move out, his gracious design being to bring us nearer to himself; and he intends, by the discipline of his hand, that all our discomforts and trials, and the making away of those things to which we are too much attached, shall be the means of strengthening the wings of our faith, to elevate our affections to him, and to fit us for enjoying that rest which remains for all the people of God.

Let me illustrate this. First, when we are in the nest of this world, we have no desire to fly towards heaven. We are of the earth, earthy. God calls to us : "Depart ye, depart ye; this is not your rest." We heed not the call; our answer practically is, "Depart from us; we desire not the knowledge of thy ways." "We find satisfaction in this present world; we do not want to be disturbed." "Let us alone." "Art thou come to disturb us before the time?" Yes, blessed be God, he does disturb our rest in the world. If he disturb us not we shall be ruined. We shall perish in the nest if he destroy it not. And God does destroy it. He destroys our hope of finding happiness merely in the *pleasures* of this life. He destroys our expectation of finding pleasure in the ways of sin. He destroys our hope of finding satisfaction in any of the *things* of this life. He destroys our hope of ever finding peace with him from anything we can do, or anything we possess. He destroys all our vain hope in trusting to our own righteousness. We cling to our own notions as to how we may be saved from the wrath to come; but all our false notions and our refuges of lies, everything in which we trusted, is swept away, and the soul is left to try its faith *alone on Christ*. God teaches us the folly of our own fancies, to trust to him, to hang upon him. Salvation is to be found alone in Christ; there is no other name under heaven by which men can be saved. Till we are brought to this point God takes away everything that keeps us from himself.

Secondly, the believer in Jesus, while travelling in the wilderness of this world, is often disposed to and is apt to settle comfortably down in some of the circumstances in which a good and gracious Providence may be pleased to place him. Job is an instance of this. Outward things prospered, family blessings were numerous, he felt his personal influence was for good; he acknowledged that health and the bread of plenteousness were God's gifts, and he thought—ah, mistaken thought!—he thought he should never be disturbed. "I shall die in my nest." Ah, if he had lived there till he had died, he never would have soared to heaven with that heaven-taught flight of faith: "Behold, I have heard of thee by the hearing of the ear, but now mine eye seeth thee; wherefore I abhor myself, and repent in dust and ashes." What did Job lose by his nest being broken up! Nothing. What did

Satan gain by his hellish challenge? "Break up his nest," said he to God; "the bird will never fly towards thee; he is sure to break down." No, never! God's people may have their nests broken up—God means to break up their nests—but the birds shall be saved, they shall never break down.

Yes, God may sometimes allow the devil to break up our nest, as he did in Job's case, and he is delighted to do it. If he has a commission to break up any of our nests, depend upon it he will soon set about it. He will do it with all his heart, "his eye will not spare;" he will make us feel it, too. But God's eye is upon him; he has his instructions, which he dare not go beyond. He wants to ruin the bird if he can. He hoped to ruin Job, he was sure he should ruin David, and he thought to have ruined Peter; but, no! God only allowed him to ruin the nest. He takes care of the bird all the while. The nest, it is true, has been shaken, dreadfully shaken; is, in fact, broken up quite; but not the bird, that is saved. God does not mean that any of his eaglets should be always in the nest; they must learn to fly towards heaven; so he takes away one thing at a time, then another, one after another in succession; that which we so much loved, that in which we so much trusted, that which gave us so much pleasure, so much delight, so much comfort, so much ease—is all taken away!

But after all, what is a nest? Is it not in itself a mere collection of rubbish? nicely arranged, it is true, according to the instinct of birds, but to the mind of man it is seen to be but mere rubbish; a thing not worth caring for; a thing of no earthly use whatever, though to the poor young birds it is everything of comfort. Just so in the mind of God is this world and all its charms, in itself considered. To the Christian, when under the teachings of the Spirit of Truth, it is a mere collection of the veriest rubbish that can be found; it is so to the eye of faith, though to the eye of sense the world seems a very comfortable place. We are apt to think so, Job thought so. Worldlings are commonly very comfortable in their nests; "they have," as Asaph says, "more than heart could wish;" and if grace prevent not, they will live and die in their nest; and then, when the fire of God's wrath against sin comes, it will burn up their nest and themselves too.

There is one thing to be observed. In the destruction of the nest, not a single feather of the young bird is destroyed or lost. Think of this, you who may be sharply tried with the loss of your outward comforts. Not a gift or a grace of God's Spirit shall suffer by any of the dealings of his hand. Rather the wings of your faith and love shall be made strong thereby, and you yourselves enabled to fly better and more swiftly to heaven. Peter thought, when he was about to be shaken in the devil's sieve, that his faith would fail and he should be lost. "No," said his Saviour; "I have prayed for thee that thy faith fail not." Peter was a gainer by the shaking he received, for it fitted him to strengthen his brethren. Believer! the shaking of the nest, while it lasts, most truly, is not joyous, but grievous, but afterwards it produces a better state of things, a better state of the mind, a better state of the heart. See Paul's opinion in his Epistle to the Hebrews, xii. 11: "Now no chastening for the present seemeth to be joyous, but grievous; nevertheless it afterward yieldeth the peaceable fruit of righteousness unto them which are exercised thereby." Blessed discipline! Happy the man who can trace the health of his soul, the strengthening of his faith, the increase of his love, to the destruction of his nest—his worldly comforts, his worldly hopes, his worldly affections. God will secure the best interests of his people while he shakes their nest, but not a single essential feather shall be lost. As the great Physician of real value, he will destroy the disease, but save the patient.

Again, we are told the parent eagle takes the eaglet on its wings, lets it fall, makes it try its own power. It does indeed try the poor little creature; but the old bird catches it on the wing while falling, and saves it. So God, in like manner, with the believer. Sometimes he appears to have quite forsaken him. How alarmed is the poor soul in such a case! Hear what David said, "My God, my God, why hast thou forsaken me? why art thou so far from helping me, and from the words of my roaring?" "Be not far from me, O Lord, for trouble is near. O my strength, haste thee to help me." And God was near to help him, and joyfully he acknowledged it. (See Psa. xxii. 11.) Look, again, at Asaph, (Ps. lxxvii.,) when he was left to try his own wing. What does he say? "Will the Lord cast off for ever? and will he be favourable no more? Is his mercy clean gone for ever? doth his promise fail for evermore? Hath God forgotten to be gracious? hath he in anger shut up his tender mercies?" But, presently, God catches him underneath; then poor Asaph, finding his support, says, "This is my infirmity." He found he was mistaken in his opinions of God's dealings with him; and he, brethren, like us, made more mistakes than one. At another time, he tells us his feet were almost gone; he had well nigh slipped, he thought there was nothing better than the worldling's nest; but being lifted into the sanctuary, then he discovered his foolishness, and acknowledged his stupidity, and said to God, "Thou shalt guide me with thy counsel, and afterward receive me to glory."

Thus was it with king Hezekiah, when his nest was disturbed. Indeed, Sennacherib, the king of Assyria, threatened to take it all away; but he only disturbed poor Hezekiah's imagination, for God put a hook in that proud man's nose, and sent him unexpectedly back. Many of God's people have their comforts threatened; but let them, like Hezekiah, spread their case before the Lord, and if it be that an enemy has done it, God will soon take up the matter for them, and settle it in their favour.

But though at first it was only Hezekiah's imagination that was really disturbed, yet we see that his excessive fear brought upon him a severe fit of sickness; it brought him almost to death's door. His nest *was* disturbed, though in another way; he was brought into deep affliction, and to try the strength of his own wing. How soon he felt his weakness; how soon he felt his life consisted not in the abundance of what he possessed; what a sudden disruption there seemed of all his happiness, his power, and glory! How easily God can disturb our nest, and show us the vanity of everything in this world! Rank, wealth, honour, sink into nothing the moment God puts his finger upon them. Our troubles form a grave in which most of our comforts are soon buried out of sight.

We see, too, what piteous complaints Hezekiah utters when left to try his own wing: he thought he should drop quite to the ground. "I said, I shall go to the gates of the grave; I shall not see the Lord, even the Lord, in the land of the living; from day even to night wilt thou make an end of me; mine eyes fail with looking upward. O Lord, I am oppressed; undertake for me." Then, when God caught him up, and he felt again the safety of being borne upon eagle's wings, how he changed his song and tune! "O Lord," says he, "by these things men live, and in all these things is the life of my spirit; so wilt thou recover me and make me to live. The living, the living, he shall praise thee as I do this day: the father to the children shall make known thy truth." (Isa. xxxviii.) Thus the Lord teaches his people to make observations in their experience; it is in the school of adversity, he teaches them their most valuable lessons, and instructs them in the most weighty truths of the gospel; they are taught more through the medium of troubles and trials than of comfort or prosperity; indeed, as Mr. Serle truly says, "God's people are seldom trusted with much prosperity; and, when they are, it very rarely appears for their good."

Poor Hezekiah, how many of God's dear people have been like him; thrown out of long-continued comforts and left to find new resources, they find no immediate answer to prayer; broken with breach upon breach, and their way hid from the Lord, apparently cast away from his presence; but says God, "for a small moment have I forsaken thee, but with great mercies will I gather thee. In a little wrath I hid my face from thee for a moment; but with everlasting kindness will I have mercy on thee, saith the Lord thy Redeemer." (Isa. liv. 7, 8.)

Nor must we pass by the case of poor Jacob; in fact, his history belongs to our text. How his nest was stirred up again and again through all his pilgrimage of life! First, he was unhomed through his mother's deceit and his own falsehood. My friends, let us take care that our difficulties and troubles do not arise from our own making. Doubtless poor Jacob, as we all do, felt leaving his parents' comfortable nest. Many young persons' first trouble is in leaving their parents' roof; but they shall not be left alone; for they shall find, when they commit their way to him whose wisdom cannot err, whose love never fails, and who is the disposer of all things, that he will be sure to provide for them and fit them for going through life.

Jacob, you remember, on his awaking from his dream of the ladder to heaven, vowed a vow, that if God would be with him and bring him again to his father's house, the Lord should be his God, and the stone that he had anointed should be God's house; meaning that there he would come to reside and worship God. Twenty years rolled on. The nest in which he had settled was made uncomfortable by his uncle; he departed, and God brought him in peace and safety to his fatherland. What was Jacob's duty, then? Clearly, I think, to have settled at the place where he vowed; but no, he went to Succoth, and there built a house for himself and booths for his cattle. Did he stay there? No; he then went to Salem, then to Shechem, bought land, and dwelt there. There he erected an altar to God, the God of Israel. In thus erecting an altar to God, where he had pitched his tent, he was right; but in going there to reside he was wrong, because Bethel was the place where he vowed should be his dwelling, and where he would worship God. Jacob seemed to have neglected and forgotten that vow; but God had not. Again, he was wrong in purchasing the land where he dwelt. God had expressly *given* him the land, and Bethel in particular. He needed not, therefore, to have purchased what was previously his own, both by gift and by inheritance; but so it is, when we forget God and our religious obligations, we make strange mistakes, and get into very sad troubles. Poor Jacob's nest at Shechem was soon stirred up by family troubles, and he was forced to leave his little freehold for his life and go to Bethel at last. But, strange to say, even at Bethel he did not remain long. There he lost his dear Rachel. Again he journeyed farther still from Bethel, and another trouble befel him in the matter of Reuben. Thus it has ever been; those who have once connected themselves with God's house find no peace or safety in wandering from it; the farther they go, the more frequently is their nest stirred up.

Neither was Jacob without his troubles when he had settled down in the place of his purchased birthright. There Joseph was stolen and sold by his brethren. This was a sore trial to lose that dear boy. 'Tis true he had twelve sons, but this one he could not spare. How often it is we are called to give up that which we cherish most! And how often it happens that God's stroke falls heaviest upon the part which can least bear it! This is our view of the case; but God knows what is right. "He stayeth his rough wind in the day of his east wind." Poor Jacob never forgot the loss of dear Joseph; and there are some of our troubles that seem to make an indelible impression upon us—we carry, as it were, the mark to our grave. We see, too, Jacob's nest was again stirred up when he had to part with Simeon. Then Benjamin also. Oh, what resistance; oh, what clinging to the nest; not a twig will he give up; he holds on tightly. He says, "All these things are against me; I shall go to the grave in sorrow." Ah, he little thought that the taking away of his darling Benjamin was to be the means of bringing him to his dear Joseph. It was God who routed the good man's nest, took him and bore him up above all his trials, as on eagle's wings; so the Lord alone did lead him. And now he says to Joseph, "I had not thought to see thy face; and lo, God hath showed me also thy seed." Yes, God gave him more than he took away. He takes away our earthly nest, our perishable nest; and gives us in place an "incorruptible crown, and an inheritance undefiled and which fadeth not away."

Brethren, if these are our views of God's dealings, and of the blessed results of his teaching, why then are we so slow to take the consolations of his grace? Why do we grieve at being called to give up any of the comforts we possess? Is it not because we are too much absorbed in the things of earth? We profess to be pilgrims, "strangers in the earth, as all our fathers were;" and yet we seem to be forgetting our high calling, forgetting the end we should have in view. Instead of travelling through the wilderness, we seem to be wanderers and loiterers in it, leading, as it were, a sort of gipsy life. Brethren, let us remember this world is only for our use *pro tem.*—for the time being; our life in this world is a life of passing on, a passing through it, not remaining in it. No permanent rest is allowed for God's people in the wilderness of this world. None are suffered to make for themselves a nest out of any of the rubbish, the perishable rubbish of the things of time. If they attempt it, they will be sure to be stirred up, and the comfort taken out of it, whatever it may be.

In the figure employed in our text, and from the remarks already made, and the illustrations adduced, we see how God teaches his people to fly towards heaven. He tries the strength of our faith. He proves to us our weakness. He shows to us our worldliness. And if his method of dealing seems to be rough, he is gentle and kind notwithstanding. 'His loving-kindnesses are ever towards us. We may be sometimes alarmed, but we shall never be really damaged. We may lose much that we loved, but we shall love him more purely. We may lose the perishable rubbish we so fondly cherished, but we shall not lose him. No, never.

> "What if our dearest comforts fall
> Before his sovereign will;
> He never takes away our all';
> Himself he gives us still."

So when God seems to leave us, as it were, to find our own way, to exercise our own wing, it is not to hurt us, neither to alarm us. God means his eaglets to fly above ground, to exercise their wings for heavenly use; he is near to us, really nearer to us when we seem most forsaken by him. Oh, how great is the difficulty of parting with the world and the things in it! It is no easy matter to part with right eyes, with right hands; it is no easy matter, without divine support, to bear the loss of property, the loss of income; it is no easy matter to give up beloved relatives or friends, an affectionate son or daughter, one's husband, or one's wife. They seem parts of ourselves, parts of our very existence. The world without them seems a blank, without its charms:

> "The fondness of a creature's love,
> How strong it strikes the sense;
> Thither the warm affections move,
> Nor can we call them thence."

The fact is, our hearts are too full of this world, our nature loves it; thus it is we find it so hard to part with it. Like foolish children who have eaten to repletion, and yet will not desist until they are nearly choked; so are we often nearly choked with the cares of life. We are unable to breathe freely in the atmosphere which God designs for us to live in; but the Lord will carry on his own work notwithstanding; he will strip us of everything that obstructs his own glory. His plan is that we shall live by faith; our plan is to live by sense, and thus, by reversing God's method, we make our own crook in the lot, and give ourselves the wounds we feel. Yet, even our own follies God will make subservient to his glory and our real good. He will make the world a complete cross to us; he will make it strike daggers to our very souls, to keep us from clinging to it; he will make it a sharp, piercing spur, to drive us nearer and faster to himself. Now, if we find the world a cross to us, it will never hurt us; if it wound us ever so deeply, our wounds shall be our health. Indeed, whatever it is that we find brings us nearer to God, and lays us low at his feet, cannot but be a blessing in itself; it may have the name of adversity, a cross, trial, stripping providence, and I know not what else beside, but these are nothing but ill names which we, in our ignorance and perversity of temper, give to what God is pleased to do, in his infinite love, wisdom, and mercy, for our soul's eternal good. We have contracted a false opinion of the world, and a false love to it and the things of it; yet at times desiring to be not of it, but to rise above it, and yet loth to give it up. Strange inconsistency; one part of us clinging to earth, the other part attempting to soar towards heaven. We feel we cannot rise above the earth. Like a bird with clipped wings, or with a clog fastened to its feet, it cannot fly or rise above the earth; so our souls are kept down by the things of time and sense. We vainly strive to free ourselves; we feel it is the world that binds us to it, and keeps us from rising higher. We dread the process that is taken to free us from our chains. We dread the stroke that is to set us at liberty; but it must be done. God will do it, and effectually too. Our sharpest sorrow shall yield us sweetest comfort; and invariably we find our greatest blessings are connected with our greatest troubles, and so God makes use of them to bring us nearer to himself. How true are the words of Dr. Young:

> " Our hearts are fasten'd to this world
> By strong and endless ties;
> And every sorrow cuts a string,
> And urges us to rise."

Let us now, in conclusion, make a few practical observations arising from what we have been considering.

1. *God's fatherly affection* which he displays towards each and all his dear children. "Like as a father pitieth his children, so the Lord pitieth them that fear him." He sympathises with them in all their wants, pities their weaknesses; "he knoweth our frame, he remembereth that we are dust." His love and affection are constant; his care is all-sufficient. Let us, then, cast all our care upon him, for he careth for us; and he hath promised he will never leave us nor forsake us. (Ps. ciii.; 1 Pet. v. 7; Heb. xiii. 5.)

2. *God's fatherly discipline* which he exercises over his children. The discipline of God's hand may seem to be severe, sometimes rough and sharp; but we must not estimate the character of his dealings by our feelings, wishes, and wills. We are apt to measure God's method by our own fleshly notions; but the Lord will sift us from all our chaffy thoughts, that we may know only the power of his truth and goodness in his providential dispensations towards us. We must be careful to not to misrepresent God's hand towards us, nor to misunderstand God's object in correcting us. The trials and afflictive dispensations which he sends are for our present and eternal benefit; "all things work together for good to them who love God and are called according to his purpose." He chastens us for our profit. He means us to see the vanity of all things beneath himself, and to bring us to a state of heart and mind which shall lead us to feel that no part of this world is to be our rest. "It is polluted."

3. *God's gracious teachings.* Like as the eagle fluttereth over her young, and spreadeth abroad her wings, so God, in like manner, by various methods, teaches his people. "All thy people shall be taught of the Lord, and great shall be the peace of thy people." "Who teacheth like him?" said Elihu to Job. This was the man who thought he should die in his nest, who cursed the day of his birth. He was taught to know he was nothing, that he was vile in the sight of God, though upright before men. God graciously teaches us the true value of the things of time, and shows to us the value of the heavenly inheritance to which he means to bring us; he leads us into all truth; he teaches us to rise from earth to heaven. We never forget what God teaches us in the school of experience; his lessons are burnt in with the fires of afflictions, trials, and sorrows of every sort and kind; but the blessedness of all this is, that all his teachings lead us to himself.

4. *God's leadings alone are effectual.* The Lord alone did lead Jacob; there was no strange god with him. When God leads us to Bethel, we soon put away all our strange gods. When once he begins a good work, he never leaves it, but carries it on to the day of Jesus Christ. "See," says God, "how I have borne you as upon eagle's wings, and brought you unto myself." My dear hearers, all God's fatherly discipline, his gracious

teaching, flows from his fatherly affection; his object is, that all his dear children, when cleansed by his Spirit from the pollution of this world, shall be brought home to himself, and live in the enjoyment of his love for ever.

Believer in Jesus, you see the end God has in view by breaking up your nest in this world; it is to bring you unto himself. He means to bear you up far above the world. You have, doubtless, often prayed that you might be brought nearer to him; you have often sighed to have more acquaintance with him " whom to know is life eternal." When you first knew God, you prayed often and fervently that you might know more of him; you have prayed that you might *grow* more in love, in faith, and in every grace; " might more of his salvation know, and seek more earnestly his face." Well, then, are you surprised because God is answering your prayers? If you are longing to live nearer to heaven, depend upon it every nest you settle in will be disturbed. He will un-comfort you in it; he will unfasten every tie that binds you to earth; he will separate everything that in-tervenes between him and yourself. You shall, indeed, be borne up above the world, far above its spirit, far above its pursuits, far above its charms. God will do all this for you *himself.* You will mount up as on eagle's wings, and thus he will blessedly bring you to himself. Say, then, to your soul:

> " Rise, my soul, and stretch thy wings,
>   Thy better portion trace ;
> Rise from transitory things,
>   Towards heaven, thy native place.
> Sun and moon and stars decay ;
> Time shall soon this earth remove ;
> Rise, my soul, and haste away,
>   To seats prepared above.
>
> " Cease, ye pilgrims, cease to mourn,
>   Press onward to the prize ;
> Soon the Saviour will return,
>   Triumphant in the skies.
> Yet a season, and you know,
> Happy entrance shall be given ;
> All your sorrows left below,
>   And earth exchanged for heaven."

SAMSON'S HISTORY A WARNING TO BACKSLIDERS.

◆

A SERMON,

BY CHARLES GORDELIER,

PREACHED AT NEW BROAD STREET CHAPEL, LONDON,

On Lord's Day Afternoon, June 9th, 1861.

" And she made him sleep upon her knees ; and she called for a man, and she caused him to shave off the seven locks of his head ; and she began to afflict him, and his strength went from him. And she said, The Philistines be upon thee, Samson."— JUDGES xvi. 19, 20.

SAMSON, the subject of our text, was certainly an extra-ordinary man. He was altogether a wonderful man. In all the biography of the Bible we have not his parallel. His history as a man of God is full of the deepest, the most terrible instruction.

Just for a moment let us refer to his parents. The short relation we have of them is pleasing and interesting. Manoah and his wife were simple-minded persons, but their faith in the God of Abraham was pure and earnest. Jehovah most graciously revealed to them his purposes of love and grace respecting his people Israel ; to them-selves, as parents, they are promised a child, a precious gift in those days ; and to the people, through them, that this child shall be the beginning of their deliverance from the oppression of the Philistines.

There is something here very striking and worthy of remark. Look at the first verse of the thirteenth chapter : " The children of Israel did evil again in the sight of the Lord ; and the Lord delivered them into the hand of the Philistines forty years." You see here is a repetition of evil doings, and a chastisement is awarded accordingly, and that for the space of forty years ; but see again, at

No. 4.—Fifth Edition, Revised.

the same time that God afflicted his people for their sins, he nevertheless, in his tender mercies, provided deliverance. All the time of their oppression there was growing up by the side of the oppressor, a deliverer. Samson was born, and at the end of forty years the Spirit began to move him at times in the camp of Dan in behalf of his nation. In this portion of history you see what you may often see in your own, that God's promises of help are oftentimes more prospective than immediate, and you are called to wait, not in suspense, but in hope; for all God's promises are certain, and if God has once made a promise, there is always ground for trust; the eternal grace is sure. The people had to wait till Samson was a full-grown man. The time, doubtless, seemed long. God's purposes, like some rivers we read of, are lost sight of for a while; they run underground a long way before they break out; but in the end the vision shall speak, it shall not tarry one moment behind the appointed time. God has not only appointed the time for chastisement against sin, but he also in mercy has appointed the time for its completion.

The character of Samson, doubtless, is one surrounded with difficulties; but we are not left in doubt as to his faith in God, or of his personal interest in the covenant of grace. The inspired writer to the Hebrews has recorded his name amongst those who " obtained a good report through faith, and who are now inheriting the promises." This one fact must quite decide any scruple we may have as to his possessing the true fear of God in his heart, whatever may be our opinion as to some parts of his conduct. We can understand how a man may be upright, moral, generous, loveable in all his deportment in life; but he may be, nevertheless, an unconverted man; that is to say, unregenerate in his mind and heart by the Spirit of God. He is a man of the world for all that. On the other hand, it is possible for a truly converted man, one whom the Spirit of God has called out of the world, to exhibit in his life a chequered, an uneven course. There may be, indeed relapses into old habits of sin, there may be numerous infirmities; but yet, for all that, there may be the power of divine grace so seen at intervals as to make it manifest that such a one may be a good man, a partaker of divine grace, though encompassed with infirmities. May the Lord keep you and me from being such

a one. Such a one is but little credit to the religion he
professes; such a one knows but little of either its power
or its comfort. Samson was such a one; but let us learn
from his history those lessons of instruction which may
be profitable for us, for which intent, indeed, the pen of
inspiration has recorded the narrative.

From the remarks already made you will not expect me
to advance any thoughts as to Samson being a type of the
Lord Jesus Christ. It is true there are some points of
resemblance between what is deemed the type and the
anti-type; but I consider the drawbacks in Samson's
general life and character so serious and so considerable,
that I cannot suppose that the honour of Jesus Christ can
either be set forth, or his people edified by any particular
comparison which might be instituted. I am aware that
my views do not accord with those generally held; but
I do not consider the common notions on this subject correct. I believe Samson to be a type of all self-willed, self-
sufficient Christians, especially such who may be called to
take the lead or prominent part in the public department
of Christian service and duty.

Samson's history, therefore, under the aspect in which
I am about to present it, is that of a man falling from a high
position, to which both the promise and the providence of
God had destined him to occupy. Now, the history of
the falls of God's people is always instructive, though
painful. Who can read the cases of David and Peter
without serious and profitable reflections upon the mutability of even the most exalted and favoured partaker of
God's rich gifts and influence? That of Samson's is fear-
fully instructive. He was largely endowed with the
Spirit of God. (See chap. xiii. 25; xiv. 6; xv. 14.) He
was, from his birth, peculiarly devoted to the service of
God, acted as his viceroy, and for twenty years was the
protector of the commonwealth of Israel; yet he fell into
the most debasing sins that mankind can be guilty of.
He possessed enormous muscular power, and probably a
large bodily frame; his animal passions were also strong.
These were, perhaps, the stronger of the two, for he evidently failed to govern them. Besides his strong natural
powers, he had imparted to him the qualifications and capabilities for a patriot. His tribe, Dan, lay next the
borders of the Philistines, and was naturally subject to the
incursions and oppressions of that warlike people. Sam-

son was, therefore, raised up for a deliverer in that part
where a deliverer was most needed. God not only knows
how to send deliverance, but the exact spot, and also
when. These things will God do for his people, and not
forsake them. And if any of you are troubled on this
matter, learn to say with the poet, Newton:

> " To his will I'll leave the rest,
> The when, the how, the where;
> His goodness will appoint it best,
> Without my anxious care."

But is it not surprising, that Samson, a Nazarite from
his birth, a man so devoted to God, the prince of his nation, should be found in the land of the enemy, under circumstances not only culpable for a man of any position,
but the most revolting to the purity of the faith he possessed. Mark this; in the last verse of the thirteenth
chapter we are told, " in the camp of Dan," his own proper place, there " the Spirit of the Lord began to move
him at times ;" and had he remained there, amongst his
own people, the Spirit would, doubtless, have continued to move him. The Lord meets his people who remember him in his ways." (Isa. lxiv. 5.) But, observe,
in the first verse of the next chapter we read, Samson, of
himself, went to Timnath ; there he saw a daughter of
the Philistines, and fell at once in love with her. His im-
patience has no bounds ; he urges his parents with a vehemence that seems to us somewhat childish. They reason with him ; but reason is of little avail where passion
is in the ascendant ; and so, against the remonstrance of
his parents and the law of God, he married her. But no
blessing was there. How could there be ? How soon a
quarrel ensued. It is true, it ended in the defeat of the
common enemy. And from the fourth verse of the four-
teenth chapter, it appears that God intended to bring
good out of evil ; but we see in Samson avenging his private quarrels nothing that indicates him to be under the
fear of the Lord. She who once pleased his eye is now
the plague of his heart. His temper is his master ; and
certainly the enemy was weakened thereby, and kept in
fear, for even a standing army could be of no use while
such a man was in the opposite camp to annoy them.

We see too that Samson was conscious of his supernatural strength, he was conscious too of his vow—he
perfectly understood the nature of his oath—his own life

had made that his own act and deed which his parents had done for him in infancy; yet he knew not his own weakness. His mind was as feeble as his body was strong; his religious energies suffered from the temperament of his mind, and so did his position and character. He had not strength to govern his own passions, though self-willed to the highest degree. He had not sufficient wit or judgment to keep within his own camp, though he perfectly understood his public relation to his own people. Nor was it from a political motive for the general peace of the nation that he did not keep in his place; self was his governing power; he did not keep in view the law of the Lord. All his troubles, his difficulties, and the viler sins into which he afterwards fell, arose from this one great defect in his character, his great love of self; he did not keep in view God's holy law.

There was one circumstance, however, in which God most mercifully interposed in his behalf. The Philistines demanded of the men of Judah Samson himself as a compensation for the injuries he had inflicted. The people of Judah, a true emblem of all heartless religious professors who value the friendship of the world, and who for fear of its frown will betray any one whom God has called to his service, gave him into the hands of the Philistines. As soon as the war shout was commenced, and Samson was in imminent danger, the Spirit of the Lord came upon him, and he burst the bonds of cord that bound him. He had no weapon; his own people forsook him, but not his God. He spied on the ground the jawbone of an ass, an article which he might have broken in his hand with the first blow; but no, with that sorry looking and undignified weapon, he dealt superhuman blows, he slew a thousand men; and, mark you, these men faced him about courageously and stood to the attack; but what is the use of ten thousand men against only one if God helps that one; however feeble and contemptible the instrument, God will help his oppressed people to do mighty things in his strength. Doubtless, some of you can say,

> " Oh, I have seen the day,
> When by a single word
> God helping me to say,
> 'My trust is in the Lord,'
> My soul has quelled a thousand foes,
> Fearless of all who did oppose."

It was the hand of God in the hand of Samson; and so with the jaw-bone of an ass he slew a thousand warriors and laid them in heaps. Samson knew who had given him such mighty strength and valour in that emergency, but he failed to give God the praise and the acknowledgment; keeping self in view, he makes his boast: " With the jaw-bone of an ass, heaps upon heaps, with the jaw of an ass have I slain a thousand men." Not one word of praise to God in all this! Now what follows? There is the reaction of all this exciting incident; he is fainting, ready to die of thirst; the God who gave him such prodigious valour to kill a thousand men does not keep him from fainting. He is left to his own weakness; he gives no glory to God; 'tis true, he prays, and he confesses the deliverance; and he expresses his fear of dying at last in the land of the enemy. Where is his faith? We see his fear; that arose from his love of self—unmortified self; there is in all this, not one word of praise to God. The very record of his casting away the jaw-bone seems to intimate the vain-glorious spirit of the man! How different was David, who, after a similar feat, laid up the weapon of his enemy as a trophy before the Lord. How unlike Samuel was Samson. Samuel set up a lasting memorial to the praise of God for the deliverance wrought at Mizpeh: "Ebenezer; hitherto hath the Lord helped us." But Samson merely calls the place by a name which referred to his own misery: "the well of him that cried;" a monument to his own self-pity! No praise is here ascribed to God. Why not an Ebenezer? surely it deserved one! Ah, my friends, the secret is now about coming out. When you see a man vainly puffed up in his own fleshly mind, depend upon it, if you look a little longer, you will soon see that man tripping up, his heart veering about towards himself. God will soon leave that man to himself for awhile and let him find out to his cost how much native strength he has got, and what it will do for him, and where it will leave him. Oh if God leaves a man to himself for awhile, it is next to being left in hell for an eternity! Pray then, as David did, for he knew well the history of Samson: "Take not thy Holy Spirit from me." Samson's boasting and vaunting was the secret of his beginning to fall; he began here to fall as a man of God, in the next step as a patriot to his country, and subsequently as a man in the common relations of society.

Now where do we find Samson after this miraculous interposition? Not making his way towards the tabernacle at Shiloh; not calling together the people, saying, " O, magnify the Lord with me, and let us exalt his name together." No; but immediately he goes, not where duty or providence call him, but into Gaza, the principal city of the enemy. Ah, yes to be sure, he is exalted now; what can hurt him? He can go anywhere. Who's afraid! He is like the giddy moth round the candle light; he is hovering around the full blaze of sin, and he thinks he can go near to it, and into it, and come out unscathed. Does he think so? Ah! he is not the only man that has thought so. Let us look again at Samson. He has gone into the stronghold of the Philistines flushed with his victory, trusting to his own strength; and what has he gone for? Is it to attack the enemy in his own person, alone, and unaided; to beard the lion in his own den? No; it is to rush headlong into sin—sin in its grossest form! He dashes and plunges into the most disgraceful circumstances in which a man can possibly be found. This is Samson the Nazarite—the patriot of the people Israel! And all this too was told in Gath, it was published in the streets of Askelon!

His going to Gaza makes a stir among the people; they all know their enemy. What an advantage to know your enemy, and to know how to use your advantage. These men of Gaza are determined at once to use their opportunity, and they are resolved to secure him. And God makes a stir too. He disturbs Samson; he gives him no peace; Samson cannot quietly enjoy his sin. No; God routes him out in the dead of the night, and this time most mercifully delivers him out of the mouth of hell. He carries off the gates of Gaza and leaves the city open and insecure; a figure, indeed, if he thought of it, of his own state of heart. We read of no song of praise from Samson for all this; there is only the bare record of what a great feat he did in a most extraordinary and perilous time, as if it had been but an amusing incident in his life. Ah! Samson appears outwardly strong, but he is really getting weaker and weaker; like the moth, he is getting nearer and nearer the flame which will scorch his strength, and soon we shall see him drop with no more power to rise!

What is the next step? Caution? taking more heed to his steps? walking circumspectly, not as a fool, but as a

wise man, and profiting by his past bitter experience ? No;
sad to tell, not at all!

Again he goes into the enemy's country, boldly defying
danger, and trusting to his natural prowess in case of
danger.   He is at least sixty years of age, and surely by
this time has come to years of discretion. He has judged
Israel twenty years, and must possess some judgment as
to what is fit and proper for him in his position; surely
he must know how to take care of his character. "No
harm," thinks he, "can happen to me; I've braved dangers before to-day.   I have no fear; I can at any time
beat a whole army at once; the Philistines are all afraid
of me.   But I don't like to be seen by my own people,
indulging my passions, and so I have come here out of
their sight for shame, because I am a Nazarite and their
prince."   Ah, Samson! "Let him that thinketh he standeth, take heed lest he fall."   This is the man who knows
his own strength, but does not know his own weakness;
O, what dangerous knowledge! O, what dangerous ignorance!

Now he is found in the vale of Sorek ; beautiful place,
no doubt, one mile and a half from the vale of Eschol,
where, perhaps, he had been to taste the gigantic and
luxurious grapes which were so famous. Well, he has
crossed the brook ; he has left his native place once more,
and is now again in the land of the enemy ; but he never
more returns.   He meant to return unquestionably; for, of
course, "he must have some relaxation from the cares of
public life; he must have a change for a season; he will be
all right when he comes back."   Yes, when he does come
back !   But he has gone too far ever to come back. He has
gone over to seek another strange woman, the woman
that flattereth with her lips; he takes up his abode with
her; he has become more devoted to this woman than to
the interests of his own people or of the cause of God.
Here he feels quite at ease. Nothing has occurred to
disturb him this time; there are no walls and gates to
enclose him, and he is not likely to be known in this
shady, secluded spot; or, if anything should arise, well,
he is very near to his own land; he has only to cross the
brook, and there he is all right at last. This woman with
whom he has taken up, like most of her class, is mercenary
to the last degree ; yet she is more a patriot to her country
than he is to his.   There, you see a bad woman, as it
were, a good patriot; and here, you see a good man,

professedly so, a bad patriot. The woman's services to her country have, however, to be bought, but by a higher price than Samson gives for his pleasures. She takes that, too, and not a mean sum either from such a visitor. The five lords of her people come to her and offer her 1,100 pieces of silver each, £600 of our money; a large sum for her truly, but a cheap bargain for them; and what for? Not to know where Samson's weakness was; no, they all knew that; nor did they want another proof of his power, they had had enough of that. What they wanted to find out was, the secret of his great strength.

Observe how cautious she is; how unsuspecting he is. Her manners of course appear different to him than they appear to us, because we know all the history. She is a fascinating woman, doubtless; no appearance of falseness— sweet tenderness of manners. She admires his fine per-son, wonders at his great strength, and is inquisitive about it. He thinks it is mere womanish curiosity, and takes it all in. She appears open and frank in her suit, and candidly tells him why she wants to know; but in such a way as to contradict her tongue. He, simple man, can say *No* up to a certain point and put her off besides; he really can say *No* again and again; but she is impor-tunate, time after time. She gains upon his resistance, and wears him out at last. He can hold out no longer; he has no more strength to say *No* now; he tells her the entire secret of his strength, and in such a way as satisfies her of its truth.

Now we are not to suppose all this was the work of a visit or two. She no doubt left enough time to intervene to disarm him of suspicion. She only appears to be play-ing with him; but she, like a fierce beast of prey, has her eye watching for the proper moment; then she will strike, and strike surely too. We have no record of the process, but only of the results.

Let us imagine, then, one sunny afternoon, when all the former conversation had perhaps been forgotten and passed out of his mind. He laid himself down to sleep, as, probably, he had often done before, with his head in Delilah's lap. To him what a sleep! it was the last sleep of the Naz-arite—it was the sleep of death! Oh, Samson, Samson! If your godly parents could have but seen you then; they would have stood aghast; they would have shrieked with horror; they would have shed tears of blood, to see you so vilely casting away the fear of God, blasting their hopes, sacrificing the welfare of your people, and not even scrupling to ruin your own soul!

Look at Samson fast asleep in her lap. Her arrangements have been all previously made against the next opportunity. She sends for the barber, and is sitting, as they all do in the East, cross-legged upon the carpet or mat, and he fast asleep upon her knees. See, the bright scissors are doing their fatal work! He does-not feel it. The invincible and sacred locks are laying scattered upon the ground; there he is, a shorn man, a degraded man. He has broken the covenant, he is no longer a Nazarite to God; he has told the enemy the secret of his great strength and how he may be deprived of it. Foolish man! Was it not enough to disclose the secret of his strength, but that he must also disclose how he could lose it? But so it was; he parted with his advantages as the patriot of his country, just he did with his honour as a man; his sacredness to God he valued no more than his own reputation. Samson is now no stronger than any other man; but, O, awful to relate, "he wist not that the Lord had departed from him!"

Delilah pretended to be facetious with him, and raised the former cry, and which had before raised his scornful laugh: "The Philistines be upon thee, Samson!" He awoke. She began to try his strength, and found out, before he did, that his great strength was gone. There lay his seven locks at his feet; and then she called out in a loud and confident tone, which not only aroused him for the last time, but was the signal for those in the next chamber: "The Philistines be upon thee, Samson!" "Ah, ah," said he, "I will go out and shake myself as at other times." Ah! he did shake himself, but in a more terrible manner than he had done before. He shook with horrible mortification. He could no longer shake himself and gather up his strength. Bitter remorse, like the Philistines, took possession of him. His great strength had gone from him, and, not unlikely, his common strength failed him too! Not that his great strength lay in his hair, but it lay in the keeping of the peculiar covenant under which he was related to God. His unshorn hair was the visible and outward sign of his being a Nazarite to God, and a pledge from God to impart the continuance of his superhuman strength. Samson suffered this sign to be removed; he broke his vow, and thus forfeited the thing signified. God abandoned him as a supernatural man, but he was not cast out of the covenant of grace. His name was not blotted out of the book of life, but he was no longer a Nazarite. He was left like any other man; he was weak like other men, as he said he should be if his hair were taken away. His eyes, which were first the occasion of his sinning, are first punished; they were put out; and thus he reaped what he sowed. But it was better for him to lose his eyes than to have his whole body cast into hell. He was made a prisoner for life, and though a prince, performed the most menial work of the prison. We will not follow him there. I doubt not but that his reflections were of the bitterest and most painful kind, and there was no relief for him in tears, because his eyes were gone. His repentance was deep and genuine. He mourned for his sins more than for the loss of his eyes. He could indeed then see better without them. It is far better for a man to lose both his natural eyes, than to be blind to his spiritual state before God. Samson's hair, howbeit, grew again; so did his piety, and so did his great strength; but not his position in life; that was gone for ever, and what he so much dreaded he had at last to endure. He died away from his native land; not unpitied, but certainly unhonoured. Would that he had lived as he died, a praying man! What a different result there would have been. As a Nazarite he would have been the more conspicuous; his nation and the cause of God would have been better served; he might have lived in honour and died in peace; his name would have been cherished in the affectionate remembrance of his people; and then his name, his history, and his character would have been handed down to posterity untarnished and without a stain.

Let us now, in conclusion, observe from all this, one great fact, and that is, that the principle of falling into sin is the same in every other case as in this of Samson. His case is not one of apostacy from religion, but of backsliding from the ways of God; and as none of us who profess the name of Christ are exempt from the influence of Satan, the world, or our own deceitful hearts, we shall do well to reflect:

1. The NATURE of backsliding. *It is dangerous;* once begun, there is no knowing where it will end. The beginning of sin is like letting out of water, there is no calling it back. It is done and cannot be undone. *It is secret;* the outward indications do not show themselves

at once. Many are backsliders in heart, though not in
open life; that has yet to come—it will come if grace prevent not. *It is deceitful.* The soul is led astray by very
subtle means, often by that which appears to belong to
religion itself; error in sentiments and false zeal in God's
cause have deluded many in the fold of the church.
Even the externals of Christianity will draw the heart
aside if the soul be not simply and constantly looking to
Christ. *It is gradual;* it is a downhill course. Backsliding often commences on the mount, even when the soul is
full of lively zeal, and especially if blessed with success
in religious effort. Self is apt to be elated, and then the
soul goes down step by step; the farther from heaven the
faster towards earth.

2. The EFFECTS of backsliding. At first there is *un-
consciousness;* like Samson, who knew not that the Lord
had departed from him. Few have any feeling of their
first declension. How insensible was David till Nathan
pointedly told him of his sin. Like Bunyan's pilgrim, who
dropped his roll some time before he discovered his loss, we
are often insensible of the value of what we lose till we are
brought to feel the need of it. We lose our joy, our comfort, our hope before we miss them; we complain of soul
desertion at such and such a time; but we are invariably
wrong, for it was before then. What we now feel is the
effect of a previous secret cause. How often Christians
may be seen insensibly to lose their power and influence,
and sometimes their character, from causes difficult to
trace or ascertain. Coldness and deadness in private
duties are often more manifest than felt. How relaxed
the attention and the desire towards heavenly things.
There is also a loss of a tender conscience. This is like a
gauge, it shows the measure of the distance we are reced-
ing from what which at one time would have given us
great anxiety. Then old habits, unsubdued sins, rise and
rebound with all the force of a spring that has long been
depressed. Then darkness of mind follows the loss of
fire in the heart. The feelings are benumbed, actual and
open sin is often the result. Then, when guilt with its horrid form stares you in the face, you are aroused with
something like a sense of what an evil and a bitter thing
it is to depart from the living God.

3. The CAUSES of backsliding. These are numerous.
Satan has a thousand baubles to induce a believer to take
off his eye from Christ. This one principle regulates

Satan in all his movements with the church of God; he is ever aiming to keep the believer from prayer and the word of God. The neglect of secret prayer has been generally traced as the cause of most of the slips and falls we see and feel in the Christian life. So also the neglect of praise for special mercies. This is not commonly observed; but watch its influence, you shall soon find that there is as much connection between praise and living near to God as there is in prayer. Prayer is said to be the life of God in the soul; so is praise; that is, they are sure evidences of life. Another cause of backsliding is the unsubdued strength of carnal affections; the conflict, instead of being maintained, is too often suffered to run into a compromise, and there is a cherishing within of what ought to have been uncompromisingly chased out. The seductiveness of our own hearts is another cause; the understanding is sometimes blinded by our feelings. The allurements of the world are endless and various in their fascinations, and bring many sincere souls into labyrinths from which it may be hard to escape. Another cause is, indulging in the pleasure we may have from either the success of any effort beyond our expectation, or when we are exalted in ourselves and become full of ourselves, and show a boasting spirit like Samson. Also wandering into forbidden paths; tampering with temptation; quenching or grieving the Spirit by whom we are sealed to the day of redemption.

Let me say, too, that another cause of backsliding is not abiding in Christ; that is, not abiding in the truth, not attending to the ordinances or keeping in the ways of the gospel. Neglecting the house of God, or the adoption of opinions derogatory to the truth and honour of the Lord Jesus Christ, will invariably lead to backsliding.

4. The RESTORATION of backsliders. Commonly, afflictions of body or estate are employed as chastisements; for when the believer becomes obtuse in his affections towards God, hardened in sin, there is no other method of making him feel but by affliction, as Samson in the prison-house. The Prodigal mentioned in our Lord's parable is another instance. Another means of restoration is a forsaking at once the sin into which one may be brought; also an honest and hearty confession of sin to God alone; let this be the first step. Backslider! go back at once to the place where the first departure commenced—secret

prayer in the closet. Neither let it be forgotten that
God must be acknowedged and praised for his constant
goodness, mercy, and grace. Seek also, more than has ever
yet been done, God's honour and glory. Pray for self to
be put back and kept down.

But the first and the efficient cause of all restoration is
God's everlasting love; it is his restoring grace: " He restoreth my soul," saith the Psalmist ; he brings back the
wanderer, his heart of stone is melted down by the fire of
God's love. The Holy Spirit revives the drooping soul and
brings it back again to himself. Were it not for the unchangeable love of God, the soul would be cast off, the
backslider would never be restored; " I am God, I change
not; therefore ye sons of Jacob are not consumed." The
final perseverance of every true believer is guaranteed by
every attribute of Jehovah.

> " Whom once he receives his Spirit ne'er leaves,
>   Nor ever repents of the grace that he gives."

But let none presume on the restoring mercy of God.
'Tis true he invites the wanderer to come back to him,
and he has graciously put words into his mouth, and encouraged him to come just as he is; but he must not presume in his heart that he will be fetched back. Were Saul,
Judas, Demas, and others who could be named. were they
brought back ? If you are a wanderer from Christ's fold
you will be brought back, but, depend upon it, it will be
on your part with bitter weeping, deep lamentation, and
humble supplication.

Lastly, let the backslider be *warned* by the sad history
of Samson. Remember, when Samson first trod the forbidden path, the land of the enemy, how his parents remon-
strated with him; then God sent a lion to check him in
his course; but he resisted both. God generally, in some
way, withstands the backslider in his first wanderings;
hedges up his way with thorns, reproves him, gives him
intimations in the conscience, warns him from his word,
warns him from the cases of others. Pray attend to this,
heed the first warning; think not that you will be brought
back like Samson in a second deliverance. The sending
of the lion was a soft whisper of reproof, and to bring
him back; the deliverance from Gaza was a voice of thunder; but he disregarded both. " God speaks once, nay,
twice, but man perceiveth it not." It may be he will
speak no more ; he spoke no more to Samson. He spake
twice, he then let him alone. Take a note of that.

" Ephraim is joined to idols; let him alone." (Hosea iv. 17.) If you are not resisted in your backslidings, if you find your way to sin easy and plain, depend upon it God means to let you alone. But O, if you find you are checked, if you are resisted, regard it as mercy; it is mercy urging you back. Go no farther, stop short, go back at once; God will receive you and restore to you the joy of his salvation. But if, like Samson, you are self-willed, blinded by your passions, and disregard the merciful intimations and resistances of God's Spirit, I say, " Beware of him, provoke him not;" for whatever may be the power of your talents, the strength of your character, the energy of your will, or your resolution of purpose, or even the loftiness of your position, like Samson, God will bring you down, and you shall not be able to rise; like Samson, " a wound and a dishonour shall you get, and your reproach shall not be wiped away."

My dear hearers, let us all take warning from Samson's history. If such dangers attend the strong, how shall it go with the weak? Guard, then, against the decline of your spiritual frame of mind. Watch and pray. Cultivate a tender conscience. Enter no forbidden path. Let your gifts and opportunities be used for God, not for self. Remember the word of truth, " Them that honour me I will honour, and they who despise me shall be lightly esteemed."

"THE GREAT PLAGUE OF THE HEART;"

BEING AN EXTRACT FROM THE AUTHOR'S SERMON ON I KINGS, VIII. 28.

THERE is another plague of the heart, more subtle, more insidious, more deceitful, than the one just named (Unbelief). It is that of *Pride*. It is more difficult to perceive. It is less difficult to hide. It assumes as many shapes, forms, and characters, with as much facility and adroitness, as those mountebanks, so noted for mimicking a variety of characters at a theatrical entertainment. So deceiving is pride, we hardly see it with the same dress or the same face twice. Pride is so mixed up with all we are and all we do, that it becomes, as it were, a part of us; if we are told of it or look for it, we see it not. Pride strives to hide itself; never shows its own face, never wears its own dress, speaks not with its own voice, and colours all its own doings, so that it shall not appear. With the natural man it succeeds well. He is well pleased with himself; and if found in the profession of religion, he is still more delighted with himself; for profession is the material which pride employs to deceive and catch unwary and unstable souls.   Pride is the spider in the house of God; it weaves its web from its own bowels, sucks out the life of all whom it catches; but it becomes the pest of all who love the Lord Jesus in sincerity and in truth.   Pride, therefore, does not succeed with the upright, for it is opposed; for where God begins his good work in the soul, he plants the grace of humility.   Humbleness of soul is that spirit which God approves.   Pride is that spirit which God abhors.   Pride is that cursed sin which cast angels out of heaven; and many a delight has it cast out of the heaven-born soul.   This, I dare say, some of you have known to your sorrow; and I can say with Dr. Watts:

> "But pride, that busy sin,
>   Spoils all that I perform;"

and with dear Mr. Hart:

> "Do what I will, it haunts me still,
>   And keeps me from the Lord."

And because this humbleness of soul, this poverty of spirit, is so blessed to feel, and is enjoyed by the believer, therefore pride comes in all its protean forms.   Does God shine in upon the soul, and speak peace, joy, and liberty?   Oh, how pride creeps in and causes the soul to be satisfied with itself; to rest upon its frames and feelings, believing they will ever continue.   Such souls think their mountain stands strong; they are lifted up.   Then soon the poor soul discovers its error in not always resting on Christ.   The light of God's countenance is lost sight of; the cause is pride, but it has hidden itself; it has, like the spider, hidden itself; it has cast its filmy web over the eye of the soul and brought it into darkness.   Then the believer comes to the throne of grace to mourn and to deplore the loss of God's presence; and still, even there, will pride creep in and show itself, aye, in some feelings of disappointment and mortification.   It will show itself even in tears of sorrow, so subtle is it and so difficult to detect.   In outward things, visible as it may be to others, it is often concealed from the view of those who are under its influence.   If such a one is favoured with gifts for public usefulness, O what a hotbed do they prove for pride.   Puffed up with fancy's airy dreams, till, as Mr. Hart very truly says,

> "The heart uplifts with God's own gifts,
>   Makes even grace a snare."

The soul is tempted by the cursed spirit of pride, to make a kind of show or dealing with those gifts for exalting self.   If with a gift for verbal prayer, what longings for the prayer meeting; always there.   If with a gift for public speaking, and some supposed knowledge of God's word, what burning desires to preach, what longings for a pulpit; and, as I once heard the late Mr. Gadsby say, "If God does not open a door for them in his providence, they will lift up the latch themselves and walk in."   Ah! this is true to the very letter, and all this under the specious pretence of doing it for the glory of God and the good of immortal souls.   But it is the spirit of Ahimaaz: "Howsoever, let me run;" (2 Sam. xviii. 22, 23;) yes, and run they do, and run fast too, very fast, and then stop short. How so? Because their brains have run out as fast as their legs ran; so they soon give over, and curse the pride of their hearts the rest of their days; for they find God never sent them. This kind of pride, however, only affects *a few* comparatively, but pride and vain glory work *in all*, more or less; they will show themselves in endless forms. If a soul thinks itself to have more trials than another, it will gather pride to itself. If more afflicted in body than another, it will make it an occasion of pride. If employed in any department of Christian service, ever so humble, pride will creep in and "swell a haughty worm." Conversation, position in society or the church, dress, any peculiarity, no matter what; pride will, like flies, feed upon anything—hot, cold, sweet, sour, clean, filthy, holiness, corruption—nothing comes amiss. But, O, to the child of God, exercised by this subtle and cursed spirit, it is the plague of his heart. Say, believer, is not this the torment, the plague of your heart? "Ah!" say you, "indeed it is. What a world of trouble it has occasioned me! How uneasy it makes all things between God and the soul!" Thus it is, that much of our discomforts arise from pride, this plague of the heart.

Closely allied to this plague of the heart is another, but it is still more difficult to detect and to subdue, and that is *Self*. Self-seeking, self-praise, self-pleasing, "Wonderful self," as Mr. Huntington styles it. This is the great idol of the heart. This is the idolatry which God's work is labouring to destroy and cut down; and it may be remarked, that if the Spirit of truth reveals the working of this subtle and insidious enemy to all righteousness, it is no small proof of his gracious teaching. I am not referring to what is usually termed self-sufficiency or self-conceit; but a seeking of self in whoever is engaged professedly for God; the preponderating ruling motive being self, self-advancement, "to be seen of men," seeking one's own glory, "loving the praise of men." Repudiate it as we may, yet there is a tendency to it even in the best of men, and the best of men have been most distressed about it; their self is the plague of their hearts. The more active the believer is for God, the more his singleness of heart is opposed by this spirit; it obstructs his honesty of purpose, sincerity of aim, even if the object be ever so praiseworthy, and ever so far removed from self; yet sometimes, when it is detected and exposed, the shame is so great that one is led almost to think there has been no simplicity of intention at all, no godly sincerity, but all self, self. This is often to be noticed in those moments of mortification and disappointment we are called upon to feel when our schemes, plans, or prospects have been thwarted or foiled.

No doubt, self-seeking creeping in thus occasions the Lord to confound our Babel-building and to smash our pet schemes; and it is only by *his so doing* with us that we learn what *we are doing*. If we were as careful as to what God did with us, as we are in what we do for him, our mortifications would be less and not so painful; but it is our self, our unmortified self, that is pained and grieved; it is our self that suffers, not his work. We sometimes think we are losing ground. No, we are not, the lower self is cut down, the higher grace rises. God's work goes on best when self bleeds most. This is painful experience, but self must fall. Dress it up as we may, and make it look like grace according to our fancy, self will be stripped off and the shame of it made to appear. God stamps upon all our nonsense and crushes it into powder; he dashes it into the cup of bitterness and makes us drink it, that we may be sick of ourselves and of our follies; then it is we find that self-seeking, flesh-pleasing, is the plague of our hearts; nothing but our own experience will prove it to us. If God blesses us in anything in which we have been concerned, self will be elated, because *we* have been employed, *we* have appeared in it, we have figured out upon the stage; if otherwise, then self is vexed. Self is never pleased if it labours and others enter into its labours; self has no liking to sowing and not reaping. Self likes to have everything in its own way, likes everything that it does to prosper, and is regardless of any one else's comfort or interest, so that it may stand foremost or prominent in some way. If self could have its way, it would wrest the sceptre from the hand of Jesus and take the crown from his head, and display them for itself. This wickedness God sees, though we do not; so God, to make us hate self in every shape, causes us to feel it to be the plague of our hearts; and when this is the case, then it is that a man grows out of love with himself and falls at Jesus' feet, making his grace his song and boast, and crowning him Lord of all. Now, mark you, this is not the work of a day or two, like Jonah's gourd, but a long life-time. I have been nearly forty years coming to this point, but seem to have made very little progress yet; if any at all, I bless God for it. If God did not make us feel the plague of our hearts in this way, it would be the death of us; but God, to save our souls alive, kills our pride, kills our self-seeking; kills everything that opposes the work of grace in the soul. God means that all his children shall be out of love with themselves, but in love with him, his grace, and his work; for this purpose he puts us into the furnace repeatedly, and when all self, pride, and everything that exalteth itself against the knowledge of God is melted down and consumed, then the true gold will shine with the Refiner's image to "praise and honour and glory, at the appearing of Jesus Christ." (1 Pet. i. 7.)

Still, there is yet another sore grief which is felt by many a believer, who would trust to Christ alone and his finished work for life and salvation; it is the offspring of both Pride and Self; I mean Self-righteousness. How many souls, when convinced of sin, attempt in their own strength to attain eternal life, on the footing of their doings. How they labour, and tug, and toil to work out their own salvation; always aiming at and going about to establish their own righteousness, yet always failing; but like Job, until they are better taught, they will maintain their own supposed integrity and their own righteousness; they will not let it go. (Job xxvii. 5, 6.) But when the Spirit of Truth opens up to them the spirituality of God's law, that Christ has fulfilled it and delivered them from its curse by his life and his death, and that they are accepted in him, his righteousness being imputed to them, O how soon they renounce their own righteousness and count it as filthy rags; glad are they to flee naked to Christ and cleave to him. Ever after, they view all notions of creature merit as the very plague of their hearts; free grace becomes their darling theme, and their prayer is now, that they "may be found in him, not having on their own righteousness, which is of the law, but that which is through the faith of Christ, the righteousness which is of God by faith." (Phil. iii. 9.)

JEHOVAH'S THRONE

THE

BELIEVER'S SANCTUARY.

A SERMON,

BY CHARLES GORDELIER.

PREACHED AT JEWRY STREET CHAPEL, ALDGATE,

On Monday Evening, July 7th, 1862.

" A glorious high throne from the beginning is the place of our sanctuary."—JEREMIAH xvii. 12.

THE apostle Peter assures us (2 Peter i. 20, 21) " that no prophecy of the Scriptures is of private interpretation, For the prophecy came not in old time by the will of man ; but holy men of God spake as they were moved by the Holy Ghost." And concurrent with this testimony is that of the apostle Paul, (2 Tim. iii. 16, 17,) wherein he says, " All Scripture is given by inspiration of God, and is profitable for doctrine, for reproof, for correction, for instruction in righteousness : that the man of God may be perfect, throughly furnished unto all good works." From these two unexceptionable witnesses we derive this important fact, that there is no part of God's word but what is divine truth, it being ALL divinely inspired; and though every part may not be equally important in matters of salvation, yet, nevertheless, the whole is to be regarded as God's word. This is a truth which every sincere believer in Jesus must hold with a firm grasp, like as the manslayer clung to the horns of the altar when the avenger of blood was at his heels. Here he will be safe though danger is near ; for in these days, sceptics and infidels, both in the world and the professing church, are perpetually aiming to un- dermine the foundations of our faith, either by pretend- ing to grapple with supposed difficulties, or making some frivolous objections which really are of no moment what-

ever. Not being themselves under the teachings of God's
Spirit, these cavillers " understand neither what they say
nor whereof they affirm ;" yet, forsooth, they will tell us
there are things in the Scriptures which *cannot* be explained, and allege there is " a defect, a mistake ;" that
the Scriptures are but *partially* inspired. Now this is
indeed marvellous on their part, for them to take upon
themselves to judge what is and what is not inspired, or
to solve the knot of a difficulty by cutting it. How
much better it would be for men to confess their inability
to deal with questions above their comprehension, than to
be finding fault with what has defied the attacks of dis-
putants for ages past. Does it not remind one of a common saying, " Bad workmen always find fault with their
tools "?   Men would, indeed, be wise above what is
written ; but such wisdom as this " descendeth not from
above, but is earthly, sensual, and devilish."

I make these remarks in consequence of the attacks on
the sacred writings which have been recently made by
one who is evidently " full of all subtlety and mischief, a
child of the devil," though under the name and wearing
the garb of a bishop. It is no small mercy to be able to
see the drift of such men, and to know the spirit they
are of.

Now, we readily grant there is in the Scriptures a
diversity of subjects, as well as of style and ability, according to the natural abilities of the several writers.
Things profound and obscure, in what belongs to God
we expect to meet ; but *partial* inspiration, insuperable
difficulties, or radical deficiencies, we cannot for one moment admit. We take our stand upon this truth : " ALL
Scripture is given by inspiration of God." We make no
pretensions to understand everything. What we know
not now, we shall know hereafter ; in the meantime let
us wait, we are perfectly safe here, for we are standing on
a rock. Variety of subject-matter is obvious to us all ; but
it is the extreme of folly to deny the divine character of
any particular part because we have at present no eyes to
see it. The supernatural element runs through the whole,
though some portions are sufficiently plain as to require
no elucidation whatever. Then, again, we find there are
some which can be easily opened up with aid close at
hand, as if the key hung by the door side, the context
being sufficient. Others, indeed, seem as though they

were enclosed in a hard case or outer shell, like a nut, which has to be broken up by external help, that is, a knowledge of history and of the manners and customs of Eastern nations being of great assistance. And there are others like choice articles deposited in a cabinet, the key of which the owner keeps in his own care, these cannot be opened and displayed until we have the key direct from Him whose province it is to take of the things of Christ and reveal them unto us.

Of the last class I consider are the words which I have read as a text for this evening's discourse. They are a sentence in itself. It does not appear to me that they are connected with either the passage that goes before or that which follows. The power of God's Spirit upon the mind of Jeremiah is thus remarkably seen. There are a loftiness and grandeur in the language that seem to bespeak something divinely precious within its hidden meaning, and which could only have been spoken under the immediate influence of the Holy Ghost. O may the same Spirit aid us in forming right conceptions of "the truth as it is in Jesus," and to a firm apprehension of it; so that we may not only escape making or receiving fanciful and mistaken impressions, but find profit and comfort in the consideration of what I believe to be a choice and delightful portion of God's holy word.

Our text speaks of a sanctuary. A sanctuary, as you know, is a sacred place, sacred to the worship of God. The word is also used for a place of protection, of retirement, of shelter. Here, doubtless, in a literal sense it refers to that inner chamber of the Jewish temple, called the Holy of holies. It was a peculiarly sanctified place; called, indeed, "a worldly sanctuary," as in Heb. ix. 1, because its materials were of a visible kind, and could be approached unto. It was ordained for the local worship of Jehovah, the Most High God, and for the congregated service of his people. Within this inner chamber, which was screened by a vail, was placed the ark of the covenant, overlaid with gold and sprinkled with blood. This was called the mercy-seat, and over it the glory of the Lord shone between the cherubim. There Jehovah took up his symbolical abode, and appeared to his servants from the time of its erection in the tabernacle to the time of the destruction of the first temple. In this sanctuary, (the Holy of holies,) on the great day of atone-

ment, the High Priest, as the representative of the
people, presented the vicarious blood of the sacrifices as
typical of an expiation for sin, and with it sprinkled the
mercy-seat, agreeably to the divine command, all which
prefigured the Saviour's intercession and the sinner's
acceptance with God.   But the Jewish dispensation has
long passed away.   The temple and the sacred ark, with
its table and candlestick, have all been destroyed.   Ichabod has been written, in large characters, on the place
where the temple stood, and on the people themselves—
" the glory has departed."

The Lord's dear people, his spiritual Israel I mean,
have, however, a sanctuary which no outward circumstances can possibly destroy.   It is a place which the
vulture's eye hath not seen; it is the secret tabernacle
of the Most High, the pavilion where the soul may hide
in the time of trouble; it is the throne of grace, where
believers in Christ may pour out their hearts before him;
it is, indeed, a hallowed place, sacred to God the Father,
sacred to God the Son, sacred to God the Holy Ghost,
and sacred to every sinner seeking for life and salvation
through Christ Jesus.   And there is also another sanctuary besides this secret sanctuary of the soul; there is
the open or public sanctuary, where the unseen Jehovah,
the uncreated I AM, Jehovah Jesus, may be worshipped
by all who love his name.   It is found in the place where
God's people meet in Christ's name to worship him in
spirit and in truth; for "God is a Spirit, and they who
worship him must worship him in spirit and in truth."
(John iv. 24.)   In all such places where the name of
Christ the eternal Son of God is recorded, he comes to
bless his people; Jesus himself is with them, and it is
his presence which constitutes a place of worship a sanctuary to the humble, believing child of God.

I have already alluded to the Jewish Holy of holies,
and in the 9th chapter of Hebrews, which was read,
sufficient has been said upon the subject.   I might,
indeed, refer you to a passage (Ezek. xi. 16) where the
Lord God declares "he will be a little sanctuary" to his
people; but I am rather desirous, as the Lord may be
pleased to help me, of presenting to your notice some
of the characteristics which constitute the *place* of our
sanctuary.   There are four things which claim our consideration :

I. A Throne.

II. It is high.

III. It is glorious.

IV. Its ancient date: "A glorious high throne from the beginning is the place of our sanctuary."

I. The place of this sanctuary is said to consist of a THRONE. This is to be understood of the elevated place and seat reserved for a monarch when presiding over an assembly of his people. It is the chief seat, as is indicated by its being raised above the common level. It is the seat of power, the place of government, the source of all authority and law. Spiritually considered, the place of our sanctuary is the throne of the heavenly King; it is Jehovah's throne, a throne of grace, a mercy-seat. From this throne the God of heaven dispenses his favours to his royal favourites. Here, wonderful to tell, "pardoned rebels sit and hold communion with their Lord." Yes, at the footstool of divine mercy every rebel made the subject of divine grace comes as an humble suppliant for life, pardon, and peace. Though once they were rebels and broke his holy law, yet now he bestows from this place mercy and pardon. It is here he gives peace to anxious penitents; it is here he bestows gifts to his children; it is here he administers justice to all who are oppressed; it is here he commands, regulates, and over-rules all things by the word of his power and his providence, both for the good of his people and the destruction of his enemies. It is here the believer comes for life, justification, sanctification, grace, power, and authority. He comes here to have a faith's view of the infinite majesty of the eternal Jehovah. It is here where he has humbling views of himself; it is here he has exalted views of the Person, work, offices, and characters of his most glorious Lord and Redeemer; it is here he rejoices that "the Lord reigneth," and that he has been made willing in the day of His power, and crowns Jesus Lord of all.

Come, believer, what think you of this throne? Does it correspond with your experience? Has it not been a throne of grace, a mercy-seat to you, when sunk in misery and despair? Was it not here you first drew, as it were, your vital breath of humble, fervent prayer: "God be merciful to me a sinner"? Is not this throne all that we say it is, ay, and much more too? How can poor finite mortals like ourselves pretend to sum up or describe the glory of this throne. It is the foundation of all our trust, all our hope. We set our seals to the truth which Newton has written:

> "When first before his mercy-seat
> Thou didst to him thy all commit,
> He gave thee warrant from that hour
> To trust his wisdom, love, and power."

II. This throne is said to be HIGH. Yes, *it is high in its own nature;* for it is holy. "Thus saith the Lord, I dwell in the high and holy place, and with him also who is of an humble and contrite spirit, and that trembleth at my word." (Isa. lxvi. 2.) O ye trembling ones, ye whom God's word has made to feel nervous, a shaking within, God is very near you. High as is his throne, it is as low as you are: your spirit is just such as is fitted for it. He raises you to his holy throne, "for he dwelleth with you, and shall be in you." "Be not afraid, only believe. You say you feel yourself sinful; but he says your iniquity is purged. Why do you doubt his word? If your iniquity is purged, you are clean," made to be partaker of his holiness. Let God be true, and unbelief be put to shame, and hide itself in the dust of self-abasement.

This throne is *heavenly.* Far above all that is earthly. "Thus saith the Lord, heaven is my throne and the earth is my footstool." (Isa. lxvi. 1.) "It is far above all principality, and power, and might, and dominion, and every name that is named, not only in this world, but also in that which is to come." (Eph. i. 21.) O what a mercy this is to the poor, tried, persecuted child of God, oppressed above measure by the sons of earth. They would not only crush the life out of him if they could, but they would rob him of his throne. But his God is in the heavens, and His throne is eternally settled in the high court of heaven. From this throne God utters his voice on behalf of all his persecuted saints: "For the oppression of the poor, for the sighing of the needy, now will I arise, saith the Lord; I will set him in safety from him that puffeth at him." (Ps. xii. 5.)

This throne is not only heavenly, but it is *spiritual.* Far above all that is material and carnal, sensual and grovelling, and of an earthly nature. They that are of the earth do mind the things of the earth, are earthly in themselves, and, like the worms of the earth, they rise no higher than the earth. To this heavenly throne they never glance an eye, they never look to Christ, they never come to the mercy-seat, they never look to this high throne with hope for mercy and pardon. But the renewed soul, the spiritually taught believer, looks to Christ, he comes to God, he minds the things of the spirit, he looks to Him who dwells in the high and holy place; and Jehovah in return looks "to him who is of an humble and contrite spirit, and that trembleth at his word."

Again, this throne is high above everything of human nature; above all human conception, high above all carnal reason. It is high above the reach of Satan's rage; above the reach of men's pride, malice, or persecuting spirit. It is high above the reach of all sin and guilt. Sin cannot enter here; for death, hell, and the grave have been completely subdued by him who sits upon this throne.

This throne is *very high*, so high, that no human merit can reach it; no self-righteousness can touch it; no, not even come near it; no, not even one's own blood. Our own blood, if it were shed for our own sin, would be but the well merited penalty. It could never, by any possible means, be a propitiation for sin. This throne is holy, and must not be polluted with the blood of a sinner; but it may be sprinkled with the blood of the spotless Lamb of God; the mercy-seat of the Jewish tabernacle was never sprinkled otherwise than with the blood of a lamb or bullock, without spot. This was the shadow of good things to come. The blood of our Immanuel is an atonement, it is a propitiation, for it was an acceptable offering in righteousness. His Person being holy and immaculate, therefore his blood, his merits did avail; and because this blood of sprinkling did avail, it speaks better things than that of Abel; for Abel's offering, good as it was in itself and acceptable, was but the type and shadow; but this is the substance, the true sacrifice for sin; and because it avails, it is accepted for every believing sinner who comes to this high throne for grace and help in every time of need; be he ever so humble, ever so lowly in himself, here is access for him, free access; but none to the high-minded and carnal professor, the sham Christian, the nominal Christian, the proud, boasting pharisee; it is out of his reach altogether.

III. This throne is not only high, but it is said to be
GLORIOUS.   It is glorious because it is the throne of the
eternal Father.   He sits here in all the glory of his
divine majesty.

> " His glories shine with beams so bright,
>   No mortal eye can bear the sight."

It is glorious because from it God's countenance shines
upon us in the face of Jesus Christ ; glorious through the
blood of the eternal covenant, the blood of the Son of
God ; glorious because of the all-sufficiency of his atonement for all who come to God by him ; glorious because
of the completeness of his atonement to the satisfaction
of divine justice.

> " Once 'twas a seat of dreadful wrath,
>   And shot devouring flame ;
>   Our God appear'd consuming fire,
>   And vengeance was his name."

But there is no wrath now.   The throne is sprinkled
with atoning blood.   The Father is well pleased with his
Son Jesus for his righteousness' sake.   He has magnified
the law and made it honourable.   The church of the
living God is accepted in him : for

> " In him the Father never saw
>   The least transgression of his law ;
>   Perfection, then, in Christ we view ;
>   His saints in him are perfect too."

This throne, then, becomes glorious through the mediatorship of our divine Lord, our ever-living Head, our
glorious substitute, our most glorious Christ.   It is
glorious to us because by this new and living way, (his
mediatorship,) we can now come to God.   We are brought
nigh by the blood of Christ ; we, who were once far off by
the sin of fallen Adam and by our own actual transgressions, are now permitted to approach this throne.   His
atonement hath both cleared the way to our approach,
and hath made it the place of our sanctuary.   This throne
is most glorious to behold with the eye of faith ; most
glorious to realise in the conscience of every sin-pardoned
rebel.   Every sinner enlightened by the Holy Ghost finds
pardon at this throne of the heavenly Father, through the
blood of Jesus Christ his dear Son ; and it is from this
throne that peace is applied to the conscience by the

same Spirit who first led him to it. Believer in Jesus, is not this your experience? I am sure that it is, if I may judge from my own. Seeking soul, are you desirous of finding pardon and peace? seek it here; seek it at this glorious high throne, the only place of your sanctuary.

Further. This throne is glorious, because it is founded and established upon the infinite and immutable holiness, justice, truth, and love of God the eternal Father. "God sitteth upon the throne of his holiness." Justice and judgment are the habitation of his throne," "Mercy and truth shall go before his face." (Ps. lxvii. 8, Ps. lxxxix. 14.) All the divine perfections combine to make this throne glorious. Whatever God is, that is his throne. The perfections of Jehovah cannot be considered apart from himself; they are not abstract qualities; and, glorious as is this fact, if I might so say, his throne is still more glorious to his Church, because these divine perfections are seen all concentrated in, and radiating through, the sinless humanity of the Lord Jesus Christ. How could we, who are fallen creatures in ourselves, approach Deity in its abstract form. Impossible. Our nature, as fallen creatures, is depraved and could by no means, in the moral fitness of things, ever be brought into contact with the divine nature. "No man hath at any time seen the Father, or ever can see him; but he that hath seen the Son hath seen the Father." This is provided for in the economy of redemption. The saints of God who are dear to him by covenant love, shall be made near unto him by the Son of God taking their nature into personal union with himself; and in virtue of this covenant engagement the Holy Spirit regenerates them, thereby making them partakers of the divine nature and meet for the heavenly inheritance. Here, then, we see the throne of Jehovah made most glorious by the personal acts of each of the ever blessed Trinity. By the Father's love, the incarnation of his Son, and the regeneration of the Holy Spirit, the people of God find this glorious high throne is made the place of their sanctuary. It is glorious in itself; it is made glorious to the saints of God—to all of them, the weak as well as the strong— to all who come thereto for life and salvation.

And, because this throne is *holy* it is *glorious*, "glorious in holiness." Where sin entered this world and ruined the nature of man, the throne of God stood immutable.

Divine justice is immutable; sin left it still as inflexible as it ever was, though dishonoured. The law being broken, the sinner must die. This was the divine decree; it had gone forth. "The soul that sinneth shall die." Shall, then, justice be dishonoured by leaving sin unpunished? Shall the authority of God's law be weakened by letting the sinner go free or escape with impunity? No! But, though God will by no means clear the guilty against the principles of his righteous government, yet, glory be to his rich, free, and sovereign grace; he hath devised means by which his banished ones may be not expelled from him. He gave his only begotten Son to take their place and stead. He became their Surety in that covenant of grace ordered in all things and sure. In the fulness of time he was made flesh, became their substitute, magnified the law by his perfect obedience; and made it honourable by his death as an offering for sin, and thereby expiated all their guilt. Thus the justice of God was satisfied, his holiness vindicated, and now the blood sprinkled upon the mercy-seat ever remains as a propitiation for sin to all believers whose consciences in this time-state, may again contract fresh guilt.

And now, because divine justice has been satisfied in the death of Christ, and the majesty of God's holiness maintained by his obedience, therefore the everlasting love of God can be set forth and divine mercy displayed to every seeking, returning, penitent sinner. It was because of God's everlasting love that the Son of God became the Surety of his church. He took their Law place, and he fulfilled, on their behalf, the law which they had broken; and his obedience is imputed to them, and becomes their righteousness; therefore are they without fault before the throne: "God commendeth his love toward us, in that, while we were yet sinners, Christ died for us." (Rom. v. 8.) "God so loved the world that he gave his only begotten Son, that whosoever believeth in him should not perish, but have everlasting life." (John iii. 16.) This throne, then, is glorious, because divine mercy can now be displayed to every poor sinner feeling his lost, ruined, rebellious state before God. O, is there a poor soul here who feels his want of mercy? See here, how rich, how full, how free it flows through the death of Christ! O may the Spirit of truth help you to lay hold of the hope set before you. This is the glorious gospel of the grace of God: "The blood of Jesus Christ cleanseth from all sin."

Well has it been said, "His glory is great in our salvation." How honourable to God; how safe to man. The Son of God has made his throne most glorious. Let me repeat it; our Lord Jesus Christ, by his perfect obedience and complete atonement, has set forth the divine perfections most gloriously:

> "Mercy and truth on earth have met,
> Since Christ the Lord came down from heaven;
> By his obedience, so complete,
> Justice is pleased, and sin forgiven."

Here, then, you see, is another precious truth set forth, making this throne glorious in every point of view—sin forgiven,—so that every sinner, every prodigal, every rebel against God's law, coming to this throne, trusting to the atoning blood of Christ, shall find pardon. There are no ifs, no buts, no may-be's; but all is positive, gracious assurance. "Let the wicked forsake his way, and the unrighteous man his thoughts; and let him return unto the Lord, and he will have mercy upon him; and to our God, for he will abundantly pardon." (Isa. lv. 7.) This is God's truth—truth from his own lips. Do you doubt it? Try it for yourself. Truth is the rock, the firm foundation, on which the throne of God rests. What can you have better for your own soul to rest upon?

God's truth is the rock on which the church's faith is built. Your doubts and your fears cannot shake it, though they often shake you and make you tremble. O, pray for strength in your soul; he will give more grace, he will strengthen your faith and your hope. May he enable you to lay hold of this precious truth: "There is forgiveness with thee;" so shall you blessedly find pardon and peace,—saved from hell; saved from sin; redeemed to God!

IV. I pass on to notice, in the fourth place, the *ancient date* of this glorious high throne. *From the beginning.* Earthly thrones have no such date. There is one throne in Europe which, indeed, has lasted nearly three hundred years in one direct line; but what is that short period of time compared to the date of this glorious, high throne of which we are speaking? for from the beginning it has been a glorious high throne.

What, then, is here intended by "from the begin-ning?" From the beginning of time? As far back as the creation? Yes; that is included, certainly; but that is not the full meaning intended. I think it means long before time began,—long before nature had its being. I believe it to mean in the beginning of the eternal cove-nant of grace. It had its beginning in the everlasting love of God the Father. It had its beginning when the glorious plan of redemption was formed by the eternal Three-One Jehovah. It had its beginning in the council of peace between the Father and the Son; and thus in eternity, from the very first of man's ruin being foreseen, was the existence of this sanctuary, this glorious high throne. It was the place of our sanctuary, as we stood in Christ, before time began; before the foundation of the world. It had its beginning from the moment when the Son of God became the Surety of his church. This was proved on earth when the first man sinned. The promise of the covenant of grace was first declared to him as the blessed result of the sanctuary being already in existence from the beginning. Christ was our sanc-tuary before Adam fell. To suppose the contrary would involve the necessity of believing God to be taken by surprise at the unforeseen event of Adam's fall, and not providing a scheme of salvation until the necessities of the case pointed out what was requisite to be done; all which is a grave imputation on the wisdom and knowledge of God, yet this is believed in and insisted upon by many of the preachers of the day. It is, I know, in harmony with the human brain, but not with the word of God. The scheme of salvation as a remedial expedient *after* the fall of man leads to free-will, gives God's word the lie, and takes the crown from off Jesus' head, and casts it to the ground. Let me ask your attention to the scripture contained in the Apostle Paul's Epistle to the Ephesians, chap. iii.: "And to make all men see what is the fellow-ship of the mystery, which from the beginning of the world hath been hid in God, who created all things by Jesus Christ; to the intent that now unto the principali-ties and powers in heavenly places might be known the manifold wisdom of God, according to the eternal purpose which he purposed in Christ Jesus our Lord, in whom we have boldness and access with confidence by the faith of him." (v. 9 to 12.) Here is revealed the eternity of the

Lord Jesus Christ. His Person is eternal, his Mediatorship is undertaken in eternity,—hid in God, revealed in his incarnation; revealed unto us by his Spirit. "Great is the mystery of godliness; God was manifested in the flesh." From the beginning, the great Head of the church was the Sanctuary of all believers, the whole church of God: "Blessed with all spiritual blessings in heavenly places in Christ Jesus, according as they were chosen in him before the foundation of the world." So that there comes out this great and glorious fact, that before Adam fell, before the earth or the heavens were made, the Church of God was safe in Christ our Sanctuary. Listen, again, to another portion of Scripture. (Col. i. 14–18.) "In whom we have redemption through his blood, even the forgiveness of sins; who is the image of the invisible God, the first-born of every creature; for by him were all things created, that are in heaven, and that are in earth, visible and invisible, whether they be thrones, or dominions, or principalities, or powers; all things were created by him and for him; and he is before all things, and by him all things consist. And he is the Head of the body, the church; who is the beginning, the first-born from the dead; that in all things he might have the pre-eminence."

We have now to consider, in the last place, a most vital part of our subject. Our text says, "A glorious high throne from the beginning is the place of OUR sanctuary." That little word *our* is of great importance in a subject like this. Jeremiah used the word *our* rightly. He, as a Jew, worshipping the only true God, Jehovah, could, on behalf of his nation, at least so far as the true Israel of God were concerned, say, "A glorious high throne from the beginning is the place of *our* sanctuary." But God is no respecter of persons, nationally so. The Jews, as a nation, are no longer the exclusive people of God; nor are *we* because born in a Christian country, so called. True religion is a personal thing; it is a matter of faith between God and the soul; an inwrought work by the power of his Spirit. Now, my hearer, can you say, "*It is my* sanctuary?" Be not afraid to examine yourself, or to commune with your own heart. I have no wish to bring you into bondage by a raking question of this sort, but rather into the glorious liberty of the sons of God. Come, let me appeal to your conscience; let me ask you plainly, have you come to this sanctuary as reclaimed rebels for mercy? Are you looking for mercy to atoning blood? If so, you have Jesus standing before the throne of his Father as your eternal Mediator, your Advocate, Intercessor: "He ever liveth to make intercession for all who come unto God by him."

If, then, the Holy Spirit has made us new creatures in Christ Jesus, he has taken of the things of Christ and revealed them unto us; he has revealed this great, grand, and glorious truth, that the throne of Jehovah is our sanctuary; a sanctuary by virtue of his immutable holiness, his inviolable justice, his everlasting love, and his adorable mercy. Again, let me tell you, by the atoning blood of Immanuel the justice of God has been satisfied and his holiness everlastingly vindicated. Now, God's eternal love can be set forth and his abundant mercy bestowed to every returning prodigal. This sanctuary is raised on purpose for all who feel their need of Christ, as a place of refuge and security from the curse due to sin, and the stings of a guilty conscience:

" No fiery vengeance now, no burning wrath comes down;
  If justice calls for sinner's blood, the Saviour shows his own."

" "Let us, therefore, come boldly to a throne of grace, that we may obtain mercy, and find help in every time of need." You who stand trembling and fearing lest you should find the door of mercy shut, O take courage; come just as you are; wait for no human fitness, no creature merit; fear not. What is it hinders? Look away from yourself; look to Christ alone:

    " The door of his mercy stands open all day,
     To the poor and the needy who knock by the way;
     No sinner shall ever be empty sent back,
     Who comes seeking mercy for Jesus' sake."

THE

MINISTRATION OF THE HOLY GHOST.

---◆---

A SERMON,

BY CHARLES GORDELIER.

PREACHED AT JEWRY STREET CHAPEL,

On Monday Evening, July 21st, 1862.

" But the Comforter, the Holy Ghost, whom the Father will
send in my name, he shall teach you all things, and bring all
things to your remembrance, whatsoever I have said unto you."—
JOHN xiv. 26.

THERE is no history in the world like that which records
the last week of our Lord's public life on earth. It is
crowded with incidents of the deepest interest to all
believers; their life and their hopes of immortality are
bound up in it. Neither is there any discourse in the
Bible like that which fell from the lips of our Lord on the
night in which he was betrayed; for it contains the
germs of all those truths which the disciples were taught
to hold as the doctrines of the glorious gospel of the
grace of God.

This verse which we have taken as a text is a portion
of that discourse. It contains a most important doctrine
—the ministration of the Spirit. Its central truth is,
that the Holy Spirit is the Teacher of the Church of
Christ.

This central truth arises out of the gracious compact
between the Eternal Three in the Covenant of Grace; it
is based on the fundamental truth of the Trinity in Unity
of the glorious Godhead, in the distinct Personalities of
Father, Son, and Holy Ghost. It is God the Father
sending the Holy Ghost, in the name of his Son, to
teach his people divine truth—the way of salvation.

Such a revelation as this by the Lord Jesus Christ to
the believer renewed in the spirit of his mind must

No. 6.

necessarily, therefore, lead him to regard the teachings of the Holy Spirit as being in the highest degree most essential and exceedingly precious. This teaching is the Sun which illuminates the whole hemisphere of divine truth, and enlightens the eye of the understanding. Divine truth can only be understood by those who are spiritually taught. The natural man does not, cannot, receive the things of the Spirit, for they are foolishness unto him; neither can he know them, because they are spiritually discerned; that is, they can only be discerned by the spiritual man (1 Cor. i. 14).

Observe, in the 16th verse, our Lord first speaks of the Holy Ghost as another Comforter; MENAHEM, PARA-CLETOS, signifying an advocate, comforter; and a sweet truth it is to feel that sinners such as we have such an Advocate and Comforter—so near to us as to be dwelling in us. Jesus our Advocate in heaven for us with the Father, and the Holy Ghost our Advocate within us while on earth. O, what a glorious Comforter! Jehovah, in each of his divine Personalities, is the one Comforter of the Church of God in its militant and triumphant state.

But we must further observe, the Holy Ghost is also called the Spirit of Truth. Here his *character and office* are first developed; then, in our text his *Person* is fully declared; while, at the same time, both his mission and the manner of it are so graciously explained that we cannot but see all the Persons of the Godhead are united in bringing the redeemed to a knowledge of the truth as it is in Jesus. What a testimony we have here, both in this, the 26th verse and also the 16th verse, to the fact of a Trinity of Persons in the Godhead. Not a Trinity of *manifestations*, as some aver, *but of persons*, really and truly. The *Son* prays the *Father* for the gift of the *Comforter*; then the *Father* sends the *Comforter* in the name of *Christ* the Son. What a glorious Trinity in Unity! The undivided One, the uncreated and eternal Jehovah; distinct in their Personality, yet one in the Unity of the incomprehensible essence; distinguished as to order of subsistence and also by their personal qualities. Each Person is God most high, and all three Persons but one undivided Godhead, the same in nature, and equal in power, glory, and eternity; so that the Eternal Father, the Eternal Son, and the Eternal Spirit are the one incomprehensible Jehovah. This great truth, however, we must remember, is more a matter of faith than of the understanding.

> " To comprehend the great Three-One,
>   Is more than highest angels can ;
>   Or what the Trinity has done,
>   From death and hell to ransom man."

I pass on to notice, in connection with our text, that the range of knowledge possessed by the disciples was extremely limited till they were specially taught by the Holy Ghost.   Their ideas of Christ's kingdom were very vague and imperfect.   Their notions were chiefly of an outward or worldly character.   They were not suddenly prepared by the Lord to receive spiritual truth ; they were slow of heart to believe all what the prophets had spoken.   His teaching was gradual, apparently at times ineffective, for oftentimes He upbraided them ; but in this discourse He assured them that their memory should be enabled to recall the things He had said, and He intimated to them that He would not then say what at a later period of their understanding and experience would be more needful and advantageous for them to know.   The principal ideas which Jesus seemed to impress upon the disciples were, that the Comforter would further unfold those truths which he had already begun to impart, and that the Spirit's teaching would not only be found to agree with that of his own, but would also have one object in particular—the displaying to them the glorious Person, work, and character of the God-man Christ Jesus, in the redemption of the Church by his atonement to God the Father for their sin.

Here, then, is our position as believers.   The inspired word is complete ; all needful truth as to our relations with God is there revealed.   We have all the advantages the disciples possessed, yet how little we know of divine truth ; we still require teaching.   What can we know without ?   We need the ministration of the Holy Spirit as much as ever the disciples did.   Now, if you and I have been made sensible of our ignorance and our need of his teaching, we shall not fail to seek his aid in helping our conceptions of divine realities, both at this and at all other times whenever we read and meditate on his holy word.

I. Let us now attempt, in the first place, to make a few remarks on

The *Person and Nature of the Holy Ghost*. The word *Person*, I am aware, is not employed in Scripture to designate the Holy Spirit, but it is nevertheless plainly implied; nor is the word *third*, but both terms are commonly used merely for distinction's sake in the human mind, and have no reference to order of time or equality. The Person of the Holy Spirit is God, equal in nature, power, and glory with the Father and the Son—distinct in his Personality, yet one in the Unity of the incomprehensible Jehovah. Of his Personality, we may say, that Christ always speaks of him as a Person, as is plainly indicated by the use of the pronouns *he, his, himself*, &c. I would fain quote a number of scriptures for proof, but this would take up too much of our time ; and besides, I must bear in mind I am not discussing with Unitarians or Socinians. I doubt not but that most of you are familiar with the word of God on this important branch of truth, and that you receive it with joy and love as well as faith. Respecting the *nature* of this divine Person, he is *Spiritual*, essentially so, hence his name; and, being in his essence spiritual, is invisible to the bodily sense of sight. He is *omnipresent*, being everywhere present in the hearts of all true believers in Jesus; he dwells in them—making their bodies his temple. He is *holiness*, essentially so, hence his name; and, being essentially holy, he is the author, source, and fountain of holiness, purity and goodness. He is *divine*, essentially so, and hence he is often spoken of as the Divine Spirit. Believers in Christ are said to be partakers of the divine nature, because all that they possess of holiness, goodness, spiritualness, truthfulness, and heavenly-mindedness is derived from him. He communicates, imparts to them of his spirit, not his essence as God, but his nature. He is *truth*, essentially so; he is called the Spirit of Truth (John xvi. 13). He that is holiness itself cannot but be truth itself; no truth can be received and known until the Spirit of Truth imparts it. He is *Almighty*, essentially so. Thus it is we use the words "God the Holy Ghost." His operations in the hearts of men fully demonstrate that he is God. What but an almighty power can renew the mind of man in the image of Him who created him ? What is your own experience on this matter ? Has it any correspondence with the declaration of God's word ? You say you were once dead in trespasses and in sins ; you were dead to God ; but now you humbly

trust you live unto God.   Well, then, who quickened your
dead soul?   Who opened your blind eyes?   Who turned
your affections to things above, where Christ sitteth, and
made them to savour of the things of God?   "O," say
you, "it was God the Holy Ghost.   His power I felt to
be almighty, invincible, and irresistible ; and it was as
gracious as it was free."   Ah, my brother or my sister in
Christ, it is so—

> " 'Tis God's inimitable hand
> That moulds and forms the heart anew."

> " Learning and wit may cease their strife,
> When miracles with glory shine ;
> The voice that calls the dead to life
> Must be almighty and divine."

On the other hand how sad, and how awful, is the state
of those churches, families, and individuals who are without the teachings of God the Holy Ghost.   Whatever
understanding there may be of Bible truth, it is but the
letter of it, not the power ; they have no vitality, no spirituality, no real godliness.   The mental or mere natural
reception of the great truth which we are speaking of, is
totally powerless in itself.   Divine and almighty power is
indispensable to receive and to acknowledge the Person
and operations of God the Holy Ghost.

II. I proceed now to notice in the second place—

*That the Ministration of the Holy Ghost is by virtue of
the Commission and Authority of God the Father.*

When we speak of the Holy Ghost as the administrator
of the Covenant of Grace, we by no means intimate or
intend to infer that he is inferior in power, nature, glory,
or authority to either of the Persons of the Father or the
Son.   The offices of each Person in the Trinity for carrying forth the great work of Salvation are as distinct as
are their Persons.   The object is one—the salvation of
the Church of God.   All are united and engaged in it
equally, even as the Godhead is one ; hence the salvation
of each and every elect vessel of mercy is of God alone.

God the Father loved the Church with an everlasting
love.   He determined on the salvation of his people ; He
chose their persons in Christ His Son, who became their
Covenant Head ; he blessed them with all spiritual blessings in heavenly places in him before time began, before
the foundation of the world, before the fall of Adam.   It

is manifest, therefore, that nothing having respect to the merits or works of the creature could have moved the mind of God. Doubtless he foresaw that *all* the race of mankind was involved in the ruin of the first transgression; but that he should save some and not save all can only be ascribed to reasons of his own sovereign goodness; and in speaking of God's sovereignty, just let me observe there can be nothing of arbitrariness in the nature of God as a sovereign. This would be absurd to suppose. He has revealed that his justice is fully satisfied in the death of his Son as the substitute of his chosen, and therefore we ascribe the work of Salvation to God's free and boundless grace.

God the Son has equally and fully manifested his grace in the Salvation of his Church, in undertaking in the fulness of time to become Incarnate. The love of Christ passeth knowledge, when we consider "that for our sakes he became poor, that we through his poverty might be made rich." That he should leave his primeval glory, the glory that he had with his Father before the world was, and take our nature into personal union with himself, is wonderful indeed. Well does he deserve the name Wonderful (Isaiah ix. 6). Wonderful in his condescension to take our nature; wonderful in his willingness to take our low place; wonderful in his love to become our Surety, Mediator, Substitute, and Redeemer. What could move him thereto but his own innate love to us? The love of Christ is as truly inconceivable even as he is in himself the "unspeakable gift" of God the Father. It is under this view of Christ's free, boundless, and eternal love to us, when made known to us under the teachings of the Holy Spirit, that our souls become animated and fired with love to him. We love him because he first loved us; and it is his love which becomes the ruling principle in us to serve him and to follow him in all that his will and word direct—the love of Christ constraineth us in all we are and do.

God the Holy Ghost is also manifested as being equally engaged in the work of Salvation as the Father and the Son. His work, if I might so say, is more demonstrative, more tangible, being brought home to our consciousness and experience. He is the Witnesser of what the Father *is*, and what the Son *has done*. His office is to testify to the believer of the truth as revealed in the Scriptures.

He does not, indeed, speak of himself in the manner that Christ speaks of himself; but all his operations in the heart, and his communications to the understanding and the affections bear ample testimony of his work, character, love, and power as being fully equal in divine grace, love, goodness, truth, and power in all that concerns the covenant of grace and the salvation of each believer in Christ.

Thus we perceive, as revealed in the Word of God and by his Spirit, the several parts of the great work of man's redemption, which each of the divine Persons of the ever-blessed Trinity have undertaken to perform. The salvation of the church, in the eternal plan and mind of God, is perfect and complete, though in the personal experience of individual believers it is not so until the spirit is dismissed from the body, and the body itself is redeemed from the power of the grave on the morning of the general resurrection. Salvation, effectively, is wrought out *in our time-state*, and in harmony with God's providence on earth. All God's people, therefore, in harmony with the manifestations of his truth on earth, and the general designs of his providence, are, in process of time, sooner or later brought to a knowledge of himself by faith in the Lord Jesus Christ; and their characters as believers in Christ, while in the world, are known by the fruits and graces of the Spirit, which they produce and exhibit in their general conduct and manners of life. Being separated from the world in its spirit, pursuits, pleasures, and maxims, they show that their sentiments, motives, and course of life are regulated by the principles of the gospel. Such only, whose outward testimony of the salvation within, can be deemed worthy of the name of Christian. O! my hearers, how stands it with you? This is a solemn question; let it come home to you, and examine yourselves. Know whether ye be in the faith.

But I must not forget to speak to the point in hand. I said that the ministration of the Holy Ghost is by virtue of the commission and authority of God the Father. I have given you a general statement of the method of salvation in the several acts of Father, Son, and Spirit, and also a brief sketch of the manner in which it is developed in those who are its participants; I have now to show more particularly *the authority* which God the Father possesses in relation to the work of the Spirit.

God the Father, by virtue of his own proper nature as

God, as the Creator of the universe, the Creator of man and of all other intelligences, has authority alone over all things which he has made. (Ps. xcv. 5; and c. 3.) "Behold, all souls are mine." (Ezek. xviii. 4.) "Shall the thing formed say to him that formed it, Why hast thou made me thus? Hath not the potter power over the clay?" (Rom. ix. 20, 21.) "Who hath directed the Spirit of the Lord, or being his counsellor, hath taught him?" (Isa. xl. 13.) "He doeth according to his will in the army of heaven, and among the inhabitants of the earth: and none can stay his hand, or say unto him, What doest thou?" (Dan. iv. 35.) "He is Lord of all." "He is King of kings, and Lord of lords." "He is the only Potentate." (Acts x. 36; Rev. xix. 16; 1 Tim. vi. 15.) The centre of all authority, therefore, is in God, and all other authority must be derived from him; for he is the source of it. As, therefore, the plan of man's redemption originated with God, he alone has the right of authority as to the method of its accomplishment. This is seen in his own choice of the persons saved, his blessing them in Christ, giving Christ to be their head, and in giving them to him as his body, the church. (John xvii. 2; vi. 9; Eph. i. 4, 22; v. 23; Col. i. 18.)

Now comes the gracious disclosure of the Redeemer himself. The promise of the Holy Ghost, as the Comforter of his sorrowing disciples, is declared to them. His Personality is revealed in the designation given of his nature—the Holy Ghost. Then we have the manner of his coming made known—*sent by the Father*. Not that his being sent implies inferiority. By no means. The part each Person of the Godhead takes in salvation is *a joint* transaction, though *personally distinct* in its accomplishment. The work of salvation in men's hearts is begun and carried on by some one, and in some manner. Can we define it in any other way than the Saviour himself has done? Being a spiritual operation in the soul, can any other person than the Holy Ghost take possession of us, create in us a new heart, renew a right spirit, dwell in us, teach us, comfort us, lead us, and preserve us unto his kingdom of glory? 'Tis true Christ dwells in our hearts, but then it is by faith, not personally; that could not be. And there is a sense, too, in which it is said both God the Father and the Son dwell and abide with the believer, (John xiv. 23,) but even this is as the spirit of love; and here is the secret, the main-spring, as it were, of the Father's authority in sending the Spirit as the Comforter of the church—he comes by virtue of his being the Spirit of love, the love of God the Father, and the love of God the Son. In all this there is equality and unity; not inferiority or priority. Jesus himself speaks of sending the Spirit; (John xvi. 7;) and in the 28th verse, of his coming forth from the Father. Hence, then, by the unity there is in the Godhead, there can be no inferiority or priority of either Personality, position, or essence in the Triune Jehovah. But seeing that we, for distinction's sake, ascribe to the Father the supremacy of all things, and that the origination of salvation was from his love, and was the moving cause of Christ coming into the world to save sinners, (John iii. 16; 1 Tim. i. 15,) so we perceive, as declared in the Scriptures of truth, the Holy Ghost proceeds from the Father with authority, the highest authority, the best authority—LOVE—being commissioned to execute the work of salvation in each believer's soul in the spirit of love. GOD IS LOVE. We are witnesses of the fact that LOVE, as a principle, is the main-spring of all good felt in the heart, or done in the life. It is the powerful lever which moves man to exercise himself in acts of kindness for the benefit of his species. And thus we find revealed in the word of truth, it is the love of God the Father which moves him to send forth the Spirit to regenerate his elect vessels of mercy—to call them out of the kingdom of darkness, and to translate them into the kingdom of his dear Son. As, therefore, love is the great moral power by which men's hearts are moved, so we find there is, in the work of redeeming love, power, efficiency, and completeness.

> " What almighty love decrees,
> Almighty power performs."

O! my soul, " his glory is great in thy salvation." (Ps. xxi. 5.)

III. *We come now to show, in the third place, that the ministration of the Holy Ghost is* IN THE NAME *of Christ.*

The Holy Ghost comes not in his name. Christ did not; he came in the Father's name. The Holy Ghost comes in the name of Christ. His own name would have been sufficient had he chosen to have come in that, but we see a propriety and unity of action in his not doing so. Our Lord declares " he shall not speak of himself;" he shall not refer to himself personally ; his own acts shall demonstrate who he is, what his work is, and from whom he proceeds. " He shall testify of me ;" (John xv. 26 ;) " he shall take of mine, and shall show it unto you ;" (John xvi. 15 ;) and, indeed, throughout the whole of this valedictory discourse—the 14th, 15th, and 16th chapters—we have most gloriously displayed the working out of our salvation by the Eternal Three. It is traced to the love of God the Father in eternity—the incarnation, life, and death of Jesus as our substitute, and the operation of the Holy Ghost in our hearts in this time-state ; so that, in the covenant of grace, which is ordered in all things and sure, we see the salvation of each believer is effectually and finally accomplished in the same unity *of action* as there was *in purpose*. It is thus the work is made most glorious. The Father's love is made known to us by Christ himself. All that Christ has done for us is made known to us by the Holy Ghost, in the name of Christ, by his authority, by virtue of what he had done—that " name which is above every name ;" that name in which we come to the throne of God for mercy, and find acceptance for his sake.

But now let us inquire what *advantages* the church of God derive by the Holy Ghost coming in the name of Christ.

1. *He represents the Person of Christ, and supplies his place.*—This, it seems, our Lord intimates is not only the intention, but that it would be better for his disciples than his own personal presence ; for he says, " If I go not away the Comforter will not come unto you," (John xvi. 7,) meaning that the comfort and advantage of his bodily presence would be supplied by the Comforter coming to them instead, and abiding with them for ever; and he tells them, in giving his charge, to go and preach the gospel everywhere. " Lo, I am with you alway, even to the end of the world." Therefore the church of God, its ministers, especially, by the abiding and indwelling of the Spirit, have that which is equivalent to the personal presence of Christ ; for they are essentially one. However advantageous it might be to have the bodily presence of Christ, yet it could only be in a limited degree, and in some particular locality, wherever he might choose to be, for it is impossible that his corporeal body could be ubiquitous —that is, in two or more places at one time. But seeing that

the Holy Ghost is not a corporeal being, but spiritual and omnipresent—present in the hearts of all believers—the advantage is to each and every member of the mystical body of Christ that HE represents the person of Christ and supplies his place in all their circumstances and conditions, the same as if Jesus Christ himself were bodily present with them.

2. *He works the works of Christ.*—As Jesus did not his own work, but the works of his Father who sent him, and in his name, so the Holy Spirit works not his own work in his own name, but he works the works of Christ, by whom he is sent, and in whose name he accomplishes it. (John xvi. 13—15.) That is to say, the work of the Spirit is not to reveal any new truth or grace, but to confirm and build up that of which Christ came to lay the foundation. The advantage of this is, that hereby we know the Spirit of truth and the spirit of error. There is a perfect harmony and unity in all divine revelation and teaching. Whatever Christ has revealed of the Father, the Spirit takes of Christ and reveals unto the church. His great work, however, is to glorify Christ in all his offices and characters, just as it was the work of Christ to glorify the Father, by whom he was sent. Let believers bear this in mind, whenever they stand in need of his assistance in their work in the church of God, and for their own growth in grace and knowledge of the truth. Truth and grace are what Christ dispenses; (John i. 17;) the meaning of which, as I understand it, is *that which is revealed and that which is effected.* Now, since Christ has ascended into the highest heavens, and is for ever sat down on the throne of his Father, what could be more appropriate, and advantageous to believers in Christ, than that the Spirit of all grace and truth should take of the things of Christ and reveal them unto us? And I say, if we are of those who believe to the saving of the soul, " God hath revealed them unto us by his Spirit."

3. *He is received as the Spirit of God the Father and of the Son—the Spirit of love.*—Believers in the Lord Jesus Christ love his name, love his person, love his work, love his word, love his house, and love his people. "We love him because he first loved us." (1 John iv. 19.) "By this we know we have passed from death unto life, because we love the brethren." (1 John iii. 14.) Believers not only love him that is begotten, but also love him that begat, for

every one who is born of God is born of the Spirit. (1 John v. 1; John iii. 5.)   They love the Spirit; they love him because of the things of which he bears testimony in their hearts and experience—the Spirit of faith, of adoption, of a sound mind; they love him because of the name and person whom he represents; they love him because he is the Spirit of truth; they love him because he is the Spirit of holiness.   Born of God, they hate all sin and all error, and are only happy and prosperous in their souls as he exercises his influence as their teacher, and sheds abroad the love of God in their hearts by his sweet influence and power: they love him because he is the author of all those gifts, graces, and fruits which indicate the life of God in the soul.   Hence it is they pray him never to depart from them; not an exercise of devotion or meditation do they find profitable without him.   Their spirituality of mind, desires, hopes, motives, joy and peace they derive alone from him; for all this and much more they pray him to bestow, and to abound in every good word and work, and therefore He is received as the Spirit of Love.   Well will it be if all of us now present have received him as the Spirit of Love.

IV.—I pass on to shew in the FOURTH place, *that the ministration of the Holy Ghost is manifested to Believers by an evidence peculiar and proper to itself.*

By the phrase, " evidence peculiar and proper to itself," I mean, as the work of grace is spiritual, so all its parts, operations, and witness are spiritual.   What is true of the whole must be true of its parts.   Every schoolboy is taught this, and it is believed in and acted on in the world.   But in Religion, men seem to have a warped understanding, and vainly endeavour to bring to bear, things that have no common principles of agreement whatever. The things of the flesh are confounded with the things of the Spirit.   What is a large part of the profession in the present day but a fleshly, carnal, empty round of performances in the name of religion.   Thousands having a name to live while they are dead, scoff at spiritual religion and call it mysticism and fanaticism.   Well, let it be so. Our Lord says, "That which is born of the flesh is flesh, and that which is born of the Spirit is spirit." John iii. 6.   They are essentially distinct in their nature, and also in their operations.   This is the teaching of Christ, and the evidence of the Holy Ghost is in his teaching the Church all things which Christ came to do and teach.

God's word reveals to us that all men by nature are dead in sin, dead to God, dead to spiritual truth. The Gospel, that Christ died for sinners is preached to all men ; some believe and some believe not. The unbeliever is condemned because his deeds are evil, he loves darkness rather than light, he hateth the light, and will not come within its influence lest his deeds should be reproved. (John iii. 19—20.) The believer is saved, but his faith is ascribed to God, being his gift, and because of the Divine power working with the truth. (Eph. ii. 8.) Here then is the immutable truth of God. Man's damnation is of himself, but salvation is all of free, sovereign grace.

1.—His soul is quickened. Divine life is imparted. He is a new creature. He possesses life in Christ Jesus. His affections and understanding are renewed, renewed in the spirit of his mind—he has a new heart, not the carnal heart new modelled, as certain of our own poets have said.* The evidence of all this is peculiar and proper to itself— " in demonstration of the Spirit, with power and much assurance ;" the object of the affections being changed, a new direction is given to the will and to the affections ; a new motive power in all the thoughts, desires and aims ; the love of Christ is constraining, being shed abroad in the heart by the Holy Ghost; hence there is joy and peace in the Holy Ghost ; partly because there is a sense of pardoned sin, and, partly, because the Soul has found its centre. Christ is his ALL IN ALL. The believer is a new man in Christ.

2.—The Holy Ghost is his Teacher ; he imparts to the understanding a knowledge of divine truth, he is taught his state of heart, his own vileness, the exceeding sinfulness of sin, its penalty, his own inability to save himself, that there is no justification by the works of the law, but only by and through the righteousness of Christ. He is taught to look to Christ, to trust in him, to come to him. He has an experience of these facts within him ; they are the exercises of a spiritual mind on spiritual things, leading him out of himself, and resting on Christ the rock of ages. Having tasted, handled and felt of the good word of life he is dissatisfied with any thing short of it ; this

---

* Watts's Hymns, B. i., H. 95,

leads him to seek and to know more of Christ, and to say
with the poet :

> " Oh, could I know and love him more,
> And all his wondrous grace explore ;
> Ne'er would I covet man's esteem,
> But part with all and follow him."

" That I may know him and the power of his resurrection ;" such a knowledge of him as would absorb all the
powers of my soul ; to feel its influence so powerful as to
feel myself risen from the dead, and never more to be
found in company with the world.   And for this the believer looks to the Spirit of all grace, and the Holy Ghost
leads the mind into *all* truth—its depths—breadth—its
heights—into higher, richer, brighter views of Christ's
person, his work, his Offices and Characters ; he takes of
the things of Christ and reveals them unto him ; hence
the believer has most exalted views of Christ, of God the
Father, and has the witness of the Spirit, such is his
blessed experience of the heavenly truth.   He is saved by
the Eternal Three One Jehovah.

3.—*The teaching of the Holy Ghost is gradual in its
method*. God's works are invariable, slow, and progressive,
that is, in their development, but they are sure and certain.   "The path of the just is as the shining light that
shineth more and more unto the perfect day." (Prov. iv.
18.)   "Being confident of this very thing that he which
hath begun a good work in you will perform it until the
day of Jesus Christ." (Phil. i. 6.)   "Until the day dawn
and the day star arise in your hearts." (2 Pet. i. 19.)
Our experience and knowledge is gradually obtained. We
are first babes in grace, desiring the pure milk of the word
that we may *grow* thereby: We are to "*grow* in grace and
in the knowledge of our Lord and Saviour Jesus Christ,"
"until we come to the full stature of a man in Christ,"
"growing up into him in all things." (1 Pet. ii. 2 ; 2
Pet. iii. 18 ; Eph. iv. 15.)   We are at best but fools
and slow of heart to believe, for "precept must be upon
precept, precept upon precept; line upon line, line upon
line ; here a little and there a little." (Jer. xxviii. 10.)
But you will say, why does not the Holy Spirit teach us
at once, the things we are to know, and efficiently, so as
not to need this repetition and continuous labour ? I can
only say, we are dealt with as are all other parts of God's
creation, animate and inanimate. Weakness, growth,

progress, strength, completion are th e characteristics and law of all things in this world. The very fact that the Holy Spirit is our Teacher proves that his work is in harmony with the proportions of all things, for he adapts his teaching to the measure of our understandings, and leads us step by step till we attain the knowledge and experience designed by our Heavenly Father.

4.—His *method is gracious*. How free and unsought, can we not say, all his teachings have been freely imparted. "He *gave* his good Spirit to instruct them." (Nehe. ix. 20.) "The inspiration of the Almighty *giveth* understanding." (Job. xxxii. 8.) "We know the Son of God is come, and hath *given* us an understanding that we may know him that is true." (1 John v. 20.)

5.—His *method is certain*. "Who teacheth like him," was the question of Elihu; young in years, but old in knowledge. What we are instructed in by him we never forget. God burns, as it were, instruction into us; he instructs us by the furnace, the flood, the cross, bereaving providences, stripping providences, painful afflictions. He tries us as silver is tried; and when he hath tried us we shall come forth as gold, that is, all gold, gold only, no dross. It is by these things men live, and in them they have the life of their spirits. His teachings are carved deep into the memory of our experience, and thus we have a blessed assurance of his work in our soul; and, when patience has had its perfect work, we admire the discipline, teaching, and the Teacher. We praise, wonder, and adore our Covenant God and Father for sending his good Spirit to instruct us.

6.—His teaching is *truthful*. He is the Spirit of Truth, essentially so; his attribute is truth itself. He leads into all truth; or, as our text says, he shall teach you all things, and bring all things to your remembrance, whatsoever I have said unto you. Time would altogether fail to speak of the Holy Ghost either as our Comforter or as our Remembrancer, blessed offices which he sustains for the use of the church in its militant state. Our main point is his ministrations as a Teacher. All truth—not the arts and sciences of human life, for that does not enter into the question, though all natural sciences are the gifts of the Spirit; (Exod. xxxi. 3; Isa. xxviii. 26;) but all truth needful to be known by revelation,—all truth as to redemption,—all truth to be known by Christ's disciples as his ambassadors,—all truth pertaining to life and godliness.

And let me observe, that as truth is the essential attribute of the Holy Spirit, so the truth is the *instrumentality* of all his operations in the soul. He operates in no other way, though his operations may be *indirect* as well as *direct*, and always *sovereignly.* "The wind bloweth where it listeth, and thou hearest the sound thereof, but canst not tell whence it cometh and whither it goeth; so is every one that is born of the Spirit." (John iii. 8.) But whether his operations be direct or indirect, they are always by means of the truth. It may be a passage of God's word, a line of a hymn, a remark of a friend, a sentence uttered in the ministry of the word, or it may be the cogitations of the mind itself, or as I have just now said, by means of the fiery furnace, the watery flood, or any other method of his providence, yet it is the truth by which he works. I do not mean, of course, the mere letter of truth, but the power which he conveys with it into the mind of the believing heart. If you are spiritual men and women, you can understand what I mean. It may be I do not sufficiently express what I mean, but I know what I do mean, and I hope you do too. Neither do I wish it to be understood as if I implied that spiritual life is in the truth. No. If I understand the matter at all in any way, I would say, spiritual life is communicated to the soul, dead in sin, as a distinct principle altogether, though the instrumentality, as I have before said, is the truth. There is life *in knowing* the truth, but the truth is not life itself. It is but the medium through which it is known and felt. Life, I believe, is an essential principle known only to the great God himself. Man cannot understand it, it is unexplainable.

But how blessed to consider, that God the Holy Ghost leads the mind to know *all* saving truth. He opens it to understand "the truth as it is in Jesus." The believer prays, "Give me understanding, and I shall live;" (Ps. cxix. 144;) and in answer to prayer he is led to further, fuller, and brighter displays of Jehovah's grace and glory. In a word, his teaching is doctrinal, experimental, and practical. He sanctifies the believer by belief of the truth, and makes him wise unto salvation. He resides in the heart, and makes the body his temple. He is the

Comforter of the believer in all the exercises of the mortal state ; he is the Author of all spiritual operations of the soul, the understanding, and the affections:

> " Leads him to Christ, the living way,
> Nor lets him from his pastures stray."

As the Remembrancer of the church of the living God, he recalls to the recollection truths received long time since and forgotten ; promises of grace are revived with fresh vigour and encouragement that had long ceased to exercise hope and joy. By his secret influences, direct or indirect, spiritual life is constantly renewed and maintained, until the soul is brought to its eternal felicity in the heavenly state. He is the source, origin, and fountain of all that is known, or can be known and experienced, of truth, holiness, or heavenly-mindedness. His office and work in the covenant of grace being the going forth of Jehovah in the manifestations of his grace and mercy, in personal acts upon the souls of each fallen son and daughter of Adam as chosen in the covenant of grace. The great truth couched in our text is, that all we know and experience of divine truth is by the operation of God the Holy Ghost, accomplished in the name of Jesus Christ our Lord, and by God the Father's commission and authority. What a thought is here presented to us ! The glorious Trinity of Persons in the Unity of the Godhead are jointly engaged in distinct acts in teaching each believer the way of life and salvation. The Lord grant that this may be the portion of all now present, for his great name's sake. Amen.

DAVID GREATLY DISTRESSED,

BUT

DIVINELY ENCOURAGED.

◆

A SERMON,
BY CHARLES GORDELIER.

PREACHED AT JEWRY STREET CHAPEL, ALDGATE,

On Monday Evening, August 18th, 1862.

" And David was greatly distressed ; ...... but David encouraged himself in the Lord his God."—1 SAMUEL xxx. 6.

I HAVE, as you perceive, omitted a portion of the verse, but do not thereby disturb its sense. The words which I have taken as a text have been presented to my mind with a considerable degree of force and sweetness; and the subject is one which I am sure the poor tried child of God will be interested in, and is likely to arrest his attention. May the Lord help us to say a few words respecting the things which we have tasted, handled, and felt of the good word of life which, with his blessing, may comfort those whose souls may be " discouraged because of the way."

Probably, however, some may suppose, that not much good can be had from preaching on the historical parts of the Old Testament; but this is a mistake. It is very true, there are many passages in which we may see that every doctrine, every admonition, and every command of which God is the Author, has all the majesty of his name, all the weight of his authority, all the inflexibleness of his justice, and all the persuasiveness of his love; yet I think most persons must be sensible how much more lively and powerful the impression is upon the mind when they see the influence of God's truth embodied in character and brought out into action under the varying circumstances of common life. Is it not the practical

No. 7.

illustration, or exhibition, of those very truths we are aiming to learn? And certainly it is easier to understand than when presented in the form of an abstract treatise or a set of short sentences. If we regard the histories and the biographies recorded in the Bible *as mere narrations*, why, we miss the very point for which they were written. Its biographies, especially, are full of the most interesting and profitable instruction. What is the life of Jacob, the history of Joseph, of Israel in the Wilderness, Samson, Hezekiah, and others, but the application of the theoretical principles of God's Word set before us and demonstrated in the actual experience and life of the man of God. It is God's truth displayed, not so much in description as it is in action. It is not the fine sentiments of the theorist, but it is the real attainments of the believer in Christ, which excite us to "give the more earnest heed to the things which we have heard, lest at any time we should let them slip."

These remarks, then, may perhaps induce you to ponder over some things with regard to David "and the times that went over him." His life and character are remarkably interesting in themselves, apart from what may be considered his typical or lineal connection with the Lord Jesus Christ. His name signifies "the beloved," "dear." Our Lord Jesus Christ is the Beloved of his Father; his dear Son, his only-begotten Son, which is in the bosom of the Father, he hath declared him. (John i. 18; Matt. iii. 17.) In David having this name given to him, who, though the last of a numerous progeny, we see is no less loved than the first-born, for it indicates the love of those who gave it. He was born at Bethlehem, as was his great anti-type, according to the flesh. In the fields of Bethlehem David kept his father's sheep. Our Jesus keeps his Father's sheep in his own hand, and none shall pluck them thence; the lion and the bear may attempt it, but shall be foiled. They may, perhaps, worry, but shall never devour.

David, no doubt, while tending his father's sheep in Bethlehem, often thought of the story of his excellent grandmother, Ruth. We can fancy David composing some of his choice Psalms, singing them to his music, in the very places where the young widow stooped to glean ears of corn for her aged widowed mother, and often, as she went along, dropping the tear of sadness; but how God changed the scene : Ruth sowed in tears but David reaped in joy. So God has often done for his people since ; in the place made memorable by their deepest sorrows, he has made it to them a remembrance of his loving-kindness and their greatest blessings. It is true, indeed, David's youthful days were gladdened and brightened by the unexpected event of being anointed to be the future King of Israel. What his hopes and expectations were in the prospect of such an event we cannot say, but this we do know, " it was through much tribulation he entered the kingdom." Yes ; and so shall it be with every one of the Lord's followers ; tribulation is the path which they are called to tread, but through it they shall be brought, and the kingdom they shall enter ; they must enter it, for they are appointed to it. The King of kings himself has trod the path before, and he has entered the kingdom ; and where he is there must also his servants be.

David is said to have been " a man after God's own heart ;" that is, David's heart was more towards God's will, his ways, his glory, than to his own self. The love of God evidently possessed his heart ; it was shed abroad by the power of the Holy Ghost. He was noted for his fidelity to God, his meekness, humility ; his love of God's cause, his zeal for his honour were remarkably apparent ; in the midst of his deepest trials, his keenest afflictions, we see more of him as the saint of God than the monarch ; great as he was as a king, we know more about his soul's intimacy with God than of his doings in the state. God called him, " David my Servant," and thus it is his character is established as a man of God. He was the servant of God, for he did God's will.

There are certainly, some points in his history quite indefensible ; his deception, his adultery and murder are utterly abhorrent ; they are stains upon him as a man, and cannot be extenuated in any degree ; yet these crimes form no part of his character, that is, his fixed character ; they may be considered rather as accidents in his life than any trait of what he really was ; he was nevertheless what God called him, " a man after His own heart," and we have no right to contradict. David was a good man, but he was not a perfect man ; he, like other men, had his failings, his infirmities, and his weaknesses ; but, from the fact of his great excellencies in other points of view, his faults appear to greater disadvantage.

But while we are talking about David, do not let us forget ourselves; neither must we forget him who knows how to act upon our weaknesses. Satan is as wise now as he was in David's time. He who knew David's weak points knows full well all our weakness and failings, and is ever plotting to turn them to our disadvantage. We are called to be sober, to be vigilant; for our adversary the devil, as a roaring lion, is going about " seeking whom he may devour." (1 Pet. v. 8.) And you will see, by consulting 1 Sam. xxvii. 1–7, how Satan betrayed David into a false step. He deceives Achish, brings himself and his men into difficulties from which they very narrowly escape.

How common it is for men to bring themselves into perplexities and distress through deviations from the plain straightforward way of truth and honour in the first instance. This is it, sin deceives, blinds the judgment—stupifies the conscience, and, if grace prevent not, leads the man to perdition. You young folks make a note of that. Always observe the plain truth; suffer any disagreeable, indeed, the greatest inconvenience, rather than deceive others to get yourself out of trouble. And just let me say to you older ones, we ought to beware how we unite ourselves with the people of the world, or in any way that would lead us to compromise our Christian character. Their friendship, however sincere it may seem, may be a snare to us; the patronage of the world can be scarcely held with a good conscience. We may be easily deterred from the discharge of our duty, easily led to some mean trick to conceal what they dislike.

We see, however, in David's history, an exemplification of God's dealings in providence with his people. Afflictions and trials often accumulate one upon another until it seems as if a man's spirit could not possibly bear such a weight of trouble. Then, at some critical moment, just as the spirits are about to break down, God comes in with his timely aid and lifts them up.

In David's case the long misery he endured before he was king seemed to reach its height, when, on his return to Ziklag, he found his city, his home, and the homes of his mighty men consumed to ashes. His troubles had been many and various, but most severe when his brave, mighty men spake of stoning him, three of whom brake through a garrison of the Philistines once to get for him

a drink of the water of Bethlehem. Oh, this was distressing indeed. "David was greatly distressed."

I. Let us now look, FIRST, *at the source of David's
distresses.*

His distresses comprised: He was an exile from his
country ; he was, in fact, an outlaw ; away from the royal
court of which he was an honourable member ; separated
from the person of his beloved Jonathan, from the society
of his loving wife Milchal ; debarred from the worship of
God at the tabernacle ; hunted out of the land of Israel
by Saul and his followers. The Philistines had just
worked him out of the protection of the king of Gath ;
the Ziphites had betrayed him ; Cush had dealt treache-
rously ; the Amalekites had spoiled and burned his own
city Ziklag ; he had, through that circumstance, lost his
other two wives ; his men had lost their wives and children,—his men had lost their all in serving him ; they
look upon him as the occasion of all their loss and misfortunes. Now they are all agreed and ready to stone
him, none to defend him ; they all conspire his death,—a
death worthy only of some vile criminal. It was not
martial law. Martial law, if he had merited it, he could
have borne ; but he was too good a soldier for a soldier's
death, so they construe their misfortunes into a crime of
his, and their satisfaction is to be had in stoning him,—a
death in which all joined and conspired. It seemed
inevitable ; nothing seemed to turn up to soften them
down. Oh, this did indeed distress the brave, bold
warrior.

But these were not all his troubles. More than all
these put together was that which he felt within ; his
own conscience accused him. David felt that the source
of his distresses laid in his deceiving Ahimelech at Nob ;
his subsequent deviation from the path of integrity and
uprightness placed him in jeopardy, and it would have
ended desperately both with him and his men, if God had
not overruled and moved the king Achish and his lords to
send them away. Their suspicions of him were un-
founded, but it was the way out of danger. God's providence is truly wonderful. David meant well, no doubt,
but found his own judgment was not to be trusted. He
has come now to his wit's end ; now he knows where to
find his God. He seeks God in the midst of all this
confusion, uproar, and strife. He has no friend, no coun-

sellor out of all these chafed spirits; they arc sworn against him, being his enemies wrongfully. He consults Abiathar the priest and Gad the prophet. They are with him, it is true, but their personal help can be of no use at such a time as this; but their sacerdotal position may. Happily David, though greatly distressed, feels bitterly the source of all his distresses, yet finds immediately the source of his encouragement—his God. There he found help; he was divinely encouraged under all his earthly distresses. "It is no marvel," says good Bishop Hall, "that God remembereth David in all his troubles, since David in all his troubles did thus remember his God." But thus it was, all David's springs were in God, from whence flowed those streams of his remembrance of God, and seeking his face; for all that leads to God, first comes from God, and leads to God again. As fountains in the valleys descend from the hills, so David felt it when he said, "I will lift up mine eyes unto the hills, from whence cometh my help." (Ps. lxxxvii. 7; cxxi. 1.)

Now, in looking at the source of David's troubles, and the manner of their being heaped up together, and appearing as if they would all fall upon him like an avalanche and bury him completely, do we not trace something like our own experience? do we not, some of us at least, feel as if we had been where David was. We feel, this is the man who has gone before us in the same dreary, dark part, the valley of the shadow of death. How near he was to it! but he walked through it. How near some of you have been to the end of your life, or your hopes, and thought you were alone, like Bunyan's Pilgrim, but the voice of another going before in the same path helps you on. You are not alone; God is with you. Evil may be about you, all around you, dangers on every side; but, O, if God speaks or whispers but one word, you are encouraged; you fear no evil, for he is with you. (Ps. xxiii. 4.) There is a "needs be that we be in heaviness through manifold temptations." (1 Peter i. 6.)

"From all our afflictions, his glory shall spring;
The deeper our sorrow, the louder we'll sing.

II. We come now to consider, in the SECOND place, *the source of David's encouragement.* "He encouraged himself in the Lord his God." And we shall perceive, too,

that his encouragement in God was based upon several
matters of fact that led him in the midst of his distresses
to feel that though all men should forsake him, yet God
would be true to him; he would be true to his own
promise, he would be true to his own character.   These
several matters which we are now about to bring together
in a focus, as it were, is what every tried believer feels he
must do, for he finds his account in it.   "In the day
of adversity consider."   Consider what ?   Why, what
grounds you have for encouragement.   This is what
David did; and in looking at these several things we
shall observe :

1. David's heart was established in the truth and providence of God, particularly in the promises made to him
of his ultimate deliverance from Saul.   2. He had been
anointed in the presence of his brethren, not privately, as
was Saul; not only so, but with a *horn* of oil, not a
phial, as in the case of Saul.   These were two significant
facts ; spiritually, they have reference to the Messiah
upon whom the Spirit was poured out without measure.
Now the remembrance of this anointing, signifying God's
gracious appointment, his setting him apart and dedica-
tion for the monarchy, must have been indelible; consequently, in all his subsequent reverses, his opposition and
persecution from Saul, we find him ever resting on Jehovah's word for deliverance.   3. His confidence that God
would deliver him was heightened from his own experience;
he still trusted that he would be delivered as on former
occasions.   His combat with Goliath, his struggle with
the bear and with the lion, he would never forget; nor
had he forgotten the amazing escape and deliverance from
the army of Saul which had encompassed him on the
mountain; but Saul, hearing of an invasion, suddenly
withdrew his troops and left David unmolested.   Certain
death seemed inevitable, and if his faith did stagger, in
the presence of such a formidable host, can we wonder at
it?   "I shall one day perish by the hand of Saul."   But
if unbelief did make his faith to stagger, God's mercy
held him up.   Oh, how often we have sung those sweet
lines of Newton:

> " The saints need never be dismay'd,
>   Nor sink in hopeless fear;
> For when they least expect his aid,
>   The Saviour will appear.

> " Once David seemed Saul's certain prey;
> But hark! the foe's at hand.
> Saul turns his arms another way,
> To save the invaded land."

And have we not found it so too? how often God has stayed his "rough wind in the day of his east wind." While there is a needs be for the rough and the east winds, he does not suffer two cold winds to blow at one time. If the enemy comes in like a flood, the promise is, the Spirit of the Lord shall lift up a standard against him. Here you see is a resistance stronger than that which the trouble brings. And do remember this, O thou afflicted and tossed with tempest, and not comforted, all troubles must be met by a stronger force than that which they bring. Here you have it in that Almighty promise just quoted; it is the believer's breakwater. No flood can come beyond the standard which the Spirit of the Lord shall lift up; he is Lord of all power and might. Your refuge and your strength are here; here is your safety. He who lifts this standard for your salvation, times all his deliverances in such a way as shall be best for his own glory, your joy and comfort, and the everlasting confusion of all your enemies.

But I am running on and forgetting David. We were speaking of the several matters of fact which formed the basis of his encouragement in God. We have mentioned three; here is another. 4. Jonathan's friendship was at this time most invaluable to him. The thought of possessing one friend in adversity is an unspeakable solace. (See 1 Sam. xx.) Then we see another important element in David's encouragements. 5. We see his constant consultation of the Divine will. I can only refer you to the several passages, which I hope you will read at your leisure: 1 Sam. xxii. 3, 23; 1 Sam. xxiii. 4, 11, 16. Then, as to his trust, see Ps. vii. 11, 12; proving as is said by the prophet, "They that wait upon the Lord shall renew their strength; they shall mount up with wings as eagles; they shall run, and not be weary; and they shall walk, and not faint." (Isa. xl. 31.) Then again, 6. We see, too, his consciousness of his own integrity and uprightness. (1 Sam. xxiv. 11, 12.) Look, too, at the 27th Psalm, which was probably written at about this time. Twice had David deceived others; he had deceived himself; he had seen and felt the bitterness of expediency and deceit; now it is his earnest prayer, " Let integrity and uprightness *continually* preserve me." Well is it to feel the exceeding sinfulness of sin; for the stronger we feel the evil of sin, the more earnest will be our prayer for salvation from it.

7. But there was one thing more than all these : God was his all. " Whom have I in heaven, but thee, and there is none upon earth that I desire beside thee." To whom could he go in the midst of his distresses? The anointed of Israel, divinely assured of the kingdom, but, humanly speaking, never was farther from it when all his brave, mighty men threatened him with immediate and an ignominious death, but

> " The mount of danger is the place,
> Where we shall see surprising grace."

God stays their hand, though he suffered them to speak of stoning him. Many of God's people have been alarmed and felt in peril from the great swelling words of furious and malignant spirits, but their hands have been held in chains. " The Lord knoweth how to deliver the godly out of temptations." (2 Peter, ii. 9.) He knew how to deliver "the man after his own heart" out of his many and grievous perplexities. God touched a secret spring in David's heart that led him to seek his help. He calls for the priest, and consults the Holy Oracle, and what does it say? " Pursue, for thou shalt surely overtake them, and without fail recover all." (verse 8.) Was this an impression on his imagination, think ye? No, indeed ; he knew well the voice of God ; he hung on that divine word—he hung on the promises ; he was always a man in earnest, and nothing but realities, divine realities, would satisfy his heart. Look at the earnestness of his prayers ; look at the earnestness of his praises ; look at the earnestness of his thankfulness, in the 27th Psalm to wit. David never lost sight of God as his guard and guide. Even in the King of Achish's court he was not without Abiathar and the Ephod, and it was a happy circumstance that he and his men were sent away so early in the morning as they were. He had placed himself in a very questionable position with the Philistine army; certainly he never was so weak in himself. Though he had Abiathar with him, there was no consulting the Ephod ; but when on his return he found himself sur-

rounded with difficulties and danger, then he knew where
to obtain courage and resolution. He did obtain it, and
at the time he most wanted it, and he applied it, too, with
good purpose, even under the very worst of circumstances.

This energy of mind, as we sometimes term it, or, as it
is expressed in the text, encouragement, is derived from
God alone; he alone imparts it. There is no enduring
energy of mind from any other source than what David
himself says about it: "In the day of my trouble, when
I called upon thee, thou strengthenest me with strength
in my soul." (Ps. cxxxviii. 3.) This is the only true
energy of mind—that which God gives. See what it
did for David; it energized him so that he recovered his
spirits, stood to his position as their captain, subdued the
mutinous spirit of those mighty men, ordered them out,
marshalled them in rank and file, and, taking the lead,
bid them follow him, and he led them on to the pursuit,
overtook the marauders, and recovered all. If you want
to know something about these brave, mighty men, read
at your leisure 2 Sam. xxiii., from the 8th to the end,
and then you will estimate David as being superior to
them all.

Now let me draw your attention to a few of the Psalms
which were written by this sweet psalmist of Israel;
they are at least eighteen in number, all showing that he
knew where his strength lay. I can only name them by
their numbers, but you will find it worth your while to
note them down: Ps. xvii., xviii., xxii., xxxi., xxxiv., xxxv.,
lii., liv., lv., lvi., lvii., lix., lxii., lxiii., lxiv., lxxxiv., cxxiv., and
cxlii. These and others were written under the inspira-
tion of God, with, if I might so say, the ink of his own
experience; and we, who have to follow in some measure
the steps he trod, feel it is true. But look again at the
following Scriptures; do not be weary with God's Word,
for this is the instrumentality God employs to strengthen
you. If you want real courage to battle with the world,
the flesh, and the devil, you must get it here. What
does Job say? (xxiii. 6): "Will he plead against me with
his great power? No! he would put strength in me,"
that is, courage, energy. "The Lord is the strength, the
energy of my life." (Ps. xxvii. 1.) "God is the
strength of my heart; God gives me courage and life."
(Ps. lxxiii. 1.) "Blessed is the man whose strength is
in thee;"' (Ps. lxxxiv. 12;) that is, who derives his
courage, his energy, his spiritual life from his God. Now, I

appeal to your own experience whether this is not the case? The Word may have come to your soul with an irresistible power, with a power that has overset all your doubts, fears, unbelief, rebellion, and I know not what beside, in one moment; or it may have come with a dove-like softness, with such a melting influence upon your spirit as to cause you to feel so deeply humbled and yet so divinely strengthened, that you have gone forth in the power of his might, and fearlessly faced the foe, and bravely conquered. I know your reply; it is so. You can say, with the Apostle: "I can do all things through Christ which strengtheneth me," and with the poet :—

> " O I have seen the day,
>   When by a single word,
> God helping me to say,
>   ' My trust is in the Lord,'
> My soul has quell'd a thousand foes,
> Fearless of all that could oppose."

I do not know that I have anything more to add except by way of practical observations, and these shall be few and brief. I trust that, under the anointing of the Spirit, some of the remarks which have been dropped may find an entrance into your heart, and have an abiding place there. We speak of those things which we do know, and testify that which we have seen. If God has appointed us to his heavenly kingdom we shall enter it most certainly, but it will be after the manner of David entering the kingdom of Israel, "through much tribu-lation." But mark the word "through;" we pass on, not staying in it, but every step of the way, whether light or dark, rough or smooth, painful or pleasing, is to bring us nearer to it. And then, as to that word "much," which seems as though it would, and does appear at times, to eclipse the believer's sun of his hopes, is it not most blessedly compensated by that delightful word "peace"? Does not our Lord say: "In the world ye shall have tribulation; but be of good cheer; in me ye have peace?" (John, xvi. 33.) Is not peace in Christ a complete compensation for all the troubles we are called to pass through? Oh, certainly it is; the troubles of this life we are *passing through*; this life is but a life of passing on to the heavenly kingdom; Christ is the be-liever's peace; enduring peace in the midst of changing scenes; and he that believes this truth hath entered into rest; his feet are on a rock, a foundation on which he

never can be moved or shaken ; be he ever so miserable
in the world he is happy in Christ. "Let earth be all
in arms abroad, he dwells in heavenly peace." "Jesus
Christ, the Eternal God, is his refuge, and underneath are
the everlasting arms." And "as his day so shall his
strength be."

But now, in conclusion, let us from this portion of
David's history which we have had before us, observe

1. That whenever we are called to pass through
troublous times, *to be instant in prayer*—at the moment.
If the believer in Christ has this spiritual habit of prayer,
he will, at any moment of his exigences, turn at once to
his stronghold. If you were a bird, the moment you saw
danger, you would use your wings and flee away ; perhaps
you do say, oh that you had wings, like a dove you would
flee quietly and swiftly away and be at rest ; well now,
the believer's prayers are his wings. With these he flies
at once to his God: and as wings are a part of the bird
itself, so prayer is a part of the believer's self ; it is his
native air, his vital breath, returning from whence it
came. As the bird has an aptitude for flight, so should
the believer have an aptitude for prayer. "Men ought
always to pray and not to faint :" if there were not
always occasions for prayer, surely our Lord, who knoweth
all things, would not have enforced its necessity. There
is always a necessity for prayer, for we are always needy ;
but never more so, than when wave upon wave, sorrow
upon sorrow, comes rolling over the soul like a tempes-
tuous sea. The thicker our dangers accumulate the more
need for immediate prayer. "Lord, help me," "O Lord,
I am oppressed, undertake for me ;" these prayers are like
anchor flukes, they are cast within the veil, they take hold
of God's strength; the soul that trusts such an anchor as
this shall never be driven from its steadfastness ; no never.

2. Suffer yourself *not to be cast down*. Cast not away
your confidence, which has great recompense of reward.
If you are perplexed with troubles of various kinds, be
not in despair; faint not, "If thou faintest in the day of
adversity, thy strength is small." (Prov. xxiv. 10.) Save
your spirit from fainting by waiting upon God at once ;
look to the strong for strength ; the rock of your strength
is in him; he will give you divine strength to bear up
against earth's trials ; the energy, courage, resolution that
you require for dealing with difficulties, oppressions, losses
and crosses in the circumstantial affairs of life, God can

impart at the precise moment you most need it ; not before
you want it, but at the time : " In your patience possess
ye your souls ;" this is your Lord's direction, a merciful
provision for anticipated trials ; in the time that your
patience is exercised, do not lose your self-possession.
Suffer yourself not to be cast down, but hope in God;
rest in him ; wait patiently for him ; true, the soul is
often cast down, but then there is no real reason for it ;
if once the spirits give way, there is no knowing what
will follow. Hope in God, look up ; trust his faithfulness
and power. His covenant promises are engaged in thy
behalf, for he hath said, " I will never leave thee, no,
never forsake thee." (Heb. xiii. 5.)

3. That we carefully avoid adopting any expedients
that may occasion us to resort to deceit and falsehood.
God does not require it at our hands. He is a God of
truth, just and right is he. He is a rock, his work is
perfect. He is immutably the same. Nor can a sincere
believer in Christ be otherwise : " surely they are children
that will not lie, and so he was their Saviour." You have
seen the difficulties and dangers David thrust himself into
by his culpable falsehood to Ahimelech ; no one can tell
where the mischief would have ended if God had not
marvellously moved the court of Achish to send him
away. Falsehoods, prevarications, equivocations are dangerous expedients for a child of God to meddle with ; they
are sure to bring the soul into distress, guilt, and darkness ; there are no distresses in the soul so severe as the
accusations of a guilty conscience ; oh, take heed as to
how you get into difficulties ; but take more heed as to
how you get out; never forget, *expediency* brings more
into difficulty and distress than it can ever get out.
David's case to wit, and Paul's case, when he shaved
himself and went into the Temple as though he still held
with the Jews in Judaism. (Acts xxi. 23–30.) It was
" expediency " that made him a prisoner for life ! It is
true, God overruled his expediency for His glory and the
good of his church, but expedients are not to be adopted
for all that. The doctrine of human expediency is not
to be found in God's Word.

4. That courage of mind which is obtained from reliance on God will positively help us through the fiercest
of foes—the deepest distress, and the most fiery trials.
You cannot have a better illustration than our own text :
" David was greatly distressed, but David encouraged

himself in the Lord his God." Happy David! did the people stone him? No; "this poor man cried, and the Lord heard him and saved him out of all his troubles." (Ps. xxxiv. 6.) When God helped him, how undaunted he stood; how firm to his proper position; how resolute to command, and his men as ready to obey; whence came this sudden change; it was God alone that made David so invincible and beat down his foes before him; thus shall it be with every soul feeling its weakness and knowing no other resource but in God; strength for the day is God's gift; it is his promise; it is his prerogative; and it is his children's privilege to have. O tried believer; prostrated with life's troubles, or with soul troubles, your refuge and the rock of your strength is in God. Vain is all your contention, in your own strength, with the things of this world, of sin, of Satan. But if armed with strength divine,

> " A feeble saint shall win the day,
> Though death and hell obstruct the way."

Thus, as it was with David, so was it with the Apostle Paul and others that might be named; has it not been so with you? I know it has been so with me; and, I am quite sure, if God brings you into trials you never had, he will give you such grace as you never had.

Believers in the Lord Jesus Christ. If earthly distresses surround you, encourage yourselves in the Lord your God. As David did, so do you; his God is yours. " Wait upon the Lord; be of good courage, and he shall strengthen thine heart; wait, I say, upon the Lord." (Ps. xxvii. 14; xxxi. 24.) This is his own advice and direction, founded upon his own experience; and is it not in agreement with the immutable promise of Jehovah himself? " He giveth power to the faint; and to them that have no might he increaseth strength." "They that wait upon the Lord shall renew their strength." (Isa. xl. 29, 31.) Wait and see what God will do for you. Tamper not with his dealings. "The Lord will give strength unto his people; the Lord will bless his people with peace." (Ps. xxviii. 11.) Things often begin to mend when they are at the worst. If your difficulties are ever so distressing, wait at once upon God, call to mind his promises, his former loving-kindnesses; there will be no time lost in prayer. "My soul, wait thou only before God; for my expectation is from him." "From him cometh my salvation." (Ps. lxii. 1, 5.)

THE DIVINE RELATIONSHIP
BETWEEN
CHRIST AND HIS CHURCH.

---◆---

A SERMON,

BY CHARLES GORDELIER.

PREACHED AT JEWRY STREET CHAPEL, ALDGATE,

On Monday Evening, December 29th, 1862.

BEING THE EIGHTH AND CONCLUDING DISCOURSE AT THAT PLACE,
ON THE MYSTICAL UNION BETWIXT CHRIST AND HIS CHURCH.

" Jesus saith unto her, Touch me not; for I am not yet ascended to my Father; but go to my brethren, and say unto them, I ascend unto my Father, and your Father; and to my God, and your God."—JOHN xx. 17.

OF all the circumstances connected with the resurrection of the Lord Jesus Christ, there is none more important and interesting to the church of God, than the one connected with our text. "He appeared first to Mary Magdalene, out of whom he had cast seven devils." (Mark xvi. 9.)

There is something very precious in the thought, that though there were no earthly witnesses to the glorious triumph of our Lord over the power of death and the grave, yet how graciously and how tenderly he discovered himself; first to Mary Magdalene, she "who loved much," then to the other women; and afterwards to his disciples, and to his disciples only; for the resurrection glories of the Redeemer are revealed only to his church. He himself is the indubitable witness of the truth that "he rose again according to the scriptures," but he will rather have this truth to be the object of our faith than for it to be demonstrated by our carnal senses.

With respect to Mary Magdalene, we cannot but perceive she was much confused and perplexed when at the sepulchre; it was partly from the excitement and

No. 8.

surprise on finding the body of Jesus had been removed, as she supposed, and partly from the twilight haziness of the morning; and probably her eyes were filled with tears, so that she could not readily recognise the appearance of her beloved Jesus. But when he spoke to her by her name, and in such a tone that there was no mistaking it, her ears were truer to her soul than her eyes; at once she was filled with rapturous emotion, and falling at his feet, to embrace them in adoration and love, she would have held him to the place, regardless of everything else, so that she might indulge her expressions of love, joy, and delight in beholding once more her Lord and Saviour. Oh, how much nearer to his saints is Christ to be found than they commonly suppose; he may be very present and near when he is not perceived by reason of our own weakness and the imperfection of our faith; but one look from our blessed Lord, one word spoken to the heart, dispels all gloom, all fear, all ignorance, strengthens our faith, enlivens hope, and excites our love; how soon it humbles us in the dust, lays us low at his feet, and we are ready to give him the highest honour of which he is worthy and that we are capable of giving.

But to our text. It would at first sight appear somewhat obscure; Mary is forbidden to touch the bodily person of the Lord, apparently on the ground of his having not yet ascended to his Father, as if immortality must not be touched by that which was mortal; while it would appear from the record in Matt. xxviii. 9, that the other women were allowed to do so, and that Thomas was desired to handle him for the purpose of identifying his crucified body. I regard, therefore, the probable sense of these words to be: "Do not stay now to embrace me for the manifestation of your feelings; this is not the time for it; I shall not yet ascend to my Father; but go immediately to my disciples, my brethren, and tell them I have indeed risen from the grave, and shortly I shall ascend unto my Father and your Father, and to my God and your God," thereby intimating his unchangeable love to them, whatever they might feel or might remember of their inconstancy. I regard, too, the obscurity of the entire passage as internal evidence of the truth of the whole narrative and of its inspiration. We have the facts and the impressions of what was seen and heard most truthfully and exactly recorded as the women and disciples felt and believed. Those who carefully *compare* the statements of the several Evangelists, instead of *confusing* them, will find no difficulty in *reconciling* them.

In this declaration of our risen Lord we have this delightful and blessed truth—the mystical union betwixt Christ and his church. Take his own words: "my brethren, my father, your father, my God, your God." Here you see, is a divine relationship acknowledged; of brotherhood, the same fatherhood, the same God conjointly with Christ—a celestial relationship in all its fulness, in all its completeness, and in all its glory. It is a joint relationship with God, by virtue of our covenant union with Christ. If children of God, then heirs of God, and joint heirs with Christ. (Rom. viii. 17.) "He that is joined to the Lord is one spirit." (1 Cor. vi. 17.) Thus it is, that Christ's father is our father, his God is our God.

This mystical union between Christ and his church is a theme that surpasses the wondrous intelligences of angelic spirits; it is, doubtless, one of the things they desire to look into; it is one of those wonders of redeeming love which eternity itself will never fully disclose, but will ever be unfolding more and more to the astonished view of the glorified church of God. How then can sinful mortals explain it. One feels how poor are all the attempts we have made to set it forth to you for the last two months. First we took *a general* or cursory view of the subject as a whole, from the words just quoted, "He that is joined to the Lord is one spirit." Then in six subsequent discourses, we took up six different similies or figures employed in scripture, by way of illustration, each shadowing out some peculiar feature of this blessed union; and now, taking another stand-point, we desire, under the leadings and teachings of the divine spirit, to call your attention to another view of this great subject, *the divine relationship* existing betwixt Christ and his church—a truth which, when experimentally known by the believer in Jesus, is a most delightful theme of contemplation, a most precious doctrine, wherein is milk for babes and strong meat for men.

FIRST, let us consider this union in relation to the import of the words "my brethren." The expression itself is worthy of note. Our Lord calls those who are believers in him—united to him by faith, in love, his "brethren," not "my friends," as he did before his death; for since the work of redemption is finished, and the price fully paid, his people enter more into their covenant union, they are now no longer considered merely as his friends, which does not imply any relationship whatever, but, as one of the blessed results of his resurrection which demands our admiration, here is a development of another truth-relationship. The appellation of brethren discovers to us more of the heart of Jesus; it is one of those resurrection glories known only to the believing members of his mystical body. He makes himself known to us as our brother. Christ is in very deed our brother, a brother born for adversity; it is a very near relationship; we cannot be nearer unto him than we are. "A people near unto him." (Ps. cxlviii. 14.) It is an endearing relationship; it is a most affectionate relationship; it is an unalterable relationship; come what will, if brotherhood do at all exist, it ever remains, it can never be altered. Time or distance cannot change it or diminish it. "I am Joseph your brother, whom ye sold into Egypt," were the words of him who appeared as the great and mighty Zaphnath-paaneah before his brethren, the children of Israel. So when Jesus makes himself known to his sorrowing disciples, he tells them who he is; he tells them his name, he tells them *what* he is, he tells them he is their brother. Joseph could make known no more than that he was their brother, and that their father was his father; he could go no higher into the region of truth; but our Jesus, though on earth, though not yet ascended to his Father, makes known to us a greater truth than even this—he tells us that his Father is our Father, his God is our God. Thus we see how far superior is the union which Christ makes known as existing betwixt him and his church. The one is earthly, the other is heavenly.

This union is a joint relationship. Jesus Christ is the Son of God. God is his Father. He is therefore of the same nature with his Father, as all sons and fathers are. He is of a divine nature; so are all the children of God; they are made partakers of a divine nature. (2 Peter i. 4.) "Blessed be the *God and Father of our Lord Jesus Christ,* who according to his abundant mercy hath begotten us again unto a lively hope by the resurrection of Jesus Christ from the dead; being born again, not of corruptible seed, but of incorruptible, by the word of God, which liveth and abideth for ever. (1 Peter i. 3, 23.) They are born of the Spirit, and being born of the Spirit *they are the* children of God, not so by a figure of speech, but really and truly; made new creatures in Christ Jesus, by the

D

quickening the regenerating power of God the Holy Ghost.

This union is first realised by the soul when it is brought to believe on the name of the Son of God; faith is imimplanted, then love is shed abroad in the heart by the power of the Holy Ghost. The *experience* of the believer agrees with the *doctrine* of God's word; "and this is his commandment, that we should believe on the name of his Son Jesus Christ, and love one another as he gave us commandment." (1 John iii. 23.) We know that we have passed from death unto life because we love the brethren. (1 John iii. 14.) Now are we the sons of God, and it doth not yet appear what we shall be, but we know that when he shall appear, we shall be like him, for we shall see him as he is; such is the joint relationship of this union. Jesus is the express image of his Father, and we shall be like him, for we shall see him as he is. Oh what a glorious union; not only relationship, a union of nature, but a likeness of features. This truth has ever been the delight of the church of God; true believers are ever praying that they may be more and more transformed into his image. David surveyed the glorious truth with a rapture beyond description when he abruptly closed his divine meditation with, "I shall be satisfied when I awake in thy likeness." (Ps. xvii.) The apostle Paul frequently dwells upon this heavenly truth. "For as many as are led by the Spirit of God, they are the sons of God. For we have not received the spirit of bondage again to fear; but ye have received the Spirit of adoption, whereby we cry ABBA—Father. (Rom. viii. 14–15.) And this word Abba, be it remembered, is Syriac; it is retained in our Bibles, because our translators could not give us the full sense of it; it intends to convey an animated affection which no word of ours can express. The nearest approach we can have of the idea, is when we hear a child lovingly calling its father, "Father, dear," as if the mere appellation of father was insufficient, and therefore it must add a word in that kind of tone which conveys a rill of affection into the heart of the father while the child speaks. And this, dear friends, "is no wild fancy of the brain, no metaphor we speak," but is a matter of indisputable experimental knowledge of the truth as it is in Christ. "The Spirit itself beareth witness with our spirit that we are the sons of God." "And if children, then heirs; heirs of God, and joint-heirs with Christ." (Rom. viii. 16, 17.) This relationship, too, let me tell you, arises out of the eternal love of God the Father; for that is the source of all the blessings of our covenant union with Christ Jesus his Son. "Having predestinated us unto the adoption of children by Jesus Christ to himself, according to the good pleasure of his will; to the praise of the glory of his grace wherein he hath made us accepted in the Beloved." (Eph. i. 5, 6.)

And not only are we the sons of God by being made partakers of the divine nature, and by adoption in the eternal predestinating love of God the Father, and made heirs of God, joint-heirs with Christ, but we are also jointly related to Christ by virtue of his assumption of our nature. He took our nature into union with his divine nature; thus he became "the God-man, Christ Jesus." He took our nature, which is human, that we might take his nature, which is divine. He took our nature that he might take our sin, and bare it away in his own body on the tree. We have in virtue thereof, taken his nature that we might be saved through him, and dwell for ever with him, in his Father's house, where there are many mansions. "When the fulness of time was come, God sent forth his Son, made of a woman, made under the law, to redeem them that were under the law, that we might receive the adoption of sons. And because ye are sons, God hath sent forth the Spirit of his Son into your hearts, crying Abba, Father." (Gal. iv. 4, 6.) Again. "Forasmuch then as the children are partakers of flesh and blood, he also himself likewise took part of the same that through death, (dying in that nature,) he might destroy him that hath the power of death, that is, the devil." (Heb. ii. 14.) Thus there is a union of natures both divine and human, essentially in the Person of Christ as related to every believing child of God.

So, by virtue of Christ having the pre-eminence in all things, he being the Eternal Son of God, the first begotten from the dead, God's first-born Son, God's only begotten Son—He is, therefore, our ELDER BROTHER.

Christ is our elder Brother; he is appointed heir of all things; we are joint-heirs with him. He, as our elder Brother, takes all the responsibility of the family of God; he became their Surety in that covenant, ordered in all things, and sure; and he is able to meet all the demands of divine justice, as well as to provide for all their necessities. Having taken our nature into personal union with himself, he is able to accomplish everything that the law requires; he brings us back safe to our heavenly Father's home, having redeemed us from all iniquity. "Behold I and the children which God hath given me." Those that thou gavest me I have kept, and none of them is lost; but the son of perdition, he is lost, that the Scripture might be fulfilled." (Heb. ii 13; John xvii. 12.)

SECONDLY.—Let us consider that, by virtue of our divine relationship to Christ as our elder Brother, his Father is our Father.

Dr. Gill says, not that I quote him as an authority, but I love to be found in such good company: "God was his Father, not by creation in any way, as he is to angels and the souls of men, &c.; nor yet as to his incarnation, for, as man, he had no father; or with regard to his office as Mediator, for as such he was a servant, and not a son; but he was his Father by nature, or, with regard to his divine Person, being begotten of him, and so his own proper Son, and he his own proper Father; which hold forth the natural and eternal Sonship of Christ, his equality with him, and distinction from him; and God was the Father of his disciples by adopting grace, in virtue of the covenant of grace made with Christ, and through their spiritual relation to him, as the natural and eternal Son of God." (*loco*.) Here is choice truth in choice words; they are like "apples of gold in baskets of silver." And yet how far below they fall the heavenly language of the dear Redeemer himself. This union is beyond our comprehension; hear how he expresses it, not to his disciples, but to his Father. We see the truth transcendently displayed, like the setting sun dipping into the ocean on a clear summer's evening, its glories cannot be expressed nor even conceived; could the disciples have been capable of receiving the truth as it is in Jesus, doubtless he would have imparted it; but they could not bear it then, and therefore they were only permitted to hear the truth declared; never were men so divinely favoured, to hear the divine communion of Christ the eternal Son with the eternal Father, speaking of those things which related to their eternal interests, their covenant and joint relationship with him and his Father. What wondrous words of grace to proceed from his mouth: "That they all may be one; as thou, Father, art in me, and I in thee, that they also may be one in us. And the glory which thou gavest me I have given them; that they may be one, even as we are one. I in them, and thou in me, that they may be made perfect in one; and that the world may know that thou hast sent me, and hast loved them, as thou hast loved me." (John xvii. 21—23.) Oh, what vast and lofty heights we perceive in this great and mighty theme! It is like the sun in the firmament; it is high, I cannot attain unto it; I feel like an infant trying to grasp the great globe in its little tiny arms; I am standing on the shore of a vast ocean. Divine union! eternal union! A union so perfect, so complete, so indissoluble, so matchless, so infinite! The church of God, one in the Father and the Son conjointly! The church of God, loved by the Father with the same love and in the same manner as the Father has loved his own Son! Oh, amazing grace! "Oh, the depth of the riches, both of the wisdom and knowledge of God! how unsearchable are his judgments, and his ways past finding out!" "As it is written, eye hath not seen, nor ear heard, neither have entered into the heart of man, the things which God hath prepared for them that love him." Oh, how gloriously exhilirating is the thought, that if our hearts have been renewed by the power of the Holy Ghost, we have the witness within that we are the sons of God—that God is our Father—our Father by covenant love and union with Christ; our Father by adoption and grace, arising from his everlasting love to us in the Person of Jesus Christ, our ever-living Head, and by virtue of which we are made partakers of the divine nature by the renewing of the Holy Ghost. We are, I say, divinely related to the Father and to the Son by our persons being chosen by the Father before the foundation of the world, and were given to his Son, being blessed in him with all spiritual blessings in him as the adopted sons and daughters of the Lord God Almighty. The apostle Paul, inspired by the Holy Ghost, gives us this precious truth in his Epistle to the Ephesians: (i. 3—6:) "Blessed be the God and Father of our Lord Jesus Christ, who hath blessed us with all spiritual blessings in heavenly places in Christ, according as he hath chosen us in him before the foundation of the world, that we should be holy and without blame before him in love; *having predestinated us unto the adoption of children by Jesus Christ to himself*, according to the good pleasure of his will, to the praise of the glory of his grace, wherein he hath made us accepted in the Beloved." How blessedly too does the same apostle speak of God's adoption in his Epistle to the Romans. (viii.

14—21.) I need not do more than refer you to the place, having already quoted a part, and so also in Gal. iv. 1–7.

But there is one thought which may be noticed, and I think it is worthy of our consideration—in the prayer of our Lord, John xvii. 6, he speaks of having *manifested the name* of his Father to his disciples; and in the 11th verse he prays that they may kept by his Father in *the Father's own name;* and then in the 12th verse he speaks of himself having *kept them in the name of the Father.* Here is a gradual development of the doctrine of the divine Fatherhood; first, there is *the name* spoken of; this we perceive through all the teachings of our Lord while with his disciples. When he speaks of *his* Father and to them of *their Father,* it is not in special relation to that intimate union which he afterwards declared so fully to Mary Magdalene after his resurrection; first *the name* of the Father is revealed, then *the relationship* is declared— first they are indoctrinated and made familiar with the truth that God is their Father, but in what way and the manner how, this was not revealed; now, in our text, and in his prayer recorded in John xvii. we have this unfolded to them. Divine light is not dashed upon them like a thunderbolt, but is poured into their understandings in such a measure as they are able to bear it. Thus it is now with the Lord's people; they are not at first taught by the divine Spirit the deep things of God, "but first principles of the oracles of God;" being suited to such as who, like babes, "have need of milk, and not of strong meat." The light of truth is like the rising sun, it shineth more and more unto the perfect day. The manner of God's Spirit in teaching his children is in harmony with all his works; it is the same in grace as it is in creation and in providence, the law of gradual development and progress rules throughout the spiritual universe as in the universe of nature. That there are different degrees of understanding we are quite aware; some are children in understanding who ought to be men; and there have been, and are now, giants, both in natural and spiritual truths, and these have not been suffered to exist as mere curiosities or specimens of vanity; but all have their essential uses in the orbits assigned to them by the great and infinite Controller of all things. But this does not affect the truth of which we are speaking. While there is evidently a gracious provision made for the understanding to receive all truth, but not all at once, there is also a growing in grace, a growing in knowledge, a knowledge too of the best kind, a knowledge of our Lord and Saviour Jesus Christ. So that you see there is not a truth revealed in God's word respecting Christ, his Person and work, but what is adapted to be known by all the church of God. Sooner or later, the deepest, the profoundest of God's deep things shall be taught: "All thy people shall be taught of the Lord, and great shall be their peace; it is to be a matter of prayer for any believing child of God, as it was with the apostle Paul for the Ephesian saints, "that the God of our Lord Jesus Christ, the Father of glory, may give unto you the spirit of wisdom and revelation in the knowledge of him: the eyes of your understanding being enlightened, that ye may know what is the hope of his calling, and what the riches of the glory of his inheritance in the saints, and what is the exceeding greatness of his power to us-ward who believe, according to the working of his mighty power, which he wrought in Christ when he raised him from the dead and set him at his own right hand in the heavenly places, far above all principality and power, and might, and dominion, and every name that is named, not only in this world, but also in that which is to come; and hath put all things under his feet, and gave him to be the Head over all things to the church, which is his body, the fulness of him that filleth all in all." Now you see what a galaxy of heavenly truths are here to be seen and understood by the church of God; the very mention of them in such a cluster seems to dazzle and confound one. They are amazing themes truly, all matters of spiritual teaching and heartfelt experience, by each and every member of the mystical body of Christ; and this is not all, for in the third chapter he prays that these Ephesians may be "strengthened with might by his Spirit in the inner man; that Christ may dwell in your hearts by faith; that ye, being rooted and grounded in love, may be able to *comprehend* with all saints what is the breadth, and length, and depth, and height; and to know the love of Christ, which passeth knowledge, that ye might be filled with all the fulness of God."

Now I hope I have not wearied you with these long quotations. The knowledge of these truths for which the apostle prayed for others to know, is or should be, the matter for our own prayer; depend upon it, my friends, whatever people may say about doctrines, contemning them as dry and insipid, the doctrines of the gospel are the solid,

spiritual food of believers, and they are only strong in
Christ, strong in grace, in proportion as they know these
things and live upon them as the meat and drink of their
souls.   This doctrine of divine relationship is the very
marrow of the gospel.   The assurance that Christ is our
elder Brother, that his Father is our Father, in the same
bond of covenant union, must be calculated, under the
sweet anointings of the Spirit, to strengthen and to settle
the believer in the knowledge of his divine sonship.

THIRDLY. We come now to notice, that by virtue of God
being the Father of the Lord Jesus Christ, and of our union
to him by the predestinating love of God, and also the
sanctification of the Spirit through the belief of the
truth—GOD IS OUR GOD.

Our joint relationship with Christ as our elder Brother,
and to his Father, leads us to the truth that God his
Father is also our God in the same joint relationship.
There is a proprietaryship which the believer possesses in
God, arising out of it, which is of the utmost importance
to all believers.   If it were not, the risen Saviour would
not have made it the first revealed truth after his resurrection.   It is a doctrine containing the most solid comfort
which the church of God can desire ; it is the rock on which
their sonship and brotherhood in Christ are built.   Many
believers in Christ are quite strangers to this assurance of
their union with Christ and his Father; they are afraid to
cherish a thought towards it, as if it were presumption.
They go about hanging down their heads like a bulrush,
looking too much within ; like Mary Magdalene, they are
so engrossed with their own matters of grief or specula-
tion, that the real spring of comfort is unseen by them,
though it be, as it were, close to their heels.   Sincere
and humble souls too often afflict themselves by searching
for that within which cannot be found until it is made
known to them from without.   It is Christ himself that
assures us of his heavenly relationship to us.   It cannot
be learned in any other way ; it is a divine revelation, a
truth applied to the heart and conscience by the power of
his Spirit, and fills the soul with all joy and peace in
believing ; and, like the women of old, such souls will be
filled with great joy, and run to bring the disciples word
"what a dear Saviour they have found."   If believers
measure their standing in Christ by the measure of their
faith, the warmth of their love, the elasticity of their
hope, the bulk of their joy or of their peace, they will

soon find they are building on sand, shifting sand; and
when our dear Lord sees we are making a Christ, as it
were, of our faith, or of any other grace, though they
may be the gracious implantings of his Spirit, he will
soon withdraw his sweet influences, and make us feel we
are building on too low a ground. We must take higher
ground. It is Christ and his finished work that we must
look to, as being wrought for us; not so much as what is
done within us, as it is that which is done for us. Now
when Christ finds us mourning his absence, how often he
reveals himself in a manner similar to that in which he made
himself known to Mary. First he spoke in an ordinary way,
then specially and personally. He speaks to the heart.
He will speak to thee, poor soul, as sure as thou art seeking him; he will manifest himself to you, and make such a
revelation of his loving heart as will astonish you. He
will reveal his brotherhood to you; he will tell you that
his Father is your Father, that his God is your God. He
will reveal to your wondering eyes that this divine relationship is the result of an eternal union, a bond of
covenant love, which nothing can break, nothing can dis-
sever. The knowledge of this union, your interest in it,
assured to you by his Spirit, will keep your heart and
mind by Christ Jesus. Angels cannot effect it for you;
your frames and feelings cannot procure it; it is the
manifestation of Christ Jesus himself.

FOURTHLY. I come now to show some of the *excellencies*
of this divine relationship.

1. *There is a holy fellowship with God the Father.*
There is a fellowship with Jesus Christ, and there is also
a fellowship with his Father. Truly our fellowship is
with the Father and with his Son Jesus Christ. (1 John
i. 5.) This fellowship is the soul having communion with
its God; it is God speaking to the soul. This exercise
does not simply consist in occasional or ejaculatory peti-
tions, as occasions arise; this of itself, though blessed, is
not soul communion. It is when the mind is stayed on
divine things, holding a continuous, holy contemplation;
a converse, if I might so say, with God. It is found in
secret prayer; meditation on God's word; in the hearing
of his word; and also with his people when we are aiming
to talk of those things, concerning the things of Christ
and the work of his grace.

2. *God's personal residence with his people.* Our Lord
himself has declared it: "If a man love me, he will keep

my words; and my Father will love him, and we will come and make our abode with him." (John xiv. 23.) He dwells in us by his Spirit; thus are we assured of his love, by the Spirit which he hath given us. (1 John iii. 24.)

3. *It is an everlasting union.* How David rejoiced in this when on his dying bed. "He hath made with me an everlasting covenant, ordered in all things and sure." How Paul rejoiced in it; he was persuaded that nothing in time, nothing in nature, nothing in the future, could "separate us from the love of God which is in Christ Jesus our Lord." The brotherhood of Christ is eternally unalterable; the divine Fatherhood is eternal and unalterable; and the believer's proprietaryship in God is immutable and everlasting. Thus the union of Christ and his Father conjointly with his church is immutable, inseparable, and eternal.

4. *Heavenly communion.* There will be a communion in glory as sure as there has been in grace on earth. This communion in grace below is but the leading step to that in glory, whether it be with the Lord's people in this time state, or with God himself; it is the ladder of the soul planted on earth, but pitched in heaven. I doubt not, but that as Moses and Elias were seen talking with Jesus on the Mount of transfiguration, so we, who now dwell on earth, shall have communion with Christ in heaven.

5. *Possession of all spiritual blessings.* Nothing can be possibly wanting. All things are yours; ye are Christ's, and Christ is God's. All grace is made to abound towards us from the fulness which is in Christ Jesus. He who hath not witheld his only Son, shall he not with him freely give us all things? Thus we have reconciliation by the death of Christ; we have sanctification by the indwelling of the Holy Ghost; we have justification by faith in Christ; and walking after the Spirit, we have peace with God through Jesus Christ.

6. *Hatred to sin.* We have thereby one of the most blessed results of this union which the church of God on earth can have, that the love of sin is destroyed; not its inbeing, it is true; nor *its power* totally; but certainly *the love* of it. Oh, this is the believer's consummation of his desires, to feel the love of sin cast out, and the love of Jesus enthroned in his heart. If there is one thing more than another that would lead the believer to realise this union, it is in the fact that the body of sin is being crucified and shall be destroyed.

In conclusion, I would just add a few words as to the *evidences* of this divine relationship. The mere knowledge of this great subject will not suffice; this doctrine must be experimentally known, and its practical results shown in some such as the following evidences:

1. *The soul has been quickened from a death in sin by the work of God the Holy Ghost.* This new life is ascertained by an evidence which is peculiar and proper to itself. "If any man be in Christ, he is a new creature; old things are passed away; behold, all things are become new." It consists in the will being renewed. There are new desires. The objects of the affections are changed, being set on things above; the image of Christ is stamped on all the faculties of the soul; the Spirit of adoption in Christ is witnessed to the heart; the love of holiness is implanted, and the fruit of holiness is produced. Beloved! do you think you have experienced such a change in your inner life?

2. *The enmity of the carnal mind to God is subdued by the power of the Holy Ghost.* The strongholds of Satan are pulled down; false and vain imaginations are cast down; self-will, self-love, self-seeking, and everything else that opposeth and exalteth itself against God will be fought against and slain. Let me ask you again, how stands this matter with you? Do you feel anything like a conflict between the new principle of grace and the old principle of sin? This enmity of the carnal mind is not known until it is opposed. If you have never felt it, I very much question if you know anything of the matter.

3. *There is mutual love.* The love of God is shed abroad in the heart by the power of the Holy Ghost. This love shed abroad is felt towards God, towards each Person in the sacred Trinity. There is love to the brethren: "By this we know that we have passed from death unto life, because we love the brethren." We love God's house; we love his word; we love his commandments. If Jesus were to put the question pointedly to you, "Lovest thou me?" do you think you could reply, "Yea, Lord; thou knowest all things; thou knowest that I love thee?" There is very little difficulty in deciding this point.

4. *There is a mutual indwelling.* "Ye are the temple of the living God, as God hath said, I will dwell in them and walk in them; and I will be their God, and they shall be my people." "The life I now live in the flesh, I live

by faith on the Son of God." "Ye shall know that I am in my Father, and ye in me, and I in you." Where this divine union exists, in all its fulness and power, the believer feels that God lives in him, and that he lives in God; Christ dwells in his heart by faith, and he lives by faith in Christ. Is this the life you desire to live? Does this life seem to you the only life worth having? I think so, and humbly hope I know something of it.

5. *The indwelling of the Spirit* is another evidence: " Know ye not that your body is the temple of the Holy Ghost?" " Even the Spirit of truth; for he dwelleth with you, and shall be in you." This Spirit of truth is also the Spirit of love: "Hereby know we that we dwell in him and he in us, because he hath given us of his Spirit." Then I would ask, what is the spirit we are of, and what is the spirit that we manifest both in the church and in the world? Let truth do its office, and conscience will determine.

6. There is still another evidence, and that is, *the maintenance of the spiritual life within.* This is done by the constant operations of the Holy Ghost, the supply of the Spirit of Christ: "Being confident of this very thing, that he who hath begun a good work in you will perform it unto the day of Jesus Christ."

My dear friends! can you not see how blessed it is to be united to Christ? united to him by covenant love, and this made known by a true and living faith in him: "Ye are all the children of God by faith in Christ Jesus;" that is, *manifested* to be so. If this be your view as the result of the Spirit's teaching, you will give God all the praise and all the glory. And O, do we not see how mean and paltry are all other unions and fellowships compared with this? There is, indeed, nothing that can be compared to it. Mere outward church union falls short of it; " but he that is joined to the Lord is of one Spirit;" "and if any man have not the Spirit of Christ, he is none of his." Whatever *evidence we have* of this divine relationship, they will be found to proceed *from the excellencies* we have adverted to; for the tree is known by its fruit. Amen.

THE TRUE KNOWLEDGE OF JESUS CHRIST A DIVINE REVELATION.

A SERMON,

BY CHARLES GORDELIER.

PREACHED ON THE RE-OPENING OF HEPHZIBAH CHAPEL, DARLING PLACE, CAMBRIDGE ROAD, NEAR MILE END GATE,

On Lord's Day Evening, April 26th, 1863.

" And Jesus answered, and said unto him, Blessed art thou, Simon Barjona ; for flesh and blood hath not revealed it unto thee, but my Father, which is in heaven.—MATT. xvi. 17.

THE occasion of these words, as most of you know, arose out of the question which our Lord put to his disciples, as to how they understood the doctrine of his person and character ; it was a question of vital importance, and a correct reply based on right views was no less important.

It was a most material element in the preparation of our Lord's disciples for the public ministry of the word, that they should be well grounded in the doctrine of the divinity and eternity of Christ's sonship. It was the rock on which they were to build their own hopes of salvation, and it was the foundation of all Christain truth which they were to teach. For without right views of the person of Christ, as well as of his work, they would have been utterly incompetent to have taught " the truth as it is in Jesus ;" nor could the church of God have been edified, or built upon either incorrect or imperfect views of so fundamental a doctrine. It was requisite that the disciples should correctly understand what they thought of Christ, and also that they should be able to express, in unmistakable sentiments, what they understood ; hence the question, ver. 15.

Our Lord did not put the question for his own knowledge, but he put it for the use of all, and for all time. He put it for the purpose of bringing out in their own words, their own belief, so that when uttered, they could see, as in a mirror, their own faith expressed in their own words. You know the answer they gave, (verse 16,) and you know the use which the dear Redeemer made of it. He most emphatically declared, that THE TRUTH then confessed WAS THE ROCK on which he would build his church, and that the ruling powers of hell should not prevail against it.

Now, it is just as important that our minds should be equally well-grounded in the truth as the disciples, and that our views should be expressed in as clear and decided a manner as theirs were. Look at our text; let us ask the important question, "What think ye of Christ?" Can you give such an answer as Peter: " Thou art the Christ, the Son of the living God." Have you and I so learned Christ? for as Mr. Newton has very rightly put it:

> "'What think ye of Christ?' is the test,
> To try both your state and your scheme;
> You cannot be right in the rest,
> Unless you think rightly of him."

Now the doctrine taught in the text before us is, that *the true knowledge of Jesus Christ is a revelation of God the Father.* I propose, then, under divine teaching, to consider the subject thus:—I. The *nature* of this revelation. II. The *method* in which it is revealed. III. The *proofs* of this revelation; and IV. The *effects* of this revelation.

I. The *nature* of this revelation. There are two kinds of religion in the world. Notional and Revealed. Notional religion is not a substitute for revealed religion. Notional religion is superficial. It is the letter of Scripture without the spirit, and though it may embrace a belief in Christ; his person, his work, his character; it is, after all, but a *dead* faith; it is not real; there is no vitality in it, for it is without experience. It is simply the influence of the truth on the mind, and not on the heart; it is a form of godliness but without the power, for as Mr. Hart says:

> "True religion is more than notion,
> Something must be known and felt."

Revealed religion is *spiritual.* The revelation of Jesus

Christ from the Father is spiritual; made to a spiritual mind. It is a shining of divine light into the renewed soul of the child of God—the believer in Jesus. The spiritually taught believer discerns the things of the Spirit, minds the things of the Spirit, and walks after the Spirit.

As God is a Spirit, and they who worship him must do so in spirit and in truth, so what God reveals to them is of a spiritual nature; that is to say, it is not carnal, not fleshy, not earthly, not worldly, but heavenly; partaking of the nature of God; spiritual because he is a Spirit; heavenly because he is heavenly. And, indeed, whatever God is in his nature, so are his revelations. They are the same to all who believe in Christ. Is he good? so are his revelations. Is he holy? so are his revelations. Is he love? so are his revelations. The revelations of God, from his very nature, must be spiritual, heavenly, and pure; diametrically opposed to all that is earthly or sensual. This revelation of the Father is of his Son Jesus Christ, both as to his eternity and his deity. Whatever God the Father is in his nature, so is the Son. This we cannot but admit, seeing that in all Creation, from human kind to the lowest form of life, the offspring is of the same nature as the parent. Do we admit the Godhead of the Father? so we must the Godhead of the Son. Do we admit the eternity of God the Father? so we must the eternity of the Son. All the attributes and perfections of God the Father belong equally and essentially to the Son of God. Hence, by his becoming the Mediator, and taking our nature, is derived his ableness, his fitness, his willingness, as the Saviour of his body the church.

Not only so, the person of the Lord Jesus Christ as the Son of the living God, is the foundation of all the offices and relations he sustains to and for the church of God; for it is in his divine person and nature that every spiritual blessing is contained which the Church can possibly require, whether on earth or in heaven: "For it hath pleased the Father that in him should ALL fulness dwell." (Col. i. 19.). What fulness? the fulness of the Godhead. (Col. ii. 9.) In what manner? bodily, concentrated, incorporated in the person of the God Man, Christ Jesus, the Mediator. And what is the design of the Father in all this? because, every believing member of the mystical body of Christ, who is brought into an experimental knowledge of his personal union to Christ as his ever-living head, shall be made a partaker of the divine nature; (2 Peter i. 4;) for spiritual life and nourishment can be derived in no other way than from his divine fulness; his mediatorship being the channel through which all blessings flow from God the Father to the church. Hence it is that Jesus hath said, "My flesh is meat indeed, and my blood is drink indeed. He that eateth my flesh and drinketh my blood, dwelleth in me, and I in him. As the living Father hath sent me, and I live by the father, so he that eateth me, even he shall live by me." (John vi. 55–57.) Now to what can the Lord Jesus refer in this figurative language? His human nature simply, or his divine person, think ye? Certainly he could not mean his human nature, for the Jews themselves, who thought so, felt the difficulty and asked, "How can this man give us his flesh to eat;" no surely, but it means unquestionably his divine nature, and also those spiritual blessings with which the church was blessed in him before the foundation of the world; and the apostle John, in speaking of these things, (John i. 12–16,) says, "and of his fulness have all we received, and grace for grace." Oh, what a glorious truth we have here revealed in the Scriptures of truth; for thus it is we see that it is the divine person of Jesus that gives glory, weight, and dignity to his whole work of salvation, for he is the author and finisher of it. Every office and character which Jesus sustains as Mediator is stamped with eternal dignity and honour from his person being essentially divine, and it is this alone which gives an immutable efficacy to all his work, for he is Jesus the Christ, the immutable, the same yesterday, to-day, and for ever, God over all, blessed for ever. Amen.

What a delightful consideration is this fact, that Jesus is "the Son of the living God;" to be enabled under divine teaching to say, "we believe and are sure." How it fills the soul with hope, love, joy, and peace, in believing. How it leads the soul from sin, from the world, from self, from Moses, and Mount Sinai. It leads to Christ. It leads the feeblest lamb in Christ's flock to find their all in him; and they who know his name will put their trust in him.

II.—*Consider the method in which this revelation of Jesus Christ is made, by God the Father, to the renewed soul.*

By consulting the 26th verse of the 14th chapter of

John, we there find at once the method by which the Father reveals the Son; namely by the Spirit, the third person of the ever-blessed Trinity: "But the Comforter, which is the Holy Ghost, whom the Father will send in my name, he shall teach you all things, and bring all things to your remembrance, whatsoever I have said unto you." Again, we read in John xvi. 13, 14, 15: "Howbeit, when he, the Spirit of truth, is come, he will guide you into all truth; for he shall not speak of himself; but whatsoever he shall hear, that shall he speak; and he will show you things to come. He shall glorify me, for he shall receive of mine, and shall show it unto you. All the things that the Father hath are mine; therefore said I, that he shall take of mine, and shall show it unto you."

Thus, we see that the revelation, or knowledge of Jesus Christ, is from the Father, by and through the Holy Ghost. The sacred Trinity, in the unity of the divine essence, are each engaged in unfolding the glories of the person, work, and character of Jehovah Jesus to the spiritually-enlightened soul, united to Christ by a true and living faith. And observe, too, the ministration of the Holy Ghost, that is, his illuminating operations in the mind of the believer, is in the name of Christ, by the authority of God the Father. The things of Christ are taken by the Holy Ghost, under the commission of God the Father, and are revealed to the soul; thus it is that the knowledge of Jesus Christ is taught to the soul seeking to know and love the Saviour. Divine truth is known in no other way; I mean that which is called a saving knowledge, an effectual knowledge; not mere head knowledge, not a verbal knowledge of scripture truths, as we learn the sciences, but a life-giving knowledge, a spiritual knowledge, such as Jesus himself said it was: "This is life eternal, to know thee, the only true God, and his Son Jesus Christ."

This knowledge of Jesus Christ, by the teachings of the Holy Ghost, is by virtue of his indwelling in the believer. The soul being quickened by the Holy Spirit; born again of the Spirit; renewed in the spirit of his mind; made a new creature in Jesus Christ; has now become the residence of the Spirit, making the body his temple; and having once taken up his abode in the heart, he never leaves it. He takes of Christ and shows it to the believer; he glorifies Christ. He exhibits and displays the glories of his person; the glories of the God-man; the glories of his work; the glories of the characters he sustains to the church of the living God, and the adaptation and suitability of his work and character to each believer by an experimental acquaintance of the truth as it is in Jesus. This is carried on from the period of the new birth till the soul is dismissed from the body, to be for " ever with the Lord."

This revelation of Jesus Christ by the Spirit is also further proved and asserted by the apostle Paul. In his 1st Epistle to the Corinthians, 2nd chapter, and at the 10th verse, speaking of the knowledge of Jesus Christ being hid from the worldly wise, he says: " Eye hath not seen, nor ear heard, neither have entered into the heart of man, the things which God hath prepared for them that love him. But God hath revealed them unto us by his Spirit; for the Spirit teacheth all things, yea. the deep things of God. For what man knoweth the things of a man, except the spirit of man, which is in him? Even so the things of God knoweth no one, but the Spirit of God. Now we have received, not the spirit of the world, but the Spirit which is of God; that we might know the things that are freely given to us of God."

So also the apostle, in his Epistle to the Galatians, i. 16, speaking of himself being brought to a knowledge of the truth, says: " When it pleased God *to reveal his Son in me;*" that is, when it pleased God the Father to reveal the knowledge of Jesus Christ by the inward teaching of the Spirit.

Again, this knowledge of Jehovah Jesus is revealed as being the same in nature as a revelation of God the Father, by the same Trinity in unity. Read, pray, and ponder over what our blessed Lord said to Philip. " Philip saith unto him. Lord, show us the Father, and it sufficeth us. Jesus saith unto him, Have I been so long time with you, and yet hast thou not known me, Philip? He that hath seen me hath seen the Father; and how sayest thou then, Show us the Father? Believest thou not that I am in the Father, and the Father in me? The words that I speak unto you, I speak not of myself, but the Father which dwelleth in me; he doeth the works." (John xiv. 8, 9, 10.)

And, again, the knowledge of Jesus Christ is revealed also to the believer by his own personal manifestation. If you turn to the 20th verse of the same chapter, you will find Jesus declaring that mysterious and wonderful union which exists between the believer and himself as being one in essence with the Father; and then he states, " He that hath my commandments, and keepeth them, he it is that loveth me; and he that loveth me shall be loved of my Father, and I will love him, and *will manifest myself* unto him." Yes, he will manifest himself in brighter, richer, fuller views of his glorious work, his immaculate person, his wonderful name, to every believing sinner in whose heart is shed abroad the love of God under the operation and influences of God the Holy Ghost.

Thus, then, we think, we have fairly proved that the method by which a saving or spiritual knowledge of Jesus Christ is revealed, is from the Father by the Spirit. Divine truth can only be received and understood by those who are spiritually enlightened; the things of the Spirit are only communicated to such. The natural man understandeth not the things of the Spirit, neither can he know them, because they are spiritually discerned.

III.—We come now to consider some of the *proofs* of this revelation of Jesus Christ from God the Father, through the Spirit.

Here I intend to confine myself to such proofs as the believer is able to test for himself from his own experience. Sufficient doctrinal proof has perhaps been advanced while considering the second branch just disposed of.

1. The believer in Jesus is made a new creature; born again—born of the Spirit. Hence he is spiritual; spiritual in his thoughts, views, and understanding of all that relates to himself—to God—to Christ—his word. He is spiritual in his feelings, motives, aims, and desires. He is renewed in the spirit of his mind. In a word, his heart is changed; his affections are toward Christ; they are set upon things above, no longer on things of the earth, because he is regenerated entirely by God the Holy Ghost.

2. He has *a feeling sense of being a sinner* in the sight of God, for being now enlightened by the Spirit, he feels the awfulness, the bitterness of sin, far different from the common acceptation of the word; indeed, very different from thousands of those who occasionally and thought-

lessly recite: "Lord have mercy upon us miserable sinners." He feels sin to exist in all his thoughts, sayings,
and doings; if he prays, reads, or hears, he feels sin is
mixed with all he does. He feels it is an evil and bitter
thing to sin against God. He feels sin to be that hate-
ful thing which keeps his soul in bondage. He has a
feeling sense he shall be lost if not saved by Christ. My
friends, real religion has to do with the feelings. Religion
without feeling may suit the dead professor, but not the
believer made alive in Christ.

3. Another proof is that of *prayer*. Here, I think,
we shall come to the easiest test of spiritual life; for I
suppose some will be saying I have not yet touched
their case, or have passed them by; but, indeed, I would
not lose sight of the feeblest of Christ's flock. I fain
would encourage them and help them onward by every
possible means in my power. Prayer is an undoubted
proof of a regenerated soul. Look at Paul's case. The
Lord himself urges upon Ananias, as a proof that he is
no longer an enemy to truth, from the very fact of his
being a praying man: "Behold, he prayeth!" I know
some of you can give such an evidence as this. You may
think you are not that spiritually-minded person which I
have been talking about, but this you know,—you do love
prayer; you cannot pray as you wish, but you do try to
pray. Perhaps, you say, this is all the hope you have;
you are seeking God. Well, then, be assured you shall
find him. Keep on seeking the Lord in prayer: "Long
as they live should Christians pray." Prayer, indeed,
is not the life of the believer, but it is an evidence of life.
It is not strictly correct: "For only while they pray,
they live;" for if we lived no longer than we prayed, I
fear few would know but little of the sense of life.
Christ is the believer's life; it can never be taken away
from him. Christ gives to his sheep eternal life, and
they shall never perish.

4. *Love* is another proof of the soul being new-born.
Love is of God—God is love. We love him because he
first loved us. The measure of love is not stated. We
must not distress ourselves about the measure of our
love; the best of us have much reason to complain.
Christ is our salvation, not our love. How can we love
God enough? Our love, like our knowledge, is imperfect,

and will be so in this time-state; but the smallest indication is sufficient to prove its existence. Have we love to
those who love Christ? Do we love those most in whom
we see the image of Christ most? Then let us rest
assured that we have passed from death unto life, because
we love the brethren. It is, indeed, truly blessed when
we are enabled to feel the love of God shed abroad in
the heart by the power of the Holy Ghost. It is the
fire of the soul; it kindles all the other graces of the
Spirit. Faith works by love, hope and joy are animated
by it, and the believer becomes cheerful and blithe in all
the ways of God. But when the poor soul is made to
feel he is more like a bruised reed or smoking flax than
a wide spreading cedar flourishing in the courts of the
Lord, how it sighs and moans over its low and weak condition. Sometimes tempted to think "there is no good
work began at all;" sometimes fearing your religion is all
a delusion. Not a spark of love can you see or feel, a
" dull and lifeless frame " is all you possess. And is this
your complaint? Is it a matter of grief? Ah! indeed
it is :

> "My best desires are faint and few;
> I fain would strive for more.
> But when I cry, My strength renew,
> Seem weaker than before."

Well, now, poor soul, take heart. Love is at the bottom
of all this; the principle is there. "It lives under
pressure and load," as Hart very truly says. I am quite
sure, if you feel your burden, it is because you have life;
and there is no life without love. God's work is there,
and ere long he will fulfil all the good pleasure of his
goodness, and the work of faith with power. In the
mean time, be assured:

> " Those feeble desires, those wishes so weak,
> 'Tis Jesus inspires, and bids you still seek."

IV. Now, dear friends, let us in the fourth place, proceed to show some of the *practical effects* of this divine
revelation in the person of the true believer in Jesus
Christ. I say *practical effects*, because wherever there is
an experimental acquaintance with the truth as it is in
Jesus, there are sure to be produced such effects as will be
unmistakably observed both in the church and in the
world.

1. The *first* is, the believer's total separation from the world. He is not, it is true, taken out of the world as to its materiality; but he is from its spirit. He is no longer governed by its principles. He loves not the world, nor the things of it. His heart is not in it, though his body is. He feels that *he is drawn out of the world*, like as Moses was drawn out of the watery grave, and was transferred to the courts of the king's palace. So the believer is transferred from death to life. He has left the world and all its charms. He is now to be found in the courts of the Lord's house. He follows Christ in the way. He loves his house, he loves his word, he loves his laws, he loves his people. He is drawn out of his self—from self-seeking; from self-justification, and he seeks now to be justified through the imputed righteousness of Christ alone. He seeks pardon for sin from the atoning work of the Redeemer. He has joy and peace in believing that Christ is his, and he is Christ's; that he is united to him by a true and living faith. His affections are set on things above, not on things of the earth. He is dead to the world, and his life is hid with Christ in God.

2. A *second* effect is, that the true believer in Christ, while in the world, is brought to serve God in newness of spirit, and not in the oldness of the letter. His conduct in the world,—for he must needs be in it, though he is not of it,—is on the principle of the love of Christ constraining him in all things, whether they relate to his secular calling, his social or family duties. In all these things he desires to be found fearing God, working righteousness, and to be accepted of him, not after the rudiments of the world, but according to the rule of the gospel. He feels how strengthless and useless are all his unaided efforts in contending with a world that lieth in the wicked one; but he looks to the strong for strength, and his prayer is, "Hold up my goings in thy paths that my footsteps slip not." "Let integrity and uprightness preserve me, for I wait on thee" "Let thy loving-kindness and thy truth continually preserve me." He feels the world is against him; he feels it hates him; he feels it is because of the truth, and he often feels that his aims, motives, and character are unrighteously aspersed. Not only is an ungodly world against him, but carnal profes-

sors of religion are bitterly against him. He is called to endure their taunts and their contradictions against himself. He is derided, ridiculed, laughed to scorn, and is bantered with all sorts of contumely; but, nevertheless, "The righteous shall hold on his way, and he that hath clean hands shall wax stronger and stronger." This is his comfort, and he remembers the words of him who said, "Blessed are ye, when men shall revile you and persecute you, and shall say all manner of evil against you, falsely, for my sake." But,

> " Whoever frowns, if Jesus smile,
> It makes amends for all."

3. Another effect produced in the believer is *humbleness of soul*. The knowledge of Jesus Christ is unlike all other knowledge, which puffeth up. This humbles the soul; it humbles the soul before God; it humbles the soul in its own estimation; and the more Jesus is revealed, the humbler it is, thus evincing the truth of the poet, who said :

> " The more thy glories strike mine eye,
> The humbler I shall lie."

The soul that is truly humbled before God on-account of sin, on account of the holiness of God's law—its immutability, its spirituality, extending to the thoughts and intents of the hearts, feels all boasting is excluded.

> " The best obedience of his hands,
> Dares not appear before God's throne."

But having no hope in himself, looking for all in Christ, he lies prostrate at the foot of the Cross, humbled in the thought that sin cost the life of the Saviour.

But further, this humbleness of soul shows itself *without*, in proportion as it is felt *within*. There is a spirit of meekness engrafted in the temper and manner of the believer, indicating whose he is, and whom he serves. He is no longer vainly puffed up in his fleshly mind. He feels poor in spirit; not the poverty of misery, but that poverty which has a blessedness attached to it. " Blessed are the poor in spirit, for their's is the kingdom of heaven." This poverty of spirit is wrought by the Spirit of

God.   He empties the believer of all his self-sufficiency, and makes him sick of his fleshly doings and self-seeking. Where this poverty of spirit is felt, it is found to be as the poverty of a little child, which, though it be the heir of a princely estate, it really has nothing it can call its own; all he possesses is supplied him for the time being; he can do nothing with what he has of his own will.   So is it with the believer.   He has a feeling sense that he has nothing, spiritually, of his own; that he can do nothing of himself.   All that he possesses is supplied him from the fulness which is in Christ Jesus.   He can do nothing spiritually of himself; for it is God that worketh in him to do and to will of his good pleasure.   This is the poverty of spirit the believer rejoices in, that though in and of himself he is nothing and can do nothing, yet Christ is everything to him, and does everything for him; and having Christ he possesses all things.   Christ is the believer's all.   This he feels most when most he feels poor in spirit.   He loves this frame of soul, and earnestly desires ever to be found in it; and knowing the blessedness of it, he sets the highest value upon it.   He would gladly part with all worldly advantages upon any consideration, so that he might have an abiding sense of being poor in spirit.   He can fully enter into the feelings of dear Mr. Romaine, where he says, in one of his letters, " If the whole world were mine, and I could purchase what I would with it, I would give it *all* to be a scholar made poor in spirit, and to sit at Christ's feet "   What a blessed state of mind for a believer in Jesus to have !   It is the result of divine teaching.   Such a soul has a true knowledge of Jesus, and has derived it only by a divine revelation.

4.   There is also another effect produced by this divine revelation of the knowledge of Jesus Christ, and that is *peace*. The believer in Christ has *peace and joy in God*, through whom he has now received the atonement,—a peace which the world can neither give nor take away.   It is the peace of God which passeth all understanding, keeping the heart and mind by Christ Jesus; so that even in the midst of tribulation, the believer has a settled peace; and he can say, if ever so miserable in the world, yet he is happy in Christ.   Happy soul! God the Father has revealed to him his unspeakable love in sending his Son to

take the sinner's place. Christ is revealed to him as the all-sufficient Saviour. His atonement is revealed as being the only propitiation for sin, and that the Father now looks complacently on every believing, returning child of God.

And what a divine assurance flows out of this peace! What a declaration is made in the Word of God by the prophet: "The work of righteousness shall be peace; and the effect of righteousness quietness and assurance for ever." (Isa. xxxii. 17.) An assurance of God's loving-kindness, an assurance of the believer's interest in Christ; of his covenant union to him; an assurance that the only true knowledge of Jesus is by a divine revelation; for as Jesus himself hath said: "If any man will do his will he shall know of the doctrine whether it be of God or whether I speak of myself." (John vii. 17.) God the Father will enlighten his mind, and he shall know the truth, and the truth shall make him free; free from error, free from human opinion, free from vain imagination; he shall "know the certainty of the words of truth." "The secret of the Lord is with them that fear him, and he will show them his covenant." Thus it is with the believer, as it was with Peter; he can say, "We believe and are sure, that thou art the Christ, the Son of the living God." The true knowledge of Jesus Christ is a revelation of God the Father by the Holy Ghost; he takes of the things of Christ, and shows them unto each believing member of the church of God. And he is also revealed to the believer as possessing all the fulness of the Godhead; as possessing every spiritual blessing that he can possibly want, and that his own completeness stands in the person of the ever-adorable Redeemer, to whom he is united in the bonds of an everlasting covenant of grace, ordered in all things and sure.

Not only has God the Father revealed Christ in us, which is Christ in us the hope of glory, but he hath blessed us *in* him. "Blessed be the God and Father of our Lord Jesus Christ who hath blessed us with all spiritual blessings, in heavenly places in Christ; according as he hath chosen us in him before the foundation of the world, that we should be holy and without blame before him in love; having predestinated us unto the adoption of children by Jesus Christ to himself, according to the good pleasure of his will, to the praise of the glory of his grace, wherein he hath made us accepted in the Beloved." (Eph. i. 2–6.)

My hearers, this is something of the blessedness of those who know Jesus Christ by a divine revelation. Let me ask you, what do you know of this revelation ?—how do you understand the Scriptures ?—have you so learned Christ ?—is Christ revealed to you as the only and all-sufficient Saviour ?—do you feel lost ?   I appeal to your conscience.   Consider what I say, and may the Lord give you understanding in all things.

Before I sit down, I would just say one word in refer-ence to my coming to this place and occupying the pulpit. I have no wish to be here as a preacher merely.   I am desirous of seeing a church of Christ formed here, accord-ing to the plan of the New Testament; and if it should be the will of God to give testimony to the word of his grace as preached here by me, I shall be happy to see a church formed of baptised believers in the Lord Jesus Christ.   I should indeed rejoice to see this place thronged, as in the days of old.   I should not only regard it as a token of the Lord thrusting me in here by his wonder-working provi-dence,—for I can truly say, in reference to it, " The Lord hath his way in the whirlwind and in the storm, and the clouds are the dust of his feet!"—but I should also regard it as an evident proof of his employing me in the work of the ministry; for my aim is " To feed the church of God, which he hath purchased with his own blood."   I have come here almost alone.   I am here in the midst of many discouragements, and some little opposition, as several of you know, but I believe this, that if God has given me to do a work which I never did, he will give me such grace as I never had.—Amen.

CHRIST'S LIFE THE FOUNTAIN

OF THE

BELIEVER'S LIFE.

---◆---

A SERMON,

BY CHARLES GORDELIER.

PREACHED AT HEPHZIBAH CHAPEL, DARLING PLACE, NEAR
MILE END GATE,

On Lord's Day Evening, May 17th, 1863.

" Because I live, ye shall live also."—JOHN xiv. 19.

THE beloved disciple who records this statement of our
Lord seems to have had its truth powerfully wrought in
his own mind ; for he commences his gospel by declaring,
first, the eternity and deity of the Lord Jesus Christ; then,
second, that the same person, Jesus Christ, whom he calls
the Word, is the creator of the universe ; and then, third,
he proclaims this great truth, "In him was life, and
the life was the light of men." (John i. 4.) Now, I believe
that this great and precious truth he learned from the
Lord's own words, as in our text : "Because I live, ye shall
live also." Indeed, the whole of the writings of this
inspired divine may be briefly comprehended in this:
CHRIST THE LIFE; CHRIST THE LIGHT. And this, let
me tell you, is the sum and substance of the believer's experience, for there is no light without life, and there is no
life without Christ.

We cannot fail to notice that the beginning of John's
gospel, the last-written portion of the inspired books,
corresponds to a certain extent with the commencement
of the Book of Genesis ; showing that the inspiration by
which the pen of the apostle was guided is precisely the
same as that which guided the pen of the prophet Moses.

No. 10.

The Alpha and Omega of Scripture is the one and the same Spirit. "The prophecy came not in old time by the will of man ; but holy men of God spake as they were moved by the Holy Ghost." (2 Peter i. 21.).

Again, in the epistle to the Hebrews: (i. 1–3 :) "God who at sundry times, and in divers manners spake in time past unto the fathers by the prophets, hath in these last days spoken unto us by his Son, whom he hath appointed heir of all things, by whom also he made the world," "and *upholding all things* by the word of his power," proving that the Lord Jesus Christ possesses life in himself in its very essence.

It is plain, then, to the spiritual understanding that Jesus Christ is at once the source and support of all created life. God the Father is the fountain of life. So is also the Son. So is also the Holy Spirit. These three persons, in the unity of the divine essence called God, is the only being who is self-existent, uncreated, and eternal. All other beings depend upon him. He depends on none. All other beings had a beginning. He had no beginning. From his existence all other beings have derived their existence. He is, in the highest and completest sense, the Living God—JEHOVAH—the great I AM.

Neither is there any difficulty to the spiritually taught disciple of the Lord Jesus to identify the Jehovah of the Old Testament with the Jesus of the New. The same God who appeared to Moses in Horeb, appeared to John in Patmos. The *same* God that proclaimed his name to the Prophet, "I AM THAT I AM," proclaimed his name to the apostle, "I AM HE THAT LIVETH." "I am he that liveth and was dead, and behold I am alive for evermore, Amen ; and have the keys of hell and of death." (Rev. i. 18.) In Jehovah Jesus, then, all life has its derivation from Him. He is the first that gives Life. He is the Original of Life. From him issues, as from a fountain, the life of every living thing that can be discovered in the universe of God. The psalmist, in surveying the wonders of teeming life in all creation, exclaims, "With thee is the fountain of life." (Ps. xxxvi. 9.) The vital principle of all animated creation is essentially, necessarily, and originally, in Jesus Christ; he is the spring and source of all kinds and degrees of life, whether it be vegetable, animal, rational, spiritual, or eternal.

It is easy to ask the question, What is life? Like as it is easy to ask, What is light? but neither of these questions can be answered with any satisfaction. Philosophers have puzzled themselves with attempting to describe *the essences* of these substances, but have failed. The *essence* of life and light cannot be known by the human intellect; but the Scriptures have revealed the *source* of both: "In him was life, and the life was the light of men." Jesus Christ is the source of all spiritual life and light; he is the fountain of life to all true believers; this is the point we have in hand.

By referring to the commencement of the chapter, you will perceive that the disciples were troubled about the immediate and unexpected death of their divine Lord. He assures them, though the world will not see him any more, yet they will; and because he lives, and his spiritual presence will ever be with them, therefore they shall live also. The life of every believer is bound up in the life of Christ by covenant and eternal union. He is the head of his body, the church; he communicates life by his Spirit to all his members: "I give unto my sheep eternal life, and they shall never perish." He gives it because it is his prerogative to give; they shall never perish, because their life is hid with Christ in God. Their life stands in a continual dependence upon his life, for he is the vine, and his members are the branches. There is, therefore, a certainty, a blessed certainty, in the doctrine of our text, for our Lord hath made the life of believers in him as certain as it is certain that he himself liveth.

Again, Christ is the life of the believer by virtue of his union with him in the covenant of grace. As Christ is the head of his body the church, so he is their life; he the head, they the members. God, the Father of our Lord Jesus Christ, having blessed the church with all spiritual blessings in him before the foundation of the world, blessed them with life in him, for this is included, spiritual and eternal, and this life is in his Son.

Now, the proof of this truth lies in its *manifestation*. Every believer is united to Christ by a true and living faith. Faith being a living principle imparted to him *in consequence* of his eternal union with Christ, it is not the source of his life, mark you, but it is a link, as it were, in the chain by which he is eternally secured to Christ Jesus, his covenant head. By virtue of his faith in him, he is *manifested* to be a child of God, as the apostle Paul very truly says : " Ye are all the children of God by faith in Christ Jesus." (Gal. iii. 26.) It is not their faith that makes them children ; no, for God the Father, in his purposes of love, grace, and mercy, sovereignly chose the persons of every believer in Christ before the foundation of the world. (Eph. i. 3, 4.) And in the fulfilment of his purposes of grace and providence, as they are born in this world, he sends his Spirit to quicken them; he regenerates them, gives them life in Christ Jesus ; and because he is their life, they are renewed in his image, the life of Christ being manifested in their mortal bodies by his Spirit which liveth in them; so that indeed it is not so much that they live in Christ as it is that Christ lives in them.

Having, by way of introduction, attempted to show you, in the *first* place, the *connexion* there is between the life of Christ and the life of the believer, we will proceed to notice, in the *second* place, that

Christ is the Believer's Life.

1. *By his own gift.* He is the fountain of life. In him was *the* life. " I am the way, the truth, and the life." As Christ is life itself essentially, so he is the dispenser of it : " I give unto my sheep eternal life, and they shall never perish :" " I am the resurrection and the life ; he that believeth in me, though he were dead, yet shall he live." And in the most emphatic manner he declares himself to be *the bread of life :* " I am the bread of life :" " I am the living bread which came down from heaven ; if any man eat of this bread, he shall live for ever ; and the bread that I will give is my flesh, which I will give for the life of the world." Thus, from these and other portions of God's Word which might be quoted, especially in the gospel and the epistles written by the apostle John, we perceive that Christ is the believer's life by his own gift. The *instrumentality* employed is his own truth, the word of God, the gospel of the grace of God, the word of truth: " Of his own will begat he us with the word of truth." (James i. 18.) It is effected by the immediate operation of God the Holy Ghost. The *method* of his operation may be, and commonly is, *circumstantially* different; but in every case it will be found to be by means

of the truth of Christ. He is truth, the essential truth of all the words of this book—the Bible. By the power of his Spirit, the soul is quickened; the understanding is enlightened; the affections are enlivened; and there is thereby in the believer a spiritual, supernatural, and heavenly life: the result is, that he lives to God, has peace in Christ, and is blessed with a hope of eternal life in him.

The channel of this life is faith; and faith is the gift of God; it is the link that connects the Saviour and the believer. The exercise of faith is the believer's act; but its bestowment is free, and it is irresistible; in its nature it is unquenchable; though damped it never dies, for it is wrought in the heart by a divine power, and by no possible means can the enemy of our peace ever eradicate it. It is never taken away:

> " Whom once he receives, his Spirit ne'er leaves,
> Nor ever repents of the grace that he gives."

Being united to Christ both by covenant union and by a true and living faith, they live because he lives; they stand by faith, but their standing is in him, not in themselves, for their faith is in him; their life is dependent on his; it is received by faith; they live by faith; they walk by faith: " For the life believers now live in the flesh, they live by the faith of the Son of God." This life is a hidden life; its essential principle is hid with Christ in God, as in a garrison, secure, and defended by a power superior to all its antagonists.

2. *Christ maintains the life he gives to his people.* This life in the believer, though imparted from Christ, is like himself: it is the same in its nature; it is divine; it can never perish. As sure as Christ cannot perish, so sure the believer cannot perish; it is eternal life that is bestowed—a gift, not a loan, as many of our time-gifts are: a gift by which we are enriched in every thing by Christ. It can never be diminished, for it is always fed and nourished from the life in Christ. The believer lives upon him by the secret communications of his grace and love, and he can say with the poet:

> " Quickened by thee and kept alive,
> I flourish and bear fruit;
> My life I from thy sap derive,
> My vigour from thy root."

No true-born child of God can ever die. The life of

every believer being eternally secured in Christ, his covenant head, his damnation is utterly impossible. It is out
of the question altogether. Satan suggests it often to the
poor, weak, trembling soul; but it is only to distress it
and worry it; and he influences the general preachers of
the day to preach it. What? A child of God to-day,
and a child of the devil to-morrow? Is this like God,
think ye? No; it is the doctrine of devils; and so is the
kindred lie—a child of the devil yesterday, and a child of
God to-day. No, never; it cannot be. 'Tis true, God's
children are all *by nature slaves* of the devil; but when
by grace divine they are called out of darkness into the
marvellous light of the gospel, they are manifested to be
the children of light, and are *redeemed* from all sin and
iniquity, and are no more to be found in the service and
captivity of the devil. But the children of the wicked
one, they are left lying in the wicked one; no divine
change ever passes over them. 'Tis true, many are converted apparently from the ways of sin, folly, and shame,
and appear as if they were "the living in Jerusalem;"
but their hearts being unrenewed, their evil heart of unbelief remains what it ever was; they hate the doctrine of
God's sovereign, eternal, electing love; they despise the
broken-hearted, humble saint of God; they scorn an experimental acquaintance with the "truth as it is in Jesus"
they denounce it as living upon frames and feelings, and
call it a morbid state of mind. This, their ignorance, is
the veil with which Satan has blinded their eyes. What
is the life of Christ in the true believer but frames and
feelings; but does he live upon his frames and feelings?
No, certainly not; he lives upon Christ. How can a believer in Christ live upon his faith, his love, his hope, his
joy, his peace, or any other grace with which he may be
blessed? Why, if the poor soul had to live upon these
things, gracious gifts as they are, it would soon find its
spiritual life decay, and it would soon have reason to sus-
pect its life would soon die out. I have no doubt, many
gracious persons try to feed upon what is done *in* them,
instead of what is done *for* them; but the Spirit of Truth
eventually leads them out of themselves, and teaches them
to look for all *in* Christ, and to live only upon him, and
that continually, for God gives his people no stock in
hand. My dear friends, if God has begun a good work in

you, you will have exercises of soul about it; and these
exercises of soul will produce frames and feelings which
you can neither hinder nor smother. There is no true
religion without frames and feelings. They are signs of
life. I mean, of course, spiritual frames and feelings, not
carnal frames and feelings: "For to be carnally-minded is
death, but to be spiritually-minded is life and peace"
Professors of religion dead in sin, buried in nature's grave,
have no frames and feelings of a spiritual kind, no exercises of soul, no experience; or else why do they ridicule
vital, experimental religion? No part of their profession
has any vitality. There is a great deal of bustling busy-
ing, plenty of bodily exercise, there is the form of godliness, but without its power. No lack of chapels and
churches, no lack of full assemblies, no lack of conversions,
no lack of money to have every thing done on an extended
scale, and at a railroad pace. But all this is nothing else
but the wood, hay, and stubble of outside religion, built
upon *the name* of Christ for a foundation; some things
they say and do, doubtless, are very good in themselves,
and may fairly be considered the gold, silver, and precious
stones of their building; but the fire shall try every man's
work of what sort it is; for it shall be revealed by fire;
every man's work shall be made manifest. Man's work
in religion and God's work in the heart of a believer are
essentially distinct and different. God's living child is
imitated by man; it looks like a child, it is dressed like a
child, but it has no life; it is only a doll. By a little
contrivance they can make it move its eyes, make a
noise, or even to move along for a few minutes; but the
action is mechanical and artificial; there is no animation.
The religion of thousands is nothing more than this—a
mere doll, a plaything. They are mightily pleased with
it, and will carry it about with them everywhere, even take
it to bed with them. They have a notion, but it is only
a notion—a notional religion, a rational religion, a carnal
religion, but not a spiritual religion. Oh, how true it is:

> " Notion's the harlot's test,
> By which the truth's reviled;
> The child of fancy finely dressed,
> But not the living child."

But to proceed. I was saying, no true-born child of
God can ever die; his damnation is utterly impossible

To assert the contrary would be to give the lie to the solemn words of our Lord Jesus Christ which he uttered in his mediatorial prayer to his Father: "Father, I will that they also, whom thou hast given me, be with me where I am;' that they may behold my glory, which thou hast given me." (John xvii. 24.) Now what glory was this, think ye? why, the glory that he had with the Father before the world was, his primeval glory. (See v. 5 of the same chapter.) I ask you now, what can such language imply? what is the blessing couched beneath this precious truth? Why, the eternal and everlasting security and salvation of every elect vessel of mercy, to be sure! Deny it who can; no one will, but the blind leaders of the blind. You see, it is by the express wish of Christ, and, considered mediatorially, *it is his demand*, that all believers, those who are united to him, given to him by God the Father, should be brought home to glory. *All* shall be with him in heaven. It is his glory that not one of them is lost, or ever can be lost; none can ever perish. "All his saints are in his hand;" that is an Old Testament truth. None can pluck them out of his hand; this is a New Testament truth. How blessedly the word of God declares their eternal security, and assures them of their final perseverance. Trembling, doubting, fearing believer, thinking that thou wilt never hold out to the end! see here what a firm foundation is laid for your hope and for your comfort. How can you die while Jesus lives. He supplies you with all spiritual existence by virtue of his own life, inherent in himself. This life is inexhaustible.

> " Millions of happy spirits live
>   On his exhaustless store;
> From him they all their bliss receive,
>   And still he giveth more."

Surely he will be true to himself, true to his own promise: "He that hath begun the good work in you will perform it until the day of Jesus Christ." Those who have once truly believed in Jesus can never totally or finally fall away. "They are kept by the mighty power of God through faith unto salvation." Nothing can separate them from the love of God which is in Christ Jesus our Lord. Again, let me repeat the blessed truth: "I give unto my sheep eternal life; and they shall never perish, neither shall any pluck them out of my hand. My Father which gave them me, is greater than all; and none is able to pluck them out of my Father's hand." Now what can faith say to this? Oh, say you, the poet shall speak for me; say on:

> "Enough, my gracious Lord,
> Let faith triumphant cry;
> My heart can on this promise live,
> Can on this promise die."

Let us now, in the *third* place, inquire *how this life is sustained*. This is an important part of our subject; it is a matter of *experience*, the believer's experience, and it is necessary that you and I should know something about it, or else, if we do not, we are in an awful state, "we are in the gall of bitterness and in the bond of iniquity." Oh, pray do look and see where you are standing; is it on the sand of your own fancies or on the rock of God's effectual calling? I assure you, when I look within, I sometimes feel afraid confidently to decide; but still, when tempted to doubt, I can adopt the words of dear old Berridge: "Lord, if I am not right, make me right; and if I am right, keep me right."

1. Then as to *how* the believer's life is sustained. For we must observe, that though Christ has given his sheep eternal life, and because he lives they live also, yet he has not given them *self existence*. That is one of his attributes which he has not communicated to his creatures. His glory is, that he is the self-existent God, and his glory he will not give to another. Were it so, that his creatures were made self existent, where would be their dependence, where would be their union, how could they draw their blessedness from him; independency of existence would isolate every creature God has made from himself. Blessed be God, his creatures have no self existence; they have no stock of life in hand; their existence is drawn from his life, and this is experienced in the true believer by the continuous communications of divine grace, like as the vine branch and its tendrils exist and thrive by its deriving sap continuously from the root. Believers are thus supplied from their ever-living head; they are his members, and while he is their divine head, they will be ever supplied with life from him, for their life is in him. Faith, hope, love, joy, and peace, are

fed, sustained, nourished, thrive, and grow from "the supply of the Spirit of Christ." These graces of the Spirit, though once feeble, become strong, vigorous, and lively. Because Christ lives his saints live. Their life is hid with Christ in God; it cannot be touched by the adversary, it is not dependent on the believer himself, none can keep alive his own soul; his sin, his weakness, would soon injure it. It is a life of grace, grace for every need, grace for every grace, all grace is made to abound, being derived from his fulness.

2. We will now look for a moment *at the means* by which this spiritual life is sustained. We find various means are used by which God communicates his grace to his people, and hence is derived the term, "means of grace," so often employed to designate the various methods by which our souls are nourished and supported. "Who holdeth our souls in life." (Ps. lxvi. 9.)

The *first* mean the Lord employs to sustain this spiritual life, is *his own word of truth.* The word of truth is the food of the soul. What else can the soul of the believer feed upon. God's word is faith's food. Christ is the truth; they live on Christ, Christ's truth in the word. It is the aliment of the spiritual life. "Except ye eat the flesh of the Son of man, and drink his blood, ye have no life in you. He that believeth on me hath everlasting life." There is no life without Christ. As the soul was quickened by the word of truth, so the soul is nourished from day to day, from hour to hour, by the word of truth. This blessed book is the storehouse of God's truth, every variety of food to suit the different stages of spiritual life. The doctrines of the gospel are designed to be the food of believers. There is milk for babes, strong meat for the men in Christ. There is doctrine and duty, precept and promise, counsel and encouragement, solemn warnings and severe rebukes, with personal and national examples of the power of God's truth. And whether the word is read in private, in the family, or in public, it becomes, under the ministration of the Spirit, the instrument of upholding and maintaining the inward and spiritual life. Meditation on God's word has ever been proved the believer's sweetest channel of spiritual life.

The *second* mean by which spiritual life is sustained is —*prayer*. Prayer is said to be "the Christian's native air." And truly so, for as the air is essential for the animal life, so prayer is essential for the spiritual life; he cannot, he would not, he must not live without it; it is his intercourse with God. Prayer is the believer's atmosphere. It has been well said, "a prayerless soul is a Christless soul." Prayer, whether ejaculatory or statedly secret, is a gracious habit of the soul, and I may say it is an excellent thermometer of the soul. How near we live to God, or how much we draw from him, can always be tested by how much and how often we draw near to him. Prayer is the believer's great privilege, his sanctuary in trouble, and his cure for all griefs. Here it is he draws new life from Christ.

Through prayer, communion with the Lord is obtained by the believer. By communion they find their spiritual life is maintained and strengthened. Where there is a holy fellowship with God, every grace of the Spirit is nourished and in lively exercise, and there will be less of earthly fellowship. Communion with God causes the soul to be withdrawn from the world. Souls who have tasted the sweets of finding access to the heart of Jesus have no relish for the things of the world; it is in communion with our beloved Lord we prove our union. The more we have communion with him the more we realize our union to him; here we learn more of him, his beauties, his love, the wonders of his love; here we learn to live upon him, upon his word, upon his work. The more we are brought to feel our dependence upon him, the more blessed we find it is to feel our need of him, and are ever desirous of being with him, longing for his company, saying:

"Talk with me, Lord, thyself reveal,
    While here o'er earth I rove;
Speak to my heart, and let me feel,
    The kindlings of thy love.

"With thee conversing, I forget,
    All time, and toil, and care;
Labour is rest, and pain is sweet,
    If thou, my God, art there."

Oh, my friends, it is want of communion with our God that makes a soul go gadding about seeking entertainment from every frivolous amusement; tea-parties, large companies, public meetings, afford the soul no profit. These things may be very well in their place, but the hungry soul will find no account in them; they may seem to have a religious bearing or tendency, but the soul who lives on Jesus cannot live on the husks which the swine do eat. "I will," says Jesus, "cause them that love me to inherit substance." This is what the true believer wants; substance, not circumstantials. The outward things of religion are not his life. He feels it is in communion, in answers to prayer, or rather, in prayer, that the life-giving, life-sustaining Spirit of Christ descends upon him and is received.

The *promises* of God are another mean of sustaining the spiritual life. The soul is often cast down, but a good word often maketh it glad. Exceeding great and precious promises is the character the apostle has given them, and so the soul finds them. Special promises applied with power to the soul by the Holy Ghost, raising the soul above earth's trials, giving new life, helping it in trouble, giving peace in the midst of tribulation, inspiring hope, strengthening faith, sweetening prayer—all this is proved to be the method the Lord takes to maintain and impart life to the soul. He speaks to the heart through the promises of his grace, and new life is inspired through all the faculties of the soul.

Even the exercises of the soul, whether through the dispensations of God's providence—dark, crooked, and rough as they sometimes are—or those operations which are carried on in the soul, in leading the soul to God: these are also made the means of spiritual life. Hezekiah was a notable instance of this kind; and in reviewing the method of God's grace and providence, he owned it was, "In all these things is the life of my spirit." And Mr. Newton, in writing as to how his prayer was answered by crosses, says:

> "These inward trials I employ
> From sin and pride to set thee free;
> And break thy schemes of earthly joy,
> That thou may'st seek thy all in me."

I might also refer you to the ordinances of God's house, as means by which the soul is sustained. It is in the ministry of the word, which the Spirit employs through the ministering servant, by which the soul is fed. This is very evident, from the variety of blessing we often see dispensed at one time to several persons by the one

speaker. I will," says God, "abundantly bless the provision of my house, and satisfy my poor with bread."
There is the public worship on the Sabbath; the prayer
meeting; the week-night services; not forgetting the
Supper of the Lord, the symbols of his body and blood—
all these remind us that Christ is our life.

Even we derive life, or rather life is strengthened, by
church fellowship. It is not a custom or a fashion, grown
up out of the common usages of society, but it is an insti-
tution authorised in the Word of God, and is made a provision for further promoting the life of God in the soul.
The work of God in the heart, when made the subject of
discourse, and not the occurrences or circumstantials of
church meetings, is well calculated to feed and nourish
the life of God in the soul.

As long as the believer is upon earth, Christ is in him
the life of grace. The in-dwelling of the Holy Spirit
secures it, and the witnessing of the Spirit *assures* it; and
when he reaches the heavenly state, Christ will be with
him as the life of heaven itself: "For me to live is Christ,
and to die is gain." The life of grace on earth will be the
life of glory in the heavenly state—the same manner of
existence, always deriving and receiving from the fulness
of Christ.

Not only is the spiritual life of the believer sustained
by virtue of his union with Christ, his glorious head, but
the *corporeal* life of every member of the church of God,
after death, in the resurrection morn, springs from and is
secured by the life of Christ: "His resurrection from the
dead is the pattern and pledge of theirs; as sure as his
dead body is raised and lives, so shall theirs; their bodies
as well as their souls are united to Christ." The soul
without the body is not the person of the believer, and it
is the person of the believer that is secured from natural,
spiritual, and eternal death, by the obedience and death of
his risen Lord; and by virtue of this union with Christ,
which death does not and cannot dissolve, their dead bodies
shall be raised and live again: "Corruption shall put
on incorruption, mortality shall put on immortality."
"Blessed is he that hath part in the first resurrection."
"When Christ, who is our life, shall appear, we also shall
appear with him in glory."

As to our life in Christ, and living on Christ, I would

only remark, the more close the union with him, the more communion with him, and the more vigorous and healthy our spiritual life. Believers in the Lord Jesus Christ, look ye to it, how live ye on Christ? Professors of the name of Christ, do you know anything about this life you have been hearing of? look ye to it. If you have only a name that you live and art dead, your profession will leave you where it found you—a life in the flesh; and what good will it do you? You who are strangers to God and strangers to yourselves, have you never thought about this life? Remember this one thing: there is no life without Christ. I repeat it: THERE IS NO LIFE WITHOUT CHRIST. May the Lord command his blessing, even life for evermore. Amen.

THE SUBSTITUTIONARY WORK

OF THE

SON OF GOD.

◆

A SERMON,

BY CHARLES GORDELIER.

PREACHED AT HEPHZIBAH CHAPEL, DARLING PLACE, NEAR
MILE END GATE,

On Lord's Day Evening, Nov. 29th, 1863.

" For he hath made him to be sin for us, who knew no sin;
that we might be made the righteousness of God in him."—
2 Cor. v. 21.

WAIVING all reference to the circumstances under which
this epistle was written, or even the immediate connection
of the text, I would at once call your attention to the
great fact, how much the love of God is displayed to poor
sinners seeking salvation. The gospel reveals how it is
they may be pardoned and freely justified from all things,
from which they could not be justified by the law of
Moses.

All mankind are sinners, all are under condemnation ;
but how few there are who are sensible of either their
guilt or their danger. To most persons, sin has no terrors ; they love it, they roll it under their tongue as a
sweet morsel, and dream of unabating happiness in the
practice of it. They have no desire for salvation ; this
their way is their folly ; like sheep they are laid in the
grave, and have no hope beyond it.

Yet it has been that when the sinner is awakened to
a sense of his condition before God, he sees and feels
sin to be an awful reality, a new light has shone into his
understanding, and he begins to have a sense of his
danger ; now he feels the need of pardon, but his inquiry

No. 11.

is, " How can a just and holy God pardon sin, seeing he hath said, 'He will by no means clear the guilty.'" (Exod. xxxiv. 7.)

This grave question is answered in the great doctrine contained in our text. Sin is pardoned, God's law is honoured, and the sinner accepted, through the substitutionary work of the Son of God. The language of the psalmist is to the same import, when he exclaimed : " If thou, Lord, shouldest mark iniquities, O Lord, who shall stand? But there is forgiveness with thee, that thou mayest be feared." (Ps. cxxx. 3, 4.)

By the term, the substitutionary work of the Son of God, is to be understood the atonement he made to God for sin, by the sacrifice of himself. For the Lord Jesus Christ, in his character and person as the Holy Lamb of God, to take upon himself the curse and sufferings of a broken law instead of sinners, and thereby delivering them from all condemnation, is something so extraordinary and wonderful, that it outshines all the glories of creation, and even the mysteries of providence—

> " God in the person of his Son,
>   Hath all his mightiest works outdone."

The substitution of an innocent person for a criminal is of very rare and uncommon occurrence in a court of law. It is too costly and too expensive to be frequently permitted. To give up the innocent for the guilty would be a moral waste—weaken the operations of justice, and would destroy the connection between crime and punishment. The *principle* is, however, admitted in minor cases of offence, as when a *fine in money* is accepted in lieu of personal imprisonment. But personal substitution is evidently the great truth set forth in the words of our text : " For he hath made him to be sin, who knew no sin; that we might be made the righteousness of God in him." Peter, to the same effect: " For Christ also hath once suffered for sins, the just for the unjust." What is this but the substitution of the innocent for the guilty ? Let us then—

I. In the FIRST place point out the circumstances which appear to invest the subject with a heavenly wisdom, and to render this grand doctrine of divine substitution the ground of our adoring gratitude and praise.

1. *The supreme power must interpose, it being the only*

authority to dispense such a proceeding as would allow the substitution of an innocent person in lieu of the guilty, and to accept the sacrifice for the punishment.

To illustrate this point, I need scarcely do other than recite a few passages, out of many; the first that strikes us is, the remarkable words of our Lord, in his youth, to his mother: "Wist ye not that I must be about my Father's business." It was the Father's business in the great work of redemption, that his Son should not only take our nature into personal union with himself, but that also, in that nature, he should begin to fulfil all righteousness. This is also seen from the following scriptures: "That the world may know that I love the Father, and as the Father gave me commandment, so I do." (John xiv. 31.) "I came into the world not to do my own will, but the will of him that sent me, and this is the will of him that sent me, that whosoever seeth the Son, and believeth on him, should have everlasting life." (John vi. 40.) "I have finished the work which thou gavest me to do." (John xvii. 4.) So that our Lord in these, and other similar phrases, plainly set forth that all he did was by the intervention of his Father, and so confirming the faith of his disciples with the highest authority.

2. *That such a transaction should be valid and proper, it should have the full consent of the party who undertakes to suffer for the guilty,*

Or else there would be an increase of irregular proceedings; for, if reason requires that laws should not be made unless fit to be executed; and if, when they are made, wisdom suggests that a departure from them would be improper, much more would every principle of law and equity be violated by the compulsory punishment of the innocent. Now Jesus, in various places, has shown that his sacrifice was from his own willingness: "He gave himself for us." "I delight to do thy will." "Father, not my will but thine be done."

3. *The substitute must be wholly innocent from the offence for which he intends to expiate for the guilty.*

For if the substitute were not free, he must pay the penalty himself; if he owes his life to justice, it cannot be accepted instead of the life of another which has been forfeited. Now, "Jesus Christ the righteous" is the propitiation for our sins; "being holy, harmless, and undefiled, and separate from sinners," his substitution could be accepted. His own declaration is sufficient : "The prince of this world cometh, and hath nothing in me." (John xiv. 30.) Of the over-punctilious Pharisees he demanded, "Which of you convinceth me of sin." (John viii. 46.) Jesus was without spot in his person and character. The law was honoured by his life, its majesty vindicated by his death; and the result was, the sinner most honourably acquitted and eternally saved.

4. *The substitute ought to be in nature common with him who is the really guilty—man for man—brother for brother—flesh for flesh—spirit for spirit.*

The more closely he is related, the more he has in common, the more natural does substitution appear reasonable. It is more fitting that one man should be admitted as a substitute for another man, than for a being of a higher nature or order of being to take the place of one that is inferior. Here "we see Jesus, who was made a little lower than the angels;" he passed by the nature of angels that he might take ours—sin only excepted; he took our nature in order that he might take our sin, but did not take our sinful nature. He came in the likeness of sinful flesh, and for sin condemned sin in the flesh. He became perfect in his mediatorial work through suffering, and therefore he is able to succour and to sympathise with those who are tempted.

5. *The substitute should be able to vindicate the law by which he is to suffer.*

He must have a sense of its righteousness, otherwise the more noble and illustrious his character and the more extraordinary his interposition, the more men's opinion would be divided between approbation of his character and disapprobation of the law by which he suffered. For if the person suffering the penalty were to complain of the law which exacted it, the honour or glory of the law would be lost,—the law would be dishonoured in the estimation of men. But in the case of Jesus we find, that never had justice so glorious an advocate ; nor did it ever have such a victim for a sacrifice. So glorious was his person and character, that his sacrifice set forth the law of God as righteous; he magnified it and made it honourable.

But I must pass on more rapidly with these various

points of substitution ; and, therefore, cannot dilate on them as might be desired.   Notice then—

6. *Substitution should be an act wisely undertaken sa well as being prompted by goodness.*

Of this we are sure, that in the eternal covenant of grace, the plan of salvation was as much ordered by infinite wisdom, as it originated in infinite love.   For if Christ, who is of God made unto us wisdom, righteousness, salvation, and redemption, we are sure the Father's wisdom and his love, was co-equal in ordering all things, and sure.

7. *There ought to be a superiority, or at least, an equivalent, between the substitute and the person released from the penalty of his offence.*

This is seen and felt in the believer in Jesus, he is not his own, he is bought with a price ; henceforth he liveth not to himself, but to him who loved him and died for him.

8. *It would not be satisfactory if there were not some after compensation, or better result, proceeding from the death of the substitute.*

This is most truly the case in the work of redemption. Man, in his primeval state, was liable to fall, and did fall. In the new covenant state there are no contingencies ; falling, or liability to fall, is out of the question.   The believer's standing in Christ is fixed, eternally fixed, on more secure grounds than ever they stood, or could have stood under the first covenant.   The church of God being blessed with all spiritual blessings in heavenly places in Christ, according as they were chosen in him before the foundation of the world, have a superior standing, in consequence of the exalted position which they hold with Jesus Christ, their ever-living head.   And what a compensation, what a reward, what everlasting glory redounds to the Lord Jesus for all his sufferings, crowned with glory and honour: "When thou shalt make his soul an offering for sin he shall see his seed, he shall prolong his days, and the pleasure of the Lord shall prosper in his hand.   He shall see of the travail of his soul, and shall be satisfied." (Isa. liii. 10, 11.) The church of God given to him as his bride, and to be ever with him in eternal glory.   His mediatorial joy and crown was, "Father, I will that they also whom thou hast given me be with me where I am, that they may behold my glory." (John xvii. 24.)

c 2

But let us, before we proceed to notice the several terms of our text in particular, make a few brief remarks on the meaning of *Atonement* and *Redemption ;* we shall then be better prepared to enter into the two profound doctrines couched in our text. These are things which the angels desire to look into ; they are the deep things of God. O, may the Lord help us to speak as the oracles of God, so that the church of God may be edified, Christ exalted, and God in all things glorified.

The words Atonement and Redemption are often used by many persons in an indiscriminate manner, as though they were synonymous terms ; but a little consideration will, I think, show that they are not. The redemption of the soul is precious ; (Ps. xlix. 8 ;) there is not a more important subject can occupy the thought of man. It is the greatest blessing God can bestow. It is the forgiveness of sins by the death of Christ : " In whom we have redemption through his blood, even the forgiveness of sins ;" (Eph. i. 7 ;) that is, the guilt and shame is put away by the atonement of Christ, and which is here called redemption. Redemption and Atonement are two distinct subjects, though both procured by Christ's death. This will be seen in several scriptures, though expressed in a variety of forms, as in our text. (1 Peter iii. 18. 1 Cor. i. 30. Gal. iii. 13. Eph. ii. 13. Col. i. 14. Titus ii. 14. Heb. vii. 25. 1 Pet. i. 18. Rev. v. 9., &c., &c.)

Atonement is offered *to* God *for* man ; Redemption is the blessing conferred upon the believing sinner. The Atonement was to satisfy divine law and justice ; Redemption liberates the pardoned sinner from its curse. Redemption has to do with sinners on earth ; Atonement with God's government in heaven. Atonement has regard to the honour of God· Redemption the captivity of the sinner. Atonement is expiation ; Redemption is the deliverance from both the penalty and the power of sin. The Atonement was effected at once when Christ offered his sacrifice on the cross, but Redemption is the application of the benefits of his death to individual believers to the end of time. The Atonement may be viewed apart from Redemption, but Redemption can never be viewed apart from Atonement. At your leisure consult the several passages just quoted, for they all show that the Redemption of the believer is effected through the Atonement made by Christ to God the Father.

Of *the nature* of the atonement, and of *the extent* of it, I shall not, at present, remark upon ; as any observations that may be called for on these points, will be made in their proper place, under the next heads of our discourse.

We will now proceed to notice in the SECOND place,

II. The condition and character of the persons here stated to be benefited by this divine act of substitution.

The apostle Paul in writing this Epistle to the Corinthians, has named specially the persons to whom he wrote,—"the Church of God which is at Corinth ;" by which we are to understand, not all the people of Corinth, or its citizens generally, nor yet all the people in whose hands his epistle might happen to come ; still less does he mean the whole race of mankind ; therefore, the pronouns, *we* and *us* employed in the text, are to be understood of the church of God, in which, of course, he includes himself. These are the persons, and the only persons, who are benefited by the substitutionary work of the Son of God—the church of God in all ages, and through all time. By keeping this point in view we shall, if taught by the Spirit of truth, be able to keep clear of the God dishonouring, and self-contradictory doctrines of the present day, which assert that "Christ died for all men, but saves only those who believe."

The apostle in writing to the churches at Galatia, expressly states that the Scripture hath concluded all under sin. In writing to "the beloved of God in Rome, called to be saints," (for it seems there was no organised church there,) he brings forward the scriptures, which declare "There is none righteous, no, not one, there is none that understandeth ; there is none that seeketh after God." "For all have sinned, and come short of the glory of God." (Rom. iii. 10, 11, and 23.) Here is there a very grave charge brought against human nature. The whole race of mankind is under condemnation, and under a sentence of death.

Now the honour and truth of God is deeply involved in this charge. For if it be not true, then the grace of God that is manifested in the Gospel is superfluous. The death of Jesus Christ has then answered no purpose. The Bible can be no more than a history of the Jews, and a view of their opinions as men ; and it would come to this, there is no religion at all, and we who preach or profess the Gospel, are found false witnesses for God. But we are not found false witnesses for God. Yea, rather let God be true, and every man a liar. All men are sinners! "If we say that we have not sinned, we make him a liar, and his word is not in us." And when it pleaseth the Holy Ghost to quicken our souls, and to convince us of our sin, we then feel the sentence of death in us; and so far from justifying ourselves before God, we are brought to feel, and to confess before him, "Behold! I am vile;" and every one so taught is brought to "the place of stopping of mouths." He is brought in guilty before God, and to find that by the deeds of the law shall no flesh be justified in his sight.

Thus it is we see that the ground of the apostle's argument is so strongly expressed in our text. Observe the foregoing part of the chapter. Sin is described as a burden, under which we groan, we have felt it so, we long for its deliverance; and knowing the condemnation, called in the 11th verse: "the terrors of the Lord," we are the more desirous of preaching unto you the salvation, which is by Christ Jesus, whom God hath set forth to be a propitiation for sin: "For he hath made him to be sin for us, who knew no sin, that we might be made the righteousness of God in him." You will see, by reference to the 11th verse on to the 19th, that this is the bearing of the apostle's interesting and important argument.

But further, let us not be satisfied with only the truth doctrinally, there is also an *experimental* acquaintance with the truth now under consideration, and without which we shall be miserably deceived. Have not some of you been convicted of sin in your own consciences? Has not sin been revealed to you as exceeding sinful? How came guilt, like a rushing stream, to be carrying you on, as it were, down to the gulf of perdition and dark despair? was it a device of your imagination? do you think it came from the infernal regions to begin the work of misery now, or do you think it was a ray of heavenly light into your dark dead soul? whence came the consciousness of your sinfulness? I again ask you, What was it that induced you to seek relief, in humble earnest prayer, at the footstool of mercy, or in the reading of God's Word? What led you to the house of God, hoping to hear words by which you might be saved? This was it! It was the testimony of God's Spirit in your conscience; it was the testimony of

God's Spirit with his word ; it was the testimony of God's Spirit in the ministry of the word, all working in you the feeling sense that you were a sinner, and that you could be justified only by the righteousness of Christ! My friends! the word of God, our own conscience, what we see and hear in the world, all prove the universality of man's depravity, all prove the fact that ALL men are sinners. ALL men, by nature, are sinners, are under condemnation, and are under sentence of eternal death.

III. I pass on to notice in the THIRD place, the character and personal merits of the Substitute, who, though he knew no sin, was made sin.

Here we approach an ocean of divinity. We enter into our little skiff and scud along the shore for a little while, admire a few ripples, then fancy we have been doing business in the great waters, seen the works of the Lord, and his wonders in the deep. O, how shallow is all our knowledge about redemption. Redemption! how vast its benefits ; Atonement! how great the sacrifice. Substitution! what infinite wisdom in the plan. The love of Christ! it passeth knowledge. The love of God! God is love. Amazing themes! too high for mortals to scale, too deep for angels to sound. They are unutterable.

> " Justice was pleased to bruise the God,
> And pay its wrongs with heavenly blood;
> What unknown racks and pains he bore;
> Then rose; the law could ask no more."

But we have to speak more particularly upon the character of the Lord Jesus Christ. He knew no sin. Had he known sin, that is committed it, or had been infected with it, he could not have saved a single soul. A man in debt could not pay the debts of others. A condemned criminal would not be accepted as bail for an accused person.

> " For he who would for sin atone,
> Must have no failings of his own."

A sinner could not save a sinner. The ransom of a captive must be paid by one having the full price in his hand, and the power to redeem from all bondage, or else failure and abortion would disgrace the attempt everlastingly. But the Lord Jesus Christ in his own person, possessed all might, power, and riches for the ransom.

" Great was the price to Justice due,
When Jesus would redeem his bride ;
Nothing but precious blood would do,
And that must flow from his own side."

Yea, great as was the price, he was equal to the demand
in every way.   In his own person as God-man, he possessed all the power that eternal redemption required.   In
his manhood being perfectly sinless, and his perfect obedience to God's holy law, he possessed the exact price that
divine justice demanded.   In his voluntary offering of
himself as a sacrifice for sin, the full penalty of a broken
law was paid and accepted.   He was holy, harmless, and
separate from sinners.   He had no practical or personal
knowledge of sin, either in thought, word, or deed.   His
human nature being created by the Holy Ghost, and his
Person being God, it was a moral impossibility for him to
sin.   So far as mere knowledge extends, he knew what sin
was, as that evil which his soul abhorred, and which he came
to take away ; for he taught the spirituality of God's law,
and how it extended to the thoughts and intents of the
heart.   No one could know so well the nature of sin.

The character of the Lord Jesus, " who knew no sin,"
evidently means, he had no participation in it, no personal experience of it, it had no place in him.   He
was not ignorant of its nature, but he was conscious of
its non-existence in himself.   It does not regard what he
discerned in others.   Being the Son of God, he is necessarily of the same nature as his Father ; hence he is holy in
his nature, in all his works, and in all his ways ; and the
human nature he took was created by the Holy Ghost ;
he condescended to take that, but not our sinful nature ;
the dignity of his person could not possibly admit of his
contamination with sin in his compassion for sinners.
There is nothing derogatory in the goodness of a king in
lifting a beggar from the dunghill, and setting him among
the princes of his people, though there might be a question as to his wisdom and the propriety of the act.   But
this grace of our Lord Jesus Christ was guided by infinite
wisdom, as well as originated in infinite love.   He, as our
merciful High Priest, has compassion on the ignorant and
the outcast ; but this, far from being a reflection on his
wisdom and goodness, it enhances both, and exalts his
character far above all blessing and praise.

By man, wicked, perverse, rebellious man, Jesus was charged with sin; but the charge he repelled, and demanded, "Which of you convinceth me of sin?" (John viii. 46.) "He did no sin, neither was guile found in his mouth." (1 Peter ii. 22.) At the close of his life on earth, he declared, "The prince of this world cometh, and hath nothing in me." (John xiv. 30.) Had he been sinful, or liable to it, he could not have saved others; an atonement would have been needful for himself; his own death would have been no atonement, but simply the penalty for himself. Atonement by the sinner for himself is an impossibility; none can by any means redeem his brother. The principle of an atonement was in this, that for the purpose of making peace where offence existed, an unblemished sacrifice had to be made of life for life, blood for blood. This was effected by the mediation of the Son of God in the union of his two natures, the divine and the human. His human nature was perfect, and "being found in the fashion of a man, he humbled himself, and became obedient to the death of the cross."

> "His life was pure, without a stain,
> And all his nature clean;"

and as his person was divine, here was its excellency, and hence our everlasting security: "Ye know that he was manifested to take away our sins, and in him was no sin." (1 John iii. 5.)

IV. We have now to consider, in the FOURTH place, The great act of grace displayed by the Father in the substitution of his Son for sin.

This is a wonderful theme to contemplate. The Father, knowing, foreseeing our state as sinners, the ruin of all the race of mankind by the sin of the first man, our federal head, did, in the infinity of his wisdom, love, grace, and mercy, provide salvation for guilty, hell-deserving rebels, by the substitution of the life of his Son instead of the souls he had created: "God so loved the world that he gave his only-begotten Son, that whosoever believeth in him should not perish, but have everlasting life. For God sent not his Son into the world to condemn the world, but that the world through him might be saved." (John iii. 16, 17.) The great grace of the Father is also spoken of by the apostle Paul, and used as an argument from the great to the less, Rom. viii. 32 : " He that spared not his own Son, but freely delivered him for us," &c.; to whom ? The claims of divine justice in his own person.

The greatness of this grace further appears in Christ Jesus stooping so low. He left the bosom of the Father, the glory that he had with him before the world was: " Ye know the grace of the Lord Jesus, who, though he was rich, yet he became poor, that we, through his poverty, might be made rich." (2 Cor. viii. 9.)   " Surely he hath borne our griefs and carried our sorrows; yet we did esteem him stricken, smitten of God, and afflicted.   He was wounded for our transgressions, he was bruised for our iniquities; the chastisement of our peace was upon him; and with his stripes we are healed; and the Lord hath laid upon him the iniquity of us all." (Isa. liii. 4–6.) So that all the sins of all his people were laid upon him by the act of the Father's grace.

Then the question returns: How could Christ be made sin, seeing he, personally, knew no sin ? Not practically so, but by imputation. Sin was punished in his person, because he voluntarily took it upon himself. In the covenant of grace he became the Surety of his people; and thus undertaking their redemption, it was necessary that he should become their Substitute. He was made legally answerable for our sin, and the Father accepted the bond. Now see how this is taught by the Holy Spirit in the Mosaic law. (Lev. xvi. 21, 22.) It is in respect of the *one offering* of the two goats on the day of atonement. No sacrifice which God commanded Moses to institute, so circumstantially sets forth atonement; it was a most comprehensive type of Christ, for it shadowed forth not only *the means* by which expiation for sin was effected, but also *the result* of that expiation, namely the removal of guilt; the *slain* goat exhibited the death of Christ, and the *scape* goat represented his bearing away the sins of his people and also their free discharge. For by virtue of the union betwixt Christ and his people, they were both implicated; the sins of the people are expressed by the hand being placed on the head of the *scape* goat, he represents *the actual* sinner; but the Lord's lot, upon which no sinful hand is laid, and therefore represented *the innocent one*, he it is that *is slain*, he it is that is *the actual sufferer*. The innocent one is made to be the substitute for the guilty, while the guilty one is sent into the wilderness *free*, and is left at large.

Here is, then, a more striking exhibition of the substitution of Christ in the sinner's stead than can be found in any illustration from the classics, which our men of learning so proudly bring forward. Jesus Christ, by taking the sinner's law place, became, by imputation, SIN; for we must bear in mind, the two goats are but one offering; the one signified atonement; the other, redemption. "He was made to be sin." Sin was represented in his body on the cross. He suffered death as a sinner. The wrath of God against sin was inflicted on him as punishment for sin: "He suffered, the just for the unjust;" "He bore our sins in his own body on the tree." As the surety and substitute of the whole election of grace, Christ suffered all the vengeance due to all their sins; it was a complete and full atonement, and therefore they are for ever freed from its curse and penalty. His sinnership was by imputation taken by himself. *The value* of his atonement was not in the amount of human pain and suffering he endured, though it was necessary that his human nature should suffer; but it was in the fact of his person being the eternal Son of God. It was this that gave a dignity and an infinite worth to his sufferings. Had his Sonship not been eternal, his sacrifice had not been an equivalent. Hence he became the author of eternal redemption. Sin is atoned for, God's law is magnified and made honourable, the sinner is righteously acquitted and honourably saved, Christ is exalted, and is now for ever sat down on the right hand of God.

V. Now we have to consider, in the FIFTH place, The end accomplished by the transfer of sin to the Lord Jesus Christ.

This is stated in the text: "That we might be made the righteousness of God in him." Elsewhere, the apostle says, "Who of God is made unto us wisdom, RIGHTEOUSNESS, sanctification, and redemption." (1 Cor. i. 30.) We are made righteous in the same way as Christ was made sin,—by imputation. In our own persons, by nature, and consciously so, we are sinful creatures; but in the person of Christ, as united to him in the covenant of grace, we are, in the eye of the divine law, righteous, accepted as such by God the Father, being "made accepted in the beloved." (Eph. i. 6.)

This righteousness is revealed to us by the Holy Spirit; by his effectual working in us, this truth is applied to us, and is received by faith; hence the believer adopts the language of the prophet: "In the Lord have I righteousness and strength." (Isa. xlv. 24, 25.) Christ being in his person and life perfectly holy, harmless, separate from sinners, needed no righteousness by the works of the law; he undertook obedience to it on our behalf. This obedience was the righteousness which he wrought out and brought in, and is imputed to us by the Father. His death was also piacular, as well as vicarious; it was the penalty paid by him for our sin. And as it was impossible that he could be holden by death, seeing that he, personally, was not a sinner, and had paid the penalty demanded by the law, so he rose again. His resurrection, therefore, is the ratification of his own personal righteousness, and becomes, therefore, in every point of fact, our justification. He rose again for our justification. (Rom. iv. 25.) Who is he that condemneth? It is Christ that died; yea, rather, that is risen again. Thus it is that the obedience, death, and resurrection of the Lord Jesus Christ is our justification before God the Father. God looks upon his people as always standing complete in the person of his Son. "Ye are complete in him."

> " In him the Father never saw
> The least transgression of his law.
> Perfection, then, in Christ we view;
> His saints in him are perfect too."

This matter of our justification is of the utmost importance to the believer in Christ. He should see that he is well grounded in it. For there are certain men crept into the professing church, who, with all cunning craftiness, are drawing away disciples after them, and stealing away the truth as it is in Christ; saying that the resurrection of Christ is the only act that avails the church of God. Now, what is this but denying the Lord that bought them? O, beware of these so-called Plymouth brethren, or Bible Christians, as they are sometimes named! They are wolves in sheeps' clothing; they are the enemies of the cross of Christ. Their apparent spiritual tone of mind and softness of manner deceive the simple hearted, but inwardly they are found to be ravening wolves. See how they bite and devour one another!

"But," says the inquiring but believing sinner, "how am I to know that I am righteous?" I answer, *Faith* is the instrument which God employs in receiving the truth. It is called the righteousness of faith, because *faith* alone is used in its application. It is not the righteousness of love, hope, or desire, but of faith. If you are seeking to be justified by the righteousness of Christ, it is because you feel your need of it. Go on seeking. They that seek shall find; and may the Lord enable you to lay hold of the hope set before you. He will certainly reveal his love and grace to you ere long. You shall realise the fact that your sins are all pardoned for Christ's sake. You will then perceive you are made righteous in him. This is realising *how* it is done. It is a glorious thing to feel that I am a pardoned sinner; but when I learn how it was procured, I have a boundless cause of joy, and can sing with the poet:

> "I'm safe! I'll shout, O law and sin,
> Ye cannot bring me guilty in;
> For Christ was crucified!"

Now, besides the point which we have just been considering,—our character and standing before God as the end accomplished by the atonement of the Lord Jesus,—there are also other actual or positive benefits derived therefrom, such in which we have a personal consciousness of; and these may be comprised in one word,—the *Redemption* itself. This is threefold,—past, present, and future. The *first*, whereby we are freed from the power of God's law and justice, and all the consequences of sin and death. It consists in the forgiveness of sins: "In whom we have redemption through his blood, even the forgiveness of sins." The *second*, from the power of inbred sin, the working of sin within us; from the causes of sin, from the love of sin, even sin itself. This is through the sanctification of the Spirit and belief of the truth. "Sin shall not have dominion over you; for ye are not under the law, but under grace." The *third*, the redemption of our bodies from the power of the grave, whereby we are put in full possession of all the blessings of redemption at the last great day of the resurrection, when our persons will be received into heaven; the reunion of the spirit with the body will be the perfecting our bliss and capability of enjoyment, and we shall be for ever with the Lord, he " having obtained eternal redemption for us."

In concluding this discourse on the great doctrine of Christ's substitution for the redeemed sinner, we would observe:

1. *The immaculate purity of God's law and government over his rational creatures.* "He is of purer eyes than to behold evil, and cannot look upon iniquity." So pure that even the heavens, the angelic intelligences, are not clean in his sight. It was his own purpose that his people should be redeemed from all sin, that they might set forth the praise and glory of his grace.

2. We also perceive *the nature and evil of sin.* This we may not only see, but also feel, when, under the teachings of the Holy Spirit, we contemplate the holy character of God. Sin gives God a flat denial of his right to govern. Sin dares to assert its own power against God. Sin refuses to obey God. Sin insults God by contradicting his law. Sin leads the sinner from God, to hide himself from God, to hate God, to love darkness rather than light, to hate holiness, and to love filthiness, to prefer serving the devil, turn his back upon God, and to say to him, "I desire not the knowledge of thy ways."

3. From the doctrine of Christ's substitution for the sinner, we perceive,—*repentance cannot expiate* sin. 'Tis true sin must be repented of; it must be forsaken; it must be confessed; it must be deplored. But repentance is not the procuring cause of pardon; it does not regain God's favour; nor does it recompense the injury done to God's broken law. A debtor's sorrow for his debt could not pay it. Nevertheless, a godly sorrow for sin is pleasing to God, and it is made the means of putting us in a fitting frame of mind to receive God's mercy and pardon with thankfulness, joy, and love.

4. We may also infer that *the sacrifice of Christ does not supersede the necessity of repentance.* The believing sinner cannot but be a penitent sinner. He has a broken and a contrite heart for his sins, and this God will not despise. He dwelleth with him who is humble and contrite of heart, and trembleth at his word. A view of the exceeding sinfulness of sin, and of the holy majesty of

God, will, under the gracious teachings of his Spirit, lead the sinner to repentance,—a godly sorrow for sin; a repentance that needeth not to be repented of.

My friends! let me ask you, What do you know of this repentance? Has it led you to seek a righteousness founded on the substitutionary work of the Son of God? Cherish no fond hopes of your own merit, nor yet of your mere belief of the truth. If you kindle a false fire, and walk in the light of your own kindling, you will at the last die in the dark, and rise in eternal sorrow.

BEHOLD THE LAMB OF GOD.

John i. 29.

Arise, ye saints of God, arise;
Tune all your powers to praise the Lord.
Come, take your stand beside the cross,
And say, "Behold the Lamb of God."

He left his throne, and dwelt with men,
To save his church from sin and woe;
His life he gave, and thus became
The sin-atoning Lamb of God.

His sacrifice for sin avails
For all who plead his precious blood;
His power to save through time prevails,—
The high, exalted Lamb of God.

Hail! sacred Lamb! We praise thy name;
Our hearts and lives to thee we yield;
We'll spread abroad thy wondrous fame,
And say, "Behold the Lamb of God."

C. G. 1838.

THE BELIEVER'S DELIGHT IN THE LAW OF GOD.

A SERMON,
BY CHARLES GORDELIER.

PREACHED AT HEPHZIBAH CHAPEL, DARLING PLACE, NEAR MILE END GATE,

On Lord's Day Evening, Sept. 25th, 1864.

"For I delight in the law of God, after the inward man."—Rom. vii. 22.

THIS is the language of every sincere believer in the Lord Jesus Christ. It arises out of his experience of God's gracious work in the heart. For having been taught by the Spirit of truth to see the spirituality of God's law, that it is holy, and the commandment is holy, just, and good ; made to feel the evil and bitterness of sin, and to know something of the power, bondage, and curse of a broken law in his conscience, he is then led under the same teachings to see that in the person of the Lord Jesus Christ God's holy law has been perfectly fulfilled on his behalf, and that a complete atonement has been made for him, a poor helpless guilty sinner. Thus it is he is brought into the liberty of the gospel, and by a sweet testimony in his own soul that he has been re-deemed from the curse of the law by the precious blood of Christ, he feels he is no longer under the law as a cove-nant of works, but serves God according to the rule of the gospel ; for through the law he is dead to the law that he may live unto God, not in the oldness of the letter, but in newness of the Spirit ; he walks not after the flesh but after the Spirit ; hence he has a joyful sense of what the apostle has declared : "There is, therefore, now no con-demnation to them which are in Christ Jesus." For the

No. 12.

law of the spirit of life in Christ Jesus hath made him free from the law of sin and death.

But the language of our text is also used by the mere professor, the hypocrite, the man who talks the gospel, but who does not live the gospel. He uses it that he may pass current in the religious world as one who knows the truth ; but alas, he knows nothing of its power, whatever he may know of the letter. He is like the electro plated articles now used in many places instead of real silver. He has all the appearance of one of God's people, but within there is no genuine work ; he has never been brought into the furnace of those heart-searching trials which distinguish the false from the real; he pretends to delight in the law of God, but he does not, he has no real love to it ; he cherishes sin in his heart ; it is true he curbs it occasion-ally, but only lest it should discover him and disgrace him, and so lose his position in society, for this, indeed, is now what is so much craved after in the professing church. Unlike the true believer, he knows nothing of the conflict within, of which the apostle describes in this chapter. Appeal to his conscience ; press him close as to his expe-rience, and you will find that the language of his lips is not the language of his heart, and the first plausible pretext he can find he will quit your company.

But we will leave the hypocrite for the present ; it is with the believer we have to do ; and here let me say,that this delighting in the law of God is a good sign of a gra-cious heart ; it is the character of the man of whom David expressly says : " Blessed is the man that walketh not in the council of the ungodly, nor standeth in the way of sinners, nor sitteth in the seat of the scornful. But his delight is in the law of the Lord, and in his law doth he meditate day and night." Here we see Old Testament truth is the same as New Testament truth. Old Testament saints and New Testaments saints unite in the same language, for they have the same experience ; and this is our mercy, we, who have been favoured with the light of God's truth, and to know something of its unction and power, know what it is to delight in the law of God after the inward man. The true believer in Jesus sees it as being the beauty of holiness. He is pleased with it. He regards its pure and spiritual precepts as being right and good, and he finds an unspeakable satisfaction in being conformed to it.

Such was the experience of the apostle Paul; it was the life and power of God's truth wrought in his heart: it was not merely a matter of the understanding; it was not by any intellectual or reasoning process obtained at the feet of Gamaliel; but it was the result of the great promise of the new covenant: "I will put my law in their inward parts, and write it in their hearts; and will be their God and they shall be my people." (Jer. xxxi. 33.)

Now, in attempting to say a few things on the passage before us, I confess there is something, at first sight, almost contradictory, or at least paradoxical, in the way the apostle speaks at different times respecting the law of God. Paradoxies, however, if I might so say, belong to the religion of Jesus. Many things are matters of the believer's experience which cannot always be readily understood by the mere theorist. Some truths indeed are not so opposite to each other as at first might be supposed, for, on a little closer examination, they are found to be but parallel truths, running side by side; as for instance, the Galatians seemed to have thought that the law was in opposition to the gospel; and the apostle, in order to show that it was not, asks the question, "Is, then, the law against the promises of God?" He replies, "God forbid." (Gal. iii. 24.) And he shows that the gospel which he preached was founded on the same principle, which as far back as Abraham's time, had been laid down by Jehovah as the rule for man's acceptance with him, that the way for men to find righteousness with God was not by the merit of any *works* to be done, but simply in the exercise of a certain *faith* prescribed; still, though the law and the promises are distinct things and have their separate uses, yet they are not contradictory to each other, for both have the same divine origin from him who is of one mind: the gospel does not set aside the law on all accounts, but in fact establishes it; (Rom. iii. 31;) nor does the law disannul the promises, but is subservient to them; and while it is strictly true that "the law came by Moses, but grace and truth came by Jesus Christ," they are, though distinct in their principles, in nowise opposed to each other, for Jesus himself says, "Think not that I am come to destroy the law. I am not come to destroy, but to fulfil;" (Matt. v. 17;) and I trust, that under the Spirit's teaching, we shall see what the apostle's meaning is in the text before us, and that we shall be able to understand how entirely his several statements agree. O may the Lord grant us in our own hearts to feel how true it is that the believer in Christ, though not under the law, but delivered from it, yet does, from his heart, love it, and delight in it.

Now in order to understand the subject before us, there are three matters that claim our consideration.

I. What is this law of which the apostle speaks?

II. What is the believer's position in relation to that law?

III. What are the exercises of his heart towards it? and then conclude by making a few inferences by way of improvement on the whole.

I. *What is this law of which the apostle speaks?*

We have no occasion to go far for an answer, the text itself supplies it. It is, unquestionably, the law of God; in other words, the revealed will of God, the Creator, as given to his creature, man. Man, as a created being, endowed with rational faculties, is doubtless under the government and providence of his Creator. God claims obedience from him; and in his first estate no more was claimed from him than he could render. The first law was that which was given to Adam in Paradise: "Of the tree of knowledge of good and evil thou shalt not eat." Simple as this law was, it was sufficient to serve the purpose for which it was given. It was a test of obedience; it was a test of love. So long as he loved his Maker, so long would he refuse to touch the tree; but when he took thereof and did eat, he gave evidence his love was gone. The disobedience existed in principle before its development in action. The heart fell from God before the hand was raised in rebellion.

From the time of Adam's fall, other laws were given; these were but parts of the original. The principle of love being gone, man was without the guiding influence of his life; he became vain in his imagination, and his foolish heart was darkened; aiming to be wise, he became a fool. Still, fallen as he was, God would not leave him to his own destruction, in following his own pernicious ways, and therefore multiplied other laws, more particular, more defined; for now, having became ignorant of God, he needed specific injunctions and specific prohibitions;

D

" For precept must be upon precept, precept upon precept; line upon line, line upon line; here a little, and there a little." (Isa. xxviii. 10.) All these were parts of his law; sometimes more fully expressed than at other times, but the substance of the original law was ever the same. A close observation of the age in which the patriarchs lived will demonstrate this; from the time of Cain to Enoch, from Noah to Job, from Abraham to Moses.

Then came the law of the ten commandments, the law that came by Moses, frequently called the *moral* law; called so in distinction from the ceremonial or Levitical law; the word *moral*, though not found in Scripture, is used by divines chiefly for distinction's sake. The apostle Paul says, "We know the law is spiritual;" and so every believing sinner finds it. No man, until he is renewed by the Holy Ghost, can have any true knowledge of the nature of God's law.

But what is the nature of this law of Moses? We find it to be everything that God would have men to do, expressed under a few heads. Here are enjoined duties toward God and toward our fellow-men. There is also expressly forbidden all sins against God, and all sins against our fellow-men. In Micah vi. 8, we find the substance of all these points is comprised thus: "He hath showed thee, O man, what is good? and what doth the Lord require of thee, but to do justly, and to love mercy, and to walk humbly with thy God?" Then, again, as is shown by the Lord Jesus himself, all that has been enjoined, both in the law and by the prophets, is contained in this summary: "Thou shalt love the Lord thy God with all thy heart, and mind, and soul, and strength; and thou shalt love thy neighbour as thyself. On these two commandments hang all the law and the prophets." Here is the whole will of God respecting man's conduct towards himself and towards each other. The apostle Paul puts it in the same way: " Owe no man anything, but to love one another; for he that loveth another hath fulfilled the law; and if there be any other commandment, it is briefly comprehended in this saying, namely, Thou shalt love thy neighbour as thyself. Love worketh no ill to his neighbour; therefore love is the fulfilling of the law." (Rom. xiii. 8–10.) To the same effect is the apostle John, throughout his First Epistle. Thus we see, from the course of the argument which we have taken, we have come back to the first principle, where we started—The love of God is the principle of perfect obedience. Now, this law of God has never been altered or relaxed; it has remained immutable; it is holy, just, and good. Man has altered; hence his position in relation to that law has placed him in another condition. This will lead us to notice the inquiry proposed in the SECOND place.

II. *What is the believer's position in relation to that law ?*

This inquiry can only be answered thus, The believer has been taught by the Spirit that the law is spiritual, and that he is carnal, sold under sin; that the law is holy, just, and good; he has been taught to see and to feel that he cannot obey God's law in any part; having failed, more or less, in some part, therefore is guilty of the whole. Is there any hope of escape from the guilt incurred ? Nay, verily, for if life could have been given by the law, verily righteousness should have been by the law. (Gal. iii. 21.)

But the believer feels under its curse. Can he make an atonement ? No; for death is the penalty; he has already forfeited his life, and the word of God is, he "will by no means clear the guilty;" all human attempts are fruitless. But will not future obedience suffice ? No. What, then ? "A fearful looking for of fiery indignation from a righteous judge that shall devour him." This is that which is so emphatically called "the terrors of the law." How it bows a man's spirit down to the earth; often it is, his "soul chooseth strangling rather than life." His soul draweth near to the gates of despair and death.

Now it is at this point that the good Spirit leads the distressed and burdened soul to seek life and salvation in the gospel. Under his gracious teachings he finds there revealed, that God has accepted the obedience and sufferings of Jesus on the sinner's behalf, for he has magnified the law and made it honourable by his perfect obedience; he sees that divine justice has been satisfied in the death of Christ, for he has paid the penalty of a broken law, and that now nothing more is demanded of either the Surety or the sinner; he sees that he is freed from the law as a covenant of works; the gospel is now his hope of salvation and his rule of life both towards God and towards man: "For, says the apostle," I, "through the law, am dead to the law, that I might live unto God." (Gal ii. 19.) Here is something apparently paradoxical in this statement; let us look at it for a moment. By referring back to the 17th verse you will perceive the apostle is showing that the doctrine of justification without the works of the law was in no wise opposed to the doctrine of sanctification, but of absolute necessity to true holiness; here, in this 19th verse, which we are now looking at, he brings his own case for proof, "for I, through the law, am dead to the law," that is, not seeking life and righteousness by it, nor yet to fear its accusations, charges, curses, and condemnation; but he was dead to the moral law as in the hands of Moses, though not as in the heart of Christ; for thus it was he lived unto God. He then asks, Was then that which is good made death unto me? He replies, God forbid. Here is, then, in the experience of the believing soul a wonderful death and a remarkable life, yet both through the law.

By referring to the chapter from whence we have taken our text, from the 10th to the 13th verse, we shall be able to discover a little of what the apostle means about being dead to the law—it is not a temporal death, for he was then living; it was not a spiritual or eternal life, for that he never had in Adam, that is, naturally; but he is dead to the law as a covenant of works, as a condition of life, for this was the covenant under which Adam stood. As the believer is dead to the law, by virtue of not being under the first covenant, he is, therefore, dead to sin; so far as it is not to bear rule over him, for he is not under the law, but under grace. (Rom vi. 14.) To be dead to sin, through being dead to the law is a mystery to unbelievers and carnal professors, and so is being dead to the law through the law, but "they are all plain to him that understandeth."

But let us look at this matter a little closer. For in looking at the believer's position in relation to the law of God, to which we have just now proved that he is dead, we have also said, that he lives unto God. How can he live unto God and yet be dead to his law? What is this life? In the first place it is not a natural life; it is not a legal life; it is not an external life, a mere pharisaic life; but it is a spiritual life, a life imparted by the Spirit of God, by which the soul is quickened, enlivened, and enlighted. · In other words, it is the understanding and the affections renewed and put in exercise towards God in Christ. Being united to Christ by a true and living faith, he has peace, hope, and joy, from a sense of pardoned sin applied to the conscience by the power of God the Holy Ghost. He is thus brought to live in the Spirit, to walk in the Spirit, to mind the things of the Spirit, and being spiritually minded he has life and peace. Mind you, I am speaking of *the result*, not of *the process ;* the first is, as a matter of fact, always the same, the other may be sooner or later, as a matter of the believer's experience.

This life of the believer consists in living in the strength and power of the Spirit, therefore called a law. " The law of the Spirit of life in Christ Jesus hath made him free from the law of sin and death."

" When Jesus' gracious hand,
Has touched our eyes and ears ;
O, what a dreary land,
This wilderness appears.
No healing balm springs from its dust,
No cooling streams to quench the thirst.

" Yet long I vainly sought,
A resting place below;
And that sweet land forgot,
Where living waters flow.
I hunger now for heavenly food,
And my poor heart cries out for God."

Such is the experience of the believer when renewed in the spirit of his mind. As natural life is evidenced by *breathing, motion, appetite,* and *sense,* so is the spiritual life. The believer lives in conformity with God. He that dwells with God, walks with God, will aim to be as he is, without it there is no communion with him. He walks before God as a child. He walks with God as a friend. This is the position of the believer in relation to the law of God. He walks in love.

III. We have now to consider in the THIRD place. *What are the exercises of the believer's heart towards the law of God ?*

Liberty from it ? No. To live as though there were no law ? No. He delights in it ; he feels delivered from it, that is, from its curse. He looks at it as God the Father looks at it—as Christ looks at it—as the Holy Spirit looks at it. Yes, he loves the law of God, and he can say with

D 2

David, " O, how I love thy holy law." " I delight to do thy will, O, God, yea, thy law is *within my heart*." " I delight in the law of God." He delights in the law of God because it is God's law, and because he believes it to be holy, just, and good, and he delights to walk according to it in the spirit of the gospel, namely, by the constraining influence of the love of Christ. "The law of God *is in his heart;* none of his steps shall slide." (Ps. xxxvii. 31.)

But so far as striving to inherit eternal life by the perfect performance of any one single duty he has no delight in it whatever, for he feels every effort towards that end is but an experience of its killing power. " The law worketh wrath."

> " In vain we ask God's righteous law,
>   To justify us now;
> Since to convince, and to condemn,
>   Is all the law can do."

Nor yet has he any delight in it so far as any personal merit is concerned ; for if it were possible to effect a justification by the works of the law, it would set aside the great end of Christ's death. It would set aside faith altogether. To trust, therefore, to one's own doings, or to plead them before God, as the reason of our justification in his sight, is to make the death of Christ and Redemption by it, altogether a vain thing. In fact, it is an appeal to the law for acceptance with God; whereas, God hath set forth his own son to be a propitiation, through faith in his blood. (Rom. iii. 25.)

Now I am aware there are several passages in Scripture which, apparently, speak very differently to all this. How shall we reconcile them? for instance, in Ezek. xviii. 5, 21, 27 : " If a man be just, and do that which is lawful and right, if he hath walked in my statutes, and hath kept my judgments, he shall surely live, saith the Lord." Certainly it would appear to some persons as if eternal life was to be obtained by one's own obedience, but look at the connection, and I think it will be seen that that is not the meaning to be attached to it. The *life* there spoken of is *not eternal* life, but the blessings of *the natural* life. The entire chapter shows that God is vindicating himself from the unjust charge, wherewith the Jews in exile had reproached him, and the rewards and punishments refer to those wherewith God ordinarily marked the obedience or disobedience of his peculiar people.

Take another instance, in fact two; the gospel by Luke records both. In the 10th chapter we read of a certain *lawyer* coming to Jesus with, " Master, what shall I do to inherit eternal life." Jesus sent him to the law, "This do, and thou shalt live." Then in the 18th chapter we read of a certain *ruler* who came with, " Good master, what good thing shall I do to inherit eternal life." He too was sent to the law, " Thou knowest the commandments," &c. Now, some will be ready to say, Surely this was as much as to teach, in both cases, that if they would enter into life eternal, they must keep the law and earn by their own doings, salvation as their reward. But no, look at it again, read both narratives through, see the issue ; see for what it was that Jesus sent both the lawyer and the ruler to the commandments. It was to show them that, by the law, neither of them could be justified. They came to him thinking that some " good thing " which they should do was to save them. They wanted to go to the law for their salvation. Jesus proves to them both that in *that* way there was no salvation for them. To the *lawyer* he proves that he had *not loved* even *his neighbour* as he ought. The *ruler* he convicts of *not loving God* as he ought. So that when Jesus pointed these men to the law, and said, " Do this, and thou shalt live," he meant, in real truth, to say, Prove that you *have* kept the law, or can keep the law, then, and not till then, speak of doing some good thing to gain eternal life. Your hope is in vain ; appeal to the law, you will find it condemn you.

In these, as in all other instances, it will be found that the doctrine of God's word is consistent with itself. The law was never given for man to save himself by keeping it. From the time of Adam's disobedience, God has never called upon man to save himself from eternal life upon the footing of his own doings. As I said before, the law was a law of love, it has never altered, nothing could alter it ; God is unchangeable, and love is the fulfilling of the law. Man's disobedience has brought the curse upon himself, he has become dead to it ; but the gospel gives him life, life in Christ Jesus, and now that he lives to God, he finds the law is just what it was before the fall, a law of love.

Under this law he now serves God, not in the oldness of the letter but in newness of spirit. In other words the gospel is the believer's rule of conduct ; the love of God being shed abroad in his heart by the Holy Ghost, he is under the constraining influence of the love of Christ. As for his soul's justification before God that is altogether another matter ; he looks to the atonement of the Lord Jesus Christ for redemption, not on the footing of his own performances ; these are but filthy rags.

> " The best obedience of my hands,
> Does not appear before thy throne ;
> But *faith* can answer thy demands,
> By pleading what my Lord has done."

But to proceed. Having somewhat cleared our way by removing some of the obstacles that commonly prevent persons from laying hold of the hope set before them in the gospel, we would observe, that the very position in which the believer stands towards the law of God is productive of those feelings that cause that law to be a delight to him. Instead of its being a terror to him, as it was in the hand of Moses, he beholds it with delight as in the heart of Christ—a law of love ; his claim to heavenly and eternal blessedness is securely established, his hopes are fixed, firm, and bright. He is perfectly free from all fears, apprehensions of guilt ; he no longer trembles at the strictness with which once the law menaced him. His standing in Christ, his covenant head, renders the law delightsome in itself. He is not only one in covenant union with the eternal three, but he is also one with the law of God, both in its nature and in its tendency; loved with an everlasting love, drawn with an everlasting love, kept by the power of God through faith unto salvation, he cannot but be delighted with that law of love which has united him in the bonds of an " everlasting covenant ordered in all things and sure." He is no longer a slave under a legal dispensation, but is redeemed from the curse of the law by the death of Christ, that he might receive the adoption of his divine sonship, and have fellowship with God his Father.

> " To see the law by Christ fulfilled,
> And hear his pardoning voice,
> Changes the slave into a child,
> And duty into choice."

The exercises of the believer towards the Son of God is also seen by the *peculiar* manner in which he delights in it. It is *after the inward man.* By the *inward man,* is to be understood the " new man;" which may be viewed either as the new principle of grace in itself considered or the soul itself considered as renewed. The phrase is peculiar to the apostle Paul, and occurs only in 2 Cor. iv. 16, and Eph. iii. 16. Analogous phrases, "the new man," as opposed to the "old man," (Rom. vi. 6; Eph. iv. 22; Col. iii. 9,) confirm this view. The use of the terms "inward man," "the law of the mind," " the Spirit," " the spiritual man;" as opposed to "the law in the members," " the old man," "the flesh," "the natural man," shows that the former all indicate the regenerated soul, or as the seat of the Spirit's influences, and the latter the soul as unrenewed. As it is the soul, when in union with the body, that constitutes *the person*, so when the soul is regenerated, it is the believer's *self* that has undergone the divine change; it is *he* who feels it; *he* has the *consciousness* of it. This is the "I" which is to be understood as being represented when the apostle speaks of himself as, " It is no more I that do it, but sin that dwelleth in me;" and this is the " I," the renewed self, that delights in the law of God. It cannot but be so from the very constitution of the case, for there is an homogeneity of nature in the Spirit that renews the soul, and in the soul that is renewed. This is how it is that John declares he that is born of God cannot commit sin. Whatever may be the conflict between the two principles of grace and sin, or laws, as the apostle terms them, in the person of the believer, he, being made spiritual, renewed in the spirit of his mind, can clearly distinguish between the nature of each principle working in him; for, being spiritually discerned, he is able *to know, as well as to feel*, the power of sin and the reign of grace. And when he says, " I delight in the law of God after the inward man," he means his self,—his renewed self. You can understand the clear distinction he makes between his flesh and his spirit as to the two principles or laws which have a conflicting rule over him. " So, then, with the mind, I myself serve the law of God; but with the flesh, the law of sin."

Now, dear friends, what can you say about this repre-

sentative pronoun, " I "?   Will this little pronoun, " I,"
be sufficient for you to use as indicative of your feelings
toward the law of God?   Can you adopt the language of
the apostle, as the result of the Spirit's work in your
heart, and say, " I delight in the law of God after the
inward man ?"   If so, happy are ye.   God has begun a
work in your soul that he will never leave ; he will carry
on his work of faith with power to the day of Jesus
Christ.

Where God's work is begun, God must be loved, and
all belonging to him must be loved.   If the believer loves
God, he loves his will.   God's will is his law; God is love;
his law is love.   The believer delights in it,—loves it.   It
is the love of God that actuates his inward man; they are
of one nature.   What a spring of happiness is here!
Here is the supply of the Spirit of Christ constantly
flowing out in the affections of the believer towards God,
delighting in his law, rejoicing in it.   To him it is a perfect law of liberty.   He has the joy of salvation; for it is
a full salvation as it is a free salvation.   He has pardon,
justification, acceptance, everlasting life, glory; all bestowed upon him by virtue of God's choice of his person
in Christ; confirmed to him by the obedience and death
of Christ, and brought to a personal participation of these
blessings by the operation of God the Holy Ghost.   This
is the man who says, " I delight in the law of God after
the inward man."

Having considered the chief points comprised in our
text and its connection, we will now conclude by making
a few inferences by way of improvement.

1. *That it is the distinguishing characteristic of the true
believer in Christ that he delights in the law of God.*
The love of Christ constrains him.   His grace has enabled him to take his yoke upon him; he finds it easy,
and the burden light.   His commandments are not grievous.   He says, with David, "Thy law is very pure,
therefore doth thy servant love it."   He has David's
heart and mind.   He prays for a clean heart when feeling
the foulness of the old-Adam heart and its desperate
wickedness.   He prays for a right spirit to be renewed
within; the former spirit under which he was governed
was all wrong, and, while it was so, everything went
wrong in his own soul and between him and his God.

When this is done, and, indeed, while it is being done, he then delights in the law of God after the inward man; for he has no fear of its curse. The law of God is in his heart.

2. *That a true delight in the law of God is an unspeakable blessing.* It proves God's gracious work in the soul. It is a good sign; for he hates *all* sin; he loves *all* God's will. He feels, though carnal by nature, yet by grace divine, he loves the spirituality of God's law. He knows it is holy, just, and good. He knows where God is he shall be:

> "The holy to the holiest leads;
> From thence his hopes arise;
> And he that in his statutes treads
> Shall meet him in the skies."

3. *That to delight in the law of God after the inward man is a clear proof of the believer's conformity to the image of the Lord Jesus.* Being united to the Lord Jesus Christ by a true and living faith, as the branch of the vine is united to the root, he daily and constantly draws all supplies from his fulness, grace for grace. He looks to Jesus for all grace, power, goodness, and willingness to serve him with the mind; though with the flesh, on account of its weakness, yet against his own inclination, his better judgment, he serves the law of sin. He finds, just as Jesus said it was, "The spirit truly is willing, but the flesh is weak."

4. *That those who delight in the law of God prove it by their general consistency of temper, habits, and deportment of life.* This is too plain to be denied. By the fruit, the tree is known. "Herein," says our Lord, "is my Father glorified, that ye bear much fruit." " Jesus gave himself for us, that he might redeem us from all iniquity, and purify unto himself a peculiar people zealous of good works." Therefore, he that thinks the gospel leaves him liberty to walk before the men of the world, or his household, according to his fleshly inclinations and habits, knows nothing truly of the gospel.

5. *That it is unjust to charge such persons who delight in the law of God, according to the apostle's doctrine, with holding loose principles, or to suppose that such sentiments promote licentious conduct.* I think it right to protest against the calumnies that are so foully spread against

the truth of God, as well as against those who love it.
The prejudice that is created against the truth and the
people themselves, is extraordinary. Nevertheless, I am
persuaded that the calumnies which pharisaic preachers
and others spread in regard to persons who hold the
views I advocate, and also in regard to the places where it
is preached, do not so much arise from their sincere belief
as it is that their object is to *make merchandise* of the people whom they thus prejudice; it is to scare them away from
the places where the truth as it is in Jesus is preached,
and to get them into their own houses. (2 Pet. ii. 3.)
We are called antinomians, and I know not what else
besides; but it is the hoarse bark of the wolf to frighten
the sheep of Christ, and to hound them away from the
fold of the true gospel. Friends, beware of these sleeky
professors of religion. It is you they want to catch. It
is these places they want to shut up,—I speak their own
words.

6. *The man of the world* never delights in the law
of God. Unregenerate, carnal, worldly in all his views,
spirit, maxims, and policies, he is governed by principles
in entire opposition to the gospel of Christ. Man of the
world! I appeal to your conscience. You know I am
speaking the truth.

The self-righteous Pharisee, he never delights in the law
of God, though seeking life and salvation by it. Proud
and boasting of his own doings, he is misled by the
blindness of his understanding.

The licentious hypocrite, he, too, never delights in the
law of God. He says he does; but he is false. Look
at his conduct! What is his character at home and
abroad? He knows he loves sin; he knows he is ever
trying to hide with his cloak of profession, and, apparently, a sound creed, a deformed and ugly image of the
man of sin. But God's curse is upon him, and it will
find him out.

May the Lord bless his own word to his own people,
establish them in the faith, and lead them to know more
and more, by sweet experience, what it is to delight in
the law of God after the inward man. Amen.

A. GADSBY, PRINTER, 10, CRANE COURT, FLEET STREET, E.C.

THE
DIVINE AND ETERNAL SONSHIP
OF THE
LORD JESUS CHRIST
ASSERTED AND DEFENDED.

———◆———

A SERMON,
BY CHARLES GORDELIER,

PREACHED AT THE ANNIVERSARY OF THE RE-OPENING OF HEPHZIBAH
CHAPEL, DARLING PLACE, CAMBRIDGE ROAD, NEAR MILE END GATE,

On Lord's Day Evening, April 17th, 1864.

———

" That all men should honour the Son, even as they honour
the Father. He that honoureth not the Son, honoureth not the
Father which sent him."—JOHN v. 23.

HAVING read the chapter whence the text is taken, you
scarcely need to be reminded of its connection; but it
will be proper to observe that these words are the words
of him who spake as never man spake; they are the words
of the incarnate God, words enjoining a most solemn
duty upon all who name the name of Christ. And when
we remember the object for which this gospel was written,
(see 20th chap., 31st verse,) we must acknowledge our
text possesses a most significant importance. These words
are recorded to the intent "that ye might believe that
Jesus is the Christ, the Son of God, and that believing ye
might have life through his name."

You will perceive from the 18th verse, that the Jews, in
their zeal to defend the doctrine of the Divine Unity, contended against Jesus for asserting his divine Sonship, his
co-essentiality and his co-equality with his Father, and
for which they conspired his death. It was, indeed, a
zeal *for* God, but not according to knowledge. Misled
and puzzled with the traditions of the elders, they understood not the Scriptures which pointed out Jesus of
Nazareth to be " he which should have redeemed Israel."
Not searching the Scriptures which testified of him, they
missed the mark, and consequently failed to see in his
Person, his doctrine, and in the works which he did,
Jehovah incarnate. Sufficient testimony had been adduced to the natural senses of these stubborn Jews, that

No. 12.—Second Edition, Revised, with Addenda.

Jesus was the Christ of God; but they refused the evidence. These builders rejected this "stone" for their foundation; they fell foul upon it; "they were snared, taken, and broken," and to this day the vail remains upon their hearts.

Corresponding with the blindness and opposition of the Jews, there have been, throughout all ages of the Christian church, men who have wholly or partially rejected and opposed the doctrine of the True and Essential Deity of the Lord Jesus Christ, and, more or less, the church of God has been deceived and injured by this old leaven of the Pharisees; hence it has always been needful to contend earnestly for the faith once delivered to the saints. Arians, semi-Arians, Sabellians, Socinians, and others, who, either from a selfish love of advancing their own notions, too proud to stoop to the simple teachings of Scripture, or purposely lying in wait to deceive with cunning craftiness, have insiduously incorporated heresy with the truth. In some instances the mischief has worked silently and unperceived for a time. In others, it has quickly shown itself rampant and destructive to all vitality in religion, not shrinking openly to blaspheme the name of the Lord Jesus.

Now, there are times and seasons when the foundation truths of our faith should be more explicitly stated and positively asserted than in ordinary. The present occasion, our first anniversary of the re-opening of this place, appears to me a fitting opportunity; and, as the subject is of the utmost importance, let me bespeak your patient and candid attention; and I pray that he whose office it is to testify of Jesus may not only open our understandings to understand the truth as it is in Jesus, but that we may each have a sweet, experimental proof of his love and goodness, and that he may complete his work of faith with power. Our subject is the most exalted we can conceive of; and if we have been led by the Spirit to hold the mystery of the faith in a pure conscience, we shall not fail to have the most exalted views of the Person of our ever blessed Lord and Saviour.

As to the plain meaning of the words before us, it appears to me thus: *The Person of the Lord Jesus Christ, the Son of God, is to be regarded, esteemed, loved, reverenced, praised as co-essential and co-equal with the Father; the same attributes that are ascribed to God the Father, such as his self-existence, eternity, omnipresence, omniscience, omnipotence, and also his wisdom, truth, love, and goodness, are also to be ascribed to the Son of God.* The man who hath low views of the deity, eternity, and self-existence of Jesus Christ, hath low views of God the Father; for Jesus Christ and the Father are essentially ONE; and whatever is affirmed of the Father is also affirmed of the Son. But, further, as there is no God but Jehovah, subsisting in the personalities of Father, Son, and Holy Ghost, so he who withholds proper homage and worship from one, withholds it from all. He who would refuse to honour the Father, could not be said to honour God; and, in like manner, he who honoureth not the Son, honoureth not the Father. Let me ask, Has not the Father declared that the Son shall be honoured? He who refuses to do it, disobeys the Father, for they are equal. He who denies the one, denies also the other. The same views and feelings which lead us to honour the Father, will also lead us to honour the Son; for the evidence of the self-existence of the Son, his deity, and his eternity, is the same as that of the Father. It is, therefore, to my mind, an absurdity to talk of honouring attributes in the Father, and not in the Son; and I cannot but regard this vindication of our Lord, of his personal honour and deity, as being worthy of the gravest consideration.

I shall now attempt to consider the text in its various aspects, and shall then endeavour to draw such inferences as I think the subject will legitimately warrant.

We cannot, of course, consider the Person of the Lord Jesus Christ without the particular relation which it bears to the doctrine of the Trinity in the Unity of the Divine Essence; and here let it be understood, I shall not attempt to explain or establish any point upon the principles of *human* analogy. I look upon the system of analogical reasoning on this subject as the fruitful source of all those wide-spread and pestilential errors which have troubled the church of God. I may, perhaps, occasionally refer to some of the analogies employed; but, so far as my own argument is concerned, I shall endeavour to keep close to the word of God, receiving it in its plain and unadulterated sense.

The proposition now before us is, that Jesus Christ, the Son of God, should be honoured even as the Father, because,

1. *That he is of the same indivisible nature and essence of subsistence with the Most High, the self-existent and ever-living God, God the Father.*

Our Lord is expressly spoken of and called the Son of God, and the only-begotten Son of God, and even God's own proper Son, the Son of the living God, all of which import his being of the same nature with his Father. Now, those who reason from analogy know very well that in all created life the offspring is of *the same nature* as the parent; but human analogy fails to explain the doctrine of Christ's Sonship, for the Lord Jesus Christ is called the only-begotten Son of God, which necessarily implies more than a son by creation or adoption. Certainly it cannot refer to his extraordinary conception as man, because it is spoken, not of the flesh or human nature, but of the WORD that was made flesh. To say that the only-begotten Son of God is meant of the extraordinary conception or birth of Christ as man, is to say that Christ is not the Son of God the Father at all, but of the Holy Ghost, for that was his work; and, consequently, Christ is not the Son of God at all with them who deny the Holy Ghost to be God; and this is a plain contradiction of the words themselves, which expressly declare that Christ is the only-begotten Son of God. The word only-begotten properly respects the nature or essence, and not at all the peculiar manner of the miraculous conception. It evidently signifies one alone begotten of that nature; such a Son as God has never another. Hence it is (Rom. viii. 32) that Christ is called God's own proper Son, which he could not possibly be if he were not of the same nature or substance with God the Father; for it is plain, he that is of another substance is no proper son, no *own* son at all; but God the Father being Christ's *own proper Father*, and Christ *his own proper Son*, this necessarily imports that Christ is God's Son, and God Christ's Father, in the most proper acceptation of the words. And if it were not so, God the Father would not be a proper Father, nor a Father from eternity; to assert which, says an old divine, would lead to atheism, for unto us believers there is but one God the Father. (1 Cor. viii. 6.) Take away God the Father, and you take away the One God. But further, Christ is such a Son of God as to have all the perfections of God the Father in him, essentially considered as God. Christ is an eternal, omnipotent, omniscient, omnipresent Son. He is such a Son of God as is himself " the only wise God;" and therefore we must, indeed, we cannot but, conclude that he is such a Son as is co-essential and co-eternal with his Father.

Oh! says one, you are a believer in' a "begotten God!" No, my friend, I am not, nor are any who hold the doctrine I am setting forth; but I am fully aware of the mischievous intent of those who make this charge. Not only is it unfair that such an inference should be drawn from the views thus taken of Christ's Person, but, generally speaking, those who so assiduously and so industriously circulate this foul slander know full well we hold no such belief. It has been contradicted times out of number; and if truth could but perform its office, we should be told that being foiled in establishing their own pernicious fancies and having their designs unmasked, they have recourse to scurrilous falsehoods and abusive language to serve their own private ends and party spirit.

But we will go on to observe:

2. *Christ the Son is of the same indivisible nature with his Father, because the same attributes of God the Father, considered as the only true God, are ascribed to him.*

Jehovah, by the prophet Isaiah, (chap. xliv. 6,) describes himself thus: "I am the first and I am the last." After the same manner Christ also describes himself to his servant John: "I am the first and the last." (Rev. i. 17.) So that the Lord Jesus Christ the Son, essentially considered, is absolutely the first Being as well as God the Father. There is none other before him or after him. He is an eternal, independent, self-existent Being, the only Potentate and sovereign Lord of the Universe, having life in himself, and "upholding all things by the word of his power." This description belongs to Christ, necessarily and evidently, as he is the first and the last. He who is the first must needs be eternal, because he hath no beginning, but hath always been, eternally and essentially. Christ is the first Being, not the first creature, as the semi-Arians assert. He is an independent Being. He is God of himself; that is, he owes his being to no other, for if he did, he could not be the first; because, if his being were from another, the other must be before him, else the effect would be before the cause. Christ, as the first Being, must needs have life in himself; because there was no other to give him life. He is life, essentially, necessarily, independently, and eternally. Thus it is that Christ is said to have life in the same manner that God the Father has it—as the Father hath life in himself. (John v. 26.) So that however perfect, however glorious the Father's life is so every way perfect and glorious is the life of the Son;

it being essentially the very same life, because it is the life in and of himself, and no being but One can so have life; for the second and every other being has life from the first. Therefore Christ, having life in himself, is the first and the last, the only independent Being. He is thus distinguished from all creatures; for they derive their life from him, and thus is he proved to be the one true God with the Father.

3. *Christ the Son is of the same nature with the Father, because he has the same glorious names, titles, and attributes expressly ascribed to him that are ascribed to God the Father.*

Our Lord Jesus Christ is not only expressly, but properly and absolutely, called God. He is called God, without limitation or restriction, John i. 1: "The Word was God," or, as Wycliffe has it, "God was the Word." Acts xx. 28: "Feed the church of God, which he hath purchased with his own blood." 1 Tim. iii. 16: "God was manifest in the flesh;" and in Heb. i. 8: "Unto the Son he saith, Thy throne, O God, is for ever and ever." These passages plainly indicate that Christ is God, not only in name, but in being essentially so. He is expressly called "the mighty God;" (Isa. ix. 6;) "God blessed over all. Amen;" (Rom. ix. 5;) "the great God;" (Tit. ii. 13;) "the true God." (1 John v. 20.) So that these expressions which are here applied to Christ are the same as those which declare the Father to be God.

But again: Christ is most properly called God, because the essential name of God—Jehovah—is expressly given to him in many places of holy writ, as in Isa. xl. 3; Jer. xxiii. 6; Gen. xix. 24; Zech. x. 12. Therefore Christ is the very same God with the only true and most high God; for Jehovah is but one essence, or one God. God's name alone is Jehovah; (Ps. lxxxiii. 18;) Christ's name is Jehovah; therefore he is God. Jehovah is that very name, the glory of which God will not give to another. (Isa. xlii. 8.) But Christ has the glory of that name, therefore he is not another being, but is, essentially considered, the very same God that the Father is. Christ has all the essential properties that God the Father has. What is proper to God the Father is proper to God the Son. Is God the Father everlasting? so is Christ. The true God knows all things; so does Christ. (John xxi. 17.) God is infinite, everywhere present; so is Christ. (Matt. xviii. 20.) He is the Almighty, who is, and was, and is to come; immu-

OF THE LORD JESUS CHRIST.

table, the same yesterday, to-day, and for ever. And where texts speak of Christ having an inferior or subordinate condition, these will be found to have reference to his human nature only, of him considered in the office or capacity of Mediator.

4. *Jesus Christ the Son of God is of the same indivisible nature or essence with the Father, because it is expressly declared in God's word that they are* ONE.

Our Lord Jesus himself says so: "I and my Father are One;" that is, one being, one substance, essence, or nature. In this sense the Jews understood him, and they believed that thereby he made himself such a Son of God as was of the very same nature with God; and therefore it was that they deemed it blasphemy, and declared that he was worthy of death. Now, if they had misunderstood the sense which Jesus intended to convey, surely he would have corrected their mistake, and he would have told them plainly that he did not mean to make himself equal with God. But Jesus does not say they mistook his meaning, but goes on to vindicate and defend what he had said in the very sense the Jews had taken it, namely, that he was one with the Father in nature or being, "because he did the works of his Father." He told them emphatically that "whatsoever things the Father did, these also he did likewise." (Verse 19.) Now this could not be said of any nor of all the creatures which God has made; therefore we find he exhorts them, from the plain and full argument of his doing the same works the Father did, that they would know and believe that "the Father is in him, and he in the Father;" that is, essentially, there being a mutual in-existence and co-existence in and with one another, else it would not prove his assertion, namely, that he did the same works the Father did. Further, that Christ the Son is of the very same nature with God the Father, is also proved from Jno. viii. 19, where it is said, "If ye had known me, ye would have known my Father also. Hence, I conclude, it necessarily follows that THEY ARE ONE. How can it be otherwise, if he who knows the one should certainly know the other also? for in no two other persons, that is, a father and his son, can it ever be said, that if we know the one, we necessarily know the other. Certainly not; for every man has the whole nature of man distinct in himself and dividedly from another man. Therefore, if by knowing God the Son we know God the Father, it is because they are one and

the very same undivided nature. Now this truth appears
to me most evidently proved from 1 John v. 7; "And
these Three are One." You see they are expressly said
to be one, and, therefore, "they are ONE"—one in being,
nature, essence, substance. The Three here spoken of are
not one Person, for they are three Persons. There cannot
be any other view of Father and Son but as of two Persons. They are not barely in agreement or consent, as
three partners in a business firm, for then it might be
said, as in the 8th verse, "and these three *agree* in one;"
but it is not said so, but that "THEY ARE ONE." There
is a plain distinction. The three that bare witness or
record in heaven are said "to be One," that is, one and
the very same God; for the record that is borne by the
three in heaven, is in verse 9 called the *witness* of God;
not witnesses in the plural, but in the singular. The
same evidence we have in the command for believers' baptism, to be administered in the *name* of the Father, and
of the Son, and of the Holy Ghost.

I hope I have made myself explicit on this important
point. I have tried to do so. To understand divine
truth in a divine light, we must give up all human analogies and carnal notions of it.

5. *That Jesus Christ is the same God with God the Father, essentially considered, because he doeth the same most
mighty works, and after the same manner that God the
Father doeth them.*

These works to which I refer are such as are truly
divine, God-like; such as no being but a being of infinite
wisdom, power, perfection, and goodness, can possibly do,
and such as are expressly and properly in the word of God
attributed to the Lord Jesus Christ, as they are to God
the Father.

The works of creation and preservation are ascribed to
Jesus Christ. He is the great Creator of all things.
"All things were made by him, and without him was not
anything made that was made." (John i. 3.) "All
things were created by him and for him, and he is before
all things, and by him all things consist." (Heb. i. 10.)
And it is also said: "He upholds all things by the word
of his power." (Heb. i. 13.) So that it is certain that
Christ hath not only done these bright and mighty works
which none but God can do, but he did them in a God-
like manner as God the Father did them, as immediately,
as easily, as irresistibly, and as independently. Look at

the miracles which he wrought in his incarnate state. One word from his mouth, one touch of his hand, sometimes without either; whatever Jesus willed, his almighty power performed, for he is God alone.

To suppose that Christ was only an instrument in the work of creation is most absurd. It is a contradiction of God's word, and it is blasphemous. Are we not expressly told that God ALONE made the heavens and earth. Therefore he had no instrument. "He spake and it was done." (Ps. xxxiii. 6, 9.) "All things were made by him" and for him, for his honour, use, and service. He is the last end of all things, but not so are instruments. I wonder sometimes that men who deny the Son, do not say that God the Father is only an instrument in creation; for all things are said to be by him. (Heb. xi. 36.) Those who receive God's word as there revealed, can easily believe that all things were made by Christ, and for him; and that "whatsoever things the Father doeth, these also the Son doeth likewise." His eternal power and God-head are clearly seen, being understood by the things that are made.

6. *That Jesus Christ is essentially and eternally the same with God the Father, because his personality is identified as the same throughout the history and work of redemption.*

In the epistle to the Ephesians (i. 4) the apostle speaks of the Church of God being chosen in Christ before the foundation of the world. Now, I cannot believe that God chose his people in a Christ that did not pre-exist—a mere name. A nominal Christ is surely not the Christ of God, though he appears to be so according to many professors. The good pleasure of the Father's will which he purposed in himself was not prospective in regard to the Person of his Son. No, surely, for his eternal purpose he purposed *in Christ*, (Eph. iii. 11,) a proof of Christ's existence before his incarnation; and in verse 12, we read: "He *trusted in Christ*." Was this a Christ only in purpose, or a Christ then in being, think you? Evidently the Person of Christ is co-eternal and co-equal with the Father, or the Father could not have chosen his people in him. He was the Son of God before he became the Christ, the anointed of God the Father. The personality of his Sonship is the basis of his mediatorship, and hence he is the author of eternal redemption.

Passing by several notable passages, we will just observe

on Zech. ii. 10.   The Lord speaking by the prophet
of the fulfillment of Eph. i. 10, (God's eternal purpose,)
saith: "Sing and rejoice, O daughter of Zion; for lo, I
come, and I dwell in the midst of thee, saith the LORD."
Here, you perceive, it is God who speaks.   And to what
period does he refer?   Certainly to no other than the incarnation of himself; the going forth of Jehovah in personal acts for the gathering together of his people and
for their redemption.

Turning now to Luke ii. 11, when the birth of the
Saviour was announced to the shepherds by the angel, he
said: "Unto you is born this day in the city of David, a
Saviour, which is CHRIST THE LORD," not *a* Lord, but
the Lord—the Lord of glory. (1 Cor. ii. 8.)   Here is the
character, the Person, and his one name declared to be *he*
who is, and was, and is to come; the personality of Jesus
as the self-existent God being too plain to be denied on
the principles of language.   Here, then, is the identity of
the same person as foretold and expected; they did not
refer to what he was to be, but to what *he is*, both in Person and character, the infinite I AM—he, "the Lord,
which is, and which was, and which is to come, the
Almighty." (Rev. i. 8.)

Now refer to Matt. xxviii. 6.   Again we have angels'
testimony to the identity of Jesus the Lord: they speak
not of his body merely, but of his Person entire, they do
not deem him as a dead man placed in the grave, but
they speak of him as what he is, *i.e.* what he ever was—
THE LORD: "Come, see the place where the Lord lay"—
his Person—his own act and deed in lying in the grave.
Ah! my friends, there is more divinity in that angelic
sentence, than has ever been uttered by mortal man; for
in it I see the God-man, during the period of death, still
the willing substitute of his church, entering the portals
of the grave to pay the last mite of their penalty to a
broken law.

Then, again, in Acts ii. 36, and 1 Cor. ii. 8, we have
the testimony of two apostles, who speak of him who was
crucified as "the Lord of glory;" "both Lord and
Christ;" and observe, too, in Eph. iv. 8–10, his ascension
to heaven is spoken of as being the same as mentioned in
Psalm lxviii. 18, and his descension is spoken of in the
same manner; both of his own will, which no creature
could do, or could be—both die and lie in the grave of his
own self.   Jesus must have been the Lord of life and

glory to have overcome death; and his triumphant entrance into heaven is celebrated in Psalm xxiv. 7–10:
"Lift up your heads, O ye gates; and be ye lift up, ye
everlasting doors, and the King of glory shall come in.
Who is the King of glory? The Lord strong and mighty,
the Lord mighty in battle. Lift up your heads, O ye
gates; even lift them up, ye everlasting doors; and the
King of glory shall come in. Who is this King of glory?
The Lord of hosts, he is the King of glory." So that
throughout the Scriptures, from the period of God the
Father choosing his people in Christ, to the time of his
incarnation, death, burial, resurrection, and ascension,
all combine to fix the identity of the Person of the Lord
Jesus Christ the same with God the Father, essentially
considered, the same God as the Father. In the contemplation of these great truths, we unite with the apostle
in exclaiming: "Great is the mystery of godliness; God
was manifest in the flesh, justified in the Spirit, seen of
angels, preached unto the Gentiles, believed on in the
world, received up into glory." (1 Tim. iii. 16.)

I pass on to notice also, under this head, that the great
and glorious *work of redemption and complete salvation*,
which is said to be God's work, is likewise said to be the
work of Christ. There is no other salvation for men but
that of Christ: "There is none other name under heaven
given among men." (Acts iv. 12.) Beside him there is
no Saviour—he is God. (Isa. lxiii. 11.) And when he
would pour in the consolations of his grace to the troubled and overwhelmed heart, he bases the promise upon
his immutableness, and declares of himself: "I am the
Lord thy God, the Holy One of Israel,"—the true spiritual Israel. It is God who hath chosen his people to
grace and glory, so has Jesus. None can forgive sins but
God only. Christ does forgive sins; therefore he is the
only true God. It is God alone who quickens sinners
when dead in sin; Christ is that great God who quickeneth whomsoever he will. Believers are called the sons of
God by virtue of God the Father's love; Christ has the
same power. (John i. 12.) He gives to his people eternal life, and he wills of himself their eternal glorification
with him and the Father. (John xvii. 24.)

7. *That Christ the Son is the same in Essence with God
the Father, because the very same things which are positively spoken of the Most High God in the Old Testament
are attributed to Christ in the New Testament.*

There can be no difficulty to the spiritually taught disciple of Christ in ascertaining that he who is called Jehovah in the Old Testament is the same as he who in the New Testament is called Jesus, the Christ. If in the Old Testament we find expressly ascribed such and such things to the great Jehovah, the only true God, and the New Testament declares these very things of Christ, it must needs follow that Jesus is the only true God. Let us just mention a few instances out of many where they occur. He who proclaimed the law on Mount Sinai was Jehovah, the Most High God. Now, it is certain that Christ was he who did so. (Acts vii. 37, 38.) The psalmist tells us that he whom the Israelites tempted and provoked was the Most High God. (Ps. lxxviii. 50.) The apostle Paul tells us expressly that it was Christ they tempted. (1 Cor. x. 9.) Therefore, Christ is the Most High God. Again, Psalm x. 2 holds out the great God in his eternity and unchangeableness, and as the Creator of all things; and the same attributes are ascribed to Christ in Heb. i. 10–12. Isaiah tells us that "the Lord of Hosts, besides whom there is no God, is the first and the last; (Isa. xliv. 6;) and John the divine tells us expressly that Jesus "is the first and the last;" therefore he is the Lord of Hosts, besides whom there is no God. "He who ascended up on high and led captivity captive," the psalmist calls God and Lord. And the apostle Paul assures us that he who ascended is he who descended into the lower parts of the earth, and he who descended is the same who ascended far above all heavens, that he might fill all things, (Eph. iv. 7–9,) which is certainly meant of Christ Jesus. And again, searching the heart, trying the reins, &c., are prerogatives which the great Jehovah ascribes to himself by the mouth of the prophet Jeremiah; (Jer. xvii. 10;) and this is what Jesus as the Son of God precisely declares of himself: "All the churches shall know that I am he which searcheth the reins and hearts; and I will give unto every one of you according to your works." (Rev. ii. 23.) This argument must needs be good with all those who take God's word as they find it, and his interpretation of it. What is spoken in the Old Testament of the only true God,—God himself interprets of Christ in the New. That in Isaiah xl. 3–5, is spoken of the great Jehovah, the Lord our God; and whosoever denies it to be spoken of Christ, contradicts all the four evangelists, for they apply it to him. Surely none can deny the Lord Jesus Christ to be the only living and true God, if they believe God's own explication of the word. If our hearts are humble we shall receive it and believe it. We cannot be deceived in so doing.

8. I come now to consider the last part of my argument, and which has a close proximity to the doctrine of my text: *That Jesus Christ is the same in nature with God the Father, because the same worship must be paid to them both.*

Not only worship, but the very same divine worship in all the parts and degrees of it must be given to the Son as to the Father. This is clear, I think, from the very words of my text. Whatever divine and excellent worship the most holy men do or can pay to God the Father, *that* worship in all its height and excellency must be given unto the Son, or else we directly deny the doctrine of our text. Here is no distinction of religious worship, nor any inequality or inferiority in the worship that is given to the Son and God the Father; but quite the contrary; we are to worship them both alike. The Son we must worship, even as we worship the Father; and unless we thus honour the Son, we honour not the Father. Their honour is inseparable. Divine worship is that honour and service we give to God, as to a Being of infinite perfection, as our Creator, Preserver, and Benefactor, and the fountain of all our happiness. Jesus Christ is a Being of infinite excellences; he is our Creator, Preserver, Redeemer, and the fountain of all divine fulness and happiness; therefore he must be worshipped. He must have paid unto him all the internal and external acts of worship. God is a Spirit, and they who worship him must worship him in spirit and in truth. Christ is God, and they who worship him must worship him in spirit and in truth, even as they worship the Father; and like as the Father seeketh such to worship him, so does our Lord Jesus Christ. Hence it is he says: "All men should honour the Son even as they honour the Father."

Again. We must *believe* in Christ, the same as we believe in God. This our Lord says himself: "Ye believe in God, believe also in me." And this is also the Father's will, that "we should believe on the name of his Son Jesus Christ." (1 John iii. 23.) Have we hope in God? Jesus Christ is expressly said to be our hope; that is, he in whose death and righteousness alone we hope for salvation. We have not our hope in Christ merely for the

things of this life, for then we were of all men the most
miserable; but we hope in Christ for the things of that
glorious life—the hope that is full of immortality. Therefore Christ is God; for to hope in any creature, would be
to bring a curse upon us and not a blessing.

Further, we must love Christ *supremely*, in all sincerity, and above all, with our highest love and affection;
and it is certain we can love but one being so. Therefore, this is to be regarded as undoubted evidence that we
believe Jesus Christ to be the only one true God. Besides, the external part of divine worship must be given
to Christ. As we must "offer unto God thanksgiving,
and pay our vows unto the Most High," (Ps. l. 14,)
so we must give honour, glory, dominion, praise, and
blessing to Christ; (Rev. v. 12;) therefore he is the Most
High God. And not only must we *praise* Jesus Christ
as God, but we must also *pray* unto him as the only true
God, and him only. Now, it is most clear that we must
pray to him. We find the apostle Paul often prayed to
him; Stephen died praying to him; and in 1 Cor. i. 2,
we find it to be a mark of a true believer, and that such
persons are reckoned among the saints of God "who call
upon the name of Jesus Christ our Lord," and how many
of the people of God can use the language of dear Mr. Hart:

> " That Christ is God I can avouch,
>   And for his people cares;
> For I have pray'd to him as such,
>   And he has heard my prayers."

Now, if Jesus Christ be only a creature, that is, a
being substantially distinct from, or made by, the only
true God, then we must either worship him who is not God,
which is idolatry, or we must cease praying unto him,
and we ought never more to use the benediction: "The
grace of our Lord Jesus Christ be with you all." We
must never more pray to him for mercy, for salvation, if
he be not the Most High God We must never more
pray : " Now our Lord Jesus Christ himself, and God,
even our Father, which hath loved us and given us everlasting consolation and good hope through grace, comfort your hearts, and stablish you in every good work."
" We must worship the Lord our God, and him only must
we serve." We cannot deny divine worship to Christ,
for he is God alone, and God only must be worshipped ;
therefore, Christ is the one and the very same God as the
Father. Amen.

My dear hearers, I shall now relieve your attention from this part of the argument. Much more, indeed, might be adduced from God's most holy book that Jesus Christ, the Son of the living God, is co-essential and co-eternal with God the Father; but sufficient, perhaps, has been stated for a public discourse of this kind. I will, therefore, proceed to notice some practical inferences, which I think are fairly deducible from the several points laid down.

1st. You may plainly perceive that *I regard the Sonship of the Lord Jesus Christ as being founded on his Deity, and not on his humanity.* This I hold to be the mind of the Spirit. This view of this most vital question, I am well aware, is objected to, and opposed by a large portion of our brethren in the ministry, who are received into the churches as men of truth, piety, learning, and principle; but we have nothing to do with men's opinions or characters where truth is at stake. The truth of God must be dearer to us than all besides. The faith of God's elect must be earnestly contended for. I am well aware, too, there is great mystery, much difficulty, singular complexity, in the controversy upon the subject. Most truly it is said, " *Without* controversy, *great* is the mystery of godliness. God was manifest in the flesh ;" and sure I am, *with* controversy, the mystery is still *greater.* For what is the fruit, in many instances, of the numerous controversies on the Sonship of Christ? Division of the brethren, and, in some cases, personal hate. It has produced such bitter strife and confusion, gross misunderstandings, and wilful perversions of each other's meanings, as remind us strongly of the Ammonites and Moabites, who, after they had blunderingly slain their Edomite ally, turned to, and " every one helped to destroy another." (2 Chron. xx. 23.) Nevertheless, the controversy has its uses. It discovers those who are on the Lord's side, and it brings into closer sympathy those who hold the unity of the faith in the bond of peace. Now, sincere believers in the Lord Jesus Christ will be in no danger of such evils, if they but carefully attend to the following things: 1. To *receive the truth* as it is in Jesus, *in the love of it;* and 2. To *rest upon it* as the only rock on which they are to stand. This I am sure they will do if they have been renewed in the spirit of their minds, and are under the teachings of the Holy Spirit. " Every word of God is pure ;" " They are all plain to him that understandeth." They must totally reject the methods men invent by attempting to explain divine truth upon human principles. For more than sixteen hundred years, men of this stamp have been blindly feeling after some analogy, which has no existence but in their own brain ! By this, they seek to illustrate the doctrine of Christ's Sonship, and thus they have forsaken the safe guidance of revelation. Now, if we will but attend to the word of God, and take it in its plain and obvious sense, apart from all human prejudices, we shall perceive that, in regard to the Person and character of the Lord Jesus Christ, all human analogy fails.

In the first place, to use the words of an excellent author, Dr. Leonard Woods: " The relation of Christ to God the Father has no real and strict analogy. It is, in various respects, unlike the relation of any created being to God. The relation of a created being to God commences in time ; but Christ was with God in the beginning, never without him. The relation of a creature originates in the derivation of his being from God. But the relation which Christ, considered as "The Word," bears to the Father, rests primarily upon his participation of the same divine nature. So that it is the relation of one who is essentially equal, and in every respect to nature, identical. Whereas, the relation of every created being to God is the relation of one essentially and infinitely inferior. The relation of Christ to the Father has no strict analogy to the relation which any created being bears to another. The relations among created beings are indeed made use of to set forth the relation of Christ to the Father; as, for example, the relations of a son and a servant. But Christ does not strictly stand in the relation of a human son to his father, or of a human servant to his master ; although these relations make known some of the properties or effects of Christ's relation to the Father. The Bible makes an essential difference between the peculiar relation of a son and that of a servant ; and represents the one as exclusive of the other. If, then, Christ were a servant, in this appropriate sense, it would be incompatible with his being a Son ; or if he were a Son, it would be incompatible with his being a servant. But he is spoken of as both a servant and a son ; which is sufficient to show that he is neither the one nor the other, in the strict and literal sense. In other words, there is no literal and strict analogy between the relation of Christ to his Father and that of a human son to his Father, or of a servant to his master. Though some of the effects and circumstances of the relation may be similar, the nature and the ground of it are materially different."

I need make no apology for this quotation; it not only expresses my view in better words than I could put it, but it shows clearly that human analogy cannot explain God's truth, and I think it strengthens my argument. I would only make another remark, in the second place, and that is, the *constitution* of the Person of the Redeemer is a *departure* from all analogy. From one class of texts we learn, that he was a true and proper man. The phrase "Son of man" is frequently used in the gospels, but mostly by himself. Other texts exhibit him as possessing all the properties of Deity. Here analogy entirely fails. In no other instance were natures and attributes, so widely different, ever united in one Person. He whose name is Wonderful is wonderful in his Person. With reference to one part of his character he is God, by whom all things were created. With reference to another part of his character, he the same Person, is called a child, a man. And when he was called "the Son of God," he not only admitted it, but approved the faith of those who thus called him, and pronounced them blessed, for their belief was the result of divine communication. (Matt. xvi. 17.) Yes, the God-man Mediator, Jesus Christ, is truly wonderful in himself; for whatever he is in himself, he is all that to him who is united to him by a true and living faith. He has life in himself; he is the same yesterday, to-day, and for ever; and yet he died and was buried. He is God over all, blessed for evermore; and yet he was a man of sorrows, and acquainted with grief. Now these representations of Christ that the Scriptures make, are a proof that there is no analogy, as to the constitution of his Person, between him and any other being.

I have detained you, perhaps, too long on this topic; but these remarks, I hope, will show, that men, who regulate their opinions respecting Christ by analogy, fall into one or another of the false notions so commonly entertained; and I think it will be seen what reason we have to be on our guard against this fruitful source of error. Every attempt men make to bring the work and character of Christ to bear a strict analogy to the character and work of any other being, is stamped with weakness, and will lead us away from the truth and the simplicity which is in Christ.

But, again, see how the folly of human analogy is ridiculed in the Scriptures of truth. Hear what the Lord himself saith by the mouth of the prophet Isaiah : "To whom, then, will ye liken God ? or what likeness will ye compare unto him ?" (Isa. xl. 18.) And : "Thou thoughtest that I was altogether such an one as thyself; but I will reprove thee." (Ps. l. 21.) Now, my friends, I ask you, is not the doctrine of my text, well sustained by the *divine forbidding* of all human analogy ? It demands " that all men should honour the Son, even as they honour the Father." O ye who fancy yourselves so wise, so clever in the argument that a Father is anterior and superior to a Son, blush for shame ! No more impugn and corrupt the doctrine of Christ by human traditions. Think me not too severe when I say, consider this, ye that yet forget the unity of God, " lest he tear you in pieces, and there be none to deliver." " Kiss the Son, lest he be angry, when his wrath is kindled but a little ;" " for ye have not spoken of him the thing that is right." " He that honoureth not the Son honoureth not the Father."

2nd. You will perceive, also, from the view I have presented, that *it is opposed to those who hold the notion of the Person of Christ as the Son of God only in his complex existence as Immanuel—God in our nature; in other words, that Jesus Christ was not the Son of God till he became the Son of man.*

I regard this notion as mere human fancy, unsustained by the authority of God's word. Doubtless there are many sincere believers in Jesus, who think it is the truth; but it appears to me, they take too low a ground. Their rock is not our rock ; and holding, as I do, the absolute essentiality and eternity of Christ with God—God in Christ, Christ in God—I could not receive it. My text forbids it. How can I honour the Son even as I honour the Father, if I limit the existence of his Person as to *time ?* Before the fulness of time—"the period when the Son of God became incarnate "—he must have existed ; for it is said, "God sent forth his Son." How could it be said he was *sent,* if he did not already pre-exist ? His being made of a woman under the law was but the *condition* in which he was to come ; a condition that was necessary in which Redemption was to be effected. The *sending* does not imply *inferiority,* any more than the sending of the Holy Spirit ; but simply means the *manifestation* of the purpose for which he came, viz., "to destroy the works of the devil." And therefore it is that I consider unless I believe and avow both the eternity and the immutability of Christ's Sonship, I cannot honour the Son even as I honour the Father.

3rd. If all men are to honour the Son even as they honour the Father, then I conceive, that *they who hold the notion of the pre-existence of Christ's human soul cannot honour the Son even as the Father is to be honoured; because they consider the Son only as a creature of the Father, though they ascribe to him a pre-existent state before all other creatures.*

The pre-existence of Christ's human soul is a notion which I nowhere find in the Scriptures expressed or implied. 'Tis true, many who hold the view of Christ being "the first of all creatures," say many excellent things of his Person, character, and work, as do those of whom I have just been speaking; but, "to the law and to the testimony." "If they speak not according to this word, it is because there is no light in them." Harsh words, 'tis true, as applied to persons who profess to love the Lord Jesus Christ in sincerity and in truth; but inasmuch as the notion they hold is opposed to the self-existence of Jesus the I AM, it must be rejected as spurious and heresy. Well does Mr. Hart say:

"Notion's the harlot's test,
By which the truth's reviled;
The child of fancy, finely dress'd,
But not the living child."

I beg pardon for calling their idea of the human preexistence a *mere doll,* but really I believe it is nothing more.*

* Since the first edition of this sermon was printed, I have had the pleasure of meeting with some remarks on pre-existerianism in a sermon by Mr. Philpot, on Prov. viii. 20, 21, No. 364 Penny Pulpit, 6th edition, which I take the liberty of inserting here, as not only confirming my own view, but as concisely setting forth in a strong light the perniciousness of that human notion.

"The dream of the pre-existerians is utterly and directly contrary to the truth of God; and those that are wrapped up in this delusion found much of their argument on this 8th chapter of the Proverbs of Solomon. I call it a delusion, and a dangerous delusion, too, because it strikes at the very root of the atonement. For if Christ's human soul existed before the foundation of world, then that human soul of Christ was never under the law; but we read that "he was made of a woman, *made under the law.*" But if that soul existed before the law was given, there could be

But lest I should make any one sad whom the Lord would not have made sad, by leading them to suppose that, because they are either under such teachings, or suppose they hold such views, and yet have felt sure in their own minds they have the witness of the Spirit that they are born of God—are united to Christ by a true and living faith, and that he is all their salvation, and all their desire—I would just say to such, far be it from me to bring a cloud between you and the Sun of your soul, by representing that all who differ from me are not partakers of saving grace. I have met with many who professed the dogma which I am condemning, who did not really believe it; arising, as I discovered, from a misconception of the peculiar idea involved. For years I verily thought I was a believer in the pre-existence of Christ's human soul, but was surprised to hear myself contradicted and told I was no Pre-existerian; and on looking more into the matter, I found it was the pre-existence of Christ's Person, founded on his self-existence I believed in, not of his human soul. I had mistaken the one for the other. This, I believe, is the case with many of the Lord's dear people, and even with some of his own sent servants in the ministry of the gospel.

Still, there is one word of caution I should like to give. Beware of men. We have had, and still have, writers and preachers who lead souls astray, and cause much confusion in the church of God by their snaky way of preaching the Person of Christ. One time they profess to teach Christ's eternal Sonship, and anon, they go off and preach either modern pre-existerianism, or some other notion intimating Christ was not the Son of God till he became man. They delight in self-made paradoxes, a little truth here, and a little truth there, and saying many pretty things about Christ; but all the while the poison of Arianism, or some other ism, is under their tongues. Their complex statements perplex, puzzle, and bewilder the minds of many, and, if it were possible, they would deceive the very elect, and *cheat* them out of the truth. There can be no objection to men honestly changing their views, if they think proper; but it is discreditable if men,

---

no subsequent *ex post facto* operation of the law upon that soul; and if it was never under the law, then Christ never could have wrought out the righteousness demanded by the law; and therefore it strikes a deadly blow at Christ's righteousness and Christ's atonement."

doing so, continue to publish and sell their contradictory writings at the same time. They may have their *pocket reasons* for so doing, they may obtain a position in certain cliques and circles, but such chamelion methods of teaching cannot promote the spiritual interests of the Church of God. He that honoureth not the Son, honoureth not the Father which sent him.

4th. *That the Sonship of the Lord Jesus Christ, being founded on his Deity, and not on his humanity, therefore this is the only true and proper basis upon which Jesus Christ, the Son of God, can be honoured as the Father.*

The apostle, in his first Epistle to the Corinthians, (viii. 6,) says: "But unto us there is but one God, the Father, of whom are all things, and we in him; and one Lord Jesus Christ, by whom are all things, and we by him." What a declaration is here of the unity of God and of Jesus Christ. The eternal, self-existent I AM, who is, and was, and is to come, the only Creator, Preserver, and Lord of all. This glorious and divine Being, so infinite in his perfections, pervading the whole universe of creation, visible and invisible, is revealed in the inspired writings as an incomprehensible and divine Spirit, and that they who worship him must worship him in spirit and in truth. In that same blessed book it is revealed that this divine and glorious Being is displayed and made known to us in the distinct Personality of Father, Son, and Holy Ghost, yet indivisible in the unity of the divine nature or substance. *The Person of God the Father is God, in the relation of a Father, sending and bringing forth his own infinitely perfect and most glorious image. The Person of God the Son is the same God, in the relation of a Son, proceeding from the Father. The Person of God the Holy Ghost is the same God, in the relation of the Holy Spirit proceeding from the Father and the Son in eternity.* This great mystery, of three Persons in One God, is plainly declared in the sacred word. Each of them is Jehovah the Most High God. All the three Persons, thus displayed, give us, as I receive it, a complete idea of the only true God. The only true God is the Father, Son, and Holy Ghost. He is revealed to us in the great scheme of Redemption by the personal acts or goings forth of Jehovah. First, we have God the Father sending forth his Son in the nature of man; then we have the Son manifesting the name of the Father; and the Son is revealed by the Holy Spirit. All this is accomplished in the mind and heart of each believer in Jesus, through the sanctification of the Spirit and belief of the truth, under his effectual teaching. Sometimes we perceive the same offices ascribed to other Persons in the sacred Trinity; by this, we mark more particularly the divine unity and essentiality of the Godhead. We believe in Christ; our sins are pardoned by Christ, and on account of Christ; we are saved by Christ; we pray to God through Christ; we praise God in Christ; we love, honour, and serve God in Christ; we know God only through Christ; we know God only *in* Christ; we are drawn to God by Christ, for none can come to the Father but by him: "He is the way, the truth, and the life." Thus, it is *by our own experience* of coming to God—loving him, knowing him, serving him—through Christ, that we attribute all the divine perfections of the Godhead to Christ, even as unto the Father. For he is God alone; besides him there is no God. We worship God in Christ. We ascribe all the glory of our salvation to him, as unto the Father. Thus it is we honour the Son even as we honour the Father, the one God over all, blessed for evermore. Amen, and amen.

Before I close this discourse, I must tax your patience for two or three more minutes; for there are one or two remarks I wish to make.

The first is *to the man who professes to believe that Jesus Christ is* NOT *co-essential and co-eternal with God the Father.*

My friend, I will give you credit for desiring to know Christ, to serve him, and to promote the knowledge of his name and will in all sincerity, and in truth; but though you may do so, yet if you are not well-grounded in the fundamental truth of the Deity of the Lord Jesus Christ, you will certainly fail to accomplish that which you are seeking. A right position, remember, if wrongly taken, will produce a wrong result. Your analogical reasoning is no substitute for the Spirit of Truth. "Who teacheth like him?" Your vain imagination has produced a creature Jesus, in opposition to the "Christ of God." If Jesus himself asserts his self-existence *prior* to his incarnation, *during* his incarnation, and *since* his incarnation,—as he does in Exodus iii. 14, John viii. 58, and Rev. i. 8—how shall mortal flesh dare to contradict and pervert the words of the infinite I AM, and add words to the inspired record that derogate the Person of the Son of the living

God, misleading and deceiving the saints of the Most High, by offering honour to a creature whom they ignorantly worship. Your whole scheme is of human invention, and must come to pieces under the hammer of God's truth. Consider what I say, and may the Lord lead you into the truth as it is in Jesus.

> "What think ye of Christ? is the test
> To try both your state and your scheme ;
> You cannot be right in the rest,
> Unless you think rightly of him."

My second remark is *to the sincere and humble believer in Jesus*, who, without entering into questions which he thinks only minister to strife and not to edification, has committed the keeping of his soul to Jesus, as unto a faithful Creator.

Dearly beloved, what a solid basis you have in the doctrine of the Essential Deity of the Lord Jesus Christ, for your salvation. This is the rock on which Christ builds his church ; here, then, rest all your hope, your faith, your love. The powers of hell may attempt to shake you, but their rage is in vain ; they shall not prevail. You may, perhaps, sometimes fear and quake *in yourself*, but not in Christ ; for you are safe and eternally secure in him. He is the Rock, his work is perfect, and you may say :

> "On Christ, the solid Rock, I stand;
> All other ground is sinking sand."

And, my brother or sister, feeling your standing so secure on such a Rock as this, what solemn weight attaches to the words of the Lord Jesus Christ as expressed in our text. You are called to honour the Son even as the Father ; you are called the children of the Lord God Almighty ; then walk as the children of the light, sons of God, holy and without rebuke, in the midst of a crooked and perverse generation. For as we have received Christ Jesus the Lord, so are we to talk in him.

> "No big words of ready talkers,
> No dry doctrine will suffice :
> Broken hearts and humble walkers,
> These are dear in Jesus' eyes."

My last remark is *to the poor seeking soul*, desiring to find Christ, believing him to be the only refuge where he can hide his guilty head from the storm of divine wrath that seems about to pour down upon him.

Poor soul! you have been driven out of all your hiding places, by the terrors of a broken law working wrath in your conscience. You are come seeking life and salvation by the death of Jesus Christ. You shall have it! Do you believe in God. Believe also in Christ. He who comes to God must believe that he—yes, Jesus Christ—is God alone. He alone can save you; his own arm brought salvation. Salvation is of God, not of a creature. Trust in him as God, the Son of God, not as the Son of man, or you will fare no better than the poor Syro-Phœnician woman; for so long as she called upon Jesus as the Son of David, all was dark, there seemed to be no hope for her, he answered her not a word; but when she came to him as the LORD alone, and dropped every plea of her own, saying, "Lord help me," that moment she took hold of God's strength, she touched his divinity, and obtained all she sought.

Are you indeed coming to Jesus? What is it that leads you to fix on him? "O," say you, "*I feel I am such a sinner, that only such a God as Christ is can save me?*" You are right; and he will save you. The Spirit has already opened your eyes. It is he who hath planted faith in your heart; he is leading you to Christ. You have been drawn by the love of the Father, and soon you shall find,

> "If you are returning to Jesus, your Friend,
> Your sighing and mourning in singing shall end."

Brethren, "These things have I spoken, that ye may know that ye have eternal life, and that ye may believe on the name of the Son of God. And we know that the Son of God is come, and hath given us an understanding that we may know him that is true; and we are in him, that is, even in his Son Jesus Christ. This is the true God and eternal life." (1 John v. 13, 20, 21.)

And now to God the Father, God the Son, and God the Holy Ghost, three Persons in one triune Jehovah, be ascribed equal and undivided honour, praise, glory, and adoration from this time forth and evermore. Amen and amen.

ADDENDA.

I HAVE no wish to revive controversy, but I think it desirable to make a few additional remarks upon the important question of the Eternal Sonship. It is well known that there are many good and gracious persons who regard the eternity of Christ's Sonship only as it respects the covenant of grace; they look upon the scheme of man's redemption originating in the mind of God before time, as an episode or parenthesis, in his eternal existence; that the personalities of the Trinity, Father, Son, and Spirit, are assumed names, and originated, for distinction sake, with that transaction only. That this notion has been put forth by some excellent men whose writings are deservedly held in estimation, I am well aware; but I feel persuaded it is contrary to the mind of the Spirit, and to the doctrine of the true and proper Sonship of Jesus Christ; and I cannot but think that while, *superficially* considered, it appears defective and to come short of the truth as it is in Jesus,—*essentially* considered, it is radically erroneous and subversive of the truth; and that the tendency of such a theory has not been sufficiently observed. To my view it inevitably leads to Sabellianism, if not to Unitarianism; yet anything approaching either of those schemes, I am sure, is utterly repudiated by the persons to whom I refer. I cannot for one moment admit that God's mercy, in respect of the fall, was the occasion or the origin of the names of the personalities in the Godhead. The covenant of grace was truly a revelation of Jehovah in his Trinity of Persons. It was a lifting up of the curtain of God's love upon the stage of time, a display of *his* mighty acts, whose goings forth, in the salvation of his people, have been from everlasting; a display to the church of the nature, glories, and eternity of the Three-One God. Surely the Scriptures do not countenance the opinion that the ever-blessed Trinity assumed to themselves names for acting out the several offices which each personality undertook in the work of redemption, as the consequence, or result, of that gracious compact? We read of God sending forth his Son, and of the Son manifesting the name of the Father, but in both instances the pre-existence of each personality in the relationship of Father and Son is implied. To suppose that a relationship did not exist until it was declared (as in Ps. ii. 7) or manifested (as in John xvii. 6) is without foundation.* The declaration and manifestation of the divine relationship arise from the fact that THERE WAS A SON—THERE WAS A FATHER—or how

* See opinions of several authors, quoted pages 27, 28.

could there be a declaration of such a relationship? A declaration of names only is something so unreal, so visionary, as to be unworthy of the character of God, and altogether unworthy of belief. Now, it is granted by our objectors, that the *personalities* are eternal; but we assert that *the relationship* of the Father and the Son is their distinct and peculiar proper personality, and that *that* relationship is eternal. How could the covenant of grace be formed by the eternal Three in the relationship of Father, Son, and Holy Spirit, as revealed, unless those relationships had a reality, and had pre-existed in the personalities by which they are designated. The question has been asked, Supposing there had been no fall of man, no covenant of grace, no redemption to effect, would there have been no Son of God, no God the Father, no God the Holy Ghost? and the answer has been emphatically, No. Now, this appears to me to involve a most grave and serious error, leading direct to Unitarianism; for if the personality of the Father be a name only, or coeval only with the covenant of grace, then there was a period in eternity, that is, antecedent to the covenant, when the Father was not the Father; if the personality of the Son be a name only, or coeval only with the covenant of grace, then there must have been a period in eternity when the Son was not the Son, — that is, when the Son was not in being, for his Sonship, according to this hypothesis, must have had a beginning; and if the Sonship was constituted only in the covenant transaction, then the Sonship is simply official, —a name only, and no personality at all; for there can be no basis for the Sonship without the personality. If there be a personality at all, it must be a reality, not a name, or else the Son of God is degraded below the brute creation; for we read, Gen. ii. 19, 20, that "Adam gave names to all the cattle and to the fowl of the air and to every beast of the field; and whatsoever Adam called every living creature that was the name thereof." That is, the creatures were in nature what they were designated. We also read that "God called the light day, and the darkness he called night." Because it was so, the light in itself is day, and the darkness in itself is night. Thus when God said, Ps. ii. 7, "Thou art my Son," the meaning is, *I am thy Father.* Are we to be told that the Sonship is only a name, and not a relationship? How contrary to all the principles of common sense! God calls Jesus his Son because he is his Son, a Son of the same nature as himself, the Son of himself, his own proper Son; not a mere name, for the name of a son is no son at all. Take away the Sonship, the personality is taken away, for *it has its name from its nature,* and, as just stated, that nature is eternal, and therefore the Sonship is eternal. So, on the same premiss which is taken as to the Sonship, the personality of God the Father is brought down to be a mere office or name; the divine Fatherhood to the Church of Christ is nothing but a name, instead of a relationship; the covenant union between Christ and his Church with his Father a mere fiction, and the believer's experience of these heavenly truths the veriest delusion. The same line of argument may be pursued as to the personality of the Holy Spirit ; so that we arrive at the conclusion that the personalities of Jehovah are nothing more than mere names, or at most *manifestations*, or different kinds of operations; thus throwing us back upon the old errors of Sabellianism, till at last, step by step, we are precipitated into the gulf of Unitarianism, one God—no Trinity of Persons. I therefore cannot but regard all views which give *data* to the Sonship of Christ as essentially erroneous, detracting from the personal glory of the Son of God, and as undermining the very basis of our common Christianity, the doctrine of our Lord's eternal generation; for on that fact is grounded the glories of his mediatorial work and character, as set forth in the Scriptures of Truth. Let this plain question be put—Is the Sonship of Christ the foundation of the covenant of grace ? or, is the covenant of grace the foundation of his Sonship ? If the latter, on what principle ? Certainly it does not exalt the person of the Son of God ; it spoils him of his crown; and the bearing to which this view inevitably leads, is to reduce him to the level of mere creatureship. As elsewhere stated (see Sermon 16 p. 40,) I regard the mediatorial work of Christ as founded on his personality, being the Son of God eternally pre-existent with his Father, antecedent to any of the covenant designs of Jehovah to save man.

I have not space here to carry out the argument as this great question well deserves, but close my remarks by simply declaring my unhesitating belief that Christ Jesus is, and ever was, the Son of God, in his own distinct personality, from all eternity. That had man never fallen, had no Church been chosen in Christ, or even this world had not been formed, the eternal God in the personalities of Father, Son, and Holy Ghost, would have self-existed in essence, nature, and relationship, in co-equal and co-eternal union, power, and glory.

QUOTATIONS REFERRED TO AT PAGE 25.

* Dr. J. A. ALEXANDER, of Princeton, America, on Ps. ii. 7, says:

"The essential meaning of the phrase, *I have begotten thee*, is simply this, *I am thy Father*, and *this day* is not to be understood as limiting the mutual relationship, though it might refer to a certain point of time for the formal recognition of it.

The declaration of our Lord's Sonship at his baptism, was but the recognition of that relation which had existed anterior to the period of his incarnation."

Dr. HODGE, of Princeton, on Rom. i. 3, 4, says:

"Christ is called the Son of God because he is consubstantial with the Father, and therefore equal to him in power and glory. The term expresses the relation of the second to the first person in the Trinity, as it exists from eternity. It is, therefore, as applied to Christ, not a term of office, nor expressive of any relation assumed in time. He was and is the Eternal Son."

Dr. GOUGE on Heb. i. 5, Section 62, says:

"This manifestation of Christ's divine generation in set and certain times, by visible and conspicuous evidences, doth no whit cross or impeach the eternity and incomprehensibleness thereof. For to declare and manifest a thing to be, presupposeth that it was before it was manifested; neither doth it necessarily imply any beginning of that before; no more than those phrases in Ps. xc. 2, Prov. viii. 25.

"The full meaning, therefore, of the apostle in alleging this testimony, 'Thou art my Son, this day have I begotten thee,' may, for perspicuity's sake, be thus paraphrased, as if God the Father had said thus to God the Son : Thou, and thou alone, art my true proper Son, not by grace or adoption, but by nature and eternal generation ; and now I do in this last age of the world declare thee so to be by thine incarnation, doctrine, works, resurrection from the dead, and ascension into heaven, whereby it manifestly appeareth that thou infinitely dost surpass all the angels in heaven."

The late Dr. SAMUEL HOPKINS, of America, Vol. I., page 308, says:

"They, therefore, who do not believe the eternal Sonship of Jesus Christ, because it is mysterious and incomprehensible,— and to some it appears to be full of contradiction,—will, if they be consistent with themselves, for the same reason reject the doctrine of a Trinity of persons in one God."

The above quotations may serve to show that my views are not unsupported by men of truth, learning, and celebrity ; to which may be added from among others the names of Drs. Owen, Goodwin, and Jacomb. The work of the latter on the 8th chapter of Romans, especially, contains an elaborate argument against the opposers of the eternal Sonship, and confutes their errors in a most masterly and scriptural manner.

October, 1866.   C. G.

LONDON: PRINTED BY ALFRED GADSBY, CRANE COURT, FLEET ST.

UNSEARCHABLE RICHES OF CHRIST.

THREE SERMONS,

BY CHARLES GORDELIER,

PREACHED AT THE SECOND ANNIVERSARY OF HIS MINISTRY AT
HEPHZIBAH CHAPEL, DARLING PLACE, NEAR MILE END GATE.

On Lord's Day Morning and Evening, April 16th, and
Lord's Day Evening, April 23rd, 1865.

I.

The Unsearchable Riches of Christ.—EPHESIANS iii. 8.

I SELDOM hear a text announced from the Epistle to the
Ephesians, or attempt to speak from one in this portion
of God's word, but what I feel something like when
one is approaching the extensive grounds of some baronial
residence. The surrounding scenery, the beautiful park,
the splendid trees, the majestic pile of buildings, the magnificent suite of rooms into which one is conducted, the
gorgeous furniture, its paintings, library, and the abundance of everything there is to supply human desires
and taste, all combine to overwhelm one with a profound
sense of the riches and greatness of the noble owner—that
is, as to his worldly possessions; and, on the other hand,
one equally feels the poverty and nothingness of one's
own position.

Now, I make no doubt but that every believer in Jesus,
when under the teachings of the Eternal Spirit, feels
there is something very rich and sublime in this Epistle
to the Ephesian "saints and faithful in Christ Jesus."
The apostle, in a very eminent degree, was inspired to
treat on such subjects as to bring believers into an
acquaintance with the deep things of God. And when,
under the rich anointing of the Holy Spirit, the soul is
led to trace his adoption in Christ Jesus to the predestinating love of God the Father, and blessed with all

No. 14.

spiritual blessings in heavenly places in him before the foundation of the world, he is constrained to acknowledge, " Oh, the depths of the riches both of the wisdom and knowledge of God! how unsearchable are his judgments, and his ways past finding out !" Like the love of Christ, it passeth knowledge.

We must not forget, however, that this epistle, so full of elevated thought and feeling, was written in the prison-house at Rome. Yet, though the apostle was an "ambassador in bonds," the word of God was not bound; his tongue, like the pen of a ready writer, speaks fluently of the transcendent excellency of the hopes and privileges of the church of God, their triumphs and glorious state of ultimate blessedness. He enters deeply into the depths of those things which are " hid in God," so far as they concern us; he brings them out, opens, explains, and sets them forth, showing whence grace and glory originate. He then goes on to show the eternal personal and unconditional election of the church in Christ, their glorious covenant head. This is shown by some of its immediate fruits and effects, as stated in the second chapter.

Then in the third chapter the apostle descends from the ancient mountains of everlasting love and free grace to speak of Christ as the eternal Head, the glorious, all-sufficient Redeemer. In the 4th verse he refers to his own personal knowledge in the mystery of Christ; and, observe, he says it was a revelation made known unto him. He knew nothing of Christ only by revelation : the only true and saving knowledge a poor sinner can have in this world is by a divine revelation. Now, how does this statement affect you ? Most of you know something of Jesus Christ, but how came you by it? Did you get it in the Sunday school, by rote? Did you acquire it by dint of study, by reading and hearing? or do you possess it by a revelation from God himself? Oh, pray do not let this vital point pass without strict examination. It matters not how long you may have made a profession of the name of Christ, you are still a poor lost perishing sinner if "God has not revealed his Son in you." There must be an inward work ; there must be the power of truth on the conscience wrought by the Spirit of God. There must be a feeling sense of what he has done in the soul; a notional or rational religion will not do. An experimental acquaintance of the truth as it is in Jesus is the only religion worth having; for, as Mr. Hart truly says,

> "Vain is all our best devotion,
> If on false foundation built;
> True religion's more than notion,
> Something must be known and *felt*."

But let us return to the apostle; see how this knowledge has humbled him in the dust of self-abasement. He has come down from those Alpine heights with a profound feeling sense of his own nothingness; he breaks through the rules of language to express himself—"less than the least of all saints." Oh, this is blessed experience, when self is laid low and words fail to utter thought and feeling; and this will be the case whenever we are led by the Spirit to take exalted views of Jesus, his glorious person and his glorious work. Dr. Watts knew something of this when he wrote,

> "The more thy glories strike mine eye
> The humbler I shall lie;
> Thus while I sink my joys shall rise
> Unmeasurably high."

Now to our text; and may he whose office it is to take of the things of Christ and to show them unto us help us to take right views of the subject before us; in his light we shall see light; without it, we shall be but stumbling in the dark, for there is no light in ourselves.

Our text speaks of Christ, his riches, and their unsearchableness.

I. FIRST, let us, with the help and blessing of the Lord, attempt to say a few things on THE PERSON OF CHRIST. This is too important a point to pass over with a glance or cursory remark. I regard it as a foundation truth, one on which every believer should see that he is well grounded. Mr. Newton has well put it in those oft-repeated lines of his—

> "What think ye of Christ is the test
> To try both your state and your scheme;
> You cannot be right in the rest,
> Unless you think rightly of him."

By the Person of Christ is to be understood the Son of God who became incarnate, he who from all eternity was the Son of God the eternal Father—God's own Son, his proper Son; (Rom. viii. 3;)—such a Son as he has never another, as Jesus himself said he was. (John iii. 16.) He was truly the Son of man; he was also truly the Son of God.   I am aware there is no question among Christians respecting the truth of Christ being a son, but about the nature and manner of his sonship there have been some fierce and bitter controversies, and will be as long as Satan is permitted to exercise his influence over the sons of men; but still truth must be maintained, notwithstanding the temporary inconvenience occasioned by it, or the heavy cross that stands connected with it; a man had better lose his dearest friends than lose his conscience.   I hold *the doctrine of Christ's eternal Sonship, irrespective of his becoming incarnate, or of the covenant of grace, to be a truth of God's Holy Word* of high import, and a most fundamental truth. Oh may the Spirit of truth help me to state my views clearly, forcibly, and concisely.

Now let us search the Scriptures; for it is there we must derive our testimony of the person of Christ; if they affirm it not, we dare not believe it; if they do affirm it, we dare not reject it.   Consult Psalm ii. 7: "The Lord hath said unto me, Thou art my Son, this day have I begotten thee;" here is plainly a declaration of Christ's eternal generation; a declaration of his personality as a SON, not of his Deity, for that does not enter into the question: "thou art," not thou shalt be; "this day," eternity, for God has no other day in respect of his self-existence than that of eternity; "ever is his time," "one eternal now;" with us time is past, present, and future; therefore this scripture which I have quoted I regard as a revelation of the truth that Christ is the Eternal Son of the Eternal Father.   I do not say a revelation of the mystery as to *how* it is that Christ is the Son of God; that I do not attempt to explain, it is not revealed, therefore cannot be explained; I am content to receive it as a revealed truth; and if men will find fault because they do not get everything explained to their own liking and fashion, they must be regarded as aiming to be wise above what is written.

Again, Jesus Christ, in several places of holy writ, is expressly stated to be the *only* begotten of the Father. (John i. 14, 16; iii. 16, 18; 1 John iv. 9.)   In these five passages the words *only begotten* show, as I have just said, such a Son as he has never another; and they also show that Christ is of the same name and essence with his Father; his Sonship is derived from that fact; his name, the Son of God, is both a name of nature and a name of relationship; hence the doctrine is founded on his Divine nature, not on his human nature, for he was the Son of God before he was born of the Virgin. The notion, therefore, that many good-meaning men hold and teach, that Jesus Christ is the Son of God only in his complex person, is without foundation in God's truth; it appears to me their view is extremely defective; not only so, it is erroneous, and is calculated to sap the comfort of all the work of Christ and the characters he bears to his church; and so also the view which many entertain, that Jesus is the Son of God *in relation only to the Covenant of grace* in man's redemption is defective; not so radically defective as the one just condemned, I admit, but, inasmuch as it gives *data* for the Sonship, it necessarily is opposed to its eternity, and therefore is not founded on truth.

But, further, we have several testimonies, which bear ample witness to this great truth, that the Person of Christ is the Son of God. In the days of his flesh, he was known to be of the root and offspring of David, as to his human nature; but as to his divine nature, he was attested to be the Son of God. John the Baptist said, "I saw and bare record, that this is the Son of God." (John i. 34.) Nathaniel said, "Rabbi, thou art the Son of God." (John i. 49.) Peter said, "Thou art the Son of the living God." (Matt. xvi. 16.) The Roman centurion acknowledged, "Truly this was the Son of God." (Matt. xxvii. 54.) The eunuch confessed, "I believe that Jesus Christ is the Son of God." (Acts viii. 37.) Martha said, "Lord, I believe that thou art the Christ, the Son of God." (John xi. 27.) Did not the devils themselves own the truth? (Matt. viii. 29.) And what is this witness they bear to? The Divine Sonship. This truth is attested by the Father himself. (Matt. iii. 17, and xvii. 5; and again 1 John v. 7, 8.) Jesus himself asserted it, and for so doing he was accused of blasphemy, condemned, and crucified for it. (John xix. 7, and Mark xiv. 64.) The apostle Paul, in writing to the Romans, (i. 4,) says Jesus was "declared to be the Son of God with power:" meaning, "He was determinately avowed, openly proclaimed, and convincingly demonstrated to be so, according to the manifest proof that was given of it, by the immediate exertion of his own divine power." (Guyse *loco*.)

Now, dear friends, may this truth be fully impressed upon your understandings by the power of the Holy Ghost. The Sonship of Christ is the foundation truth of every other truth requisite to be known for life and salvation. Christ himself is the *personal* foundation, and this truth is the *doctrinal* foundation. Upon the fact that Christ is the Son of the living God is built the faith of God's elect. It is the eternal rock on which his church is built, and the powers of hell shall not prevail against it.

Surely we shall do well to examine this momentous truth a little closer; it is the root, the trunk of that tree of life whose branches bring forth precious fruits, that feed and nourish the church of God, and whose leaves are for the healing of the nations. Observe,

1. Christ is the Coeternal Son of God. He was eternally a Son; there never was a time when he was otherwise, or began so to be. The Father is eternal, and always a Father; then the Son is eternal, and always a Son; the Son of Himself. (John xvii. 5.) If we admit the eternity of God the Father, we must admit the eternity of God the Son; the one must be coeval with the other, whatever some men may assert to the contrary. Indeed, it is a truth in nature which cannot be denied, that the relation of parent and offspring necessarily coexist, though its manifestation or development be not acknowledged till the usual time arrives for the recognition of that relationship. I make this remark because of the pertinacity with which some oppose the eternity of Christ's Sonship, on the ground that the person of a son is posterior to that of a father. Such an objection seems to me absurd. If a relationship exist at all, it must be on the ground of personality; and if the relationship is coexistent, then the personality is coexistent. Apply the argument to the doctrine of Christ being the eternal Son of God,—I think we cannot escape the conclusion that it is a truth expressly declared in God's holy word. O may the Spirit of truth help us to receive it. Let us beware of human fancies, human reason, human analogies, for they are unsafe guides to the mysteries of divine truth.

2. Jesus himself affirms his own eternity as the Son of God; see the 35th verse of the 8th chapter of John, containing a discussion on this very subject: "The Son abid-

eth ever." The words are in the present tense, and the sentence is by itself; for the word *but* is in italics, denoting that it was supplied by the translators. These words, "*The Son abideth ever,*" I take them to mean HIS SONSHIP EVER HATH BEEN AND EVER WILL BE, the sense being equivalent or similar to "I AM," "I AM THAT I AM," the eternally self-existent Son of God; being, in other words, nothing more nor less than the doctrine of Christ's eternal generation, against which some men of late have strenuously cavilled and sadly misrepresented. But, brethren, you must bear in mind we are speaking of the *personality* of Christ's Godhead, not of the Godhead abstractedly considered—a point which should be kept distinctly in view; for this is what most of our opposers like to keep out of sight, so that they may plausibly fasten upon us the odium that we are believers in Deity begetting Deity; a monstrous notion truly, but one which originated nowhere but in their own brain. It is indeed very sad to witness the painful misconstructions and perversions that have been made of the testimonies put forth on this subject by men of truth; still more is it sad to behold good men, as I believe many to be, defending their erroneous and defective views with a zeal unworthy of their character as men of God and ministers of the gospel of Christ. If we are taught by the Spirit to hold fast the Unity of the Godhead in the Trinity of Persons, I am quite sure we shall be kept free from confounding Satanic error with Divine Truth. But one remark more. Though the eternal nature and essence of Jesus Christ as the Son of God is fully asserted in the word of God, but nowhere explained, yet his office-character as the God-man Mediator is most gloriously revealed, and it is that which most of all concerns us. Pray, then, that the eyes of your understanding may be opened to perceive and to keep in view this important and most proper distinction in speaking of the Person of the Lord Jesus.

I should like to have gone a little fuller into this part of our subject, but time fails; and I must refer my hearers, if they desire more information, to my sermon on the Sonship of Jesus, preached on the former anniversary. They will find several points discussed there which we cannot here, because I must hasten to the other branches of my text; consequently, I must leave unnoticed now any remarks on the coessentiality and coequality of

Christ, the Son of God, with the Father. I trust, however, sufficient has been said to set forth the scriptural view of the Person of Jesus Christ, the Son of God, as shall enable us to apprehend something of the glories of those unsearchable riches which are treasured up in him, our ever-blessed Mediator and Redeemer.

The next subject we have to notice in connection with our text is, the great fact of the Son of God taking our nature into personal union with himself. "In the beginning was the Word;" "God was the Word;" "the Word was made flesh;" "God was manifested in the flesh." God became incarnate. Not assuming a human shape, but a real assumption of human nature: "Forasmuch as the children are partakers of flesh and blood, he also took part of the same." "He took not on him the nature of angels, but he took on him the seed of Abraham;" "He was made of a woman, made under the law, that he might redeem those who were under the law."

And observe, too, the flesh he took was not sinful flesh. *His* bodily nature was pure and sinless; he came in *the likeness* of sinful flesh, and for sin," and, in so doing, condemned sin in the flesh. The *reality* of his flesh was as much so as is ours. The necessity for the Son of God to take our flesh was because sin was committed in it, and sin must be punished in that same nature, or else the person of the sinner must be utterly lost to all eternity. But such was the love of God to man, he sent his Son into the world, not to condemn it, but to condemn *sin* and save the sinner. He who knew no sin was made sin for us. He took our law place. The guilt of our sin was transferred to him, placed to his account by imputation; and so Jesus, having become the Surety of all whom the Father had given him, became also, "in the fulness of time," their substitute. "He bore our sins in his own body," and sin was punished in his holy, immaculate Person on Calvary's bloody tree; thus it was he became the propitiation for our sins. Justice was satisfied, and could no longer demand the sinner's life. This is the joyful news of the gospel: "Christ Jesus came into the world to save sinners;" he having abolished in his flesh the curse of the law, being made a curse for us, and thereby "redeemed us from the hand of him who was stronger than we." And every believer in this great truth, trusting to that atonement then made to God for sin, is eternally saved, and shall have everlasting life. O what a grand display did Jesus make of the heart of God to that highly-favoured seeker of divine truth, Nicodemus, when he said to him, "God so loved the world, that he gave his only-begotten Son, that whosoever believeth in him should not perish, but have everlasting life;" "For God sent not his Son into the world to condemn the world, but that the world through him might be saved." It was "to damn" sin in his own flesh, but to save the sinner. Is there a poor soul here this morning distressed on account of sin in his conscience? Look at this blessed truth. Jesus died for sin. Sin is forgiven on his account. God pardons sin for his sake. What are you looking to for peace? Seek it here; it is the blood of Jesus that can alone take away sin. O may the Spirit apply his truth with power to your soul, and enable you to say, in the weighty words of old John Latchford:

"My sins were his, upon him laid;
  He all their weight sustain'd;
My debt, how vast! which yet he paid,
  And my deliverance gain'd."

But I must proceed. Jesus, in taking our nature, took the whole of it, soul and body. He had verily a human soul as well as a human body. How could he have been a man else? Impossible. When he took our flesh, he took its entirety, body and soul, sin alone excepted. As he grew in bodily stature, so he grew in the rational and moral faculties of the soul. He "increased in wisdom and in stature, and in favour with God and man." (Luke ii. 52.) This scripture confutes at once the notion that Christ's human soul pre-existed before time, and was with God in a glorified state. Of course, one scripture would not satisfy an objector; no, nor more would a thousand; but a sincere lover of God's word is quite satisfied with a single declaration upon it. The pre-existence of Christ's Person as the Son of God in eternity is a blessed truth revealed in God's word; but it is quite a distinct matter from his human soul's pre-existence. That notion, though some think they honour the Lord by it, would, if followed out to its legitimate bearings, bring the whole scheme of salvation, as well as the Person of our blessed Lord and the wisdom of God, into dire contempt. I have, however, no time to go into that dispute now. The life of Jesus on earth plainly reveals the fact of his human

*

nature being in all points, sin excepted, as we are. This divine nature being conjointly with his human nature in one Person, is that deep mystery which the apostle, under the inspiration of the Holy Ghost, calls *great:* "Without controversy, great is the mystery of godliness, God was manifest in the flesh." This is the truth, and this is godliness. Any other view of Christ's Person is not godliness; it is not the truth as it is in Jesus. I dare say some think this is severe language. No, not at all. We will not give place to Satan's lies for one moment. Let this suffice for the present.

Perhaps some may say, Was it really necessary that the Son of God should become incarnate? Yes, it was. I am not surprised at the question; for no one, unless under the teachings of the Spirit, can have the remotest idea of the real evil and danger of sin, and therefore they see not the necessity of its being put away by the sacrifice of the Lord Jesus Christ; neither do they feel the deathliness of sin within. The exceeding sinfulness of sin is only known and felt by the sinner when quickened by the Spirit; then it is he feels that satisfaction must be given to the injured Majesty of heaven, the offended God. He believes God's law is holy, just, and good; he feels condemned by it in his own conscience; and as the honour of God must be vindicated, the punishment of sin must be inflicted, either in the person of the sinner, or of a substitute whom God would accept. But where can such a proviso be found? Where can redemption be looked for? Who, of all God's created intelligences, could devise a scheme of salvation for lost man? No, not one. There was not even a single intercessor on behalf of the human race. (Isa. lix. 16.) Angels might have looked on; they might have pitied our lost condition; but, great in power as they are, and swift to do God's will, their pity and compassion would not have rendered us any real service in the ruin of our nature; and granting, just for one moment, the refined Arian scheme to be true, that the human soul of Christ was with God before time, and that he voluntarily came forward as our Surety to undertake our redemption! would God, think ye, trust the work of our salvation in the hands of a creature? No, certainly not! For, you must be reminded, these pre-exterians assert that Christ was the first of God's creatures; and, though they are desirous of giving him the pre-eminence in all things, yet, let me tell you, such a God as they make him to be is but a creature after all. A creature God forsooth! O my friends, such a Saviour as they make Jesus to be is not the Christ of God. Do you think you could trust your soul's salvation in any one's hand short of God himself? I am sure you would not. This is bringing the matter to a practical issue. Salvation, as revealed in God's word, is one which is worthy of the nature of God; it is in harmony with all his perfections; it so displays the wisdom, grace, love, and goodness in the gift of his dear Son that the soul becomes absorbed in profound admiration, and can only say what an apostle himself had before said: "Thanks be unto God for his UNSPEAKABLE gift."

Bear with me a little longer. I see time is running on, and we are only on the margin of our subject yet; but we must not think the time lost in discussing these vital points. Your life is bound up in them; and this is it, sin is an evil and bitter thing. God will punish it, he will by no means clear the guilty, except upon the righteous and honourable principles of law and justice. "The soul that sinneth it shall die." This is God's unalterable and wise decree. I say wise decree, for if man may sin and yet be permitted to live, then either sin is not so sinful as it is said to be, or God's holiness is of such a character as to be, or may be, in some way compatible with it; but this is not the case. God is of purer eyes than to behold evil. HE IS GLORIOUS IN HOLINESS; and hence it is for the comfort and salvation of every believer in Jesus that sin is condemned. It is man who has sinned; it is man who must be punished. If man is to be saved, it can only be by a method of God's devising. "His understanding is infinite." He alone could find a ransom; and this has been done; done in the Person of God's own dear Son. He became the Surety of his people; he took their sin, he took their nature, and by bearing their sins in his own body on the tree, as their Substitute, he has perfected for ever the salvation of all those whom God the Father hath sanctified. Therefore, as it was in human nature sin was committed and in that nature must be punished, so by the human nature could deliverance be effected; neither angels, nor archangels, could effect it, or else they would have been sent to accomplish it. No; their nature and their services are passed by, and these being the highest order of

God's creation, there was none to help; "therefore his own arm brought salvation unto him." So God sent his only-begotten Son into the world to take our nature, (such a nature as was possessed by the first man Adam before he fell,) pure, uncorrupted in itself, created by the Holy Ghost himself. (Matt. i. 18–20; Luke i. 35.) In this sinless flesh, the Son of God perfectly obeyed his Father's will—the law which we had broken. Yet, in the selfsame body, spotless, harmless, holy, as Jesus was in himself, he suffered for sin; he was made sin, all the sins of all his people being charged upon him; and by his death for their sin they are for ever freed and justified from all things of which they stood condemned, and are made the righteousness of God in him. (Rom. viii. 3-4; 2 Cor. v. 21.)

I hope I have made myself clearly understood on this great doctrine of divine substitution. To have a right apprehension of the unsearchable riches of Christ, we must not only have right views of his Person as the Son of God, but also of his work as the Mediator of the New Covenant. These are vast and amazing themes to contemplate. Angels cannot comprehend them. Man cannot explain them; yet it is blessed to feel that when God does reveal them to us by his Spirit, they are very precious and the choicest food of our souls. Some say they are dry doctrines; I believe them; for God never poured out upon them the bedewing influences of his Spirit. Their names may perhaps stand as members of the professing Church below, but I fear they have neither part nor lot in the mystical Church of Christ. It is quite possible for such to hold a position in the Garden of the Lord both gratifying to themselves and their friends. But alas, alas! they are but stakes in the ground, having no root; they are not trees of the Lord's right hand planting. O my hearers, beware of having a name to live while you are dead.

And now, dear friends, in drawing this part of our subject to a close, I would only say I am quite aware objections are made to the statements advanced this morning, on the Son of God taking our nature into personal union with himself. It is called the personal union because the two natures are centred in one Person. Christ took our *nature*, not our person. That would be preposterous to suppose; his own personality, that is, his individuality, consciousness, and independency, remained unchanged, unaltered. The Son of God was a perfect Person before his incarnation; but, in order that man should be redeemed, he was pleased to take the manhood into union with the Godhead, without making any personal addition to himself. Thus, though he is God and Man, he is but one Christ. I might illustrate this point thus: When believers in the Lord Jesus are renewed in the spirit of their minds, they are made partakers of a divine nature, but this new nature imparted to them makes no addition to their personality. Their own individuality, consciousness, and identity remain unaltered; each possesses two natures, the old and the new, yet but one person. So the Lord Jesus Christ in his Person possesses by his incarnation a duality of natures; and nothing can be more clear in Scripture than that Christ is not only truly man, but also that he was truly the Son of God before he was made the Son of man, perfect and complete in his Person, as is the Person of the Father or the Holy Ghost. He was the Son of God before he became incarnate. This the apostle again and again asserts. HE, a Person, speaking of Christ, God over all. (Heb. ii. 14–16.) And just let me add one remark more, and that is, I believe that the Lord Jesus Christ in his divine nature is, ever was, and ever shall be, the eternal Son of God; that had he not taken our nature, he would have been still the eternal Son of God. It was not his incarnation that made him the Son of God; it was not the covenant of grace in respect of man's redemption that made him the Son of God. As the self-existent God he is ever the same—the I AM; he who spake to Moses out of the burning bush. If sin had never existed, or man had never been formed, the Person of the Son of God would have been coessential, coeternal, and coequal with God the Father and the Holy Ghost. What is revealed to us of his Person and mediatorial work in redemption, arises out of the priority of the fact that Jesus Christ is the one true God who made all things. This is the truth, and no lie. (1 John v. 20.) Our God made man; but they who declare their man made God, utter the greatest falsehood that Satan ever invented.

Objections are made, too, to the use of the words eternal generation, eternal Son, etc.; but if the words used express our meaning, why should our opposers find fault? Are we only to use such words as are coined in their mint? The Israelites had to go down to the Philistines to have their tools sharpened, because there was no smith in the land; (1 Sam. xiii. 19, 20;) but, blessed be God, we are not in such helpless bondage. The Lord being our helper, we trust his truth will ever be defended with those weapons as he may be graciously pleased to furnish us with, even the two-edged sword of the Spirit, and not on what are framed by themselves and hammered out on their anvil.*

Thus we have attempted to say a few things upon the Person of Christ as the Son of God. This is an inexhaustible and delightful theme, and we feel how poor are all our scanty thoughts; yet let us hope they will help your conceptions of his unsearchable riches. We have also said a few things on the nature of his great work as Mediator. These two great subjects will form the basis for establishing the two remaining points of our text for this evening's consideration,—his riches and their unsearchableness. Whatever has entered into this discourse of the nature of controversy, is with a desire to place truth in a right light and souls on a right foundation, and not for the sake of controversy. I hope ever on occasions like these to be enabled to bear my humble testimony to the true doctrine of the Person and work of Jesus Christ the Son of the living God.

Let me ask you before I sit down, what think ye of Christ? Have you ever felt his love ruling in your hearts by the power of his Spirit? You may rely upon it, that if God has begun a good work in your hearts, the love of God will be shed abroad there, prompting you to know more of him, leading you to walk as he has commanded; and more than this, he has engaged to carry on that work in you amidst all the hindrances that cast your spirit down, and causes you to feel sometimes as though your profession was without principle. How did you feel when you were singing those sweet lines?—

> "Oh, could I know and love him more,
> And all his wondrous grace explore,
> Ne'er would I covet man's esteem,
> But part with all and follow him."

I felt them very precious to my own soul. I desire to know nothing among men but Christ, and him crucified; and

* See Appendix.

this is the way to it, to love Christ, to know Christ, to preach Christ, to hear Christ, to follow Christ.   Jesus is precious to those who believe; but his preciousness arises out of what he is in himself and what he is to them, not from their belief.   A theoretical knowledge will not make him so.   See to this, dear friends.   Keep it in view; be not satisfied with a mere profession in religion.   If you have no experimental acquaintance of the truths you profess, your religion will come to nothing.   The only safe religion is that which God begins and works in the heart.   Where this exists, there will be a sense of one's own ruined condition as a sinner before him, a sense of one's own helplessness, a sense of one's own nothingness, and that CHRIST IS ALL AND IN ALL.   May the Lord help you to know and to feel the power of his truth, for his name's sake.   Amen.

UNSEARCHABLE RICHES OF CHRIST.

II.

The Unsearchable Riches of Christ.—EPHESIANS iii. 8.

IT is said that young sheep like to smell the breath of the old sheep. I believe it is true; and I am quite sure in spiritual things young believers in Christ like to hear old believers speak of the Lord Jesus.

> "His name, like precious ointment shed,
>   Delights the church around."

And it is equally true that old believers like to hear the young believer talk of Jesus. How I enjoyed the singing of that 171st hymn just concluded; it did my soul good to hear our young friends singing,—

> "Take Him for strength and righteousness;
>   Make Him thy refuge in distress;
>   Love Him above all earthly joy,
>   And Him in everything employ."

That one verse contains a body of doctrinal, experimental, and practical divinity which all of you will do well to think over. Now, I know some of you young folks love the name which you have been singing about. Do you never forget that verse; have it with you everywhere; it will prove suitable for you in every condition of your life. I have found it so for thirty-six years; and I am quite sure whoever has sung that hymn from the heart this evening will sing the praises of Jesus in heaven.

The words which I have read as a text we had under consideration in the morning. We first spoke upon the Person of Christ as the Son of God, and then entered upon the threshold of that sweet truth, the Son of God taking our nature into personal union with himself. These two points are to be considered as the foundation of all that is to be said on the second and third heads of our subject. Let us now notice the SECOND head.

No. 15.

11. THE RICHES OF THE LORD JESUS CHRIST. By the word riches we ordinarily understand wealth, opulence, abundance of that which is valuable, etc. Thus we employ the word riches in reference to the Person of Christ. "Ye know the grace of our Lord Jesus Christ, who though he was rich yet for our sakes became poor, that we through his poverty might be made rich.

Observe, 1. *His riches are grounded on his Sonship.* The riches of Christ are peculiar to his Person as the Son of God. These riches are blessedly adapted to meet the wants of the most needy and bankrupt sinner. Man's nature is so constituted as to need everything that Christ *is* and everything that Christ *has.* Sin has certainly ruined every man and woman ; but, if sin had never entered this world, if man had remained perfectly obedient, innocent, and thereby immortally happy in this world, as God's creature, still he would have possessed nothing but what he derived from the fulness which is in Christ. Man at his best state is altogether vanity. (Ps. xxxix. 5.)   He is nothing, he has nothing in himself; he is less than nothing.

Now, the believer in Jesus when quickened by the Holy Ghost is made to feel his own nothingness, neediness, and helplessness. This is his first step in the divine life ; he is made to look out of himself to the Lord Jesus for everything both for time and for eternity.

> "Stripp'd of all his fancied meetness
> To approach the dread I AM,
> He is led to see all fitness
> Centring in the worthy Lamb."

" For in him," saith the apostle in writing to the Colossians, ii. 9, "dwelleth all the fulness of the Godhead bodily." " It pleased the Father that in him should all fulness dwell." (Col. i. 19.)

These stores of divine grace, without which the believer could not exist a single day,—no, not a moment,—are all treasured up in Christ for his supply, safety and security, by virtue of the covenant of grace between the eternal and ever-blessed Trinity as it is declared in that precious epistle whence we have taken our text, i. 3, 4 : " Blessed be the God and Father of our Lord Jesus Christ, who hath blessed us with all spiritual blessings in heavenly places in Christ, according as he hath chosen

us in him before the foundation of the world, that we
should be holy and without blame before him in love."

This brings us to notice,

2. *The riches of Christ are displayed to the Church of
God in the Mediatorial character and offices he sustains.*

His mediatorial character is seen in the united natures
of his Person. All the blessings of the covenant of grace
flow through the Person of the Mediator, from the gift of
the Father, and are applied by the Holy Spirit to the
heart and conscience of the believer. His Godhead and
his manhood united in one person fitted him for Mediator.
A mediator is one person undertaking with a personal
interest a cause existing between two parties. Such was
the Lord Jesus Christ; he was eminently fitted for such
a work, and such a work was needed. Man by nature is
a sinner, a rebel, a creature, and fallen from the state in
which he had been created,—a rebel against God's government, a sinner against God. It was man that could not
be reconciled to God his Creator, though God in himself
is holy, full of love and goodness. Strange as it may
appear, it is man the offender that is to be reconciled. It
reminds one of a Spanish proverb, "The man who has
injured you will never forgive you." Yes, it is the
enmity of man the offender that has to be removed. He
seeks no reconciliation; for "when we were enemies," that
is, in a state of enmity, "we were reconciled to God by
the death of his Son." This is the testimony of God
the Holy Ghost by the mouth of the apostle Paul. (Rom.
v. 8, 10.) Now, none but the Lord Jesus Christ was able
and willing for such a work. He was God-man in one
person. (Col. ii. 19.) And who could be so fit to bring
God and man together as he who was himself both God
and man? who so fit to negotiate the work of reconciliation and salvation, as he who could act between both?
Such was the Lord Jesus Christ; possessing both natures,
it showed his fitness for the work. He is truly God; he
is truly man. He was the only person that could be sent
on the errand of mercy to accomplish man's redemption;
the offices he holds in the church show his fitness for the
great work, and his fitness is grounded on his Sonship.
As we in the common concerns of life appoint a person
to hold a certain office of responsibility and trust in
consequence of his *previous* fitness personally considered,
so Jesus became the Mediator of the covenant by virtue

of his previous fitness as the Son of God. It was not the covenant of grace that made him what he was, but it was made the means of displaying what he was,—the eternal Son of the eternal Father; neither was it the fact of his being sent in the likeness of sinful flesh that became the ground of his Sonship. Before he was sent he was the Son of God, but he was not the Son of God because he was sent; his Sonship belongs to his divine person, not simply to his work. Jesus was a Son long before he was sent; from eternity he was God's own Son, (John i. 14,) as several scriptures plainly declare and intimate; but men, who have their own creeds to uphold and their own parties to serve, seem as though they would resist the Holy Ghost, and give God's word the lie. These remarks on the mediatorial character of Christ will now enable us to proceed to the consideration of the riches he possesses in his offices of PROPHET, PRIEST, and KING.

1. His *Prophetical* office. This embraces the several characters he bears to the church of God as their teacher, guide, and counsellor. Here his riches are set forth in his word as being most ample and abundant. (Ps. cxlvii. 5.) "His understanding is infinite;" (Isa. xl. 14;) "There is no searching of his understanding;" (Col. ii. 3;) "In him are hid all the treasures of wisdom and knowledge;" (Isa. liii. 11;) "By his knowledge shall my righteous servant justify many, for he shall bear their iniquities;" (Eph. i. 8;) "He hath abounded towards us in all wisdom and prudence;" (Eph. iii. 10;) "The manifold wisdom of God;" (Job xxxvi. 22;) "Who teacheth like him?" (1 Cor. i. 30;) He is of God made unto us wisdom; (1 Cor. i. 24;) the wisdom of God. These passages refer to him as God; as man, it is expressly said of him, " Grace is poured into thy lips ;" (Ps. xlv. 2;) "He was filled with wisdom;" (Luke ii. 40;) His wisdom astonished his enemies: " Whence hath this man this wisdom?" (Matt. xiii. 54.) Jude speaks of Jesus as being "the only wise God our Saviour," 25th verse. Thus we see the attribute of wisdom is a part of his riches that constitute him so eminently suited for the church of God, both on earth and before time. As our wonderful counsellor, how his wisdom shone in the plan of salvation when he undertook our cause ! Who but the Son of God could take the book of the mystery of our

redemption, and open every seal? The council of peace was between the Father and the Son. By wisdom, infinitely glorious, was the plan of salvation contrived; and by power, infinitely glorious, was it effected. Here we see in the most extensive sense the beauty of that commonplace phrase, "Knowledge is power." Not only by the wisdom of God were the worlds framed, but we see innumerable millions of the lost race of mankind are eternally saved by a wisdom which bespeaks God for its author. "Oh, the depth of the riches both of the wisdom and knowledge of God!" (Romans xi. 33.) Here is an ocean without a shore, without a bottom. This wisdom maketh wise unto salvation; it descends from above; it is imparted to his creatures for the accomplishment of his own designs, the glory of his great name, the eternal salvation of his church, and to enrich them in all knowledge. This was a matter of the apostle's earnest prayer both for the Ephesians and the Colossians, that they might have the Spirit of wisdom and revelation in the knowledge of Christ, that they might be filled with the knowledge of his will in all wisdom and spiritual understanding, (Eph. i. 17, 18; Col. i. 9.) As their divine teacher, who teacheth like him? Who can impart the wisdom of God, but the God man? How can the divine mind be communicated to the human soul, but through the union of the divine and the human natures as they dwelt in the Person of the Son of God, the Lord Jesus Christ. O, what riches are here dwelling in Christ, wisdom and knowledge in all their fulness, *treasuries* of wisdom and knowledge. *All* the treasuries, and all these to be available to and for the church of God before time, through time, and throughout eternity; every step in our divine life is directed by infinite wisdom; it guides our way through all this mortal existence, "wisdom profitable to direct," and skill to act, both come from and through Christ the Mediator. He who gave Bezaleel skill to execute works of art for the service of the Tabernacle, gives knowledge to the ploughman for casting seed into the ground, (Isa. xxviii. 23, 29.) It is owing to this great truth, "Christ is of God made unto us wisdom," that the apostle James instructs the church: "If any of you lack wisdom let him ask of God, who giveth *to all men liberally* and upbraideth not, and it shall be given him." Thus through life we are assured, "The wayfaring man though a fool shall not err therein."

The riches of Christ's *prophetical* office provide for every possible contingency or emergency of the wilderness state.

2. His *Priestly* office. This may be said to be the chiefest, the most eminent of the characters Jesus bears to the church of God. This is his great work; here is the most conspicuous element of his mediatorship. It embraces his priesthood, his sacrifice, his propitiation, his advocacy and intercessorship. First, let us consider the *constitution* of his office; this I think will help us to discover something of those riches which characterise him as our great high-priest. At your leisure consult the 7th chapter of Hebrews. The apostle uses the analogy of Melchisedec's unknown ancestry to set forth the eternity of Christ's priesthood; and, after asserting Jesus was not made a priest either by man or in this time state, he uses these remarkable words, "*made after the power of an endless life,*" and quotes, in proof, Ps. cx. 4; "Thou *art* a priest for ever after the order of Melchisedec." Now, if I understand the apostle's meaning, by the same anointing as by which he wrote, he speaks of Christ's eternal generation. "The power of an endless life" can have reference only to his possessing "life in himself;" (John v. 26;) "In him was life," (John i. 4.) The *power* of an endless life consists in possessing life in its essence, which is peculiar to God only, and this life is in his Son, for he is the Son of God; having therefore an untraceable priesthood, after the similitude of Melchisedec, and by an act of God the Father, in the covenant of grace, declared to be a Priest for ever, not merely in perpetuity, as some aver, but from eternity. His priesthood being as dateless as his sonship, for I regard the words, "Thou art a Priest for ever," as being coeval with those, in point of *existence,* as, "Thou art my Son, this day," &c. (Ps. ii. 7.) But it may be asked, why so tenacious of Christ's eternity? what has it to do with his Priesthood? Much every way; it shows a fulness of power, of merit, of mercy, as displaying such riches in his Person, as our great, high-priest, as to superabound over all the ruin and misery of man's fallen condition. If Jesus had not been our Priest before sin had its origin, we had been left poor indeed; but, O the exceeding riches of his grace, ample provision was made in the constitution of his office by his Person being eternal. The church of God was ever eternally secure in him. He was the Anti-Phineas, turning away the wrath

of God from his people. He is our propitiation, he is our peace, he has made peace by the blood of his cross. Oh the riches of this propitiation; he stood in the breach, he stayed the plague of death ; his merits being all sufficient, and grounded on the nature of his Person. The *reality* of his great work in our behalf, when in such imminent danger and ruin, became his riches to us as our priest. His propitiatory work saves us; otherwise, God had been a consuming fire, and it is indeed of his mercies that we are not consumed. But we must not stay longer here. Jesus displays his riches to us in his priestly office, in that he is also our sacrifice. Oh, here are riches indeed : "By one offering he hath for ever perfected them that are sanctified." He is our offering as well as our priest. He entered within the veil with his own blood, not the blood of others. Holy in himself as priest, holy in his person, his sacrifice is perfect and complete. He presented an offering which God our Father accepted, and was well pleased with. By the sacrifice of himself, sin was condemned in his flesh, and for ever put away. God's law was honoured and magnified, divine justice was satisfied, the sinner is saved, and glory redounds to the name of Jesus, whose name is above every name. Oh, the riches of that blood to avail for the propitiation of an offended God, to avail for the pardon of sin of so many millions of the human race; it is beyond our utmost conceptions. Oh, have you ever felt the wrath of God against sin in your own conscience ? have you ever had a sight of the numerousness, the enormity, the infinity of your own personal sins ? and have you ever had a faith's view of the blood of Jesus cleansing you from ALL sin ? If so, did you not feel his blood most rich, most precious, that it should take away all guilt from your conscience ? Oh, yes, I am sure you did; it was the greatness of his Person as the Son of God that gave such merit, such efficacy, such power to his atoning blood ; such riches as will provide for all the ransomed church of God while time shall last; and when they have ceased sinning, still his blood will be as rich as ever, and will be the theme of their adoring gratitude and praise. As in Rev. i. 5, "Unto him who hath loved us, and washed us from our sins in his own blood."

And, oh, how sweetly the riches of his priestly office are proved by the church and enjoyed, in the fact of his being their intercessor. The church in this militant state needs such an intercessor as Christ is, his Person as God-man mediator so well qualifies him for this indispensable office. He ever liveth to make intercession for all who come unto God by him. As sinners in ourselves, how could we hope for acceptance at the throne of mercy but by virtue of our great High Priest pleading for us in the high court of heaven? for so long as we are upon this earth we are within gunshot of the enemy of our souls, and shall always need the assistance, the powerful assistance, of our ever-living intercessor. We are constantly offending, but he is constantly interceding. Oh, the exceeding riches of his grace. The much incense of his prayer avails. He has prayed for us, and therefore our faith fails not; we are strengthened with strength in our souls by reason of his intercession. As man, he knows our weaknesses, he knows all our complaints; as God, he has all power in heaven and in the earth. He has power also with his Father; he pleads his own sacrifice. He pleads our cause when we have not a word to plead, and succeeds in carrying it to a safe and glorious issue.

And no less glorious are the riches of his priestly office displayed than in his being our righteous advocate with the Father. Oh, to have such an advocate in the high court of heaven, when the poor sinner is overtaken by sin, tripped up by the devil and thrown down in the mire of his guilt. Defiled and loathsome as we are, to whom can we go but to Jesus our advocate? where can we go but to the throne of mercy? But, oh, that cruel enemy of our souls, Satan, he is there to resist us, to oppose us, to accuse us; and it is all true what our indictment styles us. We are already self-condemned, but Jesus is our advocate; he rebukes the enemy of our souls, and sets us free from condemnation. Oh, wondrous riches of our advocate; his merits as "the righteous" advocate are made over to us; we are cleansed, clothed afresh, set at happy liberty. Satan is nonplussed and defeated. Then again, there is an ungodly world and a false professing church. How they accuse the true child of God! Ever and anon the poor soul is shamefully aspersed and misrepresented, thrust as it were in the stocks and cruelly treated; but Jesus is our advocate, he appears on our behalf, he bids us wait patiently for him, and not to fret because of him who bringeth wicked devices to pass. Oh, the riches of his advocacy; he brings forth in his own good time our righteousness as the noon-day light, and enables us to set the world and carnal professors at defiance, and to rejoice in him as our ever-abiding friend and pleader.

3. His *Kingly* Office. This embraces his *Government, Providence,* and *Protection.* Here we have the mediatorial character of our blessed Lord displayed in its widest and fullest extent. The worlds of nature and of grace are under his dominion, and from him have their support. His power and authority is over all creatures, whether under the earth, on the earth, or above the earth. Heaven is his throne. Justice and judgment are the habitation of his throne. The riches he possesses in his mediatorial offices as Prophet, Priest, and King are underived, eternal, coexistent, and inseparable. It would be fearful to suppose that Jesus was invested with his different offices at different times, or that he acts at one time according to one, and at another time according to another. We have already concluded that the eternity of his Person is the foundation of his riches as Mediator, and therefore from the very first he must have been possessed of the powers of all his offices; and in every part of his work they must have all come into operation: "For it pleased the Father that in him," his Son, "should all fulness dwell;" "the fulness of the Godhead bodily." At no time was he without it, and therefore perish the thought that any given point of time should make Jesus what he is. Let it, therefore, be borne in mind that his mediatorial dominion and his propitiatory sacrifice are inseparable. He sits a Priest upon his throne. Numerous are the Scriptures which set forth Christ as King, but a few shall suffice here: Heb. iv. 14; x. 12, 13; Zech. ix. 9; Song iii. 11; Isa. xxxiii. 17; Ps. cxlix. 2; Isa. vi. 5. The government is laid upon his shoulders. All power is given unto him both in heaven and on earth.

We might pursue this theme to an inconceivable extent. It cannot be fathomed. The majesty of his kingdom is glorious; it is derived from his Person as the Son of God. As it behoved Christ to suffer, so it behoved Christ to conquer; "for he must reign till he hath put all enemies under his feet." His threefold offices complete his mediatorial work and character. He is a perfect and complete Saviour. As the Priest for the sins of

God's chosen, he has made ample and all-sufficient atonement; our ransom is effected, and there is now no condemnation. As our Prophet, the glad tidings he publishes and makes known to the wounded conscience, that the curse of the law and of sin has been removed. As our King, he gives effect to all he has done by applying the word, for without the word of a king there is no power; then it is the heart believes. It is the regal authority which Christ possesses that gives such power to his sacrifice and intercession. To this end was his incarnation. (John xviii. 37.) And, oh, how this fact brings his personal dignity into near relationship with the subjects of his spiritual kingdom! Not only was it necessary he should reign over men, devils, and angels; but, to qualify him for ruling over man, it would appear requisite that he should possess human nature. The height of his personal dignity as the Son of God seems to preclude the possibility of this relationship to his subjects; but by the mystery of the incarnation this obstruction is taken away; by the Son of God taking into union our nature with his person, he became also the Son of man: "The Word was made flesh." He who, as God, was so far removed above all that was human, was, as man, qualified for possessing and exercising all the tender sympathies of humanity. He, as man, is touched with a feeling sense of our infirmities, and, as God, is fitted to rule in the hearts of his people with all the sensibilities of a brother beloved. We may, therefore, come boldly to the throne of grace, "because the King is near of kin to us."

Time would fail altogether to refer to his riches, in particular as our King. His *extensive knowledge* of all his subjects is amazing, and is truly comforting. He knows all their names, the places of their abode, their circumstances, and all their wants: "I know all the fowls of the mountain." (Psalm l. 11.) Oh what *wisdom* he possesses to direct and dispose of all our intricate affairs; what *power* to execute, what *might* and authority, what dignity, what unbounded compassion, tender mercy; what loving-kindness and bountifulness. All these regal qualifications meet in the Person of Messiah, the Prince of peace, the King of kings and Lord of lords. Of his dominion there shall be no end; his kingdom is an everlasting kingdom, and his dominion "endureth for ever throughout all generations."

Such, therefore, being the nature and character of Christ as our King, we, who are the favoured subjects of his kingdom in grace, cannot but rejoice in his divine administration. (Ps. cxlix. 2.) He rules by love and in love. He controls all events in the world for the welfare of his body, the church. The world itself, with all its nations, their national, political, and commercial affairs, are all under his government; their destinies are subjected to his will and authority; the principalities and powers of the air, the spiritual wickedness that rules in high places, are all under his surveillance, and render obedience to his almighty fiat. His church is under his government; the spiritual enemies of our souls, such as pride, unbelief, self-will, evil desires, and all the corruptions of our nature, are kept in curb by his controlling influence. He lifts up a standard against Satan, that great enemy of our souls' peace, comfort, and progress in the divine life; he is a chained enemy, and is ever held under restraint. Even death itself, the last enemy, even he shall be destroyed by the brightness of his coming, for he is the King of glory, the Lord strong and mighty, mighty in battle.

And O how the riches of his regal character are displayed in his *Providence:* "He opens his hand and satisfieth the desire of every living thing. (Ps. cxlv. 16.) While he graciously supplies his church with all their gifts, graces, and blessings as needed, he cares for all their personal necessities. Poor tried child of God, with that solitary piece of money in your pocket, how often your heart has ached in looking at it, not knowing what way to take, what to do for the best. Jesus, your King, has his kind eye over you. He will direct you and bless you. O look, look again: "He overrules all mortal things, and manages your mean affairs." Think not that your trifles are beneath his notice. O no; he made every grain of sand; he knows their number, and every grain has its appointed place. All your trials are known to him; they are dealt out to you in weight and measure by his infinite wisdom—

> " They come in his appointed hour,
> Clad with a high commission'd power,
> Perform the purpose of his heart,
> Engender good, and then depart."

Remember, he is the mighty God of Jacob; still the same God to you as he was to Jacob. O to be favoured with the spirit of wrestling prayer, in the long, dark night of trial, affliction, and poverty. May it be yours to say and know, "Happy is he that hath the mighty God of Jacob for his help." (Ps. cxlvi. 5.) Yes, if your circumstances are ever so miserable in the world, yet in Christ you have peace. He bids you remember it: "In the world ye shall have tribulation, but,"—O that blessed but!—"in me ye *have* peace." You have it now. "Ah," say you, "I wish I could feel it." Well, I wish you did; but you *have* it for all that. Come, be of good cheer, Jesus is your King; he has overcome the world; the sorrows of this life shall not take away your peace, though you are disturbed about it. All your needs shall be supplied from his riches in glory by Christ Jesus. God grant you, by his Spirit, a sweet application of his promise to your own soul, for his name's sake.

Further, how delightful to consider that, as Jesus is our King, he is our *Protector*. Speak we of power? His arm is strong. The Angel of the Lord encampeth round them that fear him, and delivereth them. He surrounds them with defence from every foe, spiritual, sensual, or worldly. He guards all his pilgrims through the desert. He is their sun and shield. Our enemies are numerous, lively, and strong, but he has a fulness of power. The Lord God is a man of war; he is competent to deal with every kind of foe, subtle as they may be; he comprehends their mischievous designs and devices, and will overthrow them in the midst. Remember, he is called King of Saints, the highest title of king. He is your king. He will act as your king. Are you timid? Does not this encourage you? Are you desponding? Does not this animate you? Are you faint and weary? He will give you strength. He will go before you, and lead you on in the way of his steps.

3. The riches of Christ are pre-eminently so, by the witness which is borne to them both in the Word of God and in our own experience.

John the Divine says, (i. 14,) "The Word was made flesh, and dwelt among us, full of grace and truth." Here is the double testimony which every true believer in Christ possesses. What God's word says, the soul may rely on; and when the Spirit applies it to the conscience, the soul is sure to believe it; indeed, there is no true belief of God's word but in this way. Come, my hearer, is this the way you are made to know God's word to be true ? There is no true knowledge of Jesus Christ but by a divine revelation of God the Father, and by the application of God the Holy Ghost. No salvation without it— no condemnation with it. Jesus is full of grace and truth. How rich he must be! What unnumbered millions of the human race have been enriched by him, in all grace, love, and goodness, and will ever continue to be, through all time and to all eternity; and yet he is as rich as ever. His bounty has not impoverished him. He is as full of truth as he is of grace. He is to be trusted for everything:

"Take him for strength and righteousness;
Make him your refuge in distress;
Love him above all earthly joy,
And him in everything employ."

You must excuse the repetition of that sweet verse. It can do you no harm to hear it again; for, if your experience corresponds to the precious doctrine it contains, your salvation is as sure as God's throne.

He is full of grace and truth; and the apostle adds, "And of his fulness have all we received, and grace for grace." O how suited is such a rich Saviour to such poor miserable sinners as we are! We are nothing without him; but by him we are enriched in every grace and gift—acceptable to God the Father through him—perfect in his righteousness, strong in his strength. All grace is made to abound toward us. *Adopting* grace. "The Spirit beareth witness with our spirit, that we are the children of God; and, because we are sons, God hath sent forth the Spirit of his Son into our hearts, whereby we cry, Abba, Father. Here, you see, is the realization of our union to Christ our Head and Elder Brother; a union of relationship. What riches can a poor soul want more, if he is made thus to feel his adoption in Christ? How easy, then, to trace the source of it to the predestinating love of God the Father, choosing his Person in Christ, blessing him with all spiritual blessings in heavenly places in him before the world began; and if, as geologists say, this world was in existence many thousand years before man was placed on it; then how glorious they unwittingly make the grace of God to appear! What treasures of grace in Christ are thereby displayed! His church secured in him,—all their persons, their grace, and their glory, all treasured up in him, ages and ages before the world began. And O, the riches of his *pardoning* grace! Did you ever have a revelation made to you of the infiniteness of your sins?—inconceivably numerous, and yet his pardoning blood has swelled above the sea of your sins, follies, and thoughts. His blood availing for all your sins, all my sins, and the whole of the sins of an elect world—millions upon millions. O how rich the grace! Thus it has ever been—thus it now is, and ever shall be, world without end. Sweet theme for the poet and every blood-bought child of God. They can sing—

> " Dear dying Lamb, thy precious blood
> Shall never lose its power,
> Till all the ransom'd church of God
> Be saved to sin no more."

3. Look, too, at the riches of his *sanctifying* grace. How it has cleansed our spotted souls from deepest dye; again and again it cleanses the conscience. And remember, too, the riches of this grace are to be viewed as the *personal* acts of Jesus, not the influence of our knowledge. Sweet as may be the knowledge of this truth, our knowledge is not the influence, not the power, by which we are freed and set at liberty. It is a personal act of God's Spirit upon the soul. O, then, how rich the grace! Repeated acts of transgression as often cleansed. This is not to allow the believer to live in sin. No, God forbid! but to save him from its commission. Sin would damn him, but grace shall save him. It separates him from the world, its company, its influence, its maxims, and its pursuits. Jesus is rich in sanctifying grace.

4. He is rich also in *justifying* grace: "In the Lord shall all the seed of Israel be justified and shall glory." (Isa. xlv. 25.) In his sight as God only, no flesh can be justified. O the riches, therefore, his people possess in him as Mediator! In him, as the God-man, they have righteousness. His justifying grace is that free gift which hath abounded unto many offences. Here we see the exceeding riches of his grace: "For if, through one man's offence, many be dead, much more the grace of God and the gift by grace, which is by one man, Jesus Christ, *hath abounded unto many.* (Rom. v. 15, 16.) O the glorious contrast between our federal head, Adam, and our ever-living Head, Jesus Christ. Adam's one offence beggared us all; but, by the righteousness of

Christ, believers stand for ever justified from all things. Satan condemns, conscience condemns, ungodly men condemn, worldly professors condemn, but Jesus acquits: "Who is he that condemneth? It is God that justifieth; it is Christ that died." Believer, here is your standing, here is your safety. If you are walking after the Spirit, and not after the flesh, there can be no condemnation to you. Walking after the Spirit may be said to be an outward sign, a proof of an inward and spiritual grace—a grace as free as it is rich.

5. *Preserving grace.* Preserved until called. The ministry of angelic hosts is employed to secure the persons of those who shall be heirs of salvation. (Heb. i. 14.) Satan seems aware of this. How low he drags some into the depths of iniquity. What easy fools some of us have been to his delusive snares. Some have been snatched as brands from the eternal burning, and they can sing with Kent—

> " Preserved in Jesus when my feet made haste to hell;
>   And there I should have gone, but thou dost all things well;
>   Thy love was great, thy mercy free,
>   Which from the pit deliver'd me."

6. *Persevering grace.* Here the riches of our Saviour God again appear. Midst numerous snares and gilded baits—with a tendency of one's old nature to draw us back to perdition—the unyielding opposition of one's old master the devil, grace is given to persevere to the end. The saints' final perseverance is guaranteed in the covenant of grace, backed by many exceeding great and precious promises. "The righteous shall hold on his way." "The path of the just is as the shining light, that shineth more and more unto the perfect day." I know many of God's dear children, if not all at times, sometimes think that this sin, or that temptation, will overcome them. It is true they are weak, but Jesus is strong; and we are confident of this very thing, "that he who hath begun a good work in you, will perform it until the day of Jesus Christ."

> " Whom once he receives, his Spirit ne'er leaves,
>   Nor ever repents of the grace that he gives."

7. *Crowning grace.* Here the riches of Jehovah Jesus are displayed in unsullied brilliancy to all his people: "The Lord will give grace and glory." (Psa. lxxxiv.) "I give unto my sheep eternal life." "Father, I *will*

that they also whom thou hast given me, be with me where I am, that they may behold my glory which thou hast given me "—(John xvii. 24)—his mediatorial glory and his primeval glory as the Eternal Son of God. Our Redeemer possesses both and dispenses both. His people shall eternally behold him crowned with glory and honour, crowned with many crowns. He possesses a fulness of glory. He has it in himself: "For it pleased the Father that in him should all fulness dwell; in his glorified presence there is fulness of joy, and at his right hand there are pleasures for evermore." O the glories that await the church of God: "The eye hath not seen, nor hath the ear heard, nor hath it entered the heart of man to conceive the things which God hath prepared for them that love him." We must die to know it. Crowns of joy and everlasting songs await each believer as he enters the pearly gates of the heavenly city. O, then, to see Jesus as he is. This will make amends for all the tribulation and anguish endured in this world. We shall lose sight of it all in one glance of the altogether loveliness of his Person.

> "His grace will be our song and boast,
> And Christ our all in all."

But I see your time is gone. I must hasten to a conclusion. My third head, the *unsearchableness* of Christ's riches, I cannot enter upon to-night, and I have one or two more things to say yet before I can dismiss this portion of the subject.

There is in Christ "*durable riches* and righteousness. Riches and honour are with him." His fruit is better than gold, yea, than fine gold; and my revenue than choice silver. I lead in the way of righteousness, in the midst of the paths of judgment, that I may cause those that love me to inherit substance, and I will fill their treasures." (Prov. viii. 21.) Now, the sum and substance of all that Christ is and can be to his people may be summed up in three words—LIGHT, LIFE, and POWER. These are durable riches, substance; it is the essence of true religion, and there is no religion worth the name if it be without these primary elements. My friends, look to yourselves, see that your religion consists of light, life, and power. If it have not, depend upon it, it is the wrong sort, it will never take you to where Christ is; and let me say too, light, life, and power are the characteristics of the ministry which God employs in his church. Wherever there is a deficiency of these elements in the preaching of the word, be it ever so sound in the letter, you may rely upon it, God is neither blessing the word nor owning the preacher as his servant. He may be a man of God, but not his servant in the Gospel. I do not, of course, mean by light, life, and power, mere intellectual acumen, loudness of voice, and forcibleness of manner. These are but natural gifts and proper in their place; were I possessed of them I could not be sufficiently thankful, but I must contend for a vital religion, a vital ministry, apart from everything that may be naturally good in itself. Nothing less will satisfy me, nor ought it to satisfy you. Now in Christ there is a fulness of spiritual light, of spiritual life and spiritual power. It is associated with and derivable from his threefold offices of Prophet, Priest, and King. When Christ reveals himself to us as our Prophet, we have light, for he is light in his essence, he is the light, the true light. Every believer renewed in the spirit of his mind, is translated from darkness to light, and is made light in the Lord. Have you any such light as this—light *in* Christ, light *from* Christ, a light *to* Christ? Thus is it when Christ is made known to us as our Priest; his sacrificial death is our life. Not only so, but he is life too in its essence. "In him was life, and the life was the light of men." (John i. 4.) Now, do pray observe this, the life in Christ becomes to us our light; therefore whatever light you have see that it is derived from life in Christ. Light without life is a very poor sort of religion, I assure you. "True religion is more than notion, something must be known and *felt*." You will ask me what I mean by power—active energy, life in activity, the Spirit of God energising the soul, it is the kingly office of Christ carried out by the Spirit under his authority. It is the soul's experience of the demonstration of the Spirit with power. If you are believers united to Christ by a true and living faith, you will know what I mean. I have my own way of expressing the truths I preach, but truth is ever the same, no matter the phraseology of the speaker. A man may be a fool, even a maniac, but if he be a child of God he knows what is light, life, and power. A few days since I was told of a poor female, a maniac; after her death, Hart's hymns, which had been in her possession, was found to have had written on the title-page, "Light, Life, and Power." When I heard it I said, "Oh how striking! the very characteristics of his hymns." Poor creature! she was bereft of reason as to this world, but her soul was perfectly sane; she knew the light, life, and power of God's truth, and I could well understand her feeling as to so express it in regard to that all but inspired book. Naturally, I expect, the *poetic* conveyance of truth to her soul was *underanged*, for I well recollect another similar case, poor John Batt. He was a lunatic; his mind was sadly out of tune with rational things, but upon soul matters, provided they were expressed in the language of Hart's or Kent's hymns, he was perfectly conscious, and exhibited superior intelligence in spiritual truths and a deep-felt experience. It was my mercy to be well acquainted with both those choice books, and it was my privilege, and there were but few others who had it, to hold sweet fellowship with this poor lunatic in this peculiar channel. Here you have, then, an illustration of the nature of divine things, how distinct and separate it is from things of this world or the religion of the flesh. The religion of the present day, that is, its public profession, is made very attractive, both to the eye, the ear, and the carnal judgment; but the circumstantials of God's worship and of the profession of his name may be made as worldly and as fashionable as any matters of business. Indeed, it is my sad lot to see that it is "*business*" which has very largely crept into religion, but, ah! there is no light, life, and power in all this. I grant there is much activity, but no life; mechanical activity, not spiritual life. I dare say you think me very harsh, but I speak the truth and lie not.

But one word more, and I have done. What riches there are in Christ as the salvation of his people, his glory is great in our salvation. What a fulness of salvation! "With the Lord there is plenteous redemption." (Ps. cxxx. 7.) "He saves to the uttermost all who come unto God by him." (Heb. vii. 25.) He saved his church before time by becoming their surety. This shows how great his riches are; for who would accept a surety but where his sufficiency was undoubted and well known? Jesus is able; he is mighty to save; he is an all-sufficient Saviour. All-sufficient was his one offering when he, as the substitute of his church, made a full expiation for all their guilt. Saved with an everlasting salvation. Saved in time from the power of inbred sin, salvation within as well as salvation without. O the riches of his mercy and his power! There is an illimitableness both as to his grace and his ability. It reaches, too, over and beyond the most extreme case of misery and danger that can be supposed. God's uttermost cannot possibly be reached by the loftiest stretch of the human intellect. The uttermost of Christ's salvation and the uttermost of the sinner's ruin are without comparison or parallel. "For as the heavens are higher than the earth, so are God's thoughts above ours;" and the riches of his grace are quite as much above our sin, misery, and poverty. We may know all the depths of our own evil, as did Hezekiah, but it is impossible ever to know the extent of the heart of Christ. The most desperate case of deep sorrow, whether of soul or of circumstances, can be met by a single promise of his grace. A line of a hymn, one word, one look, will hush the storm of the soul into a calm.

" One look from that dear Lord whose brow compassion wears,
    Will much of heavenly bliss afford, e'en in this vale of tears."

But I think I can hear some poor disconsolate soul saying, "Ah, sir, you have said many glowing things about the person of Christ and his riches, and I believe it all; but it does not remove the sense of my deep misery. I have heard all you have said for this hour past, but not one word has reached my case." Poor soul! you are indeed in a low place. I would that I could draw you out. I see where you are, and the plight you are in. You are not so much half starved as that you are half dead. It is not so much the food of the gospel that you want as it is some cordial dropped into your fainting soul; you want strength in your soul. May God help you. God only can give it. O cry mightily to him, "he will come and save you;" he has bound himself to do it. David has been where you are, and he has recorded it for your encouragement: "In the day when I cried thou answeredst me and strengthenedst me in my soul." (Ps. cxxxviii. 3.) But you say, "I am weary with crying, I have no more strength." Well then, look and look again, help will come. Jesus himself has been there before you; he knows your case. His soul was exceeding sorrowful, even unto death. His bodily weakness was extreme; his nervous power was quite gone when he fell on the ground in Gethsemane. I am sure you have never been so low as that, or ever will.

> " What he endured no tongue can tell."

He sustained a weight which none but an incarnate God could bear. Jesus knows *where* you are and *how* you are. "When your spirit is overwhelmed within you," as in deep waters drowning, sinking under, still he knows your path. (Ps. cxlii. 3.) He can see through the depth of your sorrows. He knows where to find you, and will send you help and deliverance. You will yet say, " Thou which hast showed me great and sore troubles shalt quicken me again, and bring me up again from the depths of the earth."

> " He knows how weak and faint thou art,
>   And must appear at length;
> A look from him will cheer thy heart,
>   And bring renewed strength."

I must now leave the subject for further consideration, if the Lord will, till this night week. I must pass over such inferences as might be suitable for closing this discourse. I fully intended to have said something as to the riches of the various characters Jesus bears to his people as their Shepherd, Husband, Friend, and so on, as well also of the various similitudes that are used to express what he is to us as the Bread and Water of Life, our Dwelling, our Sun and Shield, but may perhaps refer to them when we attempt to take up the remaining part, "the *unsearchableness* of his riches." " I commend you to God and to the word of his grace." Let us conclude with a word of prayer.

UNSEARCHABLE RICHES OF CHRIST.

III.

The Unsearchable Riches of Christ.—EPHESIANS iii. 8.

THOUGH this is the third time I have called your attention to these words, I trust your patience is not exhausted. The text contains a most glorious and inexhaustible subject; and, if our hearts are kept in tune by the sacred Spirit,

"No sweeter subject can invite
The sinner's heart to sing."

We proposed to treat our subject under three general heads: 1st. The Person of Christ; 2nd. His riches; and 3rd. Their unsearchableness.

We have spoken in the first discourse on *the Person of Christ,* as the Son of God; in the second, we touched a little upon *his riches,* (chiefly those of his mediatorial character,) which concern us; but I found it impossible to say all I intended; the subject grew so much in my mind while speaking. I therefore announced taking the third head, *their unsearchableness,* for this evening. O that the Spirit of all truth would again help us to see the beauties of our beloved Lord, and the unbounded love of his heart in becoming what he is to us, that we may be filled with all the fulness of God. There is something very exhilarating when, through the Spirit, we are enabled to contemplate such divine realities. It fills the soul with heavenly raptures. We can then fully enter into the feeling of the poet when he sang,

"O could I speak the matchless worth,
O could I sound the glories forth,
    Which in my Saviour shine,
I'd soar and touch the heavenly strings,
And vie with Gabriel while he sings
    In notes almost divine."

No. 16.

We come now to notice, in the THIRD place, the *unsearchableness* of Christ's riches.

The riches of Christ, as I have already intimated, are those blessings which God the Father hath bestowed upon his church, in the Person of Christ his Son, and are revealed to us in the gospel through the Spirit. They are called riches on account of their excellency, fulness, and variety. They are bestowed in such abundance as to supply all our wants, and dispensed in such manner as to be suited to all our necessities.

The riches of Christ are called *unsearchable* riches. By unsearchableness, we mean they are *undiscoverable by human reason*, and, as far as they can be known, can only be known by revelation. The men of this world cannot know them; they desire not to know them; "they say unto God, Depart from us, for we desire not the knowledge of thy ways." (Job xxi. 14.) Hence it is, "the natural man receiveth not the things of the Spirit of God; for they are foolishness unto him; neither can he know them, for they are spiritually discerned. (1 Cor. ii. 14.) Hence it is, too, they are called "mysteries,"—"the deep things of God." The apostle says, "We speak the wisdom of God in a mystery, even the hidden wisdom, which God ordained before the world unto our glory." (1 Cor. ii. 7.) In the chapter in which our text stands, (verses 3 and 4,) he tells you it was by revelation that the mystery of Christ was made known to him. It is utterly impossible for carnal reason to know anything of the unsearchableness of Christ's riches; for it is written: "Eye hath not seen, nor ear heard, neither have entered into the heart of man, the things which God hath prepared for them that love him. But God hath revealed them unto us by his Spirit; for the Spirit searcheth all things, yea, the deep things of God." (1 Cor. ii. 9, 10.)

As the riches of Christ were unsearchable to reason, so we find they were but imperfectly known to the prophets in other ages, and, in fact, unknown to the Gentiles, (like the light of some distant planet, which has been long travelling to our earth, and but recently perceived,) so Christ is more fully displayed to us in the gospel of the New Testament than in that of the Old Testament. Doubtless, the spiritual Jews, in the Levitical dispensation, understood much of Christ, both in the ceremonies of their religion and in their wilderness life; indeed, the

apostle states as much, as you will find in his 1st Epistle
to the Corinthians x. 1–4.

> " The types and shadows were a glass,
>   In which they saw the Saviour's face."

The riches of Christ are of *priceless* value.   There is
no standard or comparison by which they can be estimated.   We are "bought with a price;" "None can redeem his brother."   "Rivers of oil and thousands of rams
for a burnt-offering, nor the gift of one's first-born, could
never take away sin," (Micah vi. 7,) and ransom us from
the bondage of God's law; but the blood of Christ has
redeemed unnumbered millions of the human race.
Worlds could not save a lost soul.   It is a question that
has never yet been answered: "What shall a man give in
exchange for his soul?" (Mark viii. 37.)   Who, then, can
conceive of the love of God in the unspeakable gift of his
Son, by whose precious blood so many millions of the
human race have been redeemed." (1 Pet. i. 19.)

> " Great was the price to Justice due,
>   When Jesus would redeem his bride;
>   Nothing but precious blood would do,
>   And that must flow from his own side.

> "Not gems nor gold could bring our peace,
>   Nor the whole world's collected store,
>   Suffice to purchase our release;—
>   A thousand worlds were all too poor."

The value, then, of Christ's riches can be known only
by knowing him.   His riches and his Person are inseparable.   The one cannot be known without the other.
The knowledge of Christ is knowing something of his
riches; the more we know of him, the more we shall discover the unsearchableness of his riches.   This will lead
us to notice,

1. *His riches are unsearchable, being grounded on
his eternal Deity.*   In my last discourse you may remember I stated, " the riches of Christ were grounded *on his
Sonship*;" how they came to us through his Mediatorship; and by virtue of that relationship to his Father and
to us, as being our divine Head and Elder Brother.   This
time we have not so much to refer as to what his riches
are, as to the great fact that they are unsearchable; and
this I say, that, being grounded on his eternal Deity, they
are unsearchable.   Our Lord Jesus Christ in his divine

Person, essence, nature, and glory, is eternal, incomprehensible, omnipresent, and omnipotent. Now, we have before shown that the Son of God is eternal by virtue of that the Father is eternal, and therefore no more need be said upon this at present. It may not appear very obvious just at this moment what we mean by his riches being grounded on his eternal Sonship, and their unsearchableness being founded on his eternal Deity; the distinction, I hope, will be seen by-and-by. Pray for illumination; pray for me, that I may be able to make known unto you something of these unsearchable riches. It is impossible to *comprehend* them; but, under the Spirit's leadings, we may apprehend, that is, take hold, of a part, though we cannot grasp all. You are of course fully aware that I hold the Scriptures teach that the Sonship of Christ is founded on his divinity, not on his humanity. His divinity being essentially eternal, his personality is eternal, his Sonship is eternal. There is no material difference, it is true, between the terms Sonship and his personality; for the one is as the other; yet to us believers there is, in some respects, a distinction as to the benefits we derive from his Sonship, and from its being eternal. You may remember, perhaps, I said in the first discourse (page 5) his name, "the Son of God," is "both a name of nature and of relationship." It is in view of the latter, *of relationship*, what he is to us in that relationship, that we have what are considered the riches of Christ; and it is in respect of his *nature* being eternally divine, that we have the fact on which is founded the *unsearchableness* of his riches. This is a weighty subject. It may seem abstruse to some, but it is far from being unprofitable to consider. If the Son of God is not eternal, as some assert, then his riches are not unsearchable. If the Sonship of Christ is founded on his incarnation, as some believe, then his riches are not unsearchable. If the Sonship of Christ has only respect to the covenant of grace, as is very commonly entertained, then his riches are not unsearchable. In either case, in which the eternity of Christ's Sonship is denied, we have *data* upon which we can fix. Say, for argument sake, Christ's Person, as the Son of God, is founded on his complex nature; then his riches date, say, some 1860 years back. We have a beginning of a human calculation. I may be told, "We believe his divine nature is eternal." Yes, I know that, my friend; but you separate his divine nature from his Personality as the Son of God, for which you have no warrant. You are without a foundation. This is not the truth of God as revealed in his word.

And so I regard the opinion of those good men who hold that the Person of the Son of God is coeval only with the covenant of grace. Here, I think, as I have said before, is a very defective view of Christ's Person. He is the Son of God, irrespective of that great transaction. What! would there have been no Son of God, no God the Father, no God the Holy Ghost, if there had been no covenant of grace? O, I think we are not laying a right, a sufficient foundation for the unsearchableness of Christ's riches. Can they be bounded by the extent of his mediatorial work? Assuredly not. It is not the covenant of grace that gave rise to the existence of the ever-blessed Trinity of Persons in the Godhead; but it was the revelation of that covenant which discovered to us the previous constitution, if I might so say, of Jehovah, as the Father, the Word, and the Spirit, out of which and from whom originated the great scheme of man's redemption. Many divines deny this; but men of science would not talk thus. If they discover a planet, either by the help of some powerful optical instrument, or from its light having at length reached our earth, they would tell us the planet had existed long previously to their perception of it. I grant readily that all the blessings with which the Church is blessed in Christ their Head are coeval with the predestinating love of God the Father; but *the Person* of Christ is *anterior* to his Mediatorship, not *posterior*, or even coeval; and, therefore, the unsearchableness of his riches is over, and above, and beyond the boundary of the covenant of grace. Tell me the period when the covenant was made; tell me the number of the elect, the number of their blessings; then we have some approximation to the height, the depth, the length, and breadth of the riches of Christ.

But, again. If the Sonship of Christ is founded on *the pre-existence of his human soul*, then his riches are not unsearchable; for if these wise men after the flesh, who declare Christ's human soul to have had a pre-existence before all other creatures be correct, they must necessarily limit the extent of his riches; for with them the human soul is the foundation of their fancy Son of God. This they assert to give some pretension to his eternity. Now, if men are so wise as to be able to trace out an unrevealed fact, as this their dogma, then they are able to trace the age of Christ's riches. This, we know, is out of their ken. Secret things belong to God; but things revealed, to us and our children. To my own mind, I see the only correct view we can take of the unsearchableness of Christ's riches is from the fact of his Sonship being eternal. He is the only true and wise God. Limited views of his Person must confine us to limited views of his riches. O, my friends, why should our faith fear to tread on such high and holy ground as we are now attempting? I admit the theme is deep, it is high. What can we know? Such knowledge is too wonderful for us; we cannot attain unto it; our best thoughts are but poor. It is impossible to grasp it; it is infinite; but still we may, if only for a few minutes, survey a single drop of this eternal ocean, and see in it worlds of beauties, as revealed to the eye of faith. The divinity and eternity of Christ's Sonship and Person can be the only sure ground of his riches being unsearchable, unfathomable, inexhaustible, unknowable. All other views are contracted, and savour of human systems. I remember once hearing an anecdote of a Mexican ambassador visiting the treasurer of the Spanish kingdom. The chancellor showed him a large chest filled with coined gold. The ambassador began to dig with his hand, to find the depth of it. "What are you doing?" asked the Spaniard. "O," replied the Mexican, "I am trying to find if there is a bottom." "Of course there is," said the other. "Ah, but," rejoined the Mexican, "my master has a treasury which has no bottom. He has mines of gold in his possession. Yours will soon be spent—his will last for ever." I leave you to make the application. We will now pass on to notice,

2. *That the glorious attributes of Christ's divine Person display the unsearchableness of his riches.*

I feel to be venturing on holy ground; but we are not alone. Prophets and apostles have been before us; we have his word for our guide, and therefore we may approach this great subject, though with the most profound awe and admiration.

The apostle Paul, in 1 Cor. i. 30, says of the Church of God in Christ Jesus, "Who of God is made unto us

wisdom, and righteousness, and sanctification, and redemption." O what a revelation is here of Jesus Christ!
What he is unto us by virtue of his Godhead, not his
manhood; for, perfect as he was in his human nature,—
holy, harmless, and undefiled, separate from sinners, made
higher than the heavens,—yet that is not the source of
his riches being unsearchable. They come to us unquestionably by virtue of his Mediatorship—the God-man.
The union of our nature to his Person makes them available to us; but it is in his Person, being the eternal
God, that they are unsearchable.

Let us try, by a step at a time, with the help and blessing of the Lord, to get a nearer view of this amazing truth.
Christ is of God made unto us *wisdom*. The wisdom of
God made available to us by him. He is our wisdom.
Being blessed with all spiritual blessings in him, we are
blessed with wisdom, a fulness of wisdom; " for it
pleased the Father that in him should all fulness dwell."
" In him are hid all the treasures of wisdom and knowledge." O what heavenly wisdom was needed for such a
scheme of mercy as is revealed in the gospel! *The wisdom of God in a mystery.* The more it is pondered over,
the greater, the deeper, it appears; because the more we
search, the more vast its unsearchableness appears. It is
utterly impossible for the finite to grasp the infinite. O
what wisdom is revealed in the method by which God can
be just, and yet the justifier of him that believeth in
Jesus! Wisdom in originating the plan; wisdom in
executing it; wisdom in displaying it; wisdom in exercising his love, sovereignty, and goodness; wisdom to us
as our wonderful Counsellor, our Prophet, and Teacher;
and, as it is of his fulness that every member of his
church receives grace for grace, so wisdom is communicated to every member by the eternal Spirit as he
needs it.

Another step. He is made unto us *righteousness*. I
do not mean that righteousness which he wrought out
and brought in, and which is imputed to all, and is upon
all them that truly believe—namely, his actual obedience;
for that is our justification in fact: but I mean that
righteousness which he possesses in his divine essence as
God. "Who *of God* is made unto us *righteousness*."
Here is a vast ocean before us indeed, every drop of
which would require eternity to fathom. The church of

God have their righteousness in him. (Isa. liv. 17.) " In
Jehovah have I righteousness and strength." (Isa. xlv. 24.)
He is the source of all holiness, goodness, justice, and
truth; the spring of all our holiness, and every grace
proceeding from it, by which we walk worthy before the
Lord unto all well-pleasing, is in God. His name is *that,*
because it is the perfection of his nature. It is a name
of nature, and fully expresses his Divine nature; and it
is also a name of relationship, as well as of his Person.
This is his name whereby he shall be called, " THE LORD
OUR RIGHTEOUSNESS." (Jer. xxiii. 6.)   We are made
partakers of this divine nature by the Spirit, in being
born again, not of corruptible seed, but of incorruptible
seed, of the word of God, which liveth and abideth for
ever; and all believers vitally united to Christ as their
ever-living Head are called by the same name. (Jer.
xxxiii. 16.) This righteousness is unsearchable. As
utterly impossible as it is for the creature to measure and
know the Creator, so is it impossible to search and comprehend the righteousness of his Person.

We travel but slowly yet: another step. He is made
unto us, of God, *sanctification.* This I regard as the
third element in our salvation. To sanctify is to set
apart, to separate to holy purposes. I regard this, therefore, as meaning that God is in himself *all that* for which
God chose the church in Christ. Chosen in Christ that
we should be holy and without blame before him in love,
to the praise and glory of his grace who accepted us in
the Beloved. We are separated from the spirit of the
world, from the evil one, by an act of grace, the essence
of which he is the centre and circumference, to be partakers of that very nature; for this is the will of God,
even our sanctification—(1 Thess. iv. 3)—to the glory of
God the Father. Believers feel in themselves that they
are a mass of evil and pollution. This they do not know
till, separated by the grace of God; the Spirit of God
reveals the holiness of God's nature, and, the believer
being renewed in the spirit of his mind, he loves it,
he longs for it, it is the nature he desires to have. It
is the glory of God; he is glorious in holiness. Every
believer is sanctified by the Holy Ghost. The *treasury*
of this rich grace is in Christ, who of God is thus made
to his church sanctification, to the glory of God the
Father.

Christ is of God made unto us *redemption*. Here is
the grand climax of the whole. Here Christ is displayed
in the several acts of Jehovah, going forth for the salvation of his people, even from everlasting; God the
Father originating the plan in his infinite wisdom and
grace; God the Son possessing all power to accomplish
the work in his own Person; God the Spirit applying the
work of salvation to the hearts and consciences of the
sinners thus saved. Our redemption is effected by the
joint act of the Sacred Three, through the mediatorial
work of Christ the Redeemer, " who is of God made unto
us wisdom, righteousness, sanctification, and redemption."
It is in Christ we have redemption, through his blood,
according to the riches of his grace, which in another
place is spoken of as the *exceeding* riches of his grace—
far beyond the uttermost of all the requirements of the
church of God. Now, the unsearchableness of all these
riches was felt by the apostle himself when he said, " O,
the depth of the riches both of the wisdom and knowledge of God; how unsearchable are his judgments, and
his ways past finding out." They are unknowable, inexhaustible, ever flowing to us by Christ Jesus; yet his
fulness is as infinite as ever; for with him is *plenteous*
redemption. And it is as certain and absolute as it is
plenteous, " for Israel shall be saved in the Lord with an
everlasting salvation."

But to proceed: You have observed in all these points
to which we have referred, they are what may be considered as the main features of what Christ is to his
church, objectively and subjectively; *objectively*, their
highest wisdom being to know him, to be found in him,
to have an experimental sense of their interest in him, of
what he is to them in his various relationships he bears
to them, by virtue of his being their Head and Husband,
and their Representative; *subjectively*, in him, not in
themselves, nor yet in anything done in them or by them,
but whatever they are as believers, they are that in Christ
Jesus alone: for his riches, as they dwell in himself, are
communicable to them. Whatever they have from him,
he is all that to them; for he is the Freeholder, if I might
so say; they are but copyholders. What we are and have,
we derive from him. Our being enriched by him leaves
his riches still his own; they are none the less; their
immensity is as infinite as ever.

The riches of *all his attributes* are *unsearchable*, natural and moral. His Eternity, Spirituality, his Omnipotence, his Omnipresence, his Omniscience, and Infinity are all vast treasures peculiar to himself as the mighty God; yet, incomprehensible as these attributes are to us finite creatures, these are all exercised in behalf of and for the church of God, through the mediatorial work of Christ, their covenant and ever-living Head. None by searching can find out God; "his greatness is unsearchable." His perfections belong to his nature as God, and are incommunicable to the nature and being of a creature; yet every believer may rejoice in this great truth, that all the attributes of the Godhead are in Christ, and are his unsearchable riches. Have you never found certain seasons in your experience, when no arm but that of the great God could help you? You have committed your soul to him as your Redeemer, and in him you could feel your eternal salvation secure; but, apart from that, sometimes circumstances have been such that none but the mighty God of Jacob could act and rule for you, and you have been assured of it, realized it as a fact, it has become a part of your history, and you could say with the poet,

> " To accomplish his design
> The creatures all agree;
> And every attribute divine
> Is now at work for me."

Then as to his moral attributes; I mean those which are communicable to the creature man, and by which he is distinguished from all other creatures. I do not mean his rational or intellectual qualities, but such as mercy, love, goodness, truth, justice, holiness, &c. O what an inexhaustible source of these divine perfections is treasured up in Christ, as God. These he possesses without measure. "He is rich in *mercy;*" "from everlasting to everlasting;" rich in mercy to all who call upon him in truth. "Yea, our God is merciful;" rich in mercy from the very fact of his great love wherewith he loved us. His *love*, how great! it passeth knowledge. He gave himself for us. Being divine, it is unsearchable; yet, though it passeth knowledge, blessed be God, it does not pass our experience. We are to know the love of God, and so be "filled with all the fulness of God." His *goodness* is as unsearchable as his greatness. It must be inexhaustible, for all are assured of it. O taste and

see that the Lord is good! The Lord is good, a stronghold in the day of trouble. (Nahum i. 4.) His goodness
is as large as his power—infinite. The Lord God is
abundant in goodness. (Ex. xxxiv. 6.) It endureth continually. (Ps. lii. 1.) His *faithfulness*, how unchangeable
and inexhaustible! the same yesterday, to-day, and for
ever. He is faithful that hath promised, immutably so;
and thus we have strong consolation; for it is impossible
but that Christ is, or can be, in himself, ever faithful to
his promise and to his saints. His truth, justice, and
every other attribute flowing from the holiness of his
nature, are all alike unsearchable; but they are those
riches of which believers are made partakers in measure,
and which constitute their graces, the gifts and graces of
the Spirit, as they are sometimes called. Not a gift or a
grace do they possess but what is derived from the fulness
which is in Christ.

3. I pass on to show that Christ's riches, as *the God-
man Mediator, are unsearchable.* What Christ is in his
Person as the Mediator, in the union of his two natures,
he is all that to the Church of God. All the blessings of
the covenant of grace flow through that medium, and are
divinely imparted to them.

Access to God. "By whom also we have access into this
grace wherein we stand, and rejoice in hope of the glory
of God, made nigh by the blood of Christ;" a people
near unto him; bone of his bone, and flesh of his flesh.
We have fellowship with the Father and his Son Jesus
Christ, a privilege unknown to the highest archangel.
His saints, his separated ones, and his sanctified ones, are
brought so near unto him as to be on terms of the dearest
friendship; nay, more, a divine and eternal union exists,
such a oneness as exists between Jesus and the Father—
an unspeakable union, such a union as I believe in and
rejoice in, but I cannot fully describe it.

Peace with God. Jesus is our peace; he is our propitiation. We have peace with God through our Lord
Jesus Christ. (Rom. v. 1.) O the blessing of peace,
peace in ourselves, peace with one another; harmony of
sentiment, of feeling, of action, of purpose, showing the
security and rest possessed, which constitute peace. All
this, and more too, we possess in having peace with God,
a peace which is as eternal as it is secure. Such a peace
we have in Christ, though in the midst of tribulation. It

is his gracious assurance, in the world we shall have tribulation, but in him we have peace—a peace which the
world cannot give nor take away. Where this peace is
possessed and enjoyed, it bids defiance to the storms
without. To be miserable in the world, and yet to be
happy in Christ, is the blessed result of having peace in
Christ, peace under sorrow for sin. My dear hearers, do
you know anything of this peace in your own hearts?
Whatever you may possess in this world to make you
outwardly happy, yet, if you are without this peace with
God, peace in Christ, you are still a poor, miserable creature, blind and naked to all intents and purposes, having
no hope, without God, in the world. But O! if you are
possessors of such a divine peace, rejoice in this blessed
truth, this peace is inexhaustible, it is eternal, unsearchable. Peace when the Assyrian Death shall come. His
grim visage will not disturb us, for in Christ we shall
rest in peace.

The Promises of God. "All the promises of God in
him are yea, and in him Amen, unto the glory of God
by us." (2 Cor. i. 20) Peter calls them " exceeding
great and precious promises." (2 Peter i. 4.) Here we
see their certainty, their fulness, and value. What a
valuable treasury there is in the Word of God, even when
read merely with the eye of the rational judgment, but
when by the Spirit of God only a single promise is
applied to the heart of the spiritual believer, what an inexhaustible fulness there is! It can be made like the
single meal of the Prophet; the believer can go in the
strength of it for many days, ay, even a life-time. Some
of you can testify to the value of God's promises, even a
single one. Tell me, for what amount would you part
with one single promise that has been made dear to you,
and on which you hang your hope? "Part with it?"
say you; "no, not for thousands of worlds." Well,
then, if a single promise be so dear to you, what must
all the promises of God be to his whole church? O
what an inexhaustible fulness, what unsearchableness!

> " If such the sweetness of the streams,
>   What must the fountain be?"

Christ is the ocean of all the promises of God. His
riches are unsearchable.

His sympathetic care. Jesus having been in all points
tried as we are, he is able to succour those that are

tempted; and his knowledge and ability will last as long as his Person. In his manhood he was made perfect through suffering; (Heb. ii. 10, 18;) by virtue of his Godhead and Sonship, the riches of his sympathy with his suffering members are inexhaustible, unsearchable, illimitable, an ever-flowing fulness to the Church of God. His love is as large as his power; it is constantly exercised, without measure, without end. He has left in the world "a poor and afflicted people, and they shall trust in him." "It behoved him to be made like unto his brethren, that he might be a merciful and faithful high-priest in things pertaining to God;" such a one that could be "touched with the feeling of our infirmities, being in all points tempted like as we are, yet without sin." (Heb. ii. 17; iv. 15.) What a blessed subject for the poor distressed child of God to contemplate!—the sympathy of Christ. No sorrow of the soul but what he is perfectly acquainted with. By virtue of his human nature, and by reason of his divine nature, he can and does communicate his sympathetic care. Whatever griefs distress thy soul, they distress him; he has gone through it all, he knows all your care, he careth for you. Have you a broken heart for sin? He died of a broken heart; it was sin that broke his heart; no sorrow was like his sorrow. Though he personally knew no sin, but only representatively, yet he felt the reproach of it. He said, "Reproach hath broken my heart." His soul was exceeding sorrowful, even unto death. Jesus knew and felt the weight of sin charged upon him. It may be, you have been so overwhelmed with charges against you as to feel yourself verily guilty, and ready to believe that you are really the vile person represented. When Warren Hastings, Governor of India, was impeached, the great Edmund Burke was employed to plead against him, and he laid out the charges in such a telling manner (for he was a most masterly orator), that Hastings, when he laid his head on his pillow at night, notwithstanding his own consciousness to the contrary, actually did, for a time, really believe he had committed the crimes that were laid against him, and he looked upon himself as the greatest villain that ever lived. But, however, truth did its office, in spite of Burke's eloquence, logic, and rhetoric. He arose, put facts together, prepared his defence, and was acquitted. Now, this is just the case with many a poor soul; charges, grievous in nature and numerous, are brought against him and represented in such a light as to force the poor creature to believe it all, as if true. But the enemies' eloquence, logic, and rhetoric are not always on the side of truth. But, supposing they were, Jesus will plead; he sympathises with you; he himself has been falsely charged and accused and condemned. Come, poor, soul, have you been here? Jesus has been here before you. He feels for you, he will help you. Hear his blessed word: " For the oppression of the poor, and for the sighing of the needy, now will I arise, saith the Lord. I will set him in safety from him that puffeth at him." (Ps. xii. 5.) Take no heed to Satan's lawsuit; Jesus is your Advocate. Your cause is safe in his hands; he will be sure to succeed. His sympathies are with you, and, whether it be sin in the conscience that accuses, or whether you suffer from an ungodly world, or the false charges of carnal professors of religion, Jesus' heart is as large as your distress. You may safely confide in him; reveal everything to him, pour out your heart before him, and you shall find his resources so ample that all your enemies shall be found liars unto you, and you shall tread upon their high places." "Ah," says one, "but my sorrow rises from quite another source. I have pinching poverty. I know not how to meet the demands of my family. I am continually disappointed in my efforts to obtain the bread that perisheth, and I fear the cause of God will suffer through my inability to owe no man any-thing." O yes, I know full well these are searching trials, weighty crosses. Poverty saps the comfort of every earthly blessing, but our Lord knew poverty and bodily privations to a fearful and sad extent. He knows all the feelings of thy heart, and will provide for all thy needs, according to his will, from his divine and all-sufficient fulness. O commit your way unto him; trust also in him, and he will bring it to pass. He will not mock your distress. You have the mighty God of Jacob for your help. His sympathies for the poor and dis-tressed are unfailing in goodness, power, and timeliness. They are unsearchable.

In the promise of his presence. Jesus has promised his Church through all time, in every place, the assurance of his presence: "Lo, I am with you always, even to the end of the world." He is with us in his house;

D

with us in fellowship with his people; when we pass through the waters of affliction he is with us; with us in every place, individually as well as collectively. In the enjoyment of his presence is fulness of joy, whether in his house or in our homes. His presence sweetens every loss, soothes every pain. When he speaks to the heart, it kindles with his love. Then the face of nature changes:

"Labour is rest, and pain is sweet,"

if he be with us. This promise of his ever-abiding presence is like his Person, eternal, unsearchable in its riches.

In our completeness in him. Our completeness in Christ is by being made rich in him. Through his poverty, by his personal obedience to God's law in our flesh, we are made rich, eternally rich; completely righteous before God, without blame in love. How vast, how unsearchably great must be the righteousness which, as ample clothing, completely covers the transgressions of every member of his mystical body, the Church:

"In him the Father never saw
The least transgression of the law.
Perfection, then, in Christ we view;
His saints in him are perfect too."

In the merit of his blood. O the inexhaustible fulness of blessing there is here. On the foundation of his divinity alone rests the merit of his atonement. His blood and righteousness, as man, are our riches,—as the God-man, our unsearchable riches. Look again at the number of sinners saved, a vast multitude, a number which no man can number—in the number of each individual's sins, and the extent of their guilt. His blood cleanses from all sin, all your sins, all my sins, all the sins of all the Church of God, from the first sin of Adam, through all time, down to the last sin that shall be committed by the latest elect vessel of mercy that shall be living upon this earth. Every believing sinner must feel how rich, how precious, must be that blood which has cleansed his soul from thousands of sins; and when he reflects how it has cleansed millions of sinners, how unsearchably rich and precious must it appear! The more it is gazed upon, the more infinite does it appear. And remember, too, the riches of his blood are to be the theme of the church's song in heaven: "Unto him that loved us, and washed

us from our sins in his own blood." (Rev. i. 5 and v. 9.)
A never-ceasing song, because the riches of his blood will
never cease.   How can it be else than what it is ?   Duration will not diminish its value, but only add to its in-
finitude, and thus it will ever remain unsearchable.

In the riches of his glory.   O, this we must die to
know; the glory of his primeval state before the world
was.   No man hath seen God at any time in the fulness
of his glory.   The glories of the heavenly state can be
but imperfectly known by any created being.   What can
angels know, what can the first glorified spirit know, of
the riches of his glory ?   Vast, incomprehensible, unsearchable!   Yet on earth all our personal needs are supplied from his riches in glory, by Christ Jesus.   His riches
in glory are not the less by the supply of our needs on
earth.

4. Consider, in the next place, *what unsearchable riches
there are in all the characters Christ sustains to his
Church.*   Time will not allow of more than alluding to
them by name.   The primary offices of Prophet, Priest,
and King have already been dwelt upon.   These I refer
to now, and which are only a sample, are—our Shepherd,
Husband, Friend, the Life, the Truth, the Way, our
Hiding-place, Physician, Balm, Rest, and many others.
Not a day can pass, not a circumstance can happen, but
what the believer, who is truly alive to divine realities,
feels Christ is precious to him in all the characters and
similitudes which set him forth.   He is the chiefest of
ten thousand, the altogether lovely.

> " His beauties we can never trace,
> Till we behold him face to face."

The wilderness condition of the believer makes him feel
the necessity of looking to Jesus for everything that he
is.   There is not a title Jesus bears, but he bears it for
the believer's sake.   His are not nominal or honorary
titles, but *essential* ones, essential to every believer who
is taught to know the plague of his own heart, his own
nothingness, weakness, and emptiness.   When, like wandering sheep, we stray from the fold, we have our Shepherd's care: " He restoreth my soul."   In all time of our
soul-sickness, he is our health and cure, his blood is our
balm.   When weary and worn in the desert, he is our
hiding-place from wind and a covert from the storm, the

shadow of a great rock in a weary land, our sun and shield, our eternal rest.

What shall we say of Christ's riches as being unsearchable, when we contemplate him as the Bread of Life, the Water of Life, the Tree of Life,—our meat and drink, our clothing, dwelling, companion, our light, heat, comforter, guide and guard.   There is nothing in creation for the good of man, but Christ is that to the believer; unsearchably so, for he is our all and in all.   Can you join with me in saying,

> " He's all that's good and great,
> All that I can admire;
> All that's endearing to my soul,
> And all my soul's desire?"

And who can tell the height and depth of those vast treasures of spiritual blessings which are in him; unbounded fulness of pardoning grace, of justifying grace, of sanctifying grace; of light, hope, joy, peace, consolation, comfort; a provision for every contingency of human life and want? " In his presence is fulness of joy, and at his right hand there are pleasures for evermore."   Whether upon earth or in heaven, Christ is everything to his Church; everything in its fulness; such an abundance as is unbounded, unsearchable.

The riches of Christ are unsearchable, for he possesses in himself *eternal life*.   The gift of God is eternal life,—this life is in his Son.   "This is life eternal that they might know God, and Jesus Christ whom he has sent."   He that believeth on the Son of God hath life.   " I give unto my sheep eternal life, and they shall never perish." (John x. 2, 8.)   "As thou hast given him power over all flesh, that he should give eternal life to as many as thou hast given him." (John xvii. 2.)   "This is the promise which he hath promised us, eternal life." (1 John ii. 25.)   These passages show that he is life in its essence; "in him was life, and the life was the light of men."   If Christ be our light, it is because he is our life.   I have said it before and I repeat it, for it is a vital truth; thousands of flourishing professors, highly-esteemed in the world, know nothing of this life.   Light is not life; it is not the knowledge or *form* of truth that contents the living soul; it is the *power* of truth.   He needs it every day, every hour, every moment.   See, then, that what you have of light comes from the life in Christ. We live in a day when religion is popular; preaching is made so flexible and plausible as to suit any and every body. Crowds of professors are to be found everywhere, provided there is no searching the conscience. Doctrinal and experimental truth is eschewed, as old-fashioned and as being behind the age; but I tell you plainly, where there is no doctrinal and experimental truth in the preaching, there is no gospel at all; there is no life in it. I know it from long, sad experience.

The riches of Christ are unsearchable; for *in him is eternal salvation.* He is the author of it; he is the pro- curer of it, the dispenser of it. The church was eternally saved from Adam's apostasy, the curse of it,—saved from the present conquest of inbred sin, from the working of outward sin, from the guilt of past sins, and the curse of future sins. Often he chastises for sin,—that is our mercy; it is to save us from its power, from the love of it, from the guilt of it. "He is able to save to. the uttermost all who come unto God by him. "Who- soever shall call upon the name of the Lord, shall be saved." "There is none other name under heaven whereby men can be saved."

The riches of Christ are unsearchable; for his is *the heavenly inheritance.* This is Christ's own gift. "Father, I will that they also whom thou hast given me, be with me where I am; that they may behold my glory, which thou hast given me." (John xvii. 24.) This gift of eternal glory is over, and above, and beyond the purchased possession. Perpetuity of life and earthly happiness are what Adam and his race would have possessed, supposing he and they had never sinned. They would have enjoyed converse with God, and have delighted in him as their Creator and Lord, but not as their Redeemer. Here they have in Christ a superior life, a superior position, a superior relationship. He is their inheritance; in him is a fulness of glory; for all spiritual blessings are in him. It pleased the Father to give his adopted sons the king- dom of grace, and to Christ the kingdom of glory. Being heirs of God, joint-heirs with Christ, we have in him eternal glory. It is ours; we have an everlasting posses- sion, everlasting enjoyment. We shall have crowns of everlasting joy upon our heads. This is the portion of all the redeemed. His riches are inexhaustible; "for of him, and through him, and to him, are all things; to whom be glory for ever and ever.   Amen."

Before I conclude, I must advert to one subject specially, which has only been done incidentally, and that is, the *characters* to whom these riches are available.   There are riches in the Bank of England sufficient to make every one in this congregation easy in their circumstances, independent of labour for life; but if we have no title, no claim to those riches, of what avail are they to us?   Now, these riches that we have been speaking of are designed for the express use of certain characters,—believers in the Lord Jesus Christ.   They are persons who before God are justified, their sins pardoned; they are clothed with the righteousness of Christ, made the children of God, heirs of God, joint-heirs with Christ.   Let me ask you, in all love and faithfulness, have you any such hopes as these?

These persons have had their hearts renewed, their affections and their dispositions regenerated and sanctified by the power of God the Holy Ghost.   They have been made new creatures; they feel themselves to be new creatures.   Old pursuits, pleasures, aims, and purposes have passed away, and all things have become new.   They are enriched with the gifts and graces of God's Spirit; their affections are set on things above; they seek those things where Christ sitteth.   O my hearer, has such a change been wrought in you?

The conduct of these persons proves that they have their conversation in heaven; the life agrees with the heart.   If the heart is alive to God, it will be dead to the world.   Where these unsearchable riches are partaken of, not only are they rich in faith, hope, love, and joy in the Holy Ghost, but they are also rich in good works; for so they were created unto them in Christ Jesus, and God hath before ordained that they should walk in them. Professor of the name of Christ! let me ask you, can you prove your calling and election thus?   Does your deportment in life, before God and men, agree?   If so, in the world you will demonstrate it by living godly, soberly, and righteously in this present world. (Titus ii. 12.) In your family you will exhibit the Christian temper, and service for God.   In secret you will know something of communion with God.   Sound sentiments respecting Christ and the way of salvation can never save you; there

must be union to him, a believing in him, and a receiving
from him, or else your souls can never be enriched from
his fulness.   Examine yourselves upon this momentous
subject.   It can do you no possible harm—it may do you
eternal good.

Believers in the Lord Jesus Christ; you who are relying
on his finished work for life and salvation, what glorious
privileges, hopes, and blessings belong to you!   All that
Christ is, all that Christ has, is yours.   What think ye of
Christ?   Is he not, as the late Dr. Hawker used to say,
"a most glorious Christ"—glorious in his Person, glorious
in his riches, glorious in their unsearchableness, and glorious in his salvation?

> "His worth if all the nations knew,
> Sure the whole earth would love him too."

The half has never been told; no, not a thousandth
part.   What can finite mortals say of the Infinite.   Seeking sinner, our efforts all fail in setting forth such a
Saviour as Christ the Lord; but you will do well to
consider that the efficacy of his atonement rests alone
upon the foundation of his divinity.   It is the eternity
of his divinity that gives eternity to redemption.   It is
upon the foundation of his divinity alone that the seeking
sinner can venture to believe in him, and rest his hopes
for life and salvation.   Believers in Christ can rest upon
no other foundation than that Jesus is God, for the faithful and sure performance of the promise of his ever-abiding
presence with his people to the end of all time.   Trusting
in this great truth, we commence our third year in this
place, praying we may have some demonstration of the
Spirit with power, while we attempt to preach Christ and
him crucified, and contend earnestly for the faith of God's
elect.

"Now unto him that is able to do exceeding abundantly, above all that we can ask or think, according to
the power that worketh in us," unto him be glory in the
church by Christ Jesus, throughout all ages, world without end.   Amen, and amen.

Before I sit down I must ask your attention to one
little matter, and that is, as to my sentiments generally.
Having of late been subjected to both misunderstanding
and misrepresentation, I deem it requisite on this occasion

to declare briefly the chief points, or rather the outline, of my Articles of Faith. When this church was about being formed, 5th January, 1864, and on my being called to the pastorate, I then prepared the following summary :

"I believe that the Holy Scriptures contain every Article of Faith and Practice needful to be known for salvation. That there is One God, whose name is Jehovah, revealed in the distinct Personalities of Father, Son, and Holy Spirit, coessential, coeternal, and coequal in nature, power, and glory. That man, by disobedience to divine law, fell from his original innocency, and has thereby become totally depraved. That God, in his infinite love and wisdom, by a covenant of grace, devised a scheme of mercy, whereby a certain and specified number are everlastingly saved from all the consequences of sin, and by which the honour of divine law is fully vindicated and righteously maintained,—the Father, in the good pleasure of his will, choosing and predestinating to eternal life the persons thus saved, the Son undertaking their redemption by his atonement, and the Holy Spirit regenerating, sanctifying, and preserving them in this time state. That there will be a general resurrection of the dead, and a final judgment by the Son of God; the wicked will go into everlasting punishment, but the righteous into life eternal. That believers in the Lord Jesus Christ, being delivered from the law as a covenant of works, are henceforth to walk in all newness of life according to the rule of the gospel; that they should be united in the fellowship of the gospel for the worship of God, observing the ordinances of his house, as set forth in the New Testament, namely, baptism by immersion and the Lord's Supper, and that they should promote the knowledge of the gospel, by all scriptural means, for the salvation of their fellow-men."

These sentiments are those which I have been enabled, by grace divine, to hold for more than thirty-six years. I believe them to be the verities of the gospel. They are the substance of what I have ever taught since I was thrust into the ministry; and I trust, the Lord being my helper, that I shall not shun to declare the whole counsel of God.

APPENDIX.

THE term "Eternal Generation," (p.14) I am aware, is liable
to be both misunderstood and misrepresented; and it could
be wished that our early divines had found some other
word less obscure and more adequate to represent their
idea; but it is no easy thing to find words that could not
possibly be misconstrued, especially when persons are dis-
inclined to accept the meaning intended, or if it crosses
their own preconceived notions; but as it is, I see no reason
why one should forego the use of a term which has become
current amongst those who do receive the meaning con-
veyed. It has been well said, "The mind and meaning
of a writer should be taken from his known doctrine and
general drift; and though all writers are liable to express
themselves on some points obscurely, or at least not satis-
factorily to every mind, yet there is such a thing as
making a man an offender for a word, and imputing to
him, from some misunderstood expression, views of doctrine quite contrary to his generally known and avowed
sentiments." The word "procession," for instance, in reference to the Holy Ghost and the Father, is subject to the same
misconstruction as eternal generation, and yet it is strictly
scriptural; for it appears, in reference to the word "procession," that both Arius and Sabellius, (third century,) admitted the word, but perverted it. Arius held that the
Son and the Holy Ghost proceeded as creatures from the
Father. Sabellius held that they proceeded as offices of
the Father, or, as it were, developments. "The mistake of
both," says Mr. Peter M'Laren, "arose from supposing procession to infer motion *ad extra*; while the orthodox understood it as wholly beginning and ending within the
Godhead. Of course, from beginning and ending, we ex-
clude all idea of any era, or of time when; referring merely
to the mutual aspect of the Persons. The action in *proceeding* is immanent, not emanative."

The distinction here pointed out by this learned author

as to the word procession is important, and applies equally
to the term eternal generation, to which he also refers and
he thus states it: "Allowance must be made for obscurity
of idea and of speech in this matter; our ideas must be inadequate and obscure.   No word can be used in precisely
the same sense regarding the Creator and his creatures.
They are finite in duration and in being; he is eternal,
infinite, and unchangeable.   It must suffice that the idea
is correct, through inadequate and obscure.   Our conceptions and words are images of creatures, and yet we have
none else to use.   Were God himself to reveal all the truth
as it is, it would be unintelligible, for no human words
would be perfectly applicable.   Whatever a man knows,
he can express; and whatever man can express, man can
comprehend; but nothing else.

"But groping as best we may, we may attain certain
ideas of God, correct though obscure.   God made man in
his own image, we may assume, in his spiritual as well
as his moral nature; for God speaks of his image in man,
even after the fall had blotted out the moral likeness; as
in 1 Cor. xi. 7; James iii. 9.   It is commonly granted
that the fall erased no faculty from the essence of men.
It is also granted generally that the powers of the soul
may be reduced to two, understanding and will.   *   *   *
Of course the moral attributes fall to be classed under the
will.

"Both these, the intellect and the will, are capable of immanent action.   The immanent action of the intellect is a
proceeding of a thing conceived and understood so as to
become objective to the intellect, while still within it.
The concept, the idea, has a certain real existence, whether
it be uttered or not; so the distinction is granted between
verbum cordis and *verbum vocis:* the idea not uttered, or
uttered.

"This procession, Augustine believed, (fourth century,)
represents to us the generation of the Son, who is called
the Wisdom and the Word of God.   Others, indeed, as
Tertullian, (third century,) perceived and taught the
same thing; but Augustine set himself formally to defend
the doctrine, which is, therefore, generally traced to him.

"It is the *proprium* of the Son to be 'begotten of the
Father.'   There are two meanings attached to the word
generation,—one large, common to all corruptible things,
denoting a change from nonentity to being, the beginning

of existence; the other of more limited application, denoting the origin in the same species of one living being from another. The origin of beings in a different species, as of worms in animals, falls under the first and large meaning, but not under the second and limited meaning.

"In those living beings which proceed from possible to actual being and life, both senses of the word generation are found. But the generation of the Son of God is not in this category; in God there is no changeableness; with him there is no 'potentia passiva,'—no power to become what he is not, or to receive what he is not, or to suffer change in what he is or has proper to himself. With God, then, generation is the origin in the same species of one living being from another. But the species of God comprehends but one nature; and, therefore, to say that the generation of the Son of God is the origin in the same *nature* of one being from another, is of the same power, and is truly called generation. The origin of the manhood or human nature of our Lord was not generation by the Holy Spirit; for the human nature of Christ was not of the same species with the Holy Spirit; it was created by the Spirit.

"Voetius, to the question, Wherein does creation differ from eternal generation? answers, 'The procession of the Son from the Father is an acting, necessary, natural, emanative, eternally, within God,—a real relation signified by action. Creation is action of free-will, producing change, temporal, to without God, and external, and, considered in regard to God, is a relation to the creatures not real but nominal.' *

"We have used the words, 'one living being from another,' because we could find no other expression; but though the Son is another Person, he is not another nature from the Father; though 'alius,' he is not 'aliud.'

"We must join the two ideas, generation and conception,—understanding from the two, the origin in the same species as in generation, and the origin wholly within and immanent, as in the conception of an idea in the mind; and this procession of the Word, it must be remembered, is eternal, without beginning. The two expressions,—the conceived Word, and the begotten Son,— define the manner of substance of the Second Person in a

* Vol. I.—Prob. de Creatione i.

way that no expression alone could do it. The word of our heart, or wisdom, or an idea, is immanent, conceived, and, as it were, begotten within us; but then it is not another person. A man's son is another person, in the species of his father, and as truly subsisting as his father; but then a son is a different essence and being from his father. But the Second Person of the Trinity being scripturally named both the Wisdom and the Son of the Father, we join both ideas, and out of them compound one, if not clear, yet intelligible and practical."—*The Glory of the Holy Ghost, by Rev. Peter M'Laren, pp. 19–21.*

The author of the book containing the above extract has kindly favoured C. G. with a MS. copy of a portion of his work, intended for a second edition, from which the two following paragraphs have been selected, and are added here as tending further to explain and to elucidate this great subject, so little understood and so much misrepresented.

"My idea is, as it were, begotten within me; it is *of* me, and *in* me; but it is not another person. My son is another person, and is of me and from me; but he is not in me, he is outside of me. But God, be it repeated, for it is the thing which the assailants of eternal generation strangely forget, God has no outside. He that is God's begotten Son is everlastingly in God, as truly as my idea is in me; and he that is God's Word and Wisdom is as truly distinct from God's Being and God's Spirit, as my son is distinct from me. The Second Person of the Godhead is both the Wisdom and the Son of the first; another person though not another thing, *alius,* though not *aliud.*"

"This procession of the Son, is natural, necessary, and eternal. The Father was not before the Son, God's being was not before his knowing. His word was in him, and of him from all eternity. We cannot conceive the Father as *ever* being without the Son, of God *ever* being without his Wisdom; both are eternal, eternally distinct, eternally one. This was the archetype of two of the elements of human nature, the *I am,* and the *I think.*"

A. GADSBY, PRINTER, 10, CRANE COURT, FLEET STREET. E.C.

JESUS MORE PRECIOUS THAN THE GOLDEN WEDGE OF OPHIR.

A SERMON,
BY CHARLES GORDELIER.

PREACHED AT HEPHZIBAH CHAPEL, DARLING PLACE, NEAR MILE END GATE,

On Lord's Day Evening, 21st May, 1865.

"I will make a man more precious than fine gold; even a man than the golden wedge of Ophir."—ISAIAH xiii. 12.

OUR text appears disconnected with either the context in the foregoing or that which follows. I will just refer you to both; you see there is a sudden transition from one subject to another. The prophet announces the destruction of Babylon, and its utter desolation. Cloud upon cloud appear to accumulate, making the darkness intensely felt, with just, as it were, one ray of light suddenly darted in to make it the more palpable and awful. Some of our commentators interpret this passage as referring to the scarcity of men after the destruction of that populous city; but I confess, if we are to confine this view to the letter of Scripture, I am at a loss to discover the bearing of such a sense or the advantage of such a declaration. Others, however, looking out for Christ in his word, consider he is the man here spoken of; certain it is, many of the ancient Jews consider that it refers to "the Messiah, who shall be more precious than all the children of the world." My own impression is, that it refers only to Jesus: in point of fact it is so; it applies well to him, and can apply to no other. To employ such a simile to a mere man is most unusual, and the comparison is beyond what is needed; but if we do err in applying it to Jesus, we err on the right side; we cannot make too much of him; we had better, I was

No. 17.   B going to say, see him where he is not expressly revealed, than not to see him where he is. May the spirit of truth take of the things of Christ, and reveal them to us, and then, with his help and blessing, we shall see something of the beauties which make Jesus to the believer more precious than fine gold or the golden wedge of Ophir.

Gold has ever been esteemed as an article in commerce of great value, and, when obtained, it procures for its possessor wealth, honour, dignity, respect, and all that this world can bestow. Gold has its price; and though Jesus is compared to it, he is without price; whatever advantages the men of this world derive from the possession of gold, our Lord Jesus Christ is infinitely beyond it in his personal excellences and in the benefits and advantages which the church of God derive from their union to him, and the knowledge and enjoyment they have of him and his salvation. There is indeed no comparison between gold and Jesus. His Person and his work are incomparable to any thing on earth. Our text indeed says as much; it says, "more precious than fine gold;" so that, in fact, he is above it, even the golden wedge of Ophir. *Ophir* is a place not now known; it was once in great repute. It seems to have been located somewhere in the East, probably in the East Indies; but being exhausted of its precious metal, it has lost the name which once gave a charm and value to its produce. The gold from California is now with us in repute. Indian gold has had its day, and so have Peruvian and Mexican; these have passed away, and so will Californian and Australian gold. But the name of Jesus is ever precious to the church of God, and will be throughout all ages. The *wedge* here spoken of is not to be understood of the shape so called, but refers to some large native lump in which it had been found, and so had become famous. You may perhaps remember, that a few years ago there were exhibited in this country large masses of native gold called nuggets, meaning the same thing as wedge; one, for instance, weighed 146 lbs., called the Victoria nugget. Thus the facts of our times will illustrate those of past times; there is little that is new; we have a perpetual recurrence of the same ideas and facts generation after generation.

Let us now attempt, in humble dependence upon the divine blessing, to say a few things in the *first* place, on the GOD MADE MAN: " *I will make a man;*" and then, in the second place, notice some POINTS OF COMPARISON in which Jesus is said to be more precious "*than fine gold, even the golden wedge of Ophir.*"

I. THE GOD MADE MAN: "I will make a man." The God made man, not the man made God. This is a most important distinction to make, for there is an essential difference in the two statements; and as it lies at the basis of your faith, you will do well to inquire "What is truth?" There are those who say Christ was not the Son of God till he became the Son of man; but this notion is not only contrary to God's word, but is most derogatory to the Person of our blessed Lord. Jesus was the eternal God before he became man; he was the Son of God in his own divine and proper Personality before he became the Son of man; his taking our nature was but a revelation of his love, and that of his Father, in the salvation of man; there was a necessity for his taking our nature that he might become and perform the part of a mediator and substitute; this he did by being in himself both our Sacrifice and Priest. His divine Sonship was his qualification for the work he undertook; his manhood was but the condition in which it was effected; *his Person as the Son of God* was eternally pre-existent; his assumption of our nature was an act in time on this earth, being the fulfilment of Jehovah's purpose in the covenant transaction in eternity, whose goings have been from everlasting. Here we have God's word before us, "I will make a man," not I will make a God. This is most certainly the doctrine of the Old Testament; and the doctrine of the New Testament fully agrees with it. John, in his gospel, sets out with this truth, "In the beginning was the Word;" he then describes who and what this Word is; "and the Word was with God. The same was in the beginning with God; and the Word was God." "And the Word was made flesh, and dwelt among us;" (John i. 1, 14;) in other words, God became man. I ask you, can your own common sense put any other construction on such an obvious declaration? Then we have the same truth put forth by the apostle Paul, who, in writing to the Galatians, (iv. 4,) says, "In the fulness of time, God sent forth his Son made of a woman, made under the law, to redeem them that were under the law." Thus it was that the Son of God became the Son of man; it was not the Son of man that became the Son of God. This is reversing the word of God, indeed, a sad perversion of the truth as it is in Christ.

The doctrine of our Lord Jesus Christ being made man, was decreed and foretold to our first parents at their fall. It was afterwards more fully declared by the prophets. Isaiah especially, as in our text; and the greatly beloved Daniel had the exact time revealed to him. This fulness of time was the precise moment of its accomplishment according to God's decree; and—bear with me in repeating the Scriptures just now quoted—then it was, that God, the eternal Father, sent forth his eternally self-existent Son. "In the beginning was the Word, and the Word was with God, and the Word was God." In the fulness of time the Word was made flesh, became incarnate, made of a woman, made under the law. He came in the likeness of sinful flesh; and for sin, condemned sin in the flesh. His human nature was a creation, created by the Holy Ghost; (see Matt. i. 20;) "for that which is begotten in her is of the Holy Ghost." See also Luke i. 35: "The Holy Ghost shall come upon thee, and the power of the highest shall overshadow thee; therefore also that holy thing which shall be born of thee shall be called the Son of God." Here we have a revelation made to Joseph as to *the fact* itself, and to Mary the *manner* of its taking place. Surely the evidence of two such independent and competent witnesses ought to satisfy the most sceptical objectors; but alas it will not! for where there is no love to the truth, no amount of evidence will be received. It is not truth they are seeking, but the establishing of their own vain conceits, and to draw away disciples after them.

The doctrine of the Person of Christ, according to the Scriptures, is revealed as with a sunbeam; but it is only the spiritual eye, when enlightened by the divine Spirit, that can perceive the glory of the Son of God. He is God and Man, in two distinct, whole, and perfect natures; the Godhead and the Manhood united in one person, being very God and very Man, and constituting one most glorious Christ. He is the God-man Christ Jesus. In his mysterious incarnation we perceive him to be the first-born and the only begotten Son of God. Though made of a woman under the law, yet he was perfectly sinless, born without sin; possessing all the essential properties of immaculate humanity; made in all points like unto his brethren, sin excepted; by taking our nature he was thereby fitted to take our law place, to act as our Substitute, made to be sin for us, that we might be made the righteousness of God in him. He came to fulfil his Father's holy law; he magnified it, and made it honourable. Here the purpose of God is set forth, and the exceeding riches of his grace.

II. THE POINTS OF COMPARISON. We now proceed, in the second place, to notice some points of comparison in which Jesus is said to be "more precious than fine gold, even the golden wedge of Ophir."

Gold, in the Scriptures, is often made an emblem of what is divine, pure, solid, useful, incorruptible, or lasting and glorious. Such is our most glorious Christ, both in his Person and in his work. In the song which is Solomon's, his *head* is likened not only to gold, but the most fine gold. And the same writer, in his Book of Proverbs, sets before the young seeker of divine truth, for his encouragement, the infinite worth and value of Christ Jesus the Lord as the wisdom of his church; his own language being, "Riches and honour are with me; yea, durable riches and righteousness. My fruit is better than gold, yea, than fine gold; and my revenue than choice silver. I lead in the way of righteousness, in the midst of the paths of judgment; that I may cause them that love me to inherit substance; and I will fill their treasures." (Prov. viii. 18–21.) "In him dwelleth all the fulness of the Godhead bodily;" "for it pleased the Father that in him should all fulness dwell." The church itself is "blessed with all spiritual blessings in heavenly places in him." Thus we see the great preacher Solomon and the great apostle Paul are united in ascribing to the Lord Jesus Christ the excellency and superiority he possesses over all things esteemed good and great among men. He is the Treasure-house of all blessedness, and all who are found in union with him are enriched by him in all good things. For he is of God, made unto all true believers "wisdom, righteousness, sanctification, and redemption." (1 Cor. i. 30.) Here is, standing first in the category of blessings—WISDOM; and mark what is said of its unspeakable value: it cannot be estimated by that which is most precious to men, "it cannot be gotten for gold." "It cannot be valued with the gold of Ophir," "neither shall it be valued with pure gold." (Job xxviii. 15,

16, 19.) And again, the great preacher argues, (Prov. xvi. 16,) "How much better it is to get wisdom than gold." Here in our text Jehovah declares, "I will make a man more precious than fine gold, even the golden wedge of Ophir." This, then, we hope to put before you in several points of view, though they may not all be equally striking. 1st. Gold is the *first metal* spoken of in the Scriptures, as you will find in Genesis ii. 11, being a reference to the place where it was found, namely, Havilah, a word which signifies, "that suffers pain, that brings forth." Gold, indeed, is acquired by much toil and suffering; and Christ is first made known to the believer as being more precious than fine gold, through the sufferings and pain he has endured in his conscience by the terrors of a broken law. Pardon for sin through the atoning blood of Immanuel, he having made peace by the blood of his cross, is a truth which endears the Saviour to him more than all the riches the world could bestow. Well has the poet written:

> "Not gems nor gold could buy our peace,
> Nor the whole world's collected store
> Suffice to purchase our release;
> A thousand worlds were all too poor."

But we were speaking of gold being the first metal spoken of; and here we cannot but see the superiority of Christ; he is ALPHA, he is first, he is before all things, he is the beginning of all things, he is the creator of all things, gold was created by him, he is the beginning of the creation of God: "In the beginning was the Word, and the Word was with God, and the Word was God. All things were made by him; and without him was not any thing made that was made." (John i. 1–3.) Gold is the first metal spoken of, because it is the chiefest. So we find Christ is the chiefest of ten thousand; and how early in the beginning of creation was he manifested to our first parents as the Redeemer and Saviour of his Church; I doubt not to Adam in his state of innocency, but certainly in a way of grace and mercy after the fall, and that the atoning work of the Redeemer was set forth to them under the type of the first animal sacrificed, as may be inferred by the skins with which our first parents were clothed, the use of which setting forth the righteousness of God. In the sacrifice which Abel offered, we perceive how early in the history of man the atonement of Christ was figured forth; certainly long before the use and nature of gold was discovered or appreciated. Whatever may have been the reason which led Moses to notice the existence and locality of gold in the early history of man, there is something far superior in the thought that the love and mercy of our covenant God should reveal to the first fallen man the redemption which is in Christ Jesus.

2. *Gold is good*, goodness is its quality; it is innocuous; the use of most metals in many purposes is found to be injurious, but gold may be used with safety where the inferior metals could not; but even in gold there is a difference of quality, and the Jews have always been known as connoisseurs in this precious metal; you see in the very expression as to the first mention of gold, 1st Gen. 12—"the gold of that land is good," that they could tell the value and quality of gold; they have been always dealers in it, as they are now: so may it be said of the true Israelite, the Israelite indeed, in whom there is no guile, he will only trade with Christ; from him he derives all his goodness, Christ is precious to him, because he is good, and doeth good continually. "Oh taste and see that the Lord is good." Here we see that Christ is more precious than fine gold; for the love of gold, as it is said of money, is the root of all evil, but the love of Christ is the root of all blessedness: "blessed are all they that put their trust in him;" the seeker, the believer in Christ is counselled to "buy gold tried in the fire," for it is only such gold which has been tried, that is found to be genuine, that is good. Christ is the believer's only good. "Unto you who believe he is precious," and it is the love of Christ that constrains him to every good word and work.

3. Gold is remarkable for its *purity*. It is seldom found in a state of ore, natively it is pure. Other metals are found mixed with stones, earth, clay, and inferior metals. Native gold occurs crystallised, capillary, and massive; not unfrequently is found alloyed with silver. To separate it from the various substances with which it is mixed is the design of heating it in a furnace. Such is its purity, it suffers no change by the heating of the furnace, no exposure to the air or moisture; it is only by use and wear that its quantity or bulk decreases. So to the believer in Jesus, Christ is revealed to him as being

pure in himself; the pure, holy, harmless, spotless Lamb
of God, separated from sinners, unmixed with sins or infirmities.   He knew no sin, (2 Cor. v. 21.)   The Person
of Jesus Christ, the Son of God, was in his nature pure
and holy; it was impossible that he could sin, being holy
in his nature; and as a fountain could not send out at the
same time sweet and bitter waters, so no more could
Christ by any possibility become sinful in himself; for
when he took our nature, he took not its sinfulness; and
though he bore our sins in his own body on the tree, it
was as our Surety and Substitute, but he, in his own personality as the Son of God, remained ever the holy, spotless Lamb of God; had it been otherwise, his soul could
not have made an offering for sin, for the sacrifice must
be without defect, or otherwise it could not be accepted.
And so, as our High Priest, he was free from sin, separate
from sinners; hence his work, his priesthood avails; the
Father smiles upon him, and his people are complete in
him.   Here again is the superiority of Christ over gold;
it is liable to wear and become less in bulk; it may require refining, it may be alloyed, it may even by chemical
processes be evaporated and dissipated, but no such
changes or alterations can occur with the power and work
of Christ; if it were, where would be the foundation of a
sinner's hope?   His righteousness is everlasting, and the
redemption he has obtained is eternal.   He is more precious than fine gold.

4. *Fine gold* is a distinction well understood by dealers.
Gold is gold, but all gold is not *fine* gold.   Though gold
may be good and pure, it may not be of a kind regarded
as superior in quality, brightness, or texture.   There is a
quality known as fine gold, and this has a superior value
accordingly.   So Jesus in his Person and excellences is
known and admired as the chiefest of ten thousand, the
fairest of ten thousand fairs, the altogether lovely; he is
more precious than all that can be esteemed by man; he
had the Spirit of God without measure, no coarseness of
nature, life, or manners, nothing to deteriorate his character, being perfect in every gift and grace as God and
man united.   His head is as the *most fine* gold, the most
superior of its kind; so Jesus is the most exalted per-
sonage that can be conceived, he is head over all things
to his body the church; and in all things he has the
pre-eminence, for he is super-excellent.   As Jesus is of

God made to the church to be more precious than fine gold, so the Holy Spirit leads and teaches each individual member to find that it is indeed so of a truth; the believer is made to feel his need of him in every way, that there is no other way of salvation but by Christ, no other name under heaven by which men can be saved; that Jesus is the only Saviour. What God has made Christ to be, so the believing sinner finds that he is so, more precious than fine gold, even the golden wedge of Ophir.

5. Gold is *tried;* sometimes to prove that it is gold, and sometimes to purge it from dross or alloy. True gold suffers no loss by trial, its value is enhanced by it. Hence believers are comforted by the thought that the work of grace in their hearts suffers no loss by the trials they are called to pass through. Job said that when God had tried him, he should come forth as gold—all gold—purified from all fleshly notions, all creature dependences, all carnal things; these would be consumed or separated and made to appear what they are in themselves. Believers have their gold tried in the fire. Every gift, every grace of God's Spirit undergoes furnace work; grace must be tried, it must be tested, it shall be proved of what sort it is, and be found to the praise and honour of God. Trials strengthen every grace, as well as manifest whose work it is: and that which tends to the glory of God is found also to result in the comforting and establishing the believer in his hope and assurance of eternal bliss. Gold perisheth in the using if not in the fire, but the work of divine grace in the heart is for eternity. Every wave of trouble, every sorrow, every stroke of affliction will be found to have had its appointed work, and to have fully accomplished the design of him who sits as a refiner to purify the sons of Levi; not by washing but by melting; precious thought, the Lord will spare no pains, no exercise, till all sin, earth, and self is thoroughly purged, and his work perfected in infinite wisdom, power, and glory. Was not Jesus tried when on this earth, was he not proved as gold is proved? he was manifested to be, and declared to be the Son of God with power. As the Son of man; he learned obedience by the things which he suffered, and as the Captain of our salvation he was made perfect through suffering.

6. In ancient times *gold was plentiful.* The Jews pos-

sessed it in abundance, it seemed to be everything to them; even Job was suspected of having made it his confidence. The rich man's wealth is his strong city is a proverb. Money indeed is said to answer all things, and while it lasts it is everything to its owner, but riches make to themselves wings. Gold becomes, in process of time and wear, exhaustible; now Jesus is not only everything to the believer, possessing in him abundance, plentifulness, a fulness of blessing, (Eph. i. 3,) but there is in him an inexhaustible fulness: "In him dwelleth all the fulness of the Godhead bodily." The present Jews have lost their gold, where can it be found? but Jesus is as precious as ever, he is as rich to the believer now as ever he was to Adam, to Abel, or any other saint who lived before the flood.

> " Millions of happy spirits live,
>   On thy exhaustless store,
> From thee they all their bliss receive,
>   And still thou givest more."

7. *Gold is precious* because of its excellences. The golden wedge of Ophir was famous for its size and its quality; but it is no longer precious; where is its excellency? it has ceased to exist. The Victoria nugget, of 146 lbs. weight, its fame has dropped; these extraordinary lumps of precious metal have only a temporary name, it passes away with the flight of time; the lump is reduced, manufactured, and becomes dispersed. Here we see our text illustrated, Jesus is more precious than the fine gold, the wedge of Ophir; he remains ever what he was when first known and loved by the believer. Jesus is always precious to them who believe in all his offices and characters; he is their life, their meat, their drink, their clothing, their home, their comfort, their light, their joy, their hope; he is their all in all; they are redeemed not with silver and gold, which are corruptible, but with the precious blood of Christ. The more believers live on Christ, the more they love him, the more they delight in him, the more they feel they cannot do without him; they count everything of earth and home but as dross for the excellency of the knowledge of Jesus Christ. O my friends in the gospel, do you know anything about this feeling of high esteem for the Lord Jesus Christ? Has he been made more precious to you

than fine gold, even the golden wedge of Ophir? Come, let the question go home close to your conscience, for be you sure of this—

"None but Jesus
Can do helpless sinners good."

8. Gold *is beautiful*. It is always admired, it is always beautiful, it is always valuable, it cannot be excelled; whatever is manufactured of it has a superiority and a magnificence above any other metal. But O how superior, super-excellent is Christ to the believer in his Person as the God-man Mediator! His excellences are indescribable; he is the chiefest of ten thousand of all that can be valuable and useful; he is without comparison; he is above all that can be compared to him. How beautiful he is as the Rose of Sharon, how beautiful he is as the Lily of the Valley, as the Cedar of Lebanon; a Sun among ten thousand stars; he is altogether lovely. In all things of nature, whether on earth or in heaven, he has the pre-eminence. He is to be glorified above everything that can be named. His name shall endure for ever, and men shall be blessed in him. He is the beloved of his Father, his own Elect, in whom the eternal Jehovah delighteth; his beloved Son, in whom he is well pleased. He is most glorious in the sight of all angels in heaven, who worship and adore him, and who eternally will contemplate the wonders of his mysterious and glorious Person. And how he will be admired of all his saints, when brought to their heavenly home to behold him in his glory, the glory which he had with his Father before the world was. If faith, even now, can discover something of his inconceivable beauty, what will it be then? The very thought of it fills the heart with a joy that is unspeakable; it draws down a foretaste of the blessings, and anticipates the heavenly felicity. The fine gold, the golden wedge of Ophir shall perish when the world shall be burnt up; but the glory, the beauty of Jesus will ever shine forth more bright and more splendid.

9. Gold is noted for *its strength*. In itself its tenacity is so great that a wire the eighteenth part of an inch will bear 500 lbs. without breaking. Well, this is a remarkable property of gold; but how super-excellent is the Lord Jesus Christ above all things in nature! He who made gold so strong, did he not give it its strength?

Speak we of strength? His arm is strong. He is
strength. Happy is he who can say, " In the Lord have
I righteousness *and strength.*" "God is our refuge *and
strength.*" How infinitely strong was he when he bore
all the sins of all his people in his own body on the tree.
He upholds all things by the word of his power. The
things which are seen display his eternal power and Godhead. What a matter of eternal rejoicing is the truth
that Jesus Christ is the mighty God! The name of the
Lord is a strong tower ; the righteous runneth into it and
is safe.

10. Gold is *weighty.* Gold, when unmixed and un-
alloyed, is the most solid, and therefore the heaviest of all
metals. Its substantialness, whether for use or for ornament, makes it valuable, and causes it to be so much appreciated. Hence the Lord Jesus Christ is compared to
it. But he is infinitely beyond it in the benefits and advantages which result from the knowledge and enjoyment
of him and his salvation. The soul who is brought to
know Christ inherits substance ; his riches are unsearchable ; the knowledge of Christ Jesus is the most weighty
and durable of all sciences. It is heavenly wisdom ; it is
life eternal. The believer in Jesus has more in' him than
all the wealth which all the mines on earth could supply.
In him we have all our souls can want, or that can make
us blest and truly happy.

11. Gold is *ornamental.* It is chiefly used for splendour and ornament ; it has attractions beyond all other
metals, on account of its brilliancy. When the bright
sun shines upon the burnished gold, it has a most dazzling
glory. Thus it is, though inadequately, that gold represents the glories of our Immanuel, whether in reference to
his divine nature or his exalted and glorified manhood.
Thus the heavenly Jerusalem is described as being " pure
gold," the streets thereof being of pure gold, as it were
transparent glass. There is nothing on earth beyond
gold to which the Lord Jesus can be compared ; his
superior glory and excellency is infinitely beyond its
brightest splendour, its perfect purity, its utmost solidity
or durability. His very name is an ornament to every
true believer ; they value his name as being far more precious than fine gold, even the golden wedge of Ophir. It
is their crown of glory ; it is their diadem of beauty ; and
I can say for myself,

" So, gracious Saviour! on my breast,
 May thy dear name be worn;
 A sacred ornament and guard,
  To endless ages borne."

12. Gold is *unchangeable*. It remains essentially what
it is under all states and conditions. It will not rust nor
consume; it is indestructible by fire or air; the strongest
heat will not change its metallic qualities, nor will it lose
a grain in weight. Such is our ever adorable Lord God,
our Redeemer, Jesus Christ, the same yesterday, to-day,
and for ever. Unchangeable in his Person, unchangeable
in his mediatorial offices and characters, unchangeable in
his love, unchangeable in his will and purposes towards
his church, unchangeable in his power. He is ever the
same, who wast, and art, and is the Almighty. With him
there is no variableness, neither shadow of turning. He
is of one mind, who can turn him? Creatures change,
circumstances change, our frames and feeling vary, we
change our mind, alter our purposes; but our Jesus
changes not: "I am God; I change not, therefore ye
sons of Jacob are not consumed." We glory in an unchanging God, an unchanging salvation; thus Jesus, the
God-man is made more precious to us than fine gold,
more precious to us than the golden wedge of Ophir. The
Spirit of truth takes of the things of Christ, reveals them
to us, applies them to us; by this we discover the worth
and beauties of our ever precious and most glorious
Christ:

 " His worth, if all the nations knew,
  Sure the whole earth would love him too."

And what shall I more say? for the time would fail me
to tell of those negative points of comparison wherein
gold, however precious we may deem it, fails altogether.
Riches can procure food, raiment, every luxury, supply
every convenience and comfort the body can require; but
in the most important seasons of grief, trial, affliction, or
necessity, they can afford no aid, no support, no con
solation. Gold cannot give health of body nor peace of
mind. Without these, gold yields no enjoyment. But
here is the peculiar excellency of Jesus Christ, what gold
cannot procure, he can bestow. In the seasons of trial,
he can support the soul, bring it through, and make them
blessings indeed. By him the soul has pardon of all its
sins, and peace with God. By him the comforts of his

Spirit, the hope of everlasting glory, the assurance of an unalienable title to an inheritance incorruptible, undefiled, and that fadeth not away is imparted. These are true riches, which can never lose their value, can never fade, and never fail. They are all treasured up in Christ Jesus, and are secured for the enjoyment of true believers by the precious and never-failing promises of his own word. O, if we are united to Christ by a true and living faith, how poor and mean are all the things of this earth! How contemptible is gold! how vile in the comparison of Christ and his salvation! The earth, with all its treasures of gold and jewels, he has given to the children of men; but to his church, his beloved, his bride, he hath given himself; what can he do more? What can believers desire more? for with himself he hath given us all things; all things are ours—ours for ever—unsearchable riches—durable riches—everlasting glory. Remember, too, it is God the eternal Father who has made the Person of his Son so precious: "I will make a man more precious than fine gold; even a man than the golden wedge of Ophir." And what Jesus is in himself, he is all that to the soul renewed in his image. It is the work of the Holy Ghost to make him so to each believer living on him by precious faith. Let me ask you, dear hearer, "What think ye of Christ?" Can you lift up your heart to him and say, in the words of Newton,

> "Yes, thou art precious to my soul,
>   My transport and my trust,
> Jewels to thee are gaudy toys,
>   And gold is sordid dust."

Then if so, your title is clear to all spiritual blessings in heavenly places in him; what a rich inheritance is yours. All is yours in title; all you need now is the earnest; this you will have the more you are led to live by faith on the Son of God, who loved you and gave himself for you. May the Spirit of all grace and truth lead you on to know more of the unsearchable riches of Christ, and to know the love of Christ, which passeth knowledge. In him there is everything to love, everything that can be desired. The soul once fixed on him, lives upon him, walks with him, looks to him. Oh, the blessedness of being brought to cease from man, to be brought out of self, and away from all human things. My friends, if we want to know Christ more, it must be by daily living upon him, living by him, living in him. Not upon ourselves, not even upon what his Spirit has done in us, not his gifts in us, not his graces in us. It is himself, his Person, who is made precious to the believer, not what the believer is made to be. And until he is brought out of himself, to live quite away from himself, he knows but little of what it is to live upon Christ. This is all my salvation and all my desire. I, too, would fain walk with him, live upon him alway; but I find the world and Satan tempt me with a thousand baubles to keep me from looking to him. Too often I am sunk down within myself, and feel myself a miserable, wretched, crawling worm, as I am indeed in myself; but this is not the life of faith, it is the life of earth. I want to rise above it; I want to know more of Christ and the power of his resurrection; I am thankful to feel the desire, and I do often say :

> " O could I know and love him more,
> And all his wondrous grace explore,
> Ne'er would I covet man's esteem,
> But part with all and follow him."

Amen.

THE KINGDOM OF GOD ENTERED THROUGH MUCH TRIBULATION.

A SERMON,

BY CHARLES GORDELIER,

PREACHED AT HEPHZIBAH CHAPEL, DARLING PLACE, MILE END GATE,

On Lord's Day Morning, October 17th, 1865.

"And that we must through much tribulation enter into the Kingdom of God."—Acts xiv. 22.

THERE have been many persons who have begun to make a profession of religion, but on meeting with some obstacle or difficulty in the way, perhaps a few taunts of ridicule from their friends or old companions, or perhaps threatened with the prospect of their employment being taken away, they were so discouraged as to feel something like Bunyan's Pliable, Christian's early companion in his pilgrimage; they've got into the slough of despond, and like Pliable, they get out of it as soon as they can; but then it is with their face towards their old course, and so we see no more of them. The fact was, as good old Gurnall says, "they had a false aim in their profession, and so they soon came to the end of it." They would like to have the crown well enough, but meeting with a cross in the way, and having no will to take it up, they turn back, and so discover their true character and whose servants they are.

But with the true believer in Christ it is far otherwise. The fear of the Lord being planted within his heart by the Spirit of Truth, he is sincere in his first setting out in the divine life; he does not go very far when he begins to feel his weakness, for true religion has *feeling* in it; he soon begins to fear lest he should not hold out to the end; lest some of his old habits of sin should overthrow

No. 18.

him; lest Satan should entrap him; lest the world should allure him back: these things constrain him to cry out again and again, " Hold thou me up and I shall be safe," " Hold up my goings in thy paths." Now this is it, the love of God is shed abroad in his heart, hence he is earnest as well as sincere; his face is set Zionward because his heart is set Zionward—his aim is not centred in self, like the false professor; his delight is in God and in his service; to that all his desires are tending; he feels he has no power to persevere, but he seeks strength from on high; he seeks nothing from self, because Christ is his ALL. His judgment being established in the truth of God, his principles are well fixed; in godly simplicity and sincerity he has his conduct in the world, and thus it is the righteous shall hold on his way.

Yet it is equally true, the pilgrim to the better land is often discouraged because of the way. We read, that in the wilderness, " the souls of the people were much discouraged because of the way;" but still they went on, passing on from one station to another, from strength to strength, and at length they got through all their labour and toil and reached the promised land. So the believer in Christ, though he is often dismayed, often cast down, often perplexed, yet he has the assurance of final salvation; he is assured of an entrance being administered unto him abundantly into the everlasting kingdom of his Lord and Saviour Jesus Christ. (2 Pet. i. 11.) And this assurance of entrance is coupled with the assurance of tribulation; also, it is the pathway through the wilderness, and Mr. Hart very truly says—

> " The souls that would to Jesus press,
> Must fix this firm and sure,
> That tribulations more or less,
> They must and shall endure."

And we find Jesus forewarned his disciples of the fact: " In the world ye shall have tribulation." (John xvi. 33.) Peter reminds us, " If need be ye are in heaviness through manifold temptation;" (1 Pet. i. 6;) and here in the text before us, the disciples are exhorted to continue in the faith, and " that we must through much tribulation enter the kingdom."

This leads us to notice the connection of the text before we proceed further with our subject. Paul and Barnabas had been preaching the gospel in several cities among the heathen, and with some degree of success; then followed persecution, stirred up by the malignant Jews who tracked the holy men in their journeys. Paul himself had been so stoned as to be left for dead, but he revived, and even returned to the very places where his persecutors had come. He did not go in a spirit of bravado, but for the sake of confirming the souls of the disciples of Antioch and Iconium, lest the good seed sown should have been injured, lest they should faint at his tribulations, and be turned out of the narrow path of life—not only confirming them in the verities of the gospel, but exhorting them, notwithstanding bitter persecutions, to continue in the faith, and adding "that we must through much tribulation enter the kingdom of God."

Let us then, with the help and blessing of the Lord, in the *first* place endeavour to say a few things respecting THE KINGDOM OF GOD here spoken of in the text; in the *second* place speak of THE WAY AND MANNER OF ENTERING this kingdom; and in the *third* place state some of THE REASONS why it must be entered through much tribulation.

I. *The Kingdom of God.* I presume you all know that a kingdom is a territory of land where the people live under certain regulations, and are subject to the dominion of a man, who is their ruling head, and is styled a king. By the kingdom of God *generally*, we may understand his universal dominion over all things; for he creates, preserves, protects, and gives laws to and regulates all his creatures, and dispenses judgments and favours as he pleaseth. (1 Chron. xxix. 11; Ps. cxlv. 12.) By the kingdom of God *specially*, we are to understand it consists of persons living under the reign of God in the Person of Christ, his co-eternal and co-equal Son, being subject to his laws as made known in his word, called also the visible church of Christ. This kingdom of God, as may be supposed, is not of this world. Our Lord declared this to the Roman governor: "My kingdom is not of this world." It is a spiritual kingdom, the kingdom of God is within; it has to do with the hearts and lives of men before God. The kingdom of God is also called in the Scriptures the kingdom of heaven, the gospel of the kingdom, the gospel of Christ. These refer to the gospel dispensation, and is so designated to distinguish it from the Jewish dispensation. The Jewish dispensation was peculiar to the Jews as a nation; they were *nationally* God's people, and they worshipped God in a way and form, as prescribed by him, peculiar to themselves. The gospel dispensation is without respect to persons as a nation, and has regard to believers in the Lord Jesus Christ; but more particularly it is intended to signify the ruling power of divine grace in the soul, and the future state of glory of the blessed in heaven.

Now, our text comprises all that is intended by the terms gospel dispensation, the reign of grace, and the future blessedness. In the 9th Luke ii. we read: "And he sent them to preach the kingdom of God." In John xviii. 36: Jesus answered, "My kingdom is not of this world." The apostle Paul (Romans xiv. 17) says, "The kingdom of God is not meat and drink, but righteousness, and peace, and joy in the Holy Ghost;" and in Col. i. 13, "Who hath delivered us from the power of darkness, and hath translated us into the kingdom of his dear Son." These several passages, you perceive, refer to the work of grace in the soul. I pass by, for the present, such portions as refer to the heavenly state as being the kingdom of God, as my object, more particularly, is to lay before you that which refers to the kingdom within; this concerns us most; if we have the one, we shall have the other; for where the Lord gives grace he also gives glory. The connecting link is our own experience, and the testimony of the Holy Spirit in the conscience.

Observe, 1. The kingdom of God is one of *grace*. It originated in that heavenly compact between the Persons of the ever-blessed Trinity, the triune Jehovah, before the foundation of the world. The Father's love is the source of all grace. The love of the Son is the source of all mercy, in that having become our Surety and Ransom, mercy can now be shown to every penitent believer in him. The love of the Spirit is displayed in becoming the administrator of the covenant in harmony with the general designs of God's providence on earth. 2. The kingdom of God is one of *power*. Once the soul was dead in sin, a captive to the law of sin and death, though it was alive in the world, in league with Satan, and in his slavery. But being redeemed from the strong one by the hand of him who is stronger than he, the liberated one is free from the old yoke of sin; a complete change has been wrought in him. Once he was in a state of death, but now he is made alive and enlightened; being pardoned, he has peace and joy; he feels it to be a power of heaven over earth, Christ over Satan, grace over sin, the Spirit over the flesh and the world. 3. The kingdom of God is one of *glory*. It is a final and complete victory over sin, death, hell, and the grave. The ransomed of the Lord are everlastingly secured in the abodes of bliss and happiness. No sin or sorrow can ever find admision there. The heavenly state is one of eternal felicity, safety, joy, and peace. The blessed sing the song of providence and redemption, Moses and the Lamb. It is a place of indescribable glory, for the "eye hath not seen, nor hath the ear heard, nor hath it entered the heart to conceive the things which God hath prepared for them that love him." (1 Cor. ii. 9.)

II. *The way and manner of entrance.* In taking up the second portion of our subject, we may observe that the way and manner of the believer's entrance into the kingdom is not the least important; in fact, it is the part with which we have most to do; it has to do with our own positive experience; its realities come vividly before us, and they come within our own consciousness. The kingdom of God being partly without and partly within, it exercises all the powers of the new-born soul. Faith, hope, love, and desire are called forth; these inspire it through all the mazes of the wilderness state to that which is without, while that which is within is being manifested and unfolded more and more in and through the exercises arising out of the toils, trials, temptations, and sorrows of the present state of existence.

The doctrine of our text is founded on the truth of our Lord's statement, "In the world ye shall have tribulation." (John xvi. 33.) The idiom of the phrase itself is evidently taken from the history of David. The apostle had well proved that "bonds and afflictions abided him." "Those that will live godly in Christ Jesus shall suffer persecution." The very first step in following the Lord is on the threshold of trial; "he that will follow me let him first take up *his* cross, deny himself, and follow me." (John xvi. 24.) Thus we see there is no escaping the trials and persecutions incident to following the Lord Jesus Christ; not that there is any blind fatal necessity in the fact, but it arises out of the divine appointment and constitution of things; and this, be it remembered, is according to the good pleasure of his will; in other words, the sovereignty of God. As soon as you become a follower of the Lord Jesus Christ, immediately the world takes offence; it is naturally opposed to the Gospel of Christ; it is the way Satan works against Christ in the hearts of men. Satan has lost a slave, the world has lost a help-mate, the power of sin is checked; they are all in league against the ransomed sinner: but vain are all their efforts to recover them; as sure as they are not appointed to wrath but to obtain salvation, so sure shall they enter the kingdom of heaven, though it be through much tribulation.

You look at the history of David, see what tribulation he encountered before he entered the kingdom. He was divinely anointed, and in a larger measure than his predecessor Saul; for it is a significant fact that whereas David was anointed with a *horn* of oil, while Saul was anointed with a *phial* only; typical, doubtless, of the Lord Jesus having the Spirit poured out upon him without measure. We see also in the circumstances of David which intervened between the anointing and his coming to the throne, something which is also typical of all the Lord's people before they become possessed of the heavenly kingdom. As sure as David was divinely anointed to the kingdom, so the path to it, and every step in it, was also divinely appointed; every trial, every cross, their length, sharpness, and number. The anointing and the appointing are divinely connected, forming a circle of goodness and mercy which surrounds every believer in Christ.

> "To his church, his joy, his treasure,
>   Every sorrow works for good;
> They are dealt in weight and measure,
>   Yet how little understood:
>   Not in anger,
>   But from his dear covenant love."

Believers have to struggle through much opposition in entering the kingdom. Many things seem to threaten their destruction, God's own promise often seems a delusion; entering the kingdom of heaven with the world, sin, self, and Satan all combined against him, seems the greatest improbability. His progress is the greatest mystery; yet there is certainly some progress, an onward progress; at least, there is a divinely holding on, if there is not a sensibly going on. But eventually, all believers shall find they are more than victorious through him that hath loved them over all sin, death, hell, and the grave. They must enter the kingdom, and there is nothing on earth, above or beneath, can hinder it. Their entrance is secured by almighty destination.

It is through much tribulation we must enter the kingdom. Tribulations may be divided into two classes, those which are without and those which are within. Those without arise from the world, and those within from those exercises of soul known only to the believer in Jesus. We will speak of the first, *tribulations from without.*

1. *Opposition from the world.* Generally speaking, when the Lord's people are reclaimed from an ungodly life, their former companions will become their deadly enemies. Being haters of God, they will hate them. The world has ever hated the Lord Jesus Christ, and will continue to do so while Satan is its prince. The world will love its own, and will hate everything that savours of Christ and his gospel. And why so? Because its own works are evil; it loves darkness rather than light, and will not come to the light. The children of light are called to walk in the midst of a crooked and perverse generation, and being perverse, no wonder there is a continual collision between them and the children of light. There is a counteraction against the child of God in all his ways, his goings, and his steps; he is withstood continually, here is his tribulation. In some cases the world employs its fascinating influence without making the soul feel it for a time. It is deceitful, enticing, and imploring; hiding itself, making itself to appear on the side of truth and righteousness, as if it were impressed with a love of truth, making itself engaged in the religion of the day. How often the believer finds his great struggle is with the world; so enticing in its methods of deceit, leading the soul astray imperceptibly, as Mr. Hart says, so as not to " see the snare before we feel the smart." The world is so flexible that it will become any and everything, so that it may lead the soul away from Christ.

2. Specially do we find opposition *from carnal professors.* These are a great annoyance to sincere believers. They are " pricks in their eyes and thorns in their sides."

With fair speeches they catch the unwary, rob them of their comforts, bring them into bondage, and cause them much distress of soul. How often have we thought that we had found a true sympathising friend, cherished them in our bosoms, communed with them, when to our dismay and sorrow they have proved deadly serpents; wolves in sheeps' clothing, warm in their apparent attachments and words, but showing their teeth, ready to bite and to devour one when we have resisted their encroachments. Too often it has been worse; grievous wolves have come into the fold of Christ, not sparing the flock, and all under the name of religion. Some come into it to promote their trade; some to make friends, borrow money, never returning it; going from one place of worship to another, from one town to another, making a living out of the kindness and generosity of the unsuspecting. Some cause great tribulation by spreading pernicious errors, sowing the seeds of discord in the churches; some, evidently, mix with the people of God, under the pretence of a higher tone of spirituality and more enlightened views of truth, merely to draw away disciples after them. Some professors cause great grief in the souls of sincere disciples by their laxity of principles, indulgence of pleasure and amusements; their worldly policies in business, their craft, cunning, over reaching, oppression, knavery; all these constitute a source of much tribulation, which the disciple of Christ must pass through before he can enter the kingdom.

3. And what opposition is found often amongst even *good and gracious men.* How often mistaken views of each other's motives and purposes have given rise to serious misconstructions of each other's conduct. Paul and Barnabas, for instance; what a sharp contention there was between them, yet both designing to serve the Lord Christ, but mistaking each other till they both became unyielding, and at last part unfriendly, and never more mention each other's names. It is a great and sore trial when brethren fall out by the way, "a brother offended is harder to be won than a strong city, and their contentions are like the bars of a castle." Yet it does please the Lord, at times, to suffer bitter roots to spring up, causing much trouble and grief. To cease from man is a difficult lesson to learn; and when we find one's foes are of one's own household, to be wounded in the house of

our friends, even the church as well as the world becomes
a path of tribulation to us; but we must go through it
ere we can enter the kingdom.

4. *Tribulations in the providence of God.* These are
of a multiform character. Peter, who had a large experience of external things incident to the church of God,
speaks of manifold temptations, of their producing heaviness of spirit, and of the necessity of its being so. The
lives of Jacob, of David, and of Paul, were full of tribulation
in the world. They stand out as waymarks for the tried
believer in all ages. We refer to them as illustrations of
the great truth: "Many are the afflictions of the righteous,
but the Lord delivereth them out of them all." David
was confident his trials would never be suffered to be
above what he was able to bear: "Thou which hast
shewed me great and sore troubles shall quicken me again,
and bring up again from the depths of the earth." (Ps.
lxxi. 20.) His peculiar trials, and the number of them,
was a matter of history associated with the memory of his
name, "and the times that went over him." (1 Chron.
xxix. 30.) David, though long ago fallen asleep, still
serves his generation; the record of his deep experience,
both circumstantial and spiritual, has for ages comforted
the church of the living God, and will continue to do so
to the end of time. The experience of the apostle Paul
is perhaps more of a ministerial character, yet contains
the elements of much instruction and gracious encou-
tagement to all the church of God; (see 2 Cor. iv.
8, 9, 10;) while that of Jacob has ever and anon been
referred to throughout the word of truth for the comfort
and support of the saints in tribulation; indeed, a large
proportion of the promises to the tried and afflicted are
addressed to his spiritual seed under his name Jacob.
Troubles in early life, long servitude under oppression,
providences dark, crooked, and mysterious; disappointments, crosses, losses, failures, bereavements, painful deep
cutting sorrows, wave upon wave, form the sum of
troubles through which many a dear child of God has to
pass; long bodily affliction, fiery trials of persecutions,
overwhelming floods of bitter distress from our own mistakes and errors in life, have marked the course of many
a choice believing saint. The footsteps of the flock of
slaughter, if inquired for, will be sure to be found in the
path of tribulation; it is the way to the kingdom; there

is no exemption; it is the royal road to it; the Saviour himself has gone before us every step of the way. He is our forerunner. He has taken possession of the kingdom, his saints follow him, they are also appointed to a kingdom, and shall surely possess it; they are made kings unto God, and shall rule and reign with him. Tried believer, faint not at your present tribulations; they are all ordered for your good, your present good, your future good, your everlasting good: it is now, at this present moment, that you are entering the kingdom. Is not God now supporting you in the midst? You cannot say that he has forsaken you; you may perhaps have expected to have been borne *above* your trials, and I know many of the saints have been much blessed in them, but there is really no guarantee that it shall be so in every case. God has mercifully designed that every trial shall work its apparent end; the end, both with the degree and the number, being all appointed by his infinite wisdom in love for your soul's eternal good. Faith's estimate of tribulation, as you know, is this: " Our light affliction, which is but for a moment, worketh for us a far more exceeding and eternal weight of glory; while we look not at the things which are seen, but at the things which are not seen; for the things which are seen are temporal, but the things which are not seen are eternal." (2 Cor. iv. 17, 18.)

We proceed to notice the second class of tribulations: *those from within;* not that they are of a secondary nature in themselves, by no means. Spiritual troubles, indeed, concern the believer most, they weigh the heaviest; but our text has reference chiefly to those of an outward kind. The first soul trouble arises from the sight of sin. The Spirit of Truth commences his gracious work by convincing the believer of the evil nature of sin. He works in the heart a godly sorrow for sin, a repentance that needeth not to be repented of. The weight of guilt, the sense of unpardoned sin is often such as to sink the spirit down into the lowest depths of misery. And until the believer has some apprehension of the exceeding sinfulness of sin, with some heart rendings by reason of those terrors which a spiritual sight of God's holy law reveals, there is no entering the kingdom of grace. Then it is the Spirit leads the soul to find that by Christ his sin is purged, that for him the law has been fulfilled, that

c

God is reconciled by the death of his Son, and peace is assured him by a sweet testimony in his conscience. This is a path which no carnal professor knoweth, and which the eye of the unregenerate hath not seen; the unclean shall not pass over it; it shall be for those who must enter the kingdom; the wayfaring men, though fools, shall not err therein.

But our text says it is through *much* tribulations; soul troubles are numerous indeed; the conflict between flesh and spirit occasions more troubles than all those the world can ever produce. What fear of falling back into the world, what fear of being left to fall into some sin, of being caught in some trap or snare of the fowler. What fierce and fiery temptations from the adversary, the devil. What sore trials arise from the hidings of God's countenance, when no light shines upon the sacred word, when no unction is experienced from the ministry, when the ordinances of God's house become barren seasons, time after time; no liberty at the throne of grace; when fellowship with the saints becomes insipid; when, instead of one's peace flowing like a river, one's heart is more like the troubled sea, casting up mire and dirt. What raging of unbelief, doubt, discontent, ingratitude, pride, self-will, hard thoughts of God, misapprehension of his dealings with us; such foolishness, such baseness, such vileness, emanating from the depraved nature, indicating rather the reign of sin and corruption than the reign of grace; all these feelings creating such a disturbed and unsettled state of the soul as to cause it to feel as if the Lord had quite forsaken it, or rather had never begun a good work at all, and that the latter end of one's profession would leave one's state and being worse than the first. Such has been the discomposed state of the believer under such exercises as these as to feel tempted to give up all profession of religion, go right into the world, and never mix more with the people of God. To the human reason there seems the certain destruction of all hope; for there seems no faith, no love, no light, no life, no power; such contradictions and disappointments instead of direct answers to fervent and importunate prayer for growth in grace as is truly amazing and confounding. We think God is turned against us, and that ere long he will make us an awful example of the veriest hypocrisy that ever existed; expose all our hollow pretensions and deceit, and that we shall die at last in infamy and digrace. O how my soul has been racked with these tortures; how I have tortured myself with these instruments of torture, keeping it all to myself; or if I brought my case before the Lord, it always seemed as though the heavens were brass and the earth iron; no feeling, yet all feeling; a feeling of hardness, no tenderness. I could have been eloquent with the language of Asaph, David, Jeremiah, and others who have poured forth long and bitter complaints. The poet Newton has well described such soul troubles as these; he says:

> " I ask'd the Lord that I might grow,
>   In faith, and love, and every grace ;
> Might more of his salvation know,
>   And seek more earnestly his face.

> " I thought that in some favour'd hour,
>   At once he'd answer my request,
> And by his love's constraining power,
>   Subdue my sins, and give me rest.

> " Instead of this he made me feel
>   The hidden evils of my heart,
> And let the angry powers of hell
>   Assault my soul in every part.

> " Yea, more, with his own hand he seem'd
>   Intent to aggravate my woe ;
> Cross'd all the fair designs I schemed,
>   Blasted my gourds, and laid me low."

Thus it has been with me, and I know it has been with some of you. These exercises of soul are the tribulations which the Lord has appointed to be the way and the manner of entering the kingdom. The Lord does indeed answer prayer, but it is by crosses; in order to strengthen faith, he tries it; and this trial of our faith, as also of any other grace, is made the means of proving it, proving that it is faith, real faith, the fruit of his Spirit; and when God reveals his purposes of love to us, showing that our tribulations have not been our destructions, as we anticipated, but have been working out the very object which we at first desired, then we can rejoice, though for a season there was a needs be for our being in heaviness, through manifold temptations; the trial of our faith being much more precious than of gold, which perisheth, though it be tried with fire, it shall at last be found unto praise and honour and glory of Jesus Christ. Then it is we can glory in tribulations, because it is the entering of the kingdom; knowing that "tribulation worketh patience, and patience experience, and experience hope; and hope that maketh not ashamed, because the love of God is shed abroad in our hearts, by the Holy Ghost which is given unto us." (Rom. v. 4.)   Brethren, this is how we enter in and possess the kingdom.   There is nothing so well establishes the believer in the love and faithfulness of Jehovah as these exercises of soul about the work of God in us.   Our comforts grow out of our crosses; our gains spring from our losses; our keenest sorrows yield the sweetest comforts; our sharpest griefs are made the occasion of our highest joy.   And while on the one hand, in the brightest sky of our anticipations, we see the darkest clouds of reversion, disappointment, and dejection, we find, on the other, the windy storm and tempest hasten us towards the desired haven.   Every trial has its appropriate connection with each other, they all work together for the soul's real welfare; and, as Mr. Horne truly says,

> " Their end, triumphant, always lays
> The ground of peace for fervent praise."

III. But I must now, in the third place, state some of THE REASONS why it is that through *much* tribulation we *must* enter the kingdom.

1. That *God may draw us nearer to himself.*   Ah, say you, that is just what I have been praying for this many a long year; but I see no answer yet, and am often tempted to doubt the reality of prayer, and to say, "Where is the promise of his coming?"   Now let me call your attention to a passage or two in God's word.   In Ex. xix. 4, the Lord, by his servant Moses, speaks to his people: "Ye have seen what I did unto the Egyptians, and how I bare you on eagle's wings, and brought you unto myself."   He appeals to his own work, and to their own experience.   How did the Lord bring his people to himself?   Was it not through the way of the Red Sea, and the wilderness, with all its hardships, privations, and discouragements?   Was it not in the midst of the Red Sea that they rejoiced in the Lord? (Ps. lxvi. 6.)   Did not the Lord lead them about, and there was no strange god with them?   They did all eat of the same spiritual meat, and did all drink of the same spiritual drink; for

they drank of that spiritual Rock that followed them, and that Rock was Christ. (1 Cor. x. 3, 4.) Here we see that Christ was with his church in the wilderness; he led his people about in the waste howling wilderness, instructed them, kept them as the apple of his eye. (Deut. xxxii. 10.) Beloved, has not this been God's method with you? is it not your own experience? Have you not been completely separated from your former Egyptian state? and though brought where you are, have you not known something about serving God in the wilderness? Have not your trials brought you nearer to him? You have had some experience of his loving-kindness in the midst of your wilderness toils and life; you have found the spiritual life maintained through all the exercises of his discipline, the changes about, the wanderings round and round; who has done it? Was it not that same hand which delivered you out of darkness which is even now with you to keep you and to uphold you? He has even now brought you to himself; the end and issue of all your tribulations is now being accomplished in you You are at this very moment entering the kingdom. He has brought you nearer to himself in the wilderness state. In your former state you were quite a stranger to his grace or his mercy, being without God in the world.

2. *That we may have clearer views of his purposes of love and grace.* God's dispensations are often hidden by a cloud. His manifestations of himself are by a cloud. The glory of Jehovah cannot be seen by mortal man: "Verily thou art a God which hideth thyself." (Isa. xlv. 15.) "Why standest thou afar, O Lord, and why hidest thou thyself in times of trouble." (Ps. x. i.) This has been the experience of the saints in old time. God hides himself essentially, experimentally, and providentially, but it is to make a clearer manifestation of his goodness, his power, and his love. In our deepest straits and difficulties, he makes a way in the wilderness. He hid himself from Jacob when Joseph was sold into Egypt, but God revealed himself with greater power and glory when Jacob beheld Joseph in his exalted state, and with his two sons. God hid himself in the stripping providences which Job experienced, but the end was a clearer manifestation of his goodness by greater prosperity; seeing him with the spiritual eye, who had before but heard of him with the natural ear.

"When clouds appear to veil his face,
And clouds surround his throne,
He hides the purpose of his grace,
To make it better known."

The church had a great loss in Elijah being suddenly called away, and at a time when, apparently, he could be least spared; but the Lord sent forth Elisha, in whom was poured forth a double portion of his spirit, and who did twice as great, and many more things for Israel. See how David was stripped of his wives and goods at Ziklag, which were afterwards recovered, and enjoyed more sweetly than before. God strips us of *all* earthly comforts, that he may himself be our *only* spiritual comfort. Times of imminent danger, though enveloped in clouds of mystery, have been made the occasion of God's revealing his gracious design more clearly, and sealing home with greater power the promises of grace. As in Abraham's case, how sorely was he tried when called to offer up his *only* son Isaac, and in that word "only" was the taking away of his hope of the promise; but we see in the critical moment, not only a deliverance, but the ratifying twice and by an oath the promise to him. Beloved, have you not found the mount of danger to be the place where you have seen surprising grace?

3. *That he may strengthen our faith by the trial of our patience.* I have already touched upon this subject under the previous head, and need only to illustrate the point. See how Joseph's faith was strengthened by his trials; his giving charge concerning his bones showed that his desire was that his flesh should rest in hope in the land of promise with his fathers; *nature* would have induced him to have been buried in a splendid Egyptian mausoleum, as a monument of his own greatness, but *grace* has no affection for Egypt, it loves to lie embalmed in Canaan. See David, now on the bed of death, declaring his unabated assurance of his interest in that everlasting covenant ordered in all things and sure; "the times that went over him," he knew, were in God's hand, and that though it was through much tribulation, from the time he slew Goliah, his five years' exile from his own country, till Saul's death, the seven years in which he was opposed in being king over all Israel. And during his kingdom over all Israel, what domestic trials; yet he was brought safely through, he did enter the kingdom.

The trial of our faith is much more precious than of gold which perisheth.

4. *To discover the hidden evils of the heart.* Man by nature is as ignorant of himself as he is of God. He cannot know himself till he is brought into trial. The Israelites were brought into the wilderness to humble them, to prove them, and that they might know what was in their heart. These are fearful lessons to learn. Hezekiah, Job, and Peter, had to undergo fearful trials before they could learn what pride, self will, and other abominations were concealed in them. The use, therefore, of the furnace of trials and afflictions is to purge the child of God from all the dross and corruption of their native selves. It is in the furnace they lose that good opinion of themselves which they once cherished. To wean a man from himself is above nature, it is God's work, and he will do it too, for flesh and blood cannot inherit the kingdom of heaven. And when God has disclosed the native depravity of the heart by fiery trials, then it is the child of God learns to know and feel the plague within, and to come out of himself; and he finds that every step in this direction is to enter the kingdom of God.

5. *To wean you from the world.* This can only be accomplished by tribulation. How can we enter the kingdom of heaven until we are weaned from the world.

> " Our hearts are fastened to this world
> By strong and various ties;
> But every sorrow cuts a cord,
> That urges us to rise."

It is nature, of course, to love the world and the things of it; and the more we have of it, the more difficult the weaning. "Love not the world, nor the things of it," is the admonition of an apostle. The spirit, maxims, pursuits, and manners of the world are always hurtful to believers; they hinder their progress in the divine life; these things cannot be brought into the kingdom of heaven; yet there is something in the human nature of the child of God that cleaves to them; it is not to be wondered at, but he must "come out from among them and be separate, and touch not the unclean thing." So difficult is this self denial to exercise in nature's strength, that God himself burns the lesson into us by the fiery trial of affliction, bodily pains, or bereaving strokes; in them we learn the emptiness, the hollowness, the falsity of the world, and as we advance in this knowledge so we enter the kingdom.

6. *For the confusion of hypocrites.* Much tribulation, trials, afflictions, sorrows, discover who and what they are. "All his days he eateth in darkness, and he hath much sorrow and wrath with his sickness." (Eccles. v. 17.) Affliction is the fan wherewith God purges his floor. (Matt. iii. 12.) He will sift the house of Israel, like as corn is sifted in a sieve; (Amos ix. 9;) but the chaff he will burn with unquenchable fire. Woe, woe unto the hypocrites in Zion; the fire shall try every man's work of what sort it is; and if any man's work shall be burned, he shall suffer loss. (1 Cor. iii. 15.)

7 *For the greater vengeance on their enemies.* The tribulation of the Lord's people is a certain forerunner of the destruction of their enemies. What a strait the Israelites were in at the Red Sea; it seemed the moment of Egyptian triumph, but it was their terrible and final overthrow. Much of the tribulation which the children of Zion have to pass through is caused by their enemies, but a day of reckoning is at hand. It is a righteous thing with God to recompense tribulation to them that trouble his church, but such will never enter the kingdom. Their eternal damnation will be heavy, and it is certain. (2 Thess. i. 6, 9.)

8. *For the glory of God.* Many of our tribulations seem destructive to our present comforts and to our hopes for the future. This is the view we at first generally take, but we are often mistaken; the Saviour assured his disciples that the affliction of Lazarus was not unto death, but for the glory of God. The end of all afflictive dispensations is the glory of God; they accomplish the good of his chosen, and in that is manifested his goodness, love, and power. "Just and true are all thy ways, thou king of saints," is the ascription of praise, and the song sung by the redeemed in heaven. (Rev. xv. 3.) They there see the end from the beginning, and can justify God in all the tribulations they have passed through. They praise him for being brought into them. They praise him for his support and presence they had under them. They praise him for the good they derived from them. They praise him for being brought through them. They praise him that in them has been accom-

plished "all the good pleasure of his goodness, and the work of faith with power." You then who are in any tribulation rest with us; it is the Lord's will that we must tread this path to enter the kingdom. Our good is his object, the end is his glory.

Companions in tribulation: We enter the kingdom, though the way is not of our choosing; we must enter it, none can prevent it. Satan, the world, and our deceitful hearts have done the most they can; but "nothing, nothing" shall be written on all the attempts of the enemies of our peace. "We shall be conquerors all ere long, and more than conquerors too." Not one traveller in the rough and thorny road shall fail, the road is safe and well guarded, shoes of iron and brass for wear, strength for the day,—these are the helps by the way. If in the world we have tribulation, in Christ we have peace. We have, besides, exceeding great and precious promises; these applied to the heart by the Spirit, lift off many a load, and light up the path in a time of darkness. The kingdom of grace leads to the kingdom of glory; he that enters the kingdom of God in his gracious dealings here on earth shall possess it in heavenly glory hereafter. The cross comes first, but the crown is sure. As we must enter the kingdom, so we must be brought through all tribulations; "and so an entrance shall be ministered unto you abundantly into the ever-lasting kingdom of our Lord and Saviour Jesus Christ." To him be all the glory. Amen.

FINDING THE PEARL OF GREAT PRICE.

A SERMON,
BY CHARLES GORDELIER.

PREACHED AT HEPHZIBAH CHAPEL, DARLING PLACE, MILE END GATE,

On Lord's Day Evening, 26th November, 1865.

" The kingdom of heaven is like unto a merchant man seeking goodly pearls; who, when he had found one of great price, went and sold all that he had, and bought it."—MATT. xiii., 45, 46.

THIS chapter displays the remarkable power of illustration which our Lord possessed in teaching. The chapter is a chapter of parables; all of them exhibit some peculiar points of the gospel dispensation. Images and figures are brought before the mind with astonishing rapidity, fulness, and fitness. The first, sowing seed, sets forth the preaching of truth ; then in the others we perceive, the rise and progress of error, the collateral benefits of the truth, the permeating influence of the truth, the value of the truth, and in the last, the draw-net, the general resurrection of mankind and their final separation and destination. This variety of illustration which is here found in the chapter before us ought to lead us to investigate the particular point which is to be understood. At first sight, the parables of the " treasure hid in a field," and " the merchantman seeking goodly pearls," appear as if intended to convey one and the same truth, but they vary in one striking particular. You see, in the treasure hid in a field, a labouring man unexpectedly finds what he was not looking for. In this of the pearls, a man is looking for something good, but finds something better than all he had. The conduct of the finders, in each case, was precisely alike. Both " sold all " to make the thing found their

No. 19.

own property.   In the next, on the fishing net, bad as well
as good were gathered and much was cast away.

There is no doubt, by the parable of the treasure hid in
a field, is intended to show that a man, while engaged in
his legitimate or ordinary calling, may have unexpectedly
revealed to him the nature and importance of divine truth,
and such is its power upon the heart and conscience as to
lead him joyfully to part with all things that would hinder him from securing it for himself.

In the parable before us, we have a merchantman, a
dealer, seeking goodly pearls ; he is looking only for pearls ;
he is possessed of some already ; it is evident he under-
stands their quality, and is able to estimate their value ;
he is seeking goodly pearls, not common or ordinary ones,
but such as are better than those he has, or else he would
have been content.   In his search he unexpectedly discovers one of great price, which he appreciates more than all
he possessed or those he is looking for; he resolves to purchase it, and therefore readily sells off all he had in order
to make this exceeding rare and precious pearl his own.
Such was his estimation of this one pearl of great price
in comparison with those he possessed and of those for
which he was seeking.   •

In this parable, there seems to me a further advance in
relation to the discovery of divine truth.   A man may
possess much that is valuable in itself of a mental kind,
as a knowledge of general literature for instance; he may
have a tolerable acquaintance with the various languages
in ordinary use ; he may be laudably occupied in the search
for further acquisitions in those higher branches of the
arts and sciences which give a polish to refined society; he
may even be seeking a knowledge of Scripture truth, aiming to promote the knowledge of God and morality in a
philanthropic spirit, all which things are good and com-
mendable in themselves, and constitute ornaments to the
character ; but when the true knowledge of Jesus Christ
by a divine revelation is made known to him, immediately
he is convinced that its worth far surpasses all that he
has ever known or is seeking to know ; gladly he relin-
quishes all further search for human learning, and willingly
sacrifices the result of present attainments and every other
consideration, so that he may be truly possessed of this one
supreme object of his delight and desire.

This parable will also apply to those who are seeking

pleasure or profit in those things which at some period of their life they would be glad to part with, if perchance, something else presented itself commanding their love and desire above all that now occupies their time and attention. It may be, some of you, like our merchantman seeking goodly pearls, are looking for wealth, or are seeking happiness in the things of this life; or going about to establish your own righteousness, seeking acceptance with God on account of it; or that you are looking for salvation itself through some other misdirected channel : or perhaps some of you may be seeking a preparation for death and for judgment, and, like Martha, you are cumbered about many things in the way of good works, but ignorant of the one thing needful; which ignorance leads you to seek everything else short of right saving faith in the Lord Jesus Christ. Now, if in the course of your self-constituted search there should be, in the good pleasure of God's will, presented to your view the great truth that in Christ alone there is such a fulness of any blessing you can possibly want, would you not be ready to abandon every method of your own devising, and everything you fondly cherish, for the sake of realizing in him and in his work, that which would make you really happy now and truly blessed hereafter? I feel persuaded you would. O may the Spirit of Truth lead you to Christ, and give you understanding to discover that he is the Pearl of great price.

And there are believing souls too, sincere souls, who, like the merchantman of our text, go about seeking goodly pearls, I mean spiritual pearls, such pearls as you and I cannot do without, if ever we have known any thing of God's truth ; such souls have many evidences of a good work begun in them, but they cannot be said to be fully established in the truth as it is in Jesus ; they are only seekers, they have tasted that the Lord is gracious, they have handled and felt of the good word of life, they have known what it is to have the comforts of God's Spirit imparted to them, to have been " dandled on the knee," and to cherish a hope for which they would not exchange worlds if they were offered ; they have felt the sweetness of pardoning love and peace sealed home to the conscience, all this has been to them like life from the dead, their former misery and burden of sin and guilt they have remembered no more: in the sunshine of Jehovah's presence it has been their delight to live and walk all the day long, for indeed in his presence is fulness of joy. But when the believer finds there is night, darkness instead of light, when his day-dreams subside and vanish, when he feels he is apt to stumble, when he finds he has to walk by faith and not by sight, when the ordinances of God's house prove barren opportunities, when the ministry of the word appears unsavoury, when the word of God itself seems a sealed book, when he no longer experiences those blessed frames of soul which lifted him along the road so blithe and lightly, when, as dear good Berridge says—

" With cheerfullest praise, we tripp'd up steep ways,
And hop'd to reach Canaan in six or eight days ;"

then it is the believer sinks down into something like sadness and sorrow, he misses the presence of Jesus, the shining of whose face was everything to him; now he feels his faith is low, his love is small, his joy is gone, his hope is like a flickering light on the point of extinction, and his peace, which once flowed so sweetly from a sense of divine assurance, seems to have been withdrawn or lost he can't tell how; and when temptations set in he finds he has no strength, he is tossed about and not comforted, and he is ready to imagine the Lord has forsaken him quite, and will be gracious to him no more. Poor soul, I see how it is, thou hast been living on thy frames and feelings ; while they lasted thy happiness lasted, when they declined you declined, and now you go about seeking goodly pearls, you want to find some evidences of your faith, your hope, your love, and your joy ; well, these are good in themselves and very proper to have, but none of these things are to be compared to the pearl of great price. Christ alone is that Pearl, and naught else can ever satisfy thy soul. . To feel there is only life when we feel the graces of his Spirit in lively exercise is making a Christ of his work in us, instead of living *on what he is to us and what he has done for us.* I grant the believer has his frames and feelings, and there is no true religion without them, but they are not our life. Christ is our life ; they are goodly pearls, but he is the Pearl of great price. The truths of the gospel, the means of grace, the ordinances of God's house, the fellowship of the saints, are all goodly pearls ; and the spiritual merchant delights to trade in them; but Christ himself, his Person and his work, he alone is the Pearl of great price. He is *the object of our faith*, not ourselves, we are *the subjects* of faith; we must not live upon what we are, but upon what he is; keep this distinction in view, heavenly trading re- quires heavenly understanding, and when Christ is revealed as the Pearl of price,

> "That merchant is divinely wise
> Who makes this Pearl his own."

But it may be that there is before us another class of spiritual merchantmen seeking goodly pearls. He is seeking the way of salvation, he is seeking a knowledge of God's word, he is seeking goodly pearls, and he has come to the place where such pearls are likely to be found. Now, when the Spirit of truth leads a man to seek a knowledge of the truth as it is in Jesus, he seldom shows him in one view all the precious things of the gospel, but leads him on step by step, here a little and there a little, line upon line, line upon line. Hence he is at first convinced of his sin, then his need of righteous- ness and his ignorance of God's method of justification; he has a sense of his danger, he feels he needs a deliver- ance; he wants pardon, but which he feels he cannot merit; he wants faith, which he feels he cannot exert; he wants to be justified by a righteousness which he cannot work out; he wants a sanctification, of which he feels utterly destitute; and he wants a heavenly wisdom in place of his ignorance how to come before God in a way by which he may be accepted of him, and live a life of eternal happiness in his presence. Now these are goodly pearls he is seeking; he knows something of their value, and he is absorbed in the object of his search; he goes on seeking, and he is at length led to discover one re- markable pearl, which for size, beauty, and value exceeds all he has ever beheld; cost what it may, he feels he must have it on any consideration. In this pearl he has every- thing he can possibly want, whether for time or for eter- nity; it is the Pearl of great price; it is Christ himself, who is of God made unto this seeker of goodly pearls, wisdom, righteousness, sanctification, and redemption. In Christ it hath pleased the Father that all fulness of all blessing should dwell; in him, as the Pearl of great price, every seeker of goodly pearls is blessed with all spiritual blessings in heavenly places, according as they are chosen in him before the foundation of the world.

These few outlines will, perhaps, serve as hints as to

how the parable may be illustrated in other points of view. They are, I confess, imperfect, but it is difficult, indeed, needless, to attempt running a parallel in every particular; for instance, the buying and selling are not to be understood in the sense we generally do, value for value. What is meant is, a man will readily give up retaining any thing that prevents him possessing something else which he esteems better. Whatever may be given up for Christ cannot be an equivalent; learning, good works, the graces of the Spirit, &c., cannot be bought and sold; neither are they received as a *quid pro quo*, this for that, one thing for another; for if a man be blest in finding Christ for himself, he does not give up his human attainments, and he is still careful to maintain good works; or supposing a believer has been resting on his evidences of his being in Christ instead of Christ himself, even these, I mean, his hope, love, faith, &c., he still possesses; but all these things are estimated as inferior in worth to him who is the chiefest of ten thousand, the altogether lovely. Christ in the gospel is the Pearl of great price. Everything else, however good in itself and proper in its place, are but as goodly pearls in comparison with him, and are wholly passed by when he is discovered as the super-excellent of all excellences, for he is everything to the believer; Christ is his all, his all in all. He is the Pearl of great price.

And yet it is certainly true, that though Christ and his salvation cannot be bought, yet there must be a giving up for Christ, there must be a giving up for salvation of all such things which prevent a man realizing gospel grace for himself. A man must give up the world, he must give up himself, he must give up his self righteousness, he must give up all self seeking, he must give up all idea of creature merit, he must give up all hope of obtaining acceptance with God on the footing of his own doings; he cannot purchase eternal life by the sale, or the barter, or exchange of any of these things; none of them are the procuring causes of salvation, it is wholly of free sovereign grace; and when the seeking sinner is brought to accept it as mercy bestowed upon him in Jesus, who is the unspeakable gift of God, then he gladly parts with all creature dependences, and trusts the salvation of his soul alone to the blood and righteousness of the Lord Jesus Christ.

" His legal works and deeds the best,
     Are now in disesteem ;
For he must naked come to Christ,
     Or farewell heaven for him."

But while on the other hand the Pearl of great price cannot be purchased by any of those mistaken methods which are so often adopted by well meaning yet deluded persons, it is equally true that it cannot be had without some condition on the part of the believer himself; the Scriptures furnish us with full proof of this : " Ho, every one that thirsteth, come ye to the waters, and he that hath no money ; come ye, buy, and eat ; yea, come, buy wine and milk without money and without price." (Isa. lv. 1.) " I counsel thee to buy of me gold tried in the fire, that thou mayest be rich." (Rev. iii. 18.) These persons who are thus addressed are in extreme destitution, having no money, and are faint and famishing, yet ignorant of their poverty, misery, and wretchedness. An equivalent is not asked for, *that* is not the condition required ; they are appealed to, reasoned with, and counselled, and they are asked to buy. Why so ? Because such persons, when brought to know and feel spiritually their poverty, misery, and utter destitution of everything spiritually good, they have the capacity, the condition of mind for appreciating the provisions of the gospel ; the idea set forth by the purchase money is that of making the thing to be had one's own ; thus gospel blessings are made our own by being appropriated to our individual use, comfort, and enjoyment. The purchase of the Pearl of great price is to be understood in the same sense, it is made our own by appropriation. How so ? Through faith, " and that not of ourselves, it is the gift of God." At the same time, though no personal merits of our own, no performances that we can render, can ever secure even a single goodly pearl, yet it is certain that faith and repentance are conditions without which we cannot call the blessings we seek our own ; sin must be forsaken, the flesh must be crucified, the world must be renounced, and everything else, however dearly cherished, if we are desirous of making the Pearl of great price our own. No good works have any value in the price of our redemption, and it is just as true that we can only be manifested to be the children of God by faith in Christ Jesus ; and yet our good works have their necessary uses, for they are a proof, before now, of our belief in him who justifieth the ungodly. The pearl merchant sold all he had to possess this one pearl, and in so doing he gave himself. Oh, is there one in this assembly that can be likened to this merchant! Have you been seeking goodly pearls? have you found the Pearl of great price, and have you parted with everything else for the sake of this one Pearl? can you say with the poet,

> " Here, Lord ! I give myself away,
> 'Tis all that I can do."

But I must now draw your attention to another part of our subject. I am desirous, if the Lord shall be pleased to assist, of speaking more particularly of the Lord Jesus Christ as the Pearl of great price; and in doing so shall endeavour to point out several characteristics which he pre-eminently sustains in this beautiful and interesting similitude. I had intended to have said something about the nature of pearls in my introduction, but I think it will not be too late, even now, just to mention a few things. They are, as you may know, articles of value, and are used for ornament. A pearl is a small concretion formed within the shell of a fish of the oyster kind. It is hard, white, and shining, free from spot or stain. The largest are the most valuable. It is different from that beautiful substance called "mother of pearl," such as is used for flat surfaces, buttons, &c. The best pearl oysters are found in the fisheries at the Persian Gulf, and near the Island of Ceylon, in the East Indies; they are procured by diving, but if taken before seven years old they are imperfectly developed. It is said, in fifty years they lose their beauty, and in one hundred they are scarcely of any value. We read that Cleopatra, Queen of Egypt, had a pearl valued at £80,000 sterling. The Persian Emperor had one worth £110,000 sterling; and Philip II. of Spain, 1587, had one as big as a pigeon's egg; it weighed 250 carats, and was valued at 144,000 ducats, about £70,000 sterling. There was also one purchased by Tavernier at Catifa, in Arabia; it was rather more than half an inch in diameter, and upwards of two inches in length; the price was £110,000. The value of pearls, however, has much fallen of late years, owing to the great improvement in making artificial pearls. Beads and necklaces are commonly of this description. "Pearls have at all times been esteemed one of the most valuable commodities of the East. Their modest splendour and simple beauty appear to have captivated the Orientals even more than the dazzling brilliancy of the diamond, and have made them at all times the favourite ornament of despotic princes." A string of pearls of the largest size is an indispensable part of the decorations of an Eastern monarch. The present ruler of Persia is usually thus adorned with this elegant luxury.

Now it is not my intention to advance anything that may be regarded as curious or fanciful in the application of any of the points now stated, but shall proceed to notice,

1. *Christ is a most gracious Pearl.* This is most true of him who of old has said, "I am found of them that sought me not." Jesus is found unsought. I believe most believers can testify to this fact; some were seeking not goodly pearls, but death, and in the error of their way. I am sure it was so with me, and I can say,

> " Grace led my roving feet
> To tread the heavenly road;
> And new supplies each hour I meet,
> While pressing on to God."

The finding of Christ is a work of grace begun in the heart unlooked for; how often the outward ear has been called to listen to the voice of the preacher telling of the beauties of Christ, but the carnal eye saw no beauty in him, the unregenerated heart did not desire him. Oh, what grace was there in the display of Jesus as the Saviour of lost sinners. The heart savingly touched by the quickening influences of his Spirit; the eyes anointed with heavenly eye-salve, so that they could see divine grace leading the believer to see and to feel his lost, ruined, and undone condition before God; grace leading him to find salvation alone in Christ, salvation arising out of rich, free, sovereign, unmerited grace. Oh, what grace in the realizing of grace, leading the soul in the contemplation to exclaim,

> " What was there in you that could merit esteem,
> That could give the Creator delight;
> 'Twas even so, Father, you ever must sing,
> Because it seemed good in his sight."

And, oh, what grace there is displayed in his holy word: "I love them that love me, and they that seek me early shall find me." How gracious the promise, how sure the performance, to those who are seeking him. How encouraging to the young seeker of good pearls, Christ the heavenly wisdom of his church inviting them with his gracious voice, and secretly drawing them with his gracious influences, calling them off from the sin, errors, and follies of this life, to find in him how gracious he is to them as the Pearl of great price.

2. *Christ is a most precious Pearl.* How poor are all the pearls of which we read. Not one of them is worth our admiration in comparison with him. " Unto you that believe he is precious." The knowledge of Jesus how precious, most precious; it is above all other knowledge. The apostle Paul, who had suffered the loss of all things for Christ, counted that what things were gain to him were loss and dung for the excellency of the knowledge of Christ Jesus his Lord. Where shall we find such knowledge as the knowledge of Jesus Christ? The more we know of him the more we love him; the more we love him the more we desire to know of him.

> " Oh could we know and love him more,
> And all his wondrous grace explore,
> Ne'er would we covet man's esteem,
> But part with all and follow him."

How precious is Christ to me above all the things of time and sense. Eastern monarchs pride themselves in being adorned with pearls; but how few are adorned with Christ as a most precious pearl; he will make himself precious to every believer saved by his blood; for there is no other name under heaven whereby men can be saved. How very precious is Christ as revealed in the various offices and characters he sustains to the church of God. How precious is his atoning blood. It was " impossible that the blood of bulls or of goats could take away sin," but the blood of Christ cleanseth from all sin. How precious he is to us as our High Priest, Intercessor, and Advocate before God; in all things pertaining to the conscience he is most precious to us; for who but the God-man Mediator Christ Jesus could have stood in our law-place and taken away our sin by bearing it in his own body on the tree, being made a curse for us. How precious he is to us as our Foundation-stone; our only hope of standing before God is in being built on him; he is the Rock of ages. How precious he is as our Divine Oracle, " to whom coming, as unto a living stone, a gem of light, chosen of God and precious." In him we have life, light, and power; from him we derive all our life, all our light, all our love. He is made more precious to us than fine gold, than the golden wedge of Ophir. He is our most precious Pearl.

3. *Christ is a soul-pleasing Pearl.* Other pearls please the eye, and there is no other pleasure, no other good to be derived from them than that of beholding them with the eye. But oh the infinite delight the soul finds in beholding the beauteous charms of our adorable Christ!

> " Of him our soul delights to talk,
> With him we daily love to walk."

He is ever our delight; the things in heaven, the things on earth all fall short of his excellences. He is our hope, our joy, and crown. This we cannot say of any created things, if they were all given to us and were at our disposal. Yet if we belong to Christ, all things are ours; but what are earthly things without him? what is heaven without him? we covet it not if he be absent. Oh, when he shines into the soul, ere we are aware our souls are all on fire; we run swiftly, we catch a glimpse of his sweet face; no joy like that when his presence cheers the soul, when his love is shed abroad in the heart by the Holy Ghost. He is our soul-pleasing Pearl, for he is our peace in the midst of tribulation; he is our song and boast in the midst of conflict. He is our soul-pleasing Pearl, above all the goodly pearls of gospel ordinances, of gospel truths, of gospel fellowships; these are precious things in themselves; we delight in them, but sin can and does spoil many of our pleasures in the midst of our enjoyments. Man can deprive us of the comfort of them; they might become barren and unfruitful seasons to us; indeed how often have I found the Sabbath day to be so without my Sabbath's Lord; how often have I found his word like a sealed book; how often have brethren, dearly loved brethren, wounded and pierced me to the very quick, but Jesus is ever my soul-cheering Pearl; he cheers me in the midst of my daily calling, he cheers me under disappointments, he cheers me when cast down by fears; he cheers me when under the frowns of the world, and this makes amends for all. I am displeased with myself, in myself there is everything unsatisfactory; but in him I am complete; in him I am completely blessed. His righteousness screens me from all defilement; I shall

be satisfied when I awake in his likeness. " In his presence there is fulness of joy, and at his right hand there
are pleasures for evermore."

4. *Christ is a most distinguishing Pearl.* His name is
above every name, for he is the Pearl of great price super-
excellently. There have been but few pearls which have
obtained a world-wide notoriety; but Christ has a pre-
eminence above all, more than even the seven wonders of
the world; he is made higher than the kings of the earth.
He is distinguished by the perfections of his Godhead
and by the excellences of his manhood. He knew no sin,
neither was guile found in his mouth. He was holy,
harmless, undefiled, separate from sinners. " Thou art
fairer than the children of men, grace is poured into thy
lips." " His head is as the most fine gold; he is altogether
lovely." Oh, if you want to be distinguished in this life,
have Christ for your pearl; have Christ for your life;
this is the most distinguished life you can live; to have
his name is a most distinguishing name; hear his own
words : " Since thou hast been precious in my sight, thou
hast been honourable." (Isa. xliii. 4.) Oh what a distinguished people are the saints of God; they are distinguished above all nations in the world, for Jesus is their
most distinguishing pearl; he is distinguished as the
Eternal Son of the Eternal Father; distinguished as the
only begotten Son of God. He is distinguished as the
head of his body the church; distinguished as the Captain of their salvation; distinguished as the first-fruits of
them that slept; distinguished above all others in that
he hath conquered death, hell, and the grave. He is distinguished as the Creator and the Upholder of all things
by the word of his power. He is distinguished by a
name above every name, the only Potentate, the King of
kings and Lord of lords; who only hath immortality;
dwelling in light which no man can approach unto;
whom no man hath seen, nor can see; the only wise God
our Saviour. Thus " on his head are many crowns," his
distinguishing crown being salvation. He is the praise
of all his saints. You whom he has distinguished by his
grace in calling you out of darkness into his marvellous
light, let your life be so distinguished by Christ as your
life, as to make him the prime, principal thing in all you
enjoy, let him be your all in all, and more than all in
everything you enjoy. The princes of royal blood live

away from the common herd of mankind; they are distinguished by their high station in life. So believers,
they are called to be saints, the beloved of God, they are
to live away from the world, they are thus distinguished
from the world, because Christ is their ornament; they
have his name on their foreheads as their most distinguishing pearl.

5. *Christ is a most enriching Pearl.* I have told you
of the immense value men have put upon pearls of a large
size; but how vainly fictitious is their price. Of what
use are they, except it be to feed pride? Now here our
dear Jesus infinitely excels the comparison; he is not
only the Pearl of great price, but he really enriches its
possessor: "I will cause them that love me to inherit
substance." There is a reality in his wealth, nothing
imaginary, nothing impoverishing. He is a Pearl upon
which the soul can feed. He possesses all the fulness of
the Godhead: "For it pleased the Father that in him
should all fulness dwell." All fulness of grace, peace,
love, joy, and glory dwell in Christ. In him there is a
fulness of riches in glory which supplies all the needs of
every believer. Supposing a man were to part with everything he possessed, in houses, land, and money, to procure
the great Persian pearl, what a fool we should think him
to be; what a poor, miserable, starved wretch he would
be; how utterly destitute it would make him. Would it
feed him? would it clothe him? would it house him?
would it talk to him? would it sympathize with him in
sorrow? would it take away pain? would it ease him
when weary? No. And what are all the pearls of this
world to this Pearl of great price? His riches are durable
riches, unsearchable riches; strength for the day, grace
for every need, a balm for every wound; our joy in sorrow, our peace in trouble. He is rest for the weary, he is
our meat and our drink, our clothing, and our house. He
is our wealth, in him we possess all things; every gift
and grace, every comfort flows from him as streams from
a fountain. We are blessed with all spiritual blessings in
heavenly places in him. These are realities, nothing
imaginary, nothing supposable, nothing speculative, nothing uncertain. Christ is our all-sufficient good. All
things are ours, we are Christ's, and Christ is God's.
Life is ours; death is ours. In him is life; by him death
is conquered. Christ is the heir of all things; his people

are joint-heirs with him; heaven and eternal glory is their inheritance for ever. O the blessedness of that soul who is seeking after Christ, whose affections are set on heavenly things! You have found the Pearl of great price; he enriches all the affections of the soul; he is so rich a Pearl that he enriches the understanding of all who possess him, both for time and eternity. There is no being impoverished with Christ as our Pearl, there is enough in him to satisfy the desires of every believer; everything they have in him they enjoy in him; and, having him, they possess all things. Christ is a most enriching Pearl.

6. *Christ is a most glorious Pearl.* You have heard of the nature of pearls, how they are formed, and how they are obtained. Now their excellency lies not in what they really are, but in what men think of them. What glory, what beauty, what value can there really be in a small lump of excrescence formed by disease existing in one of the lowest class of shell fish? Yet, because of its clearness and its glossiness, men think it a beauty, and set great store by it. O that men were wise, and would look upon Christ as a most glorious pearl! They would make no mistake here. The most glorious life you can live is by living on Christ: "He is the brightness of his Father's glory." O for the revelation of the knowledge of him, the eyes of our understanding being enlightened; that we may know what is the hope of his calling, and what the riches of the glory of his inheritance in the saints. He is the most glorious Pearl. We see his glory, the glory of the only begotten Son of God, full of grace and truth. If Christ be formed in our hearts the hope of glory, we have hope the most glorious that can be realised. He is the King of glory. He is God. We glory in his holy name. We glory in that everlasting covenant union which is ordered in all things and sure. Christ is the glorious Pearl of that union; his God is our God, his Father is our Father. It is a union that can never be dissolved; it is a union, the blessedness of which all his saints must participate in, and realise in the heavenly glory as well as by faith on earth beneath. His glory is unknown to saints on earth, it cannot be seen by mortal eyes; and to make the sum of his people's happiness complete, he has willed that they shall behold him in all the magnificence of his primeval glory, the glory which

he had before the world was: "Father, I will that they
also whom thou hast given me be with me where I am;
that they may behold my glory, which thou hast given
me; for thou lovedst me before the foundation of the
world." The gloriousness of his Mediatorship, his glory
as the God-man, his glory as the Son of God, his eternal
glory, the glory of his eternal Sonship,—all this to be revealed to the glorified church of God, who shall behold
him in his glorified and eternal manhood; they shall see
him as he is, they shall be like him. O that you and I
may realise what it is to have Christ as our most glorious
Pearl by an experimental knowledge of his excellences in
a life of faith on him, a life of communion with him.
Such a life of grace on earth here will certainly lead to a
life of glory in heaven hereafter.

7. *Christ is an everlasting Pearl.* This cannot be said
of any of the finest pearls that have ever been known. It
does not appear that any retain their splendour for two
generations. Mutability, fading excellences belong to
everything of earth. What are the sons of men about, to
part with all they have for an evanescent beauty? Many
who have splendid pearls, live long enough to see them
fade; but our most glorious Christ is an everlasting
Pearl; behold him as long as you will, he will ever retain
his original splendour. He is ever the same, "the same
yesterday, to-day, and for ever." He is the everlasting
God, the everlasting Father. All his attributes, his excellences, his blessings are like himself, everlasting. He
is an everlasting Pearl. He that believeth on him shall
have everlasting life. "For God so loved the world, that
he gave his only begotten Son, that whosoever believeth
in him should not perish, but have everlasting life."
(John iii. 16.) Live as long as you may, live on him as
much as you may, you will never diminish the amount of
life he possesses, for it is everlasting: "Because I live, ye
shall live also." He is the self-existent Jehovah. He is
an everlasting Pearl; he will last for ever. Friends fail,
brethren fail; but Jesus never fails; he cannot fail. His
mercy is from everlasting to everlasting. (Ps. ciii. 17.)
His righteousness is an everlasting righteousness. (Ps.
cxix. 142.) His kingdom is an everlasting kingdom. (Ps.
cxlv. 13.) His goings forth have been from everlasting.
(Mic. v. 2.) Israel is saved in the Lord with an everlasting salvation. (Isa. xlv. 17.) They have been loved with

an everlasting love, therefore it is with loving-kindness they have been drawn to him; and he hath given them everlasting consolation, and so they find, by precious faith, that he is their everlasting Pearl.   And when the time shall come when he will descend from the heavens with a shout, and all his holy angels with him; when he will sever the wicked from the just, and take his saints to their final rest, then they will find, to their everlasting joy, that he is still their everlasting Pearl.   He will never cease to be what he has ever been, the eternal, self-existent I AM.   Eternity will only add splendour to this Pearl of great price, this most gracious Pearl, this most precious Pearl, this soul-pleasing Pearl, this most distinguishing Pearl, this most enriching Pearl, this most glorious Pearl, this everlasting Pearl.   The wonders of this Pearl can never be told; we must die to know it, we must die to see it.

Now, dear hearers, what think you of this Pearl of great price?   Do you think you can submit to part with everything you possess for the sake of possessing such a treasure?   If you are seeking goodly pearls, as you may perhaps esteem them, could you be content to give up further search for the sake of obtaining this one Pearl? If you have not found this one Pearl of great price, I ask you, what kind of pearls must they be that you are now seeking?   Whatever they are, they fall infinitely below in excellence to this one which I have attempted to describe; and if Jesus Christ possesses all these excellences, and the thousandth part has not been told you, why,

> " His worth, if all the nations knew,
> Sure the whole earth would love him too."

But you who have found him, what untold beauties have you beheld in him; what unspeakable joy have you felt in claiming him as your own, when by the Spirit of truth the great testimony has been borne to your conscience that he is yours, yours for ever; and in the hymn of Mason's, written 200 years since, you can say:

> " I've found the pearl of greatest price,
> My heart doth sing for joy;
> And sing I must, a Christ I have;
> O what a Christ have I !"

THE BELIEVER'S CONFLICT WITH INDWELLING SIN.

◆

A SERMON,

BY CHARLES GORDELIER.

PREACHED AT HEPHZIBAH CHAPEL, DARLING PLACE, NEAR MILE END GATE,

On Lord's Day Morning, 21st May, 1865.

"For I know that in me (that is, in my flesh) dwelleth no good thing; for to will is present with me; but how to perform that which is good I find not. For the good that I would I do not; but the evil which I would not, that I do. Now if I do that I would not, it is no more I that do it, but sin that dwelleth in me. I find then a law, that, when I would do good, evil is present with me." —ROM. vii. 18, 19, 20, 21.

WE have here in the language of our text, the apostle's confession of the conflict he found within himself, between the principle of indwelling sin and the principle of inwrought grace.

This is a subject which, at first sight, seems to many persons obscure, paradoxical, and mysterious. I have thought so; and I have found many of the Lord's dear people much confused, perplexed, and distressed about it. Even several of our learned Doctors of Divinity have been unable to divest the subject of its difficulties, either to the satisfaction of themselves or of others. I once thought that a knowledge of the philosophy of human nature would assist me, and I thought this was to be gained by reading books; and so for nearly twenty years I pored over the metaphysical works of those who had written upon the philosophy of the mind and the moral feelings, for I verily thought they had the key to this dark and difficult subject, as it then appeared to me; but I found, with all my painstaking, they had not; nor is it to be

No. 20.

wondered at. I was looking in the wrong place; I was looking for a spiritual light in the wisdom of this world,—a place above all others filled with nature's darkness; I was, in fact, seeking the living among the dead. At length, however, as I humbly believe, I found this key for which I had been so long searching; and where do you think I discovered it? In the garden of Gethsemane. In the garden of Gethsemane, you say; why, I never heard that you had visited the Holy Land! Perhaps not, nor indeed have I; yet many persons have travelled to this memorable place without leaving the land of their nativity. The spiritual mind, when under the leadings of the Holy Spirit, can retire to this sacred spot without the incumbrance of the body; indeed it may be said, the true disciples of the Lord Jesus love to pay frequent visits to this lovely, mournful, endearing garden of Gethsemane, both in thought and feeling; for as it was in the days of his flesh, that Jesus ofttimes resorted thither with his disciples, (John xviii. 2,) so even now, in the spirit, the disciples often resort thither with their Lord and Master, and by faith can view him agonizing in the garden, trembling under the load of guilt transferred to his sinless breast. Here it was, when meditating upon this scene of sorrow, was seen such a sight as no mortal eye could endure; for, as you know, the sight of the bleeding, suffering Lamb of God caused the companion disciples to sleep for sorrow: they beheld him drowned in sorrow. It was a fearful sight; it drowned them in sleep. "What," exclaimed the holy sufferer, "could ye not watch with me one hour! Watch and pray, that ye enter not into temptation;" and then, with a ray of divinity beaming through his lips, he explained the secret of their failure: "THE SPIRIT INDEED IS WILLING, BUT THE FLESH IS WEAK." Here it is, that in this divine sentence I find more to unravel the mystery of the believer's conflict with indwelling sin than in all the philosophical writings I have ever read. "The Spirit is willing, but the flesh is weak," is the master key of this entire seventh chapter of the Epistle to the Romans. With this key, as helped by the Spirit of Truth, we hope to unlock some of the mysteries of the kingdom. The kingdom of God is within, but the "reign of grace and the power of sin," the one so contrary to the other, perplexes the believer; he can truly say with Newton:

> " Strange and mysterious is my life,
>   What opposites I feel within;
>   A stable peace, a constant strife,
>   The rule of grace, the power of sin;
>   Too often I am captive led,
>   But daily triumph in my Head."

Before we enter immediately into our subject, I must occupy your attention with one or two prefatory remarks respecting the chapter. The apostle, in the preceding chapter, has shown that the doctrines of grace do not, as some say, give license to sin, but, on the contrary, are productive of holiness. In this chapter, he illustrates the position he laid down in verse 14,—that we are not under the law, but under grace; and he proceeds to show the results of this change in our relation to God. You perceive, he remarks, as a general fact, that there is no perpetuity in the authority of laws; as, for example, the marriage law is binding on the wife only during her husband's life-time. When he is dead, she is free from the obligations which that law imposed. So believers in Christ, being free from the law, as a covenant of works, or rule of life, are now under law to Christ. We are freed from it by his death. The fruit of our first marriage with Adam was sin. The fruit of our marriage with Christ is holiness. It is true the apostle does not carry the figure of the law of marriage through the discourse, but he has said enough to show us his meaning. As a woman is entirely free from obligation to her husband by *his* death, so believers are free from the law by *its* death. He does not indeed say in so many words that the law is dead, but this is evidently his meaning, as in verse 6. Then from the 7th verse to the 13th the apostle goes on to show the operation of the law as derived from his own experience; it was unable to produce sanctification, just as much as he had before shown that it was unable to effect justification; he shows that it produces conviction of sin. Now from the 14th verse to the 25th he shows the cause of the inability of the law to effect his sanctification. It is not in the evil nature of the law, which is spiritual, but in the power of indwelling sin. He is carnal, sold under sin. A figure of slavery is here used. His own will is opposed to that of his master; as when a slave has to beat his own wife by his master's order. Now the believer, though he denies the sufficiency of the law either to justify him or to sanctify him, and maintaining the necessity of deliverance from it, yet bears an inward testimony to its excellence. He approves it. He delights in the law after the inward man, nevertheless he finds the power of sin in his members is not destroyed; hence arises the inward conflict, which conflict the law itself cannot end. The law makes him sensible of his helpless and degraded condition; but he, who has taught him thus to know and to feel that his whole nature is fallen, corrupt, and enslaved by sin, leads him to seek deliverance and victory through the work of Jesus Christ, in whom alone he seeks salvation.

The leading doctrines of the apostle are, that believers are not under a legal system; that the consequence of their freedom is not the indulgence of sin, but of living in the service of God. And that this deliverance from the law is not effected by setting the law aside, or by disregarding its demands, but by those demands being amply satisfied in the person of Christ, namely, by his obedience and death.

Our text contains an expanding and a confirming of the preceding verses. The apostle again asserts the existence of the inward struggle, and explains the nature of it. He delights in God's law, but feels he cannot perform its conditions. Under the teachings of the Spirit of Truth, he says, *I know that in my flesh*, that indwelling, inherent sinfulness of which he is the subject, *dwelleth no good thing;* that is, there is no abiding good, no power of that kind that rules; that is to say, in his Old-Adam nature, considered apart from the divine influence which constitutes the new nature. By the term flesh, he does not mean his body corporeal, but his depraved original nature; as until a man is renewed, he is in the flesh; when renewed in the spirit of his mind, he is in the Spirit. This is how the language of the New Testament is to be understood; *a spiritual* man is one who is under the control of the Spirit of God; and *the natural* man is he who is under the control of his own nature.

To will is present with me. He has a desire to do God's will, but he finds he has no capacity, no ability, no power which he can exercise or put forth to execute the holy purposes of his heart. Here our Lord's key is of essential use; the apostle is showing us what is *the manner and nature* of the warfare, and the Lord has shown us *how* it is that the warfare is so unequal: "The spirit is willing, but the flesh is weak. As the law was weak to procure the believer a title to heaven, namely, justification; so he finds it gives him no meetness for it, namely, sanctification, because his nature is sinful; consequently the law is of no use to him in securing heaven to him as his right; it can only convince him of sin, and then condemn him for it. Now so long as a believer is unsettled on this point, he will be sure to be disturbed and distressed about his present condition of soul, as well also about his hopes as to his future state of immortality; and, therefore, seeing that the righteousness of God, which is by faith, is without the works of the law, so the sanctifying work of the Holy Ghost is also without the believer's strength. By virtue of his being regenerated, he is new born, a new creature; and consequently there is an implantation of holy desires in conformity with that new nature. He has become willing in the day of God's power, there is a readiness to do his will, a readiness to be the Lord's, body, soul, and spirit for ever. His heart is set against all sin, he hates it with a perfect hatred. This the believer should take notice of; for if he can discover certain marks or indications of desires, and a readiness of mind to those things which are spiritually good, he ought to consider they must have arisen out of that "good thing towards the Lord God of Israel," the work of God's Spirit in his heart. Let the exercised child of God examine how it is, and wherefore it is, that he has a will that is present with him, that his spirit is willing, that he has readiness of mind to all that is good; and let him, I say, be satisfied on this point. It is one thing to have these evidences of God's work, but it is another *to know that we have them*, and to perceive their actings, inefficient though they be through the flesh being weak.

But how to perform that which is good I find not. That is, he has no strength in his old nature, his fallen nature, to do that which is spiritually good. The flesh is flesh, the spirit is spirit, two distinct natures; that which is of the flesh is flesh, and that which is of the spirit is spirit, their actions or workings are essentially distinct; and until the mind is spiritually enlightened, there will be a predisposition to bring itself into bondage, because of the inequality of the conflict, and because of the inability to effect the godly desires of the heart. The old nature, from the matured habits of sin and the works of the flesh, is strong in itself; it possesses a power which is able to resist, and does resist, every motion of God's Spirit; it is always in opposition to the nature of the new man of grace, they are so contrary the one to the other. As the apostle explains to the Galatians, there can be no hope of accomplishing any good thing without opposition, vexation, and disappointment: "For the flesh lusteth against the Spirit, and the Spirit against the flesh; and these are contrary the one to the other, so that ye cannot do the things that ye would." (Gal. v. 17.) The two natures in a believing child of God have each inclinations and desires so opposite, so different, they never can harmonise. While the Spirit of God would lead him one way, his carnal nature would lead him another; so that there is impossibility of ever hoping to find help or strength from the old fallen nature, to assist the new nature in any of those motions and influences of the Spirit of God, in which the believer desires ever to cherish to live under. The apostle states, both in our text and the words just quoted, *a fact*, which is this, he cannot do the thing that he would by reason of the opposition in nature of the two principles within him. The child of God, when in a state of nature, did the works of the flesh with all his heart, his soul, and his strength; now that he is in a state of grace, he would be completely the Lord's for ever, body, soul, and spirit, but finds he cannot, because of the opposition from the old man of sin, the matured habits of sin under which he formerly lived.

For the good that I would I do not. This is an explanation of what he says in the previous verse. He, personally, is inclined to do good, but cannot; that is, *as* he should like to do it, and *when* he wished to do it; the child of God feels in bondage to his old nature as to the free exercise of his new nature; he himself cannot accomplish the desires of his heart, he cannot soar to heaven when he would; he would fain fix his affections on things above, where Christ sitteth; he would fain be always in a spirit of prayer; he would be always in a spiritual frame of mind; he would be always looking to Jesus, living in the Spirit, walking in the Spirit, but finds, alas, he is witheld by counter influences, influences from within himself. This disturbs his peace, and he is often perplexed; he humbly believes that divine grace has taken possession of his heart, and he has some sense of God's delivering power from the dominion of the devil, sin, and the flesh; but finds, when he would be wholly the Lord's in all *that he does* as well as in all that he is, he is checked, and is held back; the will is present, but not the power; his ability to do good is not equal to his inclination; he feels and experiences, that there is within that which has the force of a law, but which is contrary to the law of God; for although he would do good, he would be holy, there is this something within, drawing him quite another way; he is unable to act up to his purposes and desires. How often have we come into the house of God, the prayer-meeting, and to a throne of grace, with the earnest desire that our souls might be filled with divine things, and the things of the world shut out, so as to have close communion with our God, but this flesh has crept in and marred our enjoyment. Even sainted Watts could say,

> " Up to the fields where angels lie,
> And living waters gently roll,
> Fain would my thoughts leap out and fly,
> But sin hangs heavy on my soul."

But the evil which I would not, that I do. Here we have another view of the believer's conflict; and by taking another stand-point, we perceive a further proof of his weakness. He is compelled, against his own inclination, to do that which he regards as an evil. This is the worst condition he can be found in; for instance, he comes to the word of God with the intention of meditating thereon, and humbly looking up to him who teacheth to profit for his blessing, he desires, nay resolves to be divested of everything that would interfere with the calmness of mind so necessary for such an exercise; but the world has rushed in, and ere he has been aware, he has occupied himself in busy thoughts about everything else save that for which he took up the sacred book; he has indulged in thoughts not only irrelevant with his profitable reading, but altogether inimical to his progress in the divine life. Wandering thoughts, evil thoughts, malignant feelings, unholy desires, have possessed the soul of many who fully thought and intended to be absorbed in the things of God. And this wretchedness further consists in the fact that the believer feels he has no power to control these things, but that these things have a power to control him, and he is compelled to act against his will.

Now if I do that I would not, it is no more I that do it.
There is nothing contradictory in this statement, although
it is paradoxical; here is no extenuation for sin, although
many graceless professors have often pleaded an excuse
for their ungodliness by quoting these words. Such a
doctrine is utterly abhorrent to all right-minded persons.
The apostle in this verse repeats what he had said in the
16th and 17th verses; the repetition shows how full his
mind was of the subject, and how much inclined he was
to dwell upon it, and to place it in a variety of aspects.
He draws the same conclusion from the same premises.
And it is as if he had said, "The things which I do, when
contrary to the characteristic desires and purposes of my
heart, are to be considered as the acts of a slave in obedience to the will of his master. They are indeed my own
acts, so far as my hands and consciousness are concerned,
but not being performed with the full consent and purpose of my heart, are not to be regarded as a fair criterion
of character by which I am to be judged." The old Adam
is sold under sin, it is not renewed; sin is sin, it cannot
in its own nature be made otherwise; but in the person of
the believer in Christ it is placed under restraint, being
subdued by the power of grace. The believer often fails
in his service to God, and does those things which grieve
his heart, but his failures are not characteristic of his
habitual inclination and purpose of mind; his intentions
are to do right; he would never do wrong; but when he is
compelled by counter influences stronger than his intentions, to act contrary to them, he is in a position like the
slave whose master has bid him to flog his wife; he must
do it, he cannot avoid it; but though he is the instrument
of the act, the act is the master's, not the slave's. The
slave's will was not in the act, though he did beat his
wife. Wicked men, like graceless professors, will often
plead drunkenness as an excuse for their crimes, intimating it was under the power of the drink that they
acted against propriety; and we know that sometimes
vicious magistrates and jurymen will listen to it, I suppose from sympathy, and so pass a lenient sentence.
Nevertheless, it is right for honest and sincere believers
to commune with their own hearts, and find out the root
of the principles which act, and how they act against
each other. This is a part of our spiritual wisdom. This
is that knowledge of ourselves, which, under the Spirit's

D 2

teachings, leads a man never to trust his own heart, or his own strength, but to look to the strong for strength, and to the wise for wisdom. "Whoso is wise and will observe" the contrary principles of sin and grace acting one against the other within themselves, "even they shall understand the loving-kindness of the Lord."

But sin that dwelleth in me. That is, its habitual presence with them; it resides in their flesh; it abides in the soul, it is never absent; there is its constant residence and habitation. It is in the flesh as the plague of leprosy is in the house, there it is, in it, about it, and will be in it until the house is taken down and the materials separated and dispersed. Indwelling sin is a great plague to the child of God; it abounds in contradictions, it is treacherous, inconstant, and deceitful above all things, yea, desperately wicked; the works of the flesh proceed from the heart, the seeds of which are in it, and is the great plague of the good man's heart; it is "his own grief sore." It is enmity against God. God abates its force in the regenerated heart, but does not change its nature. Grace changes the character of the believer's person, but not the nature of sin.

I find then a law. This the believer finds by his own experience and the light of God's truth. There is a law, a force, a power against his will, desire, purposes, and resolution to do good, to follow out God's will. Thus we see two forces, two laws, two powers, acting against each other, neither of which fully succeeds; the struggle at times bewilders and discomposes the believer.

Here then we have what may be called two laws acting in the believer; the one is the law of sin, which is in his members; the other is the law of the mind, the renewed mind, the law of the Spirit of life. The law of his original nature bringing the believer into captivity by resisting the law of his mind.

The apostle states, "I find then a law;" his finding it intimates, he discovered it; it was revealed to him; he had been looking for an explanation, but not until, like Asaph, he communed with his own heart, observed his own experience, and used the Saviour's key, then he finds two distinct facts, "the Spirit is willing, but the flesh is weak." In the 23rd verse he adds, "But I see another law in my members, warring against the law of my mind, and bringing me into captivity to the

law of sin, which is in my members." He does not
mean the members of his body, for they cannot sin of
themselves, but of sin in its principle and of its workings within him. Indwelling sin is here called a law,
because of its force and power as a principle of action,
which is equivalent to a law; and as Dr. Owen well ob-
serves, "thus it is in believers; it is a law even *in them*,
but though not *to them*." No, blessed be God, "the law
of the Spirit of life in Christ Jesus hath made us free
from the law of sin and death." Wherever the soul has
been brought to know and feel the bondage of the one, he
also has been brought, or shall be brought, to know the
sweetness, power, and efficacy of the other.

That, when I would do good, evil is present with me.
Evil is ready to oppose, to obstruct, and to prevent me in
striving and aiming to effect some good purpose or desire;
as if it was determined to withstand me in the way, in
my very path, at every step, fighting against me, resisting every attempt I make in my progress to the heavenly
city. Thus the believer's pilgrimage to Zion is one of
warfare; "For the flesh lusteth against the Spirit, and
the Spirit against the flesh; and these are contrary one
to the other; so that ye cannot do the things that ye
would." "The spirit, indeed, is willing, but the flesh is
weak." The constant presence of evil in the heart is his
burden, and great grief; it is always near, nigh at hand;
it comes unbidden and undesired; its antagonistic principle demonstrates the great fact of man's apostasy, the
ruin of his moral nature, and the perpetual enmity of
Satan against Christ. But painful as is the conflict, the
victory is certain, and the triumph will be glorious. The
saints of God shall be more than conquerors through him
that hath loved them, because it will be for ever.

Thus I have gone through my text in an expository
sort of way, taking it piece by piece as the words run. I
had intended to have treated it under two distinct heads, the
first to show the nature of the two laws which the believer
finds within himself, and the second, the nature of the
conflict arising from the opposite tendencies of the two
laws. However, I have given you in substance the views
I take of this important and interesting subject: they
are, as I humbly believe, in accordance with the apostle's
doctrine, and with my own experience. May I hope that
what has been advanced has been the means of clearing
away some of those mists which sometimes hang about

the minds of the dear children of God as to the working
of sin within. I will now proceed to notice a few points
by way of practical observations.

OBS. 1. *That when believers sin, it is not with their
full and free consent at any time, or upon any occasion*.
Once they did; in their unregenerate state they were the
subjects of sin, sold unto it, sin was a law *to* them, as well
as *in* them, and they obeyed it, "fulfilling the desires of the
flesh and of the mind," but now their condition is changed.
Their relationship to God is made manifest, they are now
under the power of divine grace; it is *no more they* that
sin, but sin that dwelleth within; not that they never
sin, but that when they do, it is through the prevalence
of contrary principles of operation, so that they do not sin
with the full and entire consent of their will as when they
were enslaved by it. By reason of the principle of grace
within, they are opposed to and hate all sin, and therefore
cannot sin wilfully.

2. *That when believers sin, yet sin does not reign in
them as it once did.* Sin acts against them and frustrates
their good desires. Sin being opposed, causes it to fight
against the new principle; nevertheless grace reigns,
though sin rages; for it is always to be observed it is
grace now that has become the habit of the mind, and is
a law *to* the believer: "Sin shall not have the dominion
over you, for ye are not under the law, but under grace."
(Rom. vi. 14.) Sin has now lost its power over the believer as his tyrant, but being ever present with him, it
has thenceforward become a source of annoyance and grief;
it is the plague of his heart, he is no longer its vassal.

3. *That when believers sin, they do it not from the force
of habit and custom as they once did, for grace opposes it,
and it has become the law of their minds.* Sin is contrary
to the new nature of the child of God, and in itself it
cannot sin, though the believer himself sins at times.
"Whosoever is born of God doth not commit sin; for his
seed (the principle of grace) remaineth in him; and he
cannot sin, because he is born of God. Whosoever is
born of God sinneth not." (1 John iii. 9.) Believers find
their hearts are fully set against sin—

> "Born of God, they hate all sin,
>   God's pure word remains within."

Sin has not an abiding place as a ruler; it is grace
that reigns and has become the law of the mind. The
proof by observers must be taken from the general course

of the conduct; the character is not to be determined by an action which may be more the result of accident than of purpose, but from the habitual course of life which is followed, and which has ever marked the man.

4. *When believers sin, they do it not, as Satan does, from enmity to God.* " He that is born of God sinneth not;" " He that committeth sin is of the devil." Here are the two natures clearly defined. The believer is subject to the influence of both; the one rules, the other opposes, but he can fully distinguish between the workings of each and the effects of each; though he hates sin, he does sin; though he loves God, he does sin. The weakest saint as well as the strongest, are fully conscious that when they sin it is not from enmity to God, not from the settled love of any known sin. When they sin it is against their own light and knowledge, but not out of malice against God. This distinction, when lost sight of, has sometimes occasioned great distress of soul from the fear of having committed the unpardonable sin; but this is obviously a device of Satan himself to bring it into bondage and fear of eternal wrath.

5. *When believers sin they do not abide or continue in it and under it as they once did.* If they fall into sin it is rather from their being tripped up in their path; for if they fall, they rise again and still go on their way. They do not continue in it, or delight in it; they are ashamed of themselves, and are grieved with themselves. If there were a continuance in any particular sin, it would be a sad sign of a heart in which there was no true faith. I grant, the power of temptation in some instances may so prevail for a time as to make a man weary *in* opposing it; his want of strength may be his infirmity, and this, perhaps, is the worst case a child of God can be brought into; but he cannot go on in it, it is his distress, and not his delight. Sin is of a hardening nature, but grace brings tenderness of spirit. Grace reigns and brings the soul back to God, flies to the blood of Christ as the fountain for cleansing from all sin and iniquity.

6. *When believers sin, they sin not without the loss of their present peace and comfort, as others do, or as they themselves once did.* For if it were otherwise, what need would they have for taking heed to their steps, what necessity would there be for prayer that they might be held up in their goings, lest their safety should be endangered? When David sinned the joy of salvation was

taken from him; when Peter sinned he was soon brought
into grief; and I believe all sincere souls are exceedingly
troubled whenever they have been led out of the way of
truth and holiness. 'Tis true, graceless professors are
sometimes in trouble about their sins, but it is because
they have been found out in them and have got into disgrace; their grief is not about their wickedness, but the
exposure of their shame and the loss of their character;
if they had not been detected, they would have still continued in sin. No one, I am sure, in whose heart God
has begun a good work, can ever find a temporary delight
in the indulgence of their corrupt nature without their
consciences being wounded and experiencing the loss of
their peace. It is true, God never suffers his people to
fall into any sin at any time, but for the accomplishment
of some wise end, and which is found to result in his glory
and their eternal good; still, it is to be observed, it
arises more out of their afflictions and trials which their
sin has brought on them, and not by the sin itself. Every
scholar in the school of Christ has to learn this painful
lesson—sin and sorrow are inseparable companions.

7. *When believers sin, it is generally out of weakness,
and not out of wickedness.* It is for want of strength to
conquer; or it may be through infirmity, as it was in the
case of Asaph, who, during his fits of fainting and forget-
fulness, said many things which he afterwards acknowledged to be his infirmity, his weakness. The three disciples already alluded to, had their weakness of body,
though their spirits were willing to watch for their Lord.
We must, however, bear in mind, that though a believer's
failure is attributed to the weakness of his flesh, yet the
principle of sin is matured, and is therefore called the
" old man;" the principle of grace is immature, it is the
new nature, is not perfected yet in the believer; but we
must beware of making false conclusions upon such premises as these. Many mistakes are apt to be made;
some think their sins are infirmities, when, alas! they are
very wickedness. A sin of infirmity is not so much from
the nature of it, as it is in the manner of falling into it.
A man may be overtaken in a fault; this is different from
following after it. A man who is living in the flesh, walks
after the flesh, follows his own inclinations, because that
which is of the flesh is flesh. A man who is in the Spirit,
lives in the Spirit, walks after the Spirit, minds the things
of the Spirit, because that which is of the Spirit is Spirit;

still he finds the things of the flesh walk after him and create him much annoyance; it is that which vexes him and breaks his peace; like as when a good man is seen followed by some wretched beggar, or may be, followed by a horde of thieves, but he is distinguished from his com· pany for all that; there is no union, though there is on their part a cleaving to the good man, not because he is good, but to obtain his money for their riot and to impoverish him. We think none the less of the good man because he was followed and impoverished by the beggar or by the horde of thieves.

Dear brethren, the subject which has engaged our attention at this time is one of deep interest to every believer in Christ. He will have to learn that there is an evil principle always abiding in his heart, so that when he would do good, evil is present with him. He will have to learn that this abiding principle is not only present with him, but that it has the force and power of a law with him. The *power* which it once had over him is *weakened* indeed by the operation of the principle of grace, but *its nature is unchanged*. And the believer will find the further he proceeds in the divine life the more he will feel the force and power of the evil principle, and the more he will have to deplore it, the more spiritually minded he becomes the stronger he will feel the opposition and conflict. But though believers feel this evil principle, this law of sin is ever present with them, and they complain most when their aim is best, yet they rejoice that ere long the law of their minds, the law of God in their hearts, will ultimately triumph over the law of sin; their regenerated self, the new creature, shall be delivered from the bondage of corruption into the glorious liberty of the children of God, and the body of sin shall be totally destroyed. Oh what a glorious triumph this will be for the whole church of God; even now there is cause for rejoicing, for this triumph over all evil is already secured by the Lord Jesus Christ. We triumph by faith. We are feeble, it is true, but Christ is strong. In him is our strength. Believer, whenever you feel your weakness, look to the strong for strength; in him we shall conquer, and shall be more than conquerors too, for there will be a perpetuity of this triumph. It is recorded of one of the Roman emperors who, after gaining several decisive victories, was returning to his city in triumphant state, and was received with great acclamations and every demonstration of rejoicing, with which he was evidently delighted; and he asked a grave philosopher who was seated with him in his chariot what could be possibly wanting to make his triumph more glorious; the philosopher quietly answered — "*perpetuity!*" Yes, this is it, my friends, the saints of God are more than conquerors; they have a perpetuity of conquest, and they have a perpetuity of triumphant glory. It is otherwise with the men of this world; Time, writes "Ichabod" upon all their names and their conquests too; the glory is departed, for nothing seems to die out of memory so rapidly as martial achievements. Military glory is a thing of fits and starts, and in process of years becomes like a dream; the victories of Marlborough are forgotten, the victories of Bonaparte have vanished, the victories of Wellington are fast fading away, but the believer can exultingly exclaim, "Thanks be to God who *always* causeth us to triumph in Christ." He has triumphed over Death itself, that mighty conqueror of all conquerors. The saints of God will live for ever to enjoy their triumphs over sin; in the morning of the resurrection the upright shall have dominion over all the enemies of their peace; as sin shall not have dominion over them now because they are under grace, so even death shall not have dominion over them because he is conquered by Him who died and rose again; this is the saints' ground of rejoicing, as he rose again, so shall they, and their triumph shall be eternal; even now we triumph by faith, and our faith is more than victorious: it is through him that hath loved us; he has fought the battle with all the powers of sin; he has conquered and triumphed over the devil, death, and the grave; they are utterly vanquished; no sin shall finally triumph over the believer; the conflict within may be sharp, it may be long, but the victory is already secured by the triumphant work of Christ; through him we shall conquer and triumph over every sin. This is the saints' security, it is their strength and their encouragement; hence they stand their ground; falling is out of the question; the conflict is unequal, but the victory is certain. "Gad, a troop shall overcome him (for a time), but he shall overcome at last."

> " For here's our point at rest;
> Though hard the battle seems,
> Our Saviour stood the fiery test,
> And we shall stand through him."

THE PLEA OF
ZELOPHEHAD'S FIVE DAUGHTERS,

SPIRITUALLY CONSIDERED.

A SERMON,
BY CHARLES GORDELIER,

PREACHED AT HEPHZIBAH CHAPEL, DARLING PLACE, MILE END GATE,

On Lord's Day Evening, January 21st, 1866,

"Then came the daughters of Zelophehad . . . And they
stood before Moses, and before Eleazar the priest, and before the
princes and all the congregation, by the door of the tabernacle
of the congregation, saying, Our father died in the wilderness,
and he was not in the company of them that gathered themselves
together against the LORD in the company of Korah; but died in
his own sin, and had no sons. Why should the name of our
father be done away from among his family because he hath no
son? Give unto us therefore a possession among the brethren of
our father. And Moses brought their cause before the LORD.
And the LORD spake unto Moses, saying, The daughters of Zelophehad speak right: thou shalt surely give them a possession of
an inheritance among their father's brethren; and thou shalt
cause the inheritance of their father to pass unto them."—NUM-
BERS xxvii. 1-7.

IT is said that when the children of Israel arrived on the
borders of their inheritance "they did eat of the old corn
of the land:" (Joshua v. ii:) it was a notable circumstance to them; and though they had been divinely fed
for forty years with manna from heaven, yet it seems this
new bread made of old corn of which they had heard so
much was eaten with a peculiar relish and satisfaction.
There can be no doubt wheaten bread was a novelty to all
the people; for only two, Joshua and Caleb, remained,
who had partaken of the like before their departure from
Egypt. So sometimes even now, it may be said, God's
spiritual Israel can feed with a keen appetite upon New
No. 21.

Testament bread made of Old Testament corn; or in other
words, Old Testament truth clothed and presented in a
New Testament dress, may have the charm of novelty and
excite a laudable interest and attention to certain facts
which had been previously unobserved.

I have not taken this subject, which our text seems to
suggest, for the sake of amusing you with any vain specu-
lations. God forbid that we should ever be found trifling
with the sacred word of truth. But it does strike my
mind that our mutual edification may be promoted if, in
a spirit of humble prayer and dependence upon divine
teaching, we look at two or three points which seem sug-
gested to us, in a spiritual light. May he whose province
it is to open the understanding, open our eyes, that we
may understand the Scriptures and behold wondrous things
out of the book of God's law.

The word of God makes mention of Zelophehad's five
daughters several times. It was a remarkable case, and
we see a particular notice is taken of it. Evidently
the Holy Ghost intended something beyond its literal
history. It is true this incident shows the imperfection
of the Mosaic Law in its provisions for every human contingency, and we see that this case was made the means
of establishing a reasonable and righteous law in the
Jewish civil code as to the heirship of estates; and in
which our own nation has very wisely followed.

By a reference to the chapter preceding our text, we
observe that in the law for apportioning the Land of
Canaan no provision had been made for females in case of
there being no male issue. Consequently, this family of
Zelophehad, consisting of five daughters, were unprovided
for, and they at once saw and felt the hardship of their
destitute condition, and that their case had been overlooked. This was a hard case, and you may perhaps
remember that it was under Jehovah's sanction and
guidance, that while common and ordinary cases occurring
between man and man were adjudicated by subordinate
judges, yet all hard cases were to be brought before
Moses; but that when cases proved too difficult even for
Moses to decide upon, then the cause was to be brought
into the solemn meeting of Moses and the priests and
princes of the congregation at the door of the tabernacle,
to inquire of the Lord at the holy oracle. Such was the
case here; these five daughters, conscious of their father's

good name and of their own destitute and unprovided for estate by his death, come before this august and chief assembly to represent their cause. They very properly refer to their father as not having died under any attainder or judicial law by which his estate would have become forfeited, and therefore no legal claim might be made by his family; but they appeal on the ground that it was unreasonable that his estate should revert to his brother, their uncle, merely on the fact of their father having no son; such an accidental circumstance as this they represented as acting most prejudicial to his family of females. They plead for a possession. On what ground? relationship—Zelophehad was their father. But why plead on the ground of relationship, for Zelophehad had never an inch of ground he could call his own? True, but the promise was made to him, the reversion belonged to him and to his heirs for ever. Their faith was in the promise made to their father, their plea is founded both on the promise made to him and on their relationship to him. This was too hard a case for Moses. The law had made no provision for it. He could not act without it. He brings the case in solemn conclave before Jehovah. Their plea was admitted and approved, and an inheritance is assigned to them amongst their father's brethren.

Perhaps it may be inquired, but what is all this to us? The law came by Moses, but grace and truth came by Jesus Christ. We prefer the gospel to Moses' institutes. Well, be it so; yet, we think, under the anointing of God's Spirit, much New Testament truth may be brought out of Old Testament facts. I am persuaded good gospel grace is often to be had out of Mosaic law.

> "Israel in ancient days
> Not only had a view
> Of Sinai in a blaze,
> But learned the gospel too;
> The types and shadows were a glass,
> In which they saw the Saviour's face."

And amongst other instances, very strikingly so, as I think, in the case of Zelophehad's daughters. This is it, my object is to point out to you precious gospel truths folded within this apparently singular incident of Jewish history. Here is then the subject embraced in our text—The law of inheritance is found defective. It is appealed against. The appeal is admitted, and the inheritance is divinely secured to the appellants both by inheritance and special gift. Now I believe there is much spiritual truth underlying all this statement of literal fact, which, with the Lord's help and blessing, I trust may be of great comfort and edification to his loving family. I do not intend running a parallel on every part, but shall confine myself to a few primary points. The first we notice is,

1. *The sense these five daughters have that, by the death of their father, and they having no brother for his heir, the law has left them destitute; it has made no provision for their maintenance, for by law they are not entitled to their father's inheritance.*

Spiritually considered, this is the case of all mankind. Our first father, Adam, possessed an inheritance in himself, being created pure, holy, upright, and innocent; but for his disobedience in eating the forbidden fruit he died, forfeited his inheritance, died in his own sin, and in sinning involved his posterity in the ruin and misery of his apostasy. His inheritance passed away from them; for that by nature he left no son born before the apostasy that could inherit it; having, therefore, so to speak, no "elder brother born for adversity," the inheritance is lost to them; their father's death ruined them all, it completely beggared them, and has left them without hope in him. In the Adamic constitution the human posterity are all made sinners; the disobedience of Adam, as the head of mankind, has laid a sure foundation for the same sin and corruption to take place and spread through all the human race; just as by divine appointment, or a law of nature, as it is commonly termed, the sap of the root or original stock of a tree passes into the numerous limbs, twigs, and fruit of a tree, as they successively grow out of it. "If the sap or nature of the root or stock be bad, sour, or poisonous, the same is communicated to the whole; and every branch, and all the fruit and seed of the whole tree, is corrupt, sour, or poisonous, and of all the trees which spring from that, or are produced by the seed of it. Thus, if any tree was, when first created, of a poisonous nature, and produced such fruit, all that race of trees, or all that should spring from it, would of course be of the same nature. And if a tree or plant, which was created at first good and wholesome, did degenerate, and become corrupt and poisonous, all that should proceed from that would, of course, be equally corrupt." In this sense, the first sin is the sin of all mankind, and is the source of all the misery and woe brought into this world.

Such is the teaching of God's word, and such is our belief when our minds are enlightened by the divine Spirit. We find, by painful and bitter experience, like Zelophehad's daughters, our father has died in his own sin, his sin of unbelief; by nature, we have no brother born for adversity, "for all have sinned and come short of the glory of God," and therefore we have no inheritance in our first father; his innocency, happiness, and immortality were all forfeited by his death. By law, that is, the original constitution under which mankind were placed, there is no provision for our innocency, happiness, and immortality. We are left without hope. These five daughters felt they had no maintenance in themselves, their father's death had left them utterly destitute, and thus it was they came to make their case known. And so, brethren, when you and I are brought to feel our misery and destitution by our relation to our federal head, Adam, it will lead us to make our case known. But let me ask you in plain terms, have you ever been brought to feel that you are really a lost, ruined sinner in and of yourself? or are you so puffed up with pharisaic pride, and vainly fancy you are rich and increased with goods, and have need of nothing, being ignorant of your wretchedness, misery, and poverty, your blindness and nakedness? O if it be so, may the Lord open your eyes, and lead you to know the truth as it is in Christ!

2. *They bring their case before Moses, but it is too hard for him, and he cannot help them.*

By consulting Deut. i. 17, we find that when matters of dispute or difficulty were brought for decision in the ordinary courts of arbitration, it was said by Moses, "The cause that is too hard for you, bring it unto me, and I will hear it." There is no doubt that in the first instance, these five daughters mentioned their case to the judges in the lower courts; from thence they were sent to Moses. There is no statement of such a process, but it is implied in the result that followed, and that is, we see, Moses could not settle it; it was too hard a cause for him even; he could do nothing for them. Yet it was a very proper step for them to take; where else could they go? what else could they do? They were under Moses, and to Moses they must be sent, and then it is they learn that

Moses has no power in the present constitution of things
to give them an inheritance among their brethren. Just
so is the case with every poor sinner made sensible of his
lost, ruined condition by the death of his forefather Adam;
he comes at once to Moses for help; being born under
the law, he looks to it for pardon, peace, and righteousness, but he finds no help there. He knows the law is
holy, just, and good, but it brings him no pardon, it
brings him no peace; and as for righteousness, the more
he toils and tugs for it on the footing of his own performances, the farther he feels from it; it has only added
to his condemnation. As there is imperfection in the
best of all human institutions, so the daughters of Zelophehad found that the Mosaic constitution of things was
imperfect. "The law made nothing perfect, but the
bringing in of better hope did." (Heb. vii. 19.) They
found the law could not do everything; it had not provided for every weakness and contingency in the flesh, it
could only make them feel the more pungently their absolute doom to ruin and misery. Thus have we found it,
proved it, and have said with the poet:

> " In vain we ask God's righteous law,
>   To justify us now;
> Since to convince and to condemn,
>   Is all the law can do."

And every sinner, under a feeling sense of its condemnation, feels he is weak, and it is because he is weak
that the law cannot do anything for him; had he been a
just man, it would have justified him, but being a sinner,
it condemns him; its inability is not chargeable upon the
law, but on the sinner: " For what the law could not do, in
that it was weak through the flesh." (Rom. viii. 3.) Sin
has made us weak, made us miserably poor, stripped every
piece of righteousness from off our back. If righteousness could have come by the law, it would have given it;
" for if there had been a law given which could have given
life, verily righteousness should have been by the law;"
(Gal. iii. 21;) but being broken, it condemns us, demands
our life; it kills instead of saves. Every sinner under
the teaching of God's Spirit is made to feel that the law
can do nothing for him, that it is weak through their own
sinful flesh. The law made nothing perfect, but the
bringing in of a better hope did; this they prove by an
experimental acquaintance with the truth, and this leads

them to renounce Moses, and to seek a higher court for life and salvation. Such a soul, having the sentence of death in itself, will cease from looking to its own doings as the meritorious cause of receiving any good from the hand of God; they must look elsewhere for hope, and exclaim,

> "My soul no more attempt to draw
> Thy life and comfort from the law;
> Fly to the hope the gospel gives,
> The man that trusts the promise lives."

3. *The daughters of Zelophehad appeal on the ground of relationship, and faith in the promise made to their father.*
They claim the benefit of that relationship. An inheritance had been promised to him, but he dying in the wilderness without male issue, left it unappropriated; and as he had done nothing of himself to alienate the property from his family, but simply died in the common course of nature, decay, the effect of sin. Nor had he entered the promised land any more than any of the others, save Joshua and Caleb, through unbelief. By the accidental circumstance of these daughters having no brother, they look upon themselves as deprived of the promise, and impoverished without any just cause; and they consider their father's name dishonoured and blotted out. They not only do honour to their father in desiring that his name should not be done away, but we see also their faith in God's promise, and the esteem they have for it on their father's account. So may true believers in Christ claim an inheritance among all the sanctified, on the ground of relationship and promise; and here we see a superiority in the gospel over the law in every point of view. Believers have faith in the promises of God. God is their father. They plead his name, they plead his promise. What though the law is against them as they stand in Adam, their federal head: "Is the law, then, against the promises? God forbid?" (Gal. iii. 21.) Is the promise to be disannulled because the law is weak through the flesh? Come, Moses, answer this knotty point. No, indeed, he cannot; it is too hard a case for him: "For if the inheritance be of the law, it is no more of promise;" but God has given it to his chosen by promise. Moses has nothing to do with it; and though there is no inheritance by the law, there is by promise; and God's spiritually taught children make no attempt to claim it by

law, but by promise and untainted relationship : "Blessed
be the God and Father of our Lord Jesus Christ, which
according to his abundant mercy hath begotten us again
unto a lively hope by the resurrection of Jesus Christ
from the dead, to an inheritance incorruptible, and undefiled, and that fadeth not away, reserved in heaven for
you." (1 Peter i. 4, 5.)   And what blessedness we see in
gospel blessings.   Believers in the Lord Jesus Christ may
claim God for their father and his only begotten Son for
their brother.   Whatever may be their condition by nature
in and of themselves considered, his God is their God, his
Father is their Father, therefore he is their elder brother,
so that by no possibility can any contingency arise to
deprive them of their inheritance.   It comes to them by
virtue of covenant union to him in whom are all the promises of God. (2 Cor. i. 29.)   "The Lord knoweth the
days of the upright; and their inheritance shall be for
ever." (Ps. xxxvii. 18.)

4. *As their case is too hard for Moses, it is taken into a
higher court ; it is brought before Jehovah in solemn council and state.*

Here we see is the precedent upon which the rule is
enjoined by Moses. (Deut. xvii. 8, 9.)   All grave and
difficult matters of controversy were to be brought into
solemn conclave of priests, Levites, and judge.   In this
instance the august assembly consisted of Moses, as supreme, Eleazar, the priest, and the princes, or elders, at
the door of the tabernacle ; it was an open meeting, and
it constituted the highest court of judicature.   As there
was no law upon which this assembly could act, Moses
brings the case before Jehovah, the object being to know
his will ; in this they doubtless consulted the divine oracle
of the Urim and Thummim, in the holy place before the
Shekinah, the cloudy symbol of the divine presence.   This
we gather from the 21st verse of the chapter.   Joshua is to
" stand before Eleazar the priest, who shall ask counsel
for him after the judgment of Urim before the Lord."
Here we feel is a sweet spiritual truth.   We are brought
before God's most holy bar.   Conscious of our destitution, conscious that the law can effect no help, yet we
plead relationship, we plead the promise, and still sue for
the inheritance.   The law becomes, as it were, our schoolmaster to bring us to Christ.   It teaches us what we
were before ignorant of.   We must be made to feel that

God alone can help us. To whom can we go if Moses cannot help us. We must turn from Moses to Jesus. Truly blessed is that soul, who, having toiled at the law, hoping for acceptance on pleas of its own, and meeting with no success, finds itself brought before a mercy-seat to bow before the Lord. O this is a solemn meeting, a weighty matter, a critical moment, hoping against hope, resolving to "hear what God the Lord will speak, for he will speak peace to his saints." O Jesus! says the soul, I feel how miscrably poor I am, blind and naked, I come to thee totally helpless, O help me in this my time of need; thy holy, righteous law has made me feel all this wretchedness; I have no help there, it has stripped me naked and bare, and now to whom can I go if I should turn from thee; thou art my only refuge, I look to thee for everything; be thou my advocate in heaven's high court; O take up my case, and save me from all I feel and fear; in thy grace alone is all my hope.

> "The help of men and angels joined,
> Could never reach my case;
> Nor can I hope relief to find,
> But in thy boundless grace."

5. *Their plea is heard, and Jehovah, in his rich mercy and grace, assigns an inheritance to them among their father's brethren.*

And what was the nature of their plea that it should be entertained before Jehovah? They had done nothing personally by which they could claim an inheritance; they were not numbered amongst the people; and it was only to such who were numbered that the inheritance could be divided; these five daughters knew that, and therefore they did not expect it, and so they ask for it as a gift; they could not claim it on the ground of merit, for had it been so, the law would have dealt with them as the case required; they could not claim it as a matter of right, for otherwise the law could not have denied them; but the nature of their plea is such, that it can be brought into the high court of heaven, and it can be heard and is received by Jehovah himself. What is it? DESTITUTION and HELPLESSNESS! Merit and right in the sinner's own name have no place either in the court of God's law or in the gospel plan. The plea of Zelophehad's daughters is approved; hear the judgment: "And the Lord spake unto Moses, saying, The daughters of Zelophehad speak

E

right; thou shalt surely give them a possession of an inheritance among their father's brethren; and thou shalt cause the inheritance of their fathers to pass unto them." They speak right—their plea is according to God's word and will. Destitution and helplessness capacitates ruined, undone sinners for the grace of God, and when made sensible of it by the teachings of his Spirit he will surely lead them to seek it on that footing. "The Spirit maketh intercession within us according to the will of God." We are commended to God and to the word of his grace, which is able to build us up and to *give* us an inheritance among all the sanctified. The inheritance which the saints of God possess is a deed of gift by an act of grace. It cannot be had by the law, because it has been forfeited; it cannot be had only by the gift of the Father: "It is your father's good pleasure to give you the kingdom." (Luke xii. 32.) It is a promised inheritance, therefore a gift, not of merits, not of works, lest any man should boast. "Boasting is excluded. By what law? The law of faith." This family of daughters asked for an inheritance as a deed of gift; it was bestowed as a gift, and they received it as a gift. Now I would ask you, my hearers, have you ever been brought before the Lord with a sense of *your* destitution and *your* helplessness, and to sue for an inheritance in the heavenly Canaan as a deed of gift, as an act of Jehovah's grace? This is a solemn, momentous question. Do you really feel what ruined, bankrupt sinners you are, in and of yourselves? and are you sensible that you have no hope of eternal life except by the gift of God through Jesus Christ our Lord? These are weighty matters, and I appeal to your conscience as to how these matters stand in your estimation and your experience; think them over, and may the Lord grant you the blessedness of knowing how sure his salvation is to all who are taught to feel their own destitution and helplessness. "It is not by works of righteousness which we have done, but according to his mercy he saved us by the washing of regeneration, and renewing of the Holy Ghost." (Titus iii. 5.)

6. *So now they possess their lot in Canaan by promised inheritance, and a divine gift; by which they inherit the promise more securely and more gloriously than if they had possessed it by a legal title under the law of Moses.*

In the answer which the Lord spake unto Moses, he

gives commandment that this family shall have an inheritance: "The promise made to their father in which
their faith rested before his death shall be fulfilled towards them; the inheritance which would have fallen to
their brother, if there had been one, they shall possess
notwithstanding; and though under Moses, the first covenant, they had no legal right, they shall have it now by
virtue of my own free sovereign gift of grace." O the
blessedness of those whom Jehovah causeth to approach
unto him, they shall be satisfied with the goodness of his
house, even of his holy temple; and this was indeed a
gift worth coming for; how super-excellent the glory of
such an inheritance, a divine gift, a glorious gift, a heavenly gift; for, figuratively, they claimed an inheritance
in the kingdom of heaven, and it was the Father's good
pleasure to give them the kingdom; how everlastingly
secure the gift; his kingdom is an everlasting kingdom,
his gifts are without repentance, he never changes his
mind, for he is of one mind, and who can turn him; he
will confirm the inheritance unto his chosen; it is confirmed in the Person of Christ, his only begotten and
eternal Son. "Blessed be the God and Father of our
Lord Jesus Christ, who hath blessed us with all spiritual
blessings in heavenly places in Christ, according as he
hath chosen us in him before the foundation of the world.
In whom also we have obtained an inheritance, being
predestined according to the purpose of him who worketh
all things after the counsel of his own will." (Eph. i.
3, 9.) Here we see the basis of the inheritance—
predestination and sovereignty, those two mountains of
brass which so many professors are always kicking at;
nevertheless there they are, they cannot be overthrown;
here is the saints' security, here is their glory—the inheritance is a *most ancient* gift, for it was before time; it is
a most *extensive* gift, for all things are their's; it is a
most *beneficial* gift, for it has saved them from the curse
of sin, the slavery of the devil, and the fascinations of the
world; it is a most *dignifying and exalting* gift, for its
being in the Person of Christ, who hath by inheritance
obtained a more excellent name than all the archangels
of heaven, the church of God partake with him in all
its excellency, fulness, and glory; and it is an *eternal*
inheritance, incorruptible and undefiled, and that fadeth
not away, reserved in heaven for them who are kept by

the power of God through faith unto salvation, and have been sealed with that Holy Spirit of promise which is the earnest of the inheritance, the promise of eternal inheritance which they which are called shall receive. (Eph. i. 13, 14; Heb. ix. 15.) How super-excellent is the glory of the gospel over that of the law. The law was a ministration of condemnation, yet in itself it had a glory, for it is holy, just, and good. But grace reigns through righteousness; and "if the ministration of condemnation be glory, much more doth the ministration of righteousness exceed in glory. For even that which was made glorious had no glory in this respect, by reason of the glory that excelleth. For if that which is done away was glorious, much more that which remaineth is glorious." (2 Cor. iii. 9–11.) Do we not see how far superior the "gift by grace" is over any legal title which might have been obtained. Our heavenly inheritance stands upon no legal footing, but on the security of a divine promise and eternal covenant union with Jesus Christ; our adoption in him as the children of God renders us "heirs, heirs of God and joint heirs with Christ."

7. *Being now possessed of an inheritance in their own right, they are thereby more eligible for marriage, and to have a better standing in society.*

These five daughters in all probability would have remained unmarried if their father's inheritance had not been bestowed upon them. The family and name would have naturally died out; and as the Jews were careful to preserve by marriage family names, distinctions, and inheritances, no possible advantage could arise by a marriage with any of these destitute and forlorn orphans. This they themselves felt, and they did honour to their father in urging their plea upon the argument, "why should the name of our father be done away from among his family because he had no son;" or in other words, to speak plainly, "why should we be debarred from being married." Well, we see "the Lord commanded to give the inheritance of Zelophehad to his daughters." (Numb. xxxvi. 2.) They did possess it, and thus they became heiresses in their own right; they were married, (see v. 11th,) and what is remarkable, they were married upon their own choice, "whom they thought best;" (v. 6;) they married their cousins. (Ver. 11.) They did not go out of their tribe, for it was the law that every one of the tribes should keep themselves to their own inheritance. (Ver. 9.) Zelophehad's inheritance remained in the tribe of the family of their father; (v. 12;) and the sequel of this interesting circumstance was, that under the ministration of Joshua, who succeeded to Moses, these five daughters were put into actual possession of the inheritance. (Joshua xvii. 4.)

Here, then, we see these daughters who had, under the law of Moses, no dowry, are now, through the divine gift of inheritance, able to give one themselves. God having blessed his people with all spiritual blessings in Christ, they possess in him a rich dowry; they choose him for their heavenly husband. This is part of their heavenly wisdom, they marry whom they think best; they think best of him who is altogether lovely. She becomes the bride, the Lamb's wife; she is the king's daughter; she is "all glorious within; her clothing is of wrought gold. She shall be brought unto the king in raiment of needlework. * * * Instead of thy fathers shall be thy children, whom thou mayest make princes in all the earth. I will make thy name to be remembered in all generations; therefore shall the people praise thee for ever and ever." (Ps. xlv. 13, 17.) God's church is married to Christ; and by virtue of covenant union to him, God is their Father, so that she is now by her dowry honourable, and by marriage a king's daughter; God gave her to Christ, being precious to him: "for since thou hast been precious in my sight thou hast been honourable." (Isa. xliii. 4.) How delightful the thought, every believer in Christ, united to him by a true and living faith, is an "honourable"—the son or daughter of a lord, the Lord God Almighty. How glorious our standing in the gospel to that when under the law! destitute and helpless orphans and no prospect of an inheritance; but now delivered from that under which we were held, our standing, by grace divine, is eternally secure in that everlasting covenant which is ordered in all things and sure; raised to the highest pinnacle of glory and happiness; to be with Jesus enthroned in the heavenly state, to praise his name for ever and ever. We look back to our former estate, and can say with the poet:

" He raised me from the deeps of sin,
    The gates of gaping hell,
And fix'd my standing more secure
    Than 'twas before I fell."

But I must now draw my remarks on the several features of this remarkable and interesting incident to a close; there is much mystical and spiritual truth yet to be eliminated, but time forbids; I shall only detain you a few minutes by making two or three more observations by way of improvement. I may perhaps be accused of repetition, but risking that, I would remark,

1. We see that as the faith of these females in God's promise was manifested by their appeal to Moses in the face of the law being against them, and the inheritance secured to them by a special gift, so believers in Christ have glory promised them by a gift of grace. It is claimed by faith on the plea of covenant union. God honours their faith, while at the same time he secures his church's everlasting welfare. God's promise was the ground of the faith of Zelophehad's daughters; their altered circumstances by the death of their father did not lessen it. The promise made to Abraham was the ground of his faith; there were certain things against it, nevertheless he staggered not through unbelief, for where God has promised there is always ground for hope. "Is the law against the promises? God forbid;" but it is against the impenitent and unawakened sinner, he is under its curse.

Awakened sinners though fleeing to the law for help, claim what it cannot give; they seek life and salvation by it; they know the law is against them, it has condemned them, and yet they vainly strive for pardon and peace, they sin and stumble but the more until they are led to Christ. Then it is they look to him, from him they receive the promise, they claim it by faith in him; by living on him by faith they rejoice in hope of the glory of God; Christ dwells in their heart by faith, which is Christ in them the hope of glory. "The Lord will give grace and glory, and no good thing will he withhold from them who walk uprightly." (Ps. lxxxiv. 11.) The promise of the heavenly inheritance is secured by our Lord's own will, a security founded in everlasting love and covenant union with the eternal Jehovah in his Trinity of Persons, so that it is impossible ever to miss of it: "Father, I will that they also whom thou hast given me, be with me where I am; that they may behold my glory, which thou hast given me; for thou lovest me before the foundation of the world." (John xvii. 24.) Thus it is that God, through

Christ, gives us grace, he gives us glory. We shall have a certain realization of our faith.

2. We see that though the Lord's people may at first be under a legal yoke while in the wilderness state, yet it is by faith they are raised far superior to it, and are delivered from all the beggary to which they were reduced.

It is sheer folly to suppose that because a soul may be exercised with what pertains to a legal work in the conscience, therefore no good work is begun in the heart; the reverse is true, the law is our schoolmaster to bring us to Christ, like as Moses brought Zelophehad's family before the Lord. It is through the faith of Christ that believers seek deliverance from the bondage under which they are held; their seeking it through the law is their mistake: "Christ is the end of the law for righteousness to every one that believeth" that he is the only way to God. "Before faith came, we were kept under the law, shut up unto the faith which should afterwards be revealed, but that after faith is come we are no longer under a schoolmaster," for then it is that we are manifested to be the "children of God by faith in Christ Jesus." (Gal. iii. 23–26.) "But now we are delivered from the law, that being dead wherein we were held; that we should serve in newness of spirit, and not in the oldness of the letter." (Rom. vii. 6.) The life of faith is the work of grace, and is completed in eternal glory.

3. We see Jehovah's love and grace towards his people in bestowing the blessings they need, and for which they plead.

Salvation by grace is a theme which delights the redeemed sinner to contemplate; its blessings, like a mighty stream, flow down to them from a source which is to be traced to the fountain of God's everlasting love, whose goings forth have been of old. Our experience of his goodness commences in time; we have his promise of all needful good, grace here, glory hereafter, grace for every need, strength for the day, wisdom for every exigency; we seek these in faith, we plead his promise, we plead the name of Christ, "our elder brother," "our brother born for adversity;" we are blessed through him, blessed in him. Here on earth we are straitened in ourselves, but in the rest beyond, "there the glorious Lord will be unto us a place of broad rivers and streams." There will be an ample sufficiency of every blessing to make our bliss eternally complete.

4. We see also that as it was under Joshua Zelophehad's daughters were put into actual possession of their
inheritance, so it is by Jesus Christ we are made partakers
of the heavenly inheritance.

Joshua, the servant of the Lord, was an eminent type of
the Lord Jesus Christ; his name is the Hebrew word for
Jesus, a Saviour. As he brought the people through the
wilderness and the Jordan into the land of Canaan, and
gave to each their inheritance, so Jesus brings us safely
through the gospel wilderness state, supplying all our
wants, protecting us from every danger, preserving to us
unimpaired all our interests, and at last brings us through
the Jordan of death to the heavenly state, and puts us in
full possession of all the blessings promised. This is our
rejoicing, we will speak it to his praise: "For this God
is our God for ever and ever; he will be our guide even
unto death." (Ps. lxxxiv. 14.)

5. We see, too, the faithfulness of a covenant Jehovah
to his promise and to his people.

God is faithful who has promised. As Abraham received a divine call to leave his own country and kindred
to go into the land of Canaan, it is said, "and they went
forth to go into the land of Canaan, and into the land of
Canaan they came;" (Gen. xii. 5;) so the Lord will certainly perform his covenant to all his redeemed family,
and not one good thing of all he has promised shall ever
fail.

> " His truth he inviolably keeps,
> The largest promise of his lips."

He is a promise making and a promise performing God.
As sure as the good work of divine grace has been begun
in your hearts, he will carry it on and perfectly perform it
unto the day of Jesus Christ; and "so an entrance shall
be ministered unto you abundantly into the everlasting
kingdom of our Lord and Saviour Jesus Christ." (2 Pet.
i. 2.)

Dear friends, I have thus aimed to put before you some
of the corresponding gospel truths, which I think may be
fairly traced in this portion of Old Testament history. I
feel conscious there is much that is defective and imperfect, but nevertheless what has now been stated may serve
as an outline for your further meditation and improvement. A spiritual insight into the meaning of God's
word is the exclusive gift of him by whom it was inspired.
The natural man discerneth not the things of the Spirit,

and, therefore, it is unlikely that he will approve those things having a spiritual significancy. Our Lord when on earth spoke " unto them that were without in parables." And when he was with his church in the wilderness under Moses, he displayed his gracious designs and his infinite wisdom to the spiritually enlightened in all the types and figures which were employed in that ceremonial dispensation. "They were all," says the apostle Paul, "baptized unto Moses in the cloud and in the sea; and did all eat the same spiritual meat, and did all drink of the same spiritual drink; for they drank of that spiritual Rock that followed them, and that Rock was Christ." (1 Cor. x. 2–4.) And the same apostle, in writing to the Colossians, takes up the facts of the circumcision, baptism, and resurrection of the Lord Jesus as an argument in matters of real spiritual importance; so that whenever the Lord's people are led to contemplate the truths of the Bible, whether they be in figures, persons, or historical facts, they will find delightful and profitable subjects leading them to further discoveries of the unsearchable riches of Christ. May the Lord lead your minds to search God's word for yourselves, and to examine yourselves as to whether you have right saving faith in God's promise of the heavenly inheritance which is given to all the sanctified. Do you feel your spiritual destitution and helplessness? and do you think you can claim a divine relationship, and plead the promise of God in the face of his law being against you? Oh, if you can, the inheritance is yours,—yours by promise, yours by gift, yours by inheritance.

> "Brethren, by this your claim abide,
>   This title to your bliss;
> Whatever loss you bear beside,
>   Oh, never give up this."

JEHOVAH'S POWER CONCEALED IN THE HORNS OF HIS HAND.

———◆———

A SERMON,
BY CHARLES GORDELIER.

PREACHED AT HEPHZIBAH CHAPEL, DARLING PLACE, MILE END GATE,

On Lord's Day Evening, 18th February, 1866.

———

"He had horns coming out of his hand, and there was the hiding of his power."—HABAKKUK iii. 4.

WE have no certain information respecting the prophet Habakkuk; but it is evident that he prophesied in Judea before the captivity, and probably in the reign of Jehoiakim, and therefore co-temporary with Jeremiah. As a poet Habakkuk holds a high rank among the Hebrew prophets. There is a beautiful connection between the parts of his prophecy; its diction, imagery, spirit, and sublimity are remarkably striking, and well deserve our admiration. His prayer, in particular, from whence we have taken our text, is considered by competent judges to be a masterpiece of its kind, and one of the most perfect specimens of Hebrew poetry. His name signifies, " one that embraces, a wrestler ;" a name that befits him well. Shigionoth, a word used in the title, appears to be either the name of the tune to which the prayer was set, or else the name of the musical instrument employed when the prayer was used, it being sung in the service of God; for you observe the word "selah" occurs three times, and at the conclusion it is addressed to the leader of the choir.

I would also remark, that this prayer of Habakkuk arises out of his prophecy. The prophet, foreseeing the judgments of God, the calamities which were to befall his country from the Chaldeans, and afterwards the punishments which awaited the Chaldeans themselves;

No. 22.

being partly struck with terror and partly inspired by
his confidence in God's faithfulness and character, he
prays that God would hasten the deliverance of his people:
" O Lord, I have heard thy speech, and was afraid; O
Lord, revive thy work in the midst of the years, in the
midst of the years make known; in wrath remember
mercy." He then alludes to the Egyptian deliverance in
language so sublime as is totally beyond my power to describe: " God came from Teman." Teman is the name
of the southern country, where Moses fled when he left
Egypt, and was afterwards recalled to deliver the people
of Israel; he represented God; he did God's work.
"Paran" is the northern extremity of the wilderness
Sinai, from whence the law was proclaimed. Then we
have the word " selah." At this point the musical chorus
breaks out, or rather, as I am inclined to think, a sym-
phony is played, while the voices are silent, and meditation is promoted. The miraculous incidents in the wilderness history, the most noble and important are displayed in the most splendid colours, embellished with
magnificent and sublimest imagery, figures, and diction.
The singular elegance of the conclusion crowns the whole
with a superior dignity. It is the language of faith,
filled with divine energy, rejoicing in Jehovah Jesus, the
fountain of all true joy when the streams of creature comforts have all failed.

With regard to the first part of this verse, "His
brightness was as the light," it is probable there is an
allusion to the exceeding glory which Moses saw on the
mount at the giving of the law: " So terrible was the
sight that Moses said, I exceedingly fear and quake." As
to the second part of the verse: " He had horns coming
out of his hand," I am aware that the marginal reading
is, " beams coming out of his side;" and this rendering is
generally received by expositors; but I confess I am not
inclined to it, for having had my mind impressed with a
different view in rather a remarkable way, yet not of sufficient importance to state here, I feel I must in this instance walk out of the common road and keep to the ordinary reading, which I certainly prefer.

The material point of difference in the view generally
taken of this passage and in the one which I hold is in
the term " horns." By " horn," strength is signified
everywhere in Scripture; as, the horn of salvation, the

strength of salvation. (Ps. xviii. 2.)   The exalting of the
horn is the advancing of power. (1 Sam. ii. 1; Ps. lxxxix.
17.)   Here, in our text, these are said to be in the hand,
because the hands and arms are the powers of the body;
and, indeed, as they are the instruments of power, they
are well called "the strong men of the body."   Then,
again, horns are for use, not for display; beams are ema-
nations of light, a display of the source of light; which,
to my mind, as applied to the marginal rendering, is but
a repetition or amplification of the first portion of the
verse, "his brightness was as the light," which I imagine
is not the intention of the prophet.   That Jehovah reveals himself in the glories of his various attributes is
strictly true :

> " His glories shine with beams so bright,
>   No mortal eye can bear the sight."

But in the passage before us we think we can discover
more than that which simply confounds and dazzles us,
though it be to admiration.   The word of God reveals
to us the glories of Jehovah in a way that is to be of
essential advantage to the church of God; not for our
admiration only, but for our positive salvation.   The
horns coming out of his hand is for the salvation of his
people: "Thou wentest forth for the salvation of thy
people."   "His brightness was as the light," shows us
what God is: "God is light; in him is no darkness at
all."   The "horns coming out of his hand" shows us
what God does—the goings forth of Jehovah in acts of
mercy, love, and grace.

I said, horns are for use; they are used for defence, by
reason of the power they possess.   Zedekiah, the false
prophet, forged horns of iron, and brought them to King
Ahab, intimating thereby the power he possessed, the
power of driving his foes from him.   The timid kinds of
cattle, you observe, are provided with horns for defence;
thus, weak as they appear to be, they possess a source of
strength which is hidden.   The horn is but a small portion that is displayed; but its roots are spread over a
wider surface than can be traced.   Here, I think, is the
true idea of the text, and which we are to keep in view as
we go along with our subject.   We see but a small portion of what God does for us, for there is much more
concealed than we can trace.

Horns are for positive service.   We see it in the service of the sanctuary. The altar on which the sacrifices were to be placed were to be provided with horns at each corner. The primary use to which they were put was for fastening with cords, so as to keep secure, the sacrifices laid upon it. The accumulation of the people's sacrifices on the great days of the tabernacle service would necessitate it; hence we have the words, Ps. cxviii.: "God is Jehovah, who hath showed us light; bind the sacrifices with cords to the altar." (Ex. xxvii. 2; xxx. 10; Ps. cxviii. 27.) There was also another use to which the horns of the altar were put, and that was for the salvation of the manslayer. If the avenger of blood was close, even to his heels, yet if the manslayer could only grasp the horns of the altar, he was safe; it was his place of refuge, it was his salvation, for so had God appointed it. (See 1 Kings ii. 28; Ps. xxii. 21.) In the Book of the Revelation horns are explained to represent kings.

The horn, as you are aware, is an instrument that stands out prominently, presenting something to be laid hold of; in itself it appears small, but it is well adapted for the use intended—the defence of the body. It is large enough to be laid hold of; it is strong enough to be depended on, for the power of its roots are stronger and deeper than can be traced, for it is hidden and concealed from common inspection.

By the hand of God we are to consider is meant his providential government and the dispensations of his goodness; the horns coming out signifying the manifestation of his power, still having much that is hidden and concealed. An illustration of this is afforded us in the history of Elijah, when, after a long drought of rain for three years, he foretold Ahab of a sound of abundance of rain, yet successively the faith of the prophet was tried upon there being no appearance of it. His servant looked and looked again, but in vain. At length a sign of rain did appear, a cloud was visible; but it was a small cloud, a very small cloud, no larger, apparently, than a man's hand; yet that was the power of God, his hand was seen, the horn was displayed; what God had begun to do was as yet nothing compared to what he purposed doing. The promise and the fulfilment vary for a time; but the smallest indication of mercy is a token of his infinite mercy and goodness.

The hand of God is often seen in what is frequently

designated his purposes.   The purposes of God are more commonly concealed by what he is doing than can possibly be judged of by mortal eye.   The events in your life that may be transpiring at the present time, small as they appear, may have greater purposes to be revealed. Hope, for instance, is the laying hold of something small in itself, but behind is concealed the substance of that which is hoped for.   A promise is the ground of hope, the performance is concealed; but the reality, how far superior!   The promise made to Abraham was a small horn in the hand of Jehovah's purposes; but O what a hiding of his power as revealed in the performance to his seed!   Faith lays hold of that which secures the hand of God to itself.   God reveals but a part of himself at a time; his hand of supply has horns coming out of it; in this there is the hiding of his power.   More is concealed than revealed.

Having laid before you the ideas which I consider are intended by the words "horns" and "hand," as employed in the text, I shall proceed now to set forth a few particulars, in which the meaning of the text may be illustrated.

1. *The hiding of Jehovah's power is concealed in the works of creation.*

By referring to the Epistle to the Romans, i. 19, 20, you will there perceive that the apostle proves that though God had discovered himself to mankind by the works of the creation, they did not serve him, but fell into inexcusable idolatry and every kind of disorder and enormous vices: "Because that which may be known of God is manifest in them; for God hath showed it unto them.   For the invisible things of him from the creation of the world are clearly seen, being understood by the things that are made, even his eternal power and Godhead; so that they are without excuse."   From which we see that much of the nature and properties of God may be known by the light of nature; his infinite wisdom, power, and goodness are manifest in the minds and consciences of all men ; *for God hath showed it unto them,* partly by imprinting these ideas of himself upon the hearts of all men, and partly by the works of creation ; so that in the order, contrivance, and design displayed in the creation there is proved that in the works of nature there is more than what we really see.   We perceive that

in the works of creation there must be a Being of stupen-
dous power, infinite wisdom, and knowledge above what
we see in man, and that he must stand in relation to us
and all that we see as the maker does to the thing which
he has made. The operations of God's hand are, indeed,
displayed to man in much that they disregard; and this
disregard of God in the works of nature is their wickedness, and will prove to be their destruction: "Because
they regard not the works of the Lord, nor the operation
of his hands, he shall destroy them, and not build them
up." (Ps. xxviii. 5.) But how much more is hidden
than they can perceive, partly, it is true, from the blindness of their depraved hearts; (Rom. i. 21;) yet to the
intelligent and contemplative mind there is much more
deduced, for they have eyes to see; while to the spiritually taught disciple of Jesus still more is discerned. I
say, the works of creation show much that indicate the
hidden power of God; and that which we see is the horn,
as it were, of our reliance on a power which is beyond our
ken to discover. The very rain from heaven and fruitful
seasons, filling our hearts with food and gladness, are
witnesses of the goodness of God and of his power,
though, by reason of our native ignorance, they lead not
our souls in gratitude and praise to him as he deserves.
The revolution of our earth round the sun; the moon,
planets, and stars display infinite skill, wisdom, and
power; but we cannot possibly conceive the amazing
omnipotence that must be exerted in the centrifugal and
centripetal forces by which these bodies are kept in their
proper orbits, and that for thousands of years, without
the slightest deviation of time, as is fully proved from
the regularity of the daylight which "wakeneth morning
by morning." So with regard to life and light in their
essences, which it is impossible for man to explain; they
are the horns of the hand of him who created both. We
see much to admire; they witness the goodness of God.
It is his hand of supply; but in those essences, the horns
of his hand, there is the hiding of his power. We take
hold of those horns, for on them, the life and light by
which we are daily supplied, it is that we rely for
our own existence as the creatures of his power and
goodness.

That the omnipotence of Jehovah is concealed in his
works is further evident by the vegetable substances

which we have all about us.   The seeds, plants, and trees
all witness his eternal power and Godhead.   Every seed,
plant, and tree has precisely the same body, as to its
nature and form, as when first created; their colour, taste,
and influence are what they ever were.   What is this but
the horns of his hand, and in which there is the hiding of
his power?   We sow and plant year after year, relying on
the fact that every seed has its own body, and will produce
its like.   Grass seed produces grass, wheat produces
wheat; the combination of light, heat, and moisture producing its like by a law of nature which the concealed
power of Omnipotence unvaryingly displays.   If we look
at second causes, we can account for most things that we
see or hear of; but first causes are commonly overlooked
because they are concealed.   Omnipotence is concealed
within itself.   God in his essence can be seen by no man;
we see his hand, we take hold of his horns, his goodness;
and we can say with Job, (xxvi. 14,) "Lo, these are part
of his ways; but how little a portion is heard of him?
but the thunder of his power who can understand?"

> " When thunders shake the ground,
>   None wonder at the shock;
>   A weighty cause is found,
>   And we no further look;"
> But if a feather shake the earth,
> That feather sets Jehovah forth."

2. *The hiding of Jehovah's power is concealed in the
ordering of his Providence.*

This we can best trace out in the word of God; the
illustrations are so vivid that the eye is at once rivetted
with the sight.   We see the hand of God in the history
of his saints; we take hold of the horns and feel there is
more concealed than has been revealed.   You see it in
Job's case, his great reverses and deep poverty unshift
him from his pinnacle of pharisaic pride before God; his
friends attempted with Herculean strength to accomplish
it, but they failed.   Yet in those reverses of outward
good, of family joys, and the estimation of his character,
there was a secret working of divine power by which Job
learned a truth he had not known before—that in himself,
as a sinner before God, he was vile; he no longer persisted
in maintaining his creature righteousness; he lets it go,
and abhors himself in dust and ashes.   "Lo, all these
things worketh God ofttimes with man, to bring back

his soul from the pit, to be enlightened with the light of the living." Many a man besides Job has learned a spiritual truth, and has taken hold on God, through the ordering of his providence; the hand of God was plainly seen, but the working it out was hidden; for in those very things by which he took hold on God, there was the hiding of his power.

See it in Abraham being called to offer up his son Israel; at first he saw not the power displayed which he after discovered. Unbelief, like distant thunder, was heard to rumble unutterable things, but his faith staggered not; what mighty words were they when he replied, "My son, God will provide himself a lamb for a burnt offering." Oh, that was a cloudy and dark day; how he took hold of God's promise as the horn of his hand; he was strong in faith; at the very last moment of hope's existence, his faith still kept its hold; it was the trial of love, hope, and faith; the source of his strength was in the power concealed, the deliverance displayed it. He discovered a deep spiritual truth in the strong exercises of his soul; he saw the day of Christ; he saw in the offering up his son, in the substitution of the ram caught in the thicket, the great doctrine of the substitutionary atonement of Christ for his church; he rejoiced to know that truth, though it was by the sharp and bitter exercise of prospectively sacrificing his son, in whom all the promises were made. Believers often find that God burns his truth into them by the fierce furnace of their experience.

Good old Jacob had, too, a severe trial in the giving up of his Benjamin; but it was the means of bringing him to see his long long-lost Joseph and his children, as well as Benjamin being restored to him: "I had not thought to have seen thy face, and lo God hath showed me thy seed." There was a hiding of God's purpose to make it better known, and in this fact there was a hiding of his power, there was more concealed than revealed.

David, the man after God's own heart, passed through extraordinary vicissitudes—"the times that went over him"—what sad breakings down! and broken bones too! but he was saved out of all his troubles. How often he could lay hold on God's hand even when he could not see his face: "Why standest thou afar off, O Lord? why hidest thou thyself in times of trouble?" (Ps. x. 1, and xiii. 1–5.) You see no answer is given; the reason he asks for he has to find in his own experience; there was a divine holding on God, though he was walking in darkness, and had no light. And what was the secret, think ye? was it not that the mercy he was trusting was the hiding of Jehovah's power? That which lay concealed in the purposes of his love, grace, and goodness, was the source of David's strength; this he ever found, and in the closing scene of his life, when reviewing what a ruler ought to be, he could say, "Although my house be not so with God, yet he hath made with me an everlasting covenant, ordered in all things, and sure;" for this is all my salvation and all my desire." You see, he took hold of God's covenant, it was the horn of his salvation. Who can trace the roots of God's faithfulness and power? they are in himself, it is the hiding of his power.

Joseph is another instance. The dreams of his youth apparently come to nothing, but his faith never seems to have been lost; young as he was, he took hold of God's horn; it was coming out of his hand, it was developing itself, though slowly, yet surely; for notwithstanding his slavery and bondage, his faith was stronger than ever, his "feet were hurt with fetters, he was laid in irons; until the time that his word came, the word of the Lord tried him;" he is still an interpreter of dreams, he had not lost confidence in his early dreams, they were horns to him in the hand of Jehovah, and certainly he could not be lower in adversity than when in the dungeon; yet all this was a part of the way in which God had sent him before his father and his brethren to find them food in a time of famine, and to bring them into Egypt. Oh, what power was here concealed, and yet how marvellously Joseph could see the truth which we have just sung in our hymn of praise:

> "His purposes will ripen fast,
>   Unfolding every hour;
> The bud may have a bitter taste,
>   But sweet will be the flower."

Elijah, whose case we have referred to, took hold of God's word as to the rain; yet how he must have been exercised in prayer; all seemed dark as to the fulfilment; he continued in prayer; the promise was delayed; what a concealment, I say, of God's power; in that very promise, in the time of its performance, what a trial of Elijah's faith, yet it kept its hold. He took hold of God's strength—his faithfulness; nor did it fail him in the dark hour of trial; providence contradicting the prophecy.

Hezekiah was a man who took hold of God by the horns of his hand, and was strengthened in God. He was weak in some points of his character, and was humbled on account of his vanity, but he became thereby to know all that was in his heart; he had great bitterness for peace, when he was suddenly brought into the valley of the shadow of death, and was exercised with strong fits of unbelief; then the Lord sent Isaiah with good and comforting words. (See Isa. xxxviii. 5–7.) These were the horns coming out of his hand, but the power was hid. He was recovered in his health, he was delivered from the king of Assyria, and his life was prolonged fifteen years. And how many of the Lord's believing family have been exercised with sharp trials, reversion of circumstances, dark and mysterious; they have been amazed at the wonder-working providence of God; the causes have been entirely secret to them, though the hand was visible; yet in that very hand there were some things which kept their faith alive, these were the horns on which they had hold; they were his promises, his past dealings; they were their Ebenezers, confirming their faith, strengthening their hope and helping them along the rest of their way.

3. *The hiding of God's power is concealed in the incarnation of his eternal Son.*

Here we approach a profound mystery; God was manifested in the flesh. The infancy of the Lord Jesus was marked with all the helplessness and weakness of other infants; he was nursed and carried, yet he was at the same moment the mighty God, though a babe in Bethlehem.

> " No less Almighty at his birth,
>   Than on his throne supreme;
>   His shoulders held up heaven and earth,
>   When Mary held up him."

And how marvellously was his omnipotence concealed during the days of his boyhood and his manhood, until the days of his showing unto Israel; but the days of his humanity are the horns coming out of his hand, his people take hold of them; their faith, hope, and love are strengthened and increased; his human experience becomes the hidden source of his divine sympathy and tenderness for all his suffering saints from his glorious high throne in heaven. What omnipotence was concealed in all his public life; yet occasionally there were glimpses, as in his wilderness state, fasting forty days, *then* hungering, contrary to ordinary cases of the kind, for loss of appetite and exhaustion commonly supervenes long fasting. 'Tis true we know not how long a sinless mortal could have gone without food, but this we know from the Saviour's own lips, "Man shall not live by bread alone, but by every word that proceedeth from the mouth of God." Here is the unseen power of Jehovah exerted in the visible life of our Lord's humanity; you see it in his miracles, three shall suffice. Hushing the storm with the word of peace. Believer in Jesus, cannot you set your seal to this. One word from Jesus has hushed the storm in the soul, his word has been the born, his hand you see, his power you feel; it is hid, but you have been strengthened and comforted. The demoniac on the cliff of the sea affords us an interesting proof. Jesus saw him afar off while sailing on the billowy deep, and he spoke to the demon, who evidently heard his voice and knew his Person. The disciples heard not the voice though they were with him in the ship, but the unclean spirit did; and hence, believer, take comfort from this, he hides his great power but displays his loving heart. Take hold of that fact. Possibly you may have some great fears distressing you, and though Jesus speaks not to you personally, he may secretly remove the cause by a power you little think.

Then there is the palsied man, who was borne of four and let down through the awning into the court yard where the assembly had met to hear Jesus preach. At first it seemed an untimely and unwise interruption, but Jesus knew it was an urgent pressing case, and he divinely spoke to the distressed heart while he declared with his human voice that his sins were all forgiven him. The burden of his sins and his exercises of his soul as to his sonship had brought on extreme palsy; but when Jesus gave him an assurance of his sonship and an assurance of forgiveness, it gave him peace of soul, and restored his nervous system. Here was much of his power displayed, but much more concealed. What was seen gave umbrage to the scribes; but, said Jesus, "that *ye may know* that the Son of Man *hath power* on earth to forgive sins, he saith to the sick of the palsy, arise, take up thy bed, and go to thine house." (Matt. ix. 2, 6.)

So through all the mediatorial life on earth. The Son of God displayed his eternal power through his manhood:

" He was made of the seed of David according to the flesh ;
and declared to be the Son of God with power, according to the Spirit of holiness, by the resurrection from the
dead." (Rom. i. 3, 4.) His obedience to the law of God
was a personal obedience rendered in human nature untainted by sin, according to the Spirit of holiness which
he possessed as the Son of God and his manhood being
underived from sinful flesh; thus it was his obedience
was perfect, for it was the righteousness of God; much
was displayed but more was concealed. Great is the mystery of godliness, God was manifest in the flesh. That
which was displayed is the horn which his people take
hold of, they trust his righteousness founded on his obedience for their complete justification; his obedience, to
keep to the figure of our text, having its roots in the
concealed divinity of his Person; here is the hiding of his
power, he is God as well as man.

In his agony in the Garden of Gethsemane there was
everything that indicated his true manhood, sorrow of
soul, bodily suffering. O what a concealment of his
omnipotence was here! bowed down with weakness, prostrate with suffering :

" Bore all incarnate God could bear,
With strength enough, and none to spare."

Yet these sufferings, his very weakness, are the horns of
his Almighty hand of love; they were substitutionary
sufferings, yet real personal sufferings; these are as horns
for the believer's faith, something for the believer to lay
hold of; here is salvation for the lost, strength for the
weak, and hope for the wretched. This blessed truth is
also seen in his sufferings and weakness when on the cross.
What a concealment of omnipotence was there when by
rude and violent hands he was laid prostrate on the cross
and fastened thereto with iron nails torn through his
flesh, and then suspended with the whole weight of his
frame upon his wounded hands. He suffered from the
exhaustion it caused, and yet he was perfectly conscious
of his divine Personality, and exercised his power in the
salvation of the thief. Here was something of it displayed, but how much more was hidden; this that was
seen has become the horn of salvation to many thousands
saved in the eleventh hour. We see his power concealed
while lying in the grave; his human nature did die, it was
the Son of God that was crucified, it was the Son of God

that was buried; for he rose again by his own power. "Thou wentest forth for the salvation of thy people, even for salvation for thine anointed; thou woundest the head out of the house of the wicked, by discovering the foundation unto the neck." (Hab. iii. 13.) His life, from the period of his resurrection to his ascension, was a concealment of his Godhead, hidden from the world entirely, but was particularly declared to his church. In his ascension he led captivity captive, he received gifts for men, and thus by the mysterious union of his two natures we have the horn of our salvation; it is in the hand of a Mediator, we take hold of it, and feel security and comfort; for unto us who believe he is the power of God unto salvation. The incarnation of Jehovah is a display of goodness, mercy, and power; but much more is concealed than is revealed.

4. *The hiding of Jehovah's power is concealed in the various operations of his grace in the heart of every believer.*

(1.) Let us begin where God begins—*In the regeneration of the soul.* Here is the unseen power of the divine hand in giving spiritual life to the soul dead in trespasses and in sins, he only who has life in himself can impart it. Where it is imparted its power is soon manifested. The life of God in the soul can no more be hidden than can the light of the sun when once it appears above the horizon. The divine calling from a state of sin is an act of divine sovereignty; it is a power exerted upon every faculty of the soul, renewing the person of the believer in the spirit of his mind, manifesting a power truly almighty in its nature, but concealing much more than it reveals. The beginnings of divine grace appear at first very tender and feeble, but the hiding of his power is found in the fact that nothing can quench the living spark; its power is felt, seen, and known both in the believer and by the observer; it becomes, as it were, the horn of hopefulness, it produces a change in the heart, life, and character; there is something so remarkable in the turning of a sinner from the error of his ways and bringing him under the power of divine truth, that causes one to own the hand of God, and from what we have seen to expect still more. It is the horn growing out of his hand, an almighty fact, something to take hold of, though conscious that there is still more concealed.

(2.) *As to the revelation of truth.* Wherever there is a true and a saving knowledge of Jesus Christ, there is an evidence of the teachings of God's Spirit, it is a divine revelation, a revelation of God the Father. This is a horn coming out of his hand; it is a display of his love to the sinner, a display of his heart as well as of his hand; this the believer takes hold of; he has the spirit of wisdom and revelation in the knowledge of him; every truth by which the eyes of his understanding are enlightened, is a further display of God the Father's goodness and power, but still concealing much more than it reveals. The more we advance in divine knowledge the more we perceive its incomprehensibleness; our apprehension of divine truth is a power by which we lay hold on God, a taking of the horns coming out of his hands, and conscious that there is the hiding of his power; by this it is we " know what is the hope of our calling, and what are the riches of the glory of his inheritance in the saints, and what is the exceeding greatness of his power to us-ward who believe, according to the working of his mighty power." This knowledge, if I may so say, is incorporated with our experience. Divine teaching follows divine calling. It is the light of life. The gospel is the power of God unto salvation to every one that believeth. Faith lays hold of the hope set before it; it brings the soul into contact with the divine hand, and partakes of every blessing which a good and gracious God can give.

(3.) *In the soul's conflict with sin.* The mystery of grace is more perceived in the opposition which the believer feels from the workings of in-bred sin than in anything else. What an unequal conflict! The old man of sin against the new man of grace, the matured root of sin opposing the tender buddings of grace; yet grace reigns through righteousness. What is the power by which it maintains the contest? It is divine power. How is it supplied? That is concealed. What is it that the soul takes hold of? The promise, " sin shall not have dominion over you; ye are not under the law but under grace." The conflict is the fight of faith, faith against unbelief, hope against doubt, love against enmity; it is the works of the flesh against the fruits of the Spirit; it is the carnal mind against God; it is Satan against Christ. Still the victory is certain. This assurance of hope unto the end is the horn which the believer takes hold of; the power by which he fights and maintains his standing is from the hand of God; there is the hiding of his power; from thence he derives all his strength; he looks to the Lord with steadfast eye; he fights with hell by faith, and through the blood of the Lamb is at length more than victorious.

(4.) *In the life of grace sustained.* This is no less true than *in the commencement* of the divine life. The hiding of Jehovah's power is manifest by the continual supply of spiritual life to the renewed soul; much is manifested, but more is concealed. The horn which the believer takes hold of is, " I give unto my sheep eternal life, and they shall never perish." This is Christ's own word; it is faith's warrant; it is the believer's experience; every day his strength is as his day; often he feels like as Bunyan has represented, a fire upon which water is continually poured to quench it, but still it burns higher and hotter; we go to the back of the screen, and there the secret is explained, there is one continually feeding the fire with oil; " it shall," says Jehovah, (Lev. vi. 13,) " never go out;" the influences of the world, the carnality of the human heart, the enmity of the devil, are all in league against the life of God in the soul, but it is maintained and shall be maintained: " Being confident of this very thing, he that hath begun the good work will perform it unto the day of Jesus Christ." " The righteous shall hold on his way." " The path of the just is as the shining light, that shineth more and more unto the perfect day." " Who are kept by the power of God through faith unto salvation." " Your life is hid with Christ in God," guarded and preserved by the power and providence of God as in an impregnable garrison, no violence or stratagem of the enemy shall ever surprise or overcome those who are in Jehovah's hand; none shall pluck them out of his hand. This assurance is the horn of his power; it is the believer's security; it is the horn of his salvation; much is displayed for his present comfort, but more is concealed for his everlasting security and consolation. The work of salvation is a divine work; the work of God's hand; the production of his power; it was begun in grace, it is carried on with power, and will be completed in glory. The final perseverance of the saints is by the unseen power of God the Holy Ghost. They take hold of his word, and are strong in the consolations of his

grace. The psalmist says, " The Lord will perfect that
which concerneth me," being confident that it is nothing
but Almighty power that can carry on the work of grace
in the soul. " He will rest in his love." The supply
of the Spirit of Christ feeds, nourishes, and cheers the
soul continually, restores him when fainting, strengthens
him in his weakness, and lightens up his path when walking in darkness.

> " His grace shall to the end
> Stronger and brighter shine,
> Nor present things, nor things to come,
> Shall quench the spark divine."

(5.) *In the spirit of prayer.* What a secret power there
is in prayer. It is the taking hold of God's strength—
the horns of his hand, the promises of his grace. " He
giveth power to the faint, and to them that have no
might he increaseth strength. They that wait upon the
Lord shall renew their strength; they shall mount up
with wings as eagles; they shall run and not be weary;
they shall walk and not faint." " Likewise the Spirit also
helpeth our infirmities; for we know not what we should
pray for as we ought; but the Spirit itself maketh intercession for us with groanings which cannot be uttered.
And he that searcheth the heart knoweth what is the
mind of the Spirit, because he maketh intercession for
the saints according to the will of God." Oh what blessed
horns are these for the believer to take hold of; he takes
hold of God. " Will he plead against me," says Job,
" with his great power? No; but he would put strength
in me." " In the day when I cried thou answeredst me,
and strengthened me with strength in my soul." How
secret is the supply of the believer's strength in prayer,
yet how sure; the rock of his strength is in God; there
is the hiding of his power, like the strength of a rock,
more is concealed than displayed. The invitations and
promises of the gospels are as horns coming out of his
hand; there is more blessedness concealed than the soul
has ever experienced. Believer, take hold of these horns,
they are expressly for your faith, your hope, your comfort,
your strength, and your encouragement.

(6.) *In backsliders restored to his favour.* I must just
say a word to the wanderer from the fold of Jesus. Poor
soul, where are you now? Where has your light and
comfort fled? You come to the house of God, you listen

F

to the voice of praise, but your voice is silent; you listen
to the voice of supplication, but a sigh is all that escapes
you; you hear the preacher, but his word fails to touch
any of those chords which once produced the music of
your soul. Your harp is unstrung, hanging on the wil-
lows, and you cannot sing the Lord's song in a strange
land. Now listen once more to God's word: " O Israel,
return unto the Lord thy God; for thou hast fallen by
thine iniquity. Take with you words, and turn unto the
Lord; say unto him, Take away all iniquity, and receive
us graciously." And hear, too, what the gracious words
of the Lord are: " I will heal their backsliding, I will love
them freely; for mine anger is turned away from him."
Now what are these words but the horns coming out of
his hand? they are for you to take hold of; the hiding of
his power you will find in the restoration of your peace
and joy; it is at present concealed from you, but he reveals his love and grace. O may the Lord bring you to
his feet with weeping and with supplications, and cause
you to find rest in coming to his mercy-seat. " Who is
wise, and he shall understand these things? prudent, and
he shall know them? for the ways of the Lord are right,
and the just shall walk in them; but the transgressors
shall fall therein." (Hos. xiv. 9.)

   5. There is also another point which may be illustrated
by the words of our text—" He had horns coming out of
his hand, and there was the hiding of his power." This
will be seen *in the preservation of the saints' bodies whilst
in the grave.* The doctrine of the resurrection is plainly
revealed in the word of God. The resurrection of Christ
is an indubitable truth; it is the pledge of ours; what a
longing there is in the renewed soul for it. Why is this?
is it for the sake of immortality? is it for the sake of incorruption? Not simply for these things, for these are but
means to an end. We have no desire for immortality
unless we have strong hopes that our life, divested of its
corruption and all its sins, shall rise into the likeness of
the image and into the enjoyment of our ever-adorable
Redeemer God. The resurrection of Christ is the pledge of
a truth which has an influence in us desiring to realise it.
The Saviour we love is the risen Saviour; the Saviour we
have fellowship with is the living Jesus, he is our ever-
living friend; in this present life we are planted spiritually in the likeness of his resurrection; in the influences

of his resurrection we are desirous " if by any means we may attain unto the resurrection of the dead." (Phil. iii. 11.) Now there are two things which set the longing soul to realise this great truth ; the first is, a complete and final separation from the world ; the other is, to be for ever with the Lord : " With him is the fountain of life, in his presence is fulness of joy; at his right hand there are pleasures for evermore." In the first he is striving now to attain unto this resurrection of our Lord ; when he rose from the dead, it is to be observed, he never more mixed with the world ; the unregenerate never more saw his face or heard his voice; his resurrection glories were confined exclusively to his church. This is what believers would like to attain unto if it were possible, a complete and total separation from the spirit and tendencies of this world in this time state, for now it is we are the sons of God ; there is displayed to them in the hand of God, his truth and power, such glories of the resurrection life as fills the soul of the believer with holy longings to depart and to be with Christ, which is far better ; these glories which they view by faith are as horns coming out of his hand, and there is the hiding of his power, truths for them to take hold of. As the identity of the risen Saviour's Person was fully proved to the disciples, so we believe that the bodies of the saints will be preserved to and restored at the day of the resurrection in all the identity and personal consciousness of each individual. Our present hope is that we shall be like him, and see him as he is, and shall be satisfied when we awake in his likeness. O what a hiding of his power is here, the truth we take hold of, as he rose so will all his followers ; he is our forerunner, and where he has entered we shall enter too. He will preserve every atom of our sleeping dust during our incarceration in the tomb; those who sleep in Jesus will God bring with him. Marvellous power, inconceivably great and glorious, it is hidden until the morn of the resurrection ; he reveals the truth that it shall be so, and by faith we take hold of it as the horn coming out of his hand; for Jesus has willed that all his saints shall be where he is, to behold his glory. (John xvii. 24.) Here is our hope, our horn, something for us to take hold of, which hope we have as an anchor of the soul, sure and stedfast, which entereth into that within the veil. Happy souls, who with a well grounded hope can say—

" My flesh shall slumber in the ground,
'Till the last trumpet's joyful sound ;
Then burst the chains with sweet surprise,
And in my Saviour's image rise."

6. But before I conclude I must advert to one more illustration of our text; it contains a gospel truth which has not been sufficiently and distinctly set forth in the preceding particulars—*the Atonement of our Lord Jesus Christ is the believer's horn of salvation, in which there is the hiding of Almighty power.*

The hand of redemption which is displayed in the Scriptures of truth, is the hand of God ; the horns coming out of it are the blessings of the atonement by the sacrifice of his only begotten Son, the taking hold of which is the salvation of all who come unto God by him. This is the seeking sinner's great mercy : he has been wounded, but it was in the house of his friends ; his conscience bears him witness of aggravated sins, of an accumulated load of guilt too heavy for him to bear ; he goes about seeking deliverance but finds none. The arrow of truth which has pierced his soul " was quick and powerful, and sharper than any two-edged sword, piercing even to the dividing asunder of soul and spirit, and of the joints and marrow, and is a discerner of the thoughts and intents of the heart," and only he who gave the wound can heal it and make the spirit whole. This is the work of God's Spirit in the heart ; the entrance of his words giveth life. Here is repentance towards God ; faith in Jesus Christ leading the believer to find that there is forgiveness with him that he may feared. He finds in Christ the only way of salvation, his atoning blood is the price of his redemption from the curse of a broken law; it is the propitiation for his sins ; he has no hope in himself, merits he has none ; he looks for all in Christ, he is the sinner's only hope ; his blood and righteousness stand out as horns in the hand of Jehovah, whose covenant of redemption is everlasting, ordered in all things and sure. The believing sinner, whose conscience has followed him close, as the avenger of blood pursued the manslayer, lays hold of these horns; here is his certain salvation ; justice cannot strike him here, mercy holds him fast, he is made nigh by the blood of Christ, he is saved in the Lord with an everlasting salvation. But O what a glorious and divine power is concealed in the horns of the sinner's salvation !

Redemption is the work of Almighty power " which in other ages was not made known unto the sons of men as it is now revealed unto his holy apostles and prophets by the Spirit ;" " so that in the ages to come he might show the exceeding riches of his grace in his kindness towards us through Christ Jesus." Here is still more concealed than is revealed. He saves to the uttermost all who come unto God by him ; and him that cometh he will in no wise cast out. The strength of Israel will not lie. Here is power to save from a host of sins, from the worst of sins. O if there is here a trembling sinner seeking mercy, here is room, here is hope ; take hold of these horns, " trust ye in the Lord Jehovah, for in the Lord Jehovah is everlasting strength."

And this is the believer's mercy,—that through all his journey in the wilderness state, the blood of the atonement is available for his hope and comfort. Not only is the truth that "Christ died for him" a horn of salvation to him, and on which he holds for eternal life, but it is a source of everlasting consolation to him ; though saved from the curse of sin, and saved from the power of inbred sin, he still sins and will be liable to sin as long as he is in the flesh ; this is his grief and sore wounding, but the precious blood of atonement is the healing balm of all his sorrows and the cordial of his cares ; he seeks no healing but in and through atoning blood. Oh what a hiding of Jehovah's power is here ; again and again, through all life, to its latest moment, the blood of Jesus Christ is all-sufficient to cleanse from all sin ; it is infinite in value, infinite in strength, infinite in its efficacy. Atoning blood is the glory of the gospel. It is the mercy of God to fallen man, the horn of salvation in his hand of redeeming love, and there is the hiding of his power.

Now may the Lord command his blessing on such remarks as may be in harmony with his own word of truth for his great name's sake. Amen.

THE DIVINE ENGRAVING OF SEVEN EYES ON ONE STONE.

◆

A SERMON,

BY CHARLES GORDELIER,

PREACHED AT HEPHZIBAH CHAPEL, DARLING PLACE, MILE END GATE,

On Lord's Day Evening, March 11th, 1866.

"For behold the stone that I have laid before Joshua; upon one stone shall be seven eyes; behold, I will engrave the graving thereof, saith the Lord of hosts."—ZECH. III. 9.

IT may be said of Zechariah's prophecies, as Peter said of Paul's epistles, "in which are some things hard to be understood." This seems to have been felt by our laborious and painstaking Puritan commentators, for scarcely any, as I am aware, have left us any distinct or elaborate exposition of this choice and remarkable book. Perhaps the reason may be that within the transparent outer covering of prophecy and vision is perceived deep spiritual truth which is difficult to unfold. That there are evidently many precious truths displayed to us in these prophecies there can be no question, but they are like choice fruit on the topmost branches of trees, which way-side travellers can see as they pass, but being out of their reach they can do no more than look at it.

This prophecy is designated SEPHER ZECHARIAH, or the book of Zechariah, from its being written by him. His name signifies *the memory of the Lord*, or *the Lord remembers*. His prophecies singularly accord with his name, for there is indeed a wonderful remembrance of God's covenant love and promises of the Messiah's coming and of salvation by him. While there are many dark and obscure prophecies, yet we find a cluster of prophets almost contemporary in their prophetic work, confirming the authority of each other's prophecy, and thereby

No. 23.

the more effectually to comfort and encourage the Jews against the present opposition and future difficulties in re-building their temple. For on their return from captivity to their own land, they had to encounter the jealousies and annoyances of the strangers who had become settlers and occupants of Jerusalem; consequently the wall of the city and the temple were built in troublous times. Of the hindrances in their work we have an interesting record in the books of Ezra and Nehemiah, as also of the debased state and condition the people had fallen into in conse-quence of being "many days without a king, and without a prince, and without a sacrifice, and without an ephod." Zechariah was cotemporary with Haggai the prophet, Joshua the high priest, and Zerubabel the leader. The two prophets were evidently sent forth to stir up the people to repentance and to build the temple; it seems they were both required for the same work, so that the one might help the other in his arduous work. God ever watches over his people's needs and adapts his aid as they require it. There is this difference in the prophecies of these two men. Haggai speaks more briefly and plainly, and Zechariah more largely and mysteriously, and in a way of vision, yet with many precious promises of the Messiah's coming. Herein is set forth the Lord Jesus Christ in his glory and kingdom, in his death, offices, and priesthood; the price for which he should be betrayed, the effusion of his Spirit, the calling of the Gentiles, the many spiritual privileges of God's people, and the final and effectual expulsion of all sin and iniquity, showing with what confidence we may expect the certainty of the promised purity, victory, and happiness of the church of Christ in the latter day.

In the chapter from whence our text is taken, we have a fourth vision which the prophet had; it is concerning Joshua the high priest, the object being to encourage the priests in respect of their office and their work in the ser-vice of the temple, the building of which being then in progress but obstructed by their enemies. The vision represents Joshua the high priest in the execution of his vocation in the tabernacle service. He is accused by Satan on the ground that he is ceremonially unclean; but Satan is rebuked by Jehovah in the Person of God the Father, and Joshua is vindicated, "Though he be not cleansed according to the purification of the sanctuary."

Then we perceive there is a restoration of the priestly purity and a renewal of the covenant as to the office of the priesthood itself. Here is, then, Satan not only non-suited but rebuked, for it was not his place to bring an accusation into that court. Joshua has his priesthood confirmed to him both in its dignity and perpetuity by a divine and heavenly commission.

Besides this, we perceive in the 8th verse, something like precious balm for the healing and comforting Joshua's wounded spirit. What a sweet promise is made to him of the Lord Jesus Christ: "Thou and thy companions in the priesthood are men wondered at for their zeal and steadfastness in my service. The men of this world cannot understand how it is or why it is that they engage and persist in a work apparently so unprofitable, so unwise, so contemptible, but I will reveal my covenant designs towards my chosen. I will bring forth my servant THE BRANCH. My Mediator, of which thou art a type, he shall take a nature having its roots in the earth of humanity, and he shall be the Mediatorial Priest, Prophet, the BRANCH, the stem that shall come out of Jesse's roots, whose superiority and peculiarity shall be that Satan hath nothing in him, he shall not find in him any cause for resisting him in his mediatorial work." Now, Joshua and thy fellows, behold him, look to him; he is the substance of all the ceremonial law and dispensation. Thou art but an imperfect representative of the people, but "his work shall be honourable and glorious." And have I not spoken by my servant the prophet Haggai, "I will fill this house with glory? The glory of this latter house shall be greater than of the former, saith the Lord of hosts; and in this place will I give peace, saith the Lord of hosts." (Haggai ii. 7, 9.)

Now come the words of our text: "For behold the stone that I have laid before Joshua; upon one stone shall be seven eyes; behold, I will engrave the graving thereof, saith the Lord of hosts." These are certainly very remarkable words, and I am fully aware of the various interpretations given by commentators and preachers generally. But I confess none of them has ever satisfied me, and I feel I must eschew the fanciful, and indeed the whimsical notions, which have been uttered by good-meaning men; though there is one thing in which I agree with them all, and that is, Christ is evidently set forth in the passage before us. The points of difference in my view and those generally held are as to *the kind* of stone, and *the use* made of it. I have no desire to set up my judgment in opposition to men of learning, especially of those whose writings are well received by the church of God; but if it be so, that the light which I have upon this portion of God's word harmonises more with the general features of the vision, and displays more of the character and work of the Lord Jesus Christ than is generally given of it, why should I shrink from showing my opinion? Favour me then, dear friends, with your attention, and I trust that, with the Lord's help and blessing, we shall be able to see something of the meaning of these precious words proposed for our consideration.

FIRST. As to the Stone itself: "Behold the stone that I have laid before Joshua." I do not regard the stone here spoken of as referring to *a foundation* stone. That the Scriptures set forth Christ as a foundation stone is an indubitable and a most glorious truth; but I think that is not the mind of the Spirit in this instance. Indeed the foundation stone of the temple was already laid, as stated in the 9th verse of the 4th chapter, and this 3rd chapter has reference to the priesthood, and not to the building of the temple at all. Bear in mind, Joshua is in the exercise of his priestly office, before the Lord, that is, within the veil, in the holy of holies; not in a council for building the temple, and therefore let us not be misled by departing from the unity of the subject as revealed, though every item be not fully declared. And we must also bear in mind, that Joshua the high priest, and his fellows, the priesthood, were lamentably deficient and imperfect in several important things pertaining to the service of the sanctuary, and it was, doubtless, the absence of these things being keenly felt, occasioned the grief and weeping when the foundation was laid. (Ezra iii. 12.) We are told these five things were wanting in the second temple, namely, 1. *The ark*, with the mercy-seat and cherubims. 2. The *holy fire* from heaven for consuming the sacrifice. 3. The *Shekinah*, or the divine presence, indicated by the cloud over the mercy-seat. 4. The *Holy Ghost*, or spirit of prophecy. 5. The *Urim and Thummim*. Then we perceive the habiliments of the high priest were such as furnished Satan with a pretext for resisting Joshua in the exercise of his sacred functions, for he will catch at any-

thing, be it ever so trifling. Ah, he is a staunch Pusey-
ite, exceedingly tenacious where religious vestments and
ceremonies are concerned. These garments, in which
Joshua officiated, are said to be filthy, that is, unconse-
crated with the peculiar holy anointing oil. (Ex. xxx. 30.)
Probably he was without the purple robe, as he was without the proper mitre. A golden censer he might have
had, and he had, no doubt, with all fidelity, the blood of
the offerings with him to present before the Lord. But
there was one article of dress he was without, most essential, and that was the Ephod containing the Urim and
Thummim, the breastplate of twelve precious stones, on
which were engraved the names of the twelve tribes, and
when worn before the Lord represented the people. This
breastplate, at the time of the destruction of the temple
and the dispersion of the people, was lost, and the stones
destroyed or scattered, a true emblem of their national
condition. The absence of the Ephod with the Urim and
Thummim, must indeed have been felt a sore grief to the
devout Jew; it was the holy oracle by which Jehovah
revealed his mind and will on all important occasions
whenever it was sought. In what peculiar manner Jehovah
answered by Urim and Thummim it is impossible to say.
Scripture is silent as to how it was done, and therefore it
is useless to discuss the question. This we believe, God
spake by his holy oracle from off the mercy-seat. There
was a divine authority in it, and there was safety in obey-
ing its voice. Now, the loss of these precious stones,
both as a breastplate representing the people and as a
divine oracle, must have been felt to be an incalculable grief
and an irreparable loss; it's very name signifying light
and perfection. See Ezra ii. 63.

We must take it for granted that, from the nature of
the encouraging words and the wonderful displays which
God made to Joshua, he had come before the Lord in
a dejected state of mind, and that the nature of his
prayer and intercession is to be inferred from the communication made to him by Jehovah. We have no record,
it is true, of such a process, but this is immaterial, we
have the results. This is quite in harmony with a large
part of the word of God, the process of a thing is often
omitted, and only the result is given. Joshua's person
and office are accepted, as is seen by the change of raiment bestowed, and the renewal of the covenant. Then

there is the promise of the Messiah. This is in lieu of the mercy-seat; the shadow has been lost, but in place thereof shall be the living BRANCH. Then as to the breastplate being lost, it cannot now represent the twelve tribes on the great day of atonement, or for the special purposes of the Urim and Thummim; but see how God wondrously displays his grace, and calls him to notice *a stone* which is laid before him in place of those which are lost. Though the high priest can no longer bear upon his breast the names of the twelve tribes before the Ark of the covenant, yet now there is something far superior, a glory that excelleth. This ONE STONE shall far exceed the twelve, both in lustre and in dignity, and also in the divine uses to which it shall be put.

There is, therefore, now before Joshua this ONE STONE for his beholding ; he is to look upon it. It is not to be worn, but is laid before him. This stone is to be understood as being laid upon the golden table in the holy of holies, supplying the place of the Ark, the Mercy-Seat, and in lieu of the Breastplate. This ONE STONE is to set forth the Person of the Lord Jesus Christ in his mediatorial character and work. He is ever in the holy of holies. He, in himself, represents his people. Whether the high priest enters in once a year, or oftener if needs be, God's people are ever represented in the Person of Christ. He is their Oracle also ; they are represented in him, in that place. When the high priest enters the holy place, he sees this Stone; there it is laid before him for his beholding. It indicates the constant union and representation of the church of God existing in the Person of Christ. Not as before, which was but partial, occasional, and official, but a superior standing altogether. Before, their representation before the Lord was by virtue of the high priest coming there in his official costume and capacity; but now this STONE has a position assigned for it by Jehovah himself: "The law made nothing perfect, but the bringing in of a better hope did." O what deep spiritual truth is figured forth in this symbolical stone! The glorious Person of the Mediator, the God-man Christ Jesus; the Urim and Thummin of ancient Israel are now found in Christ.

But now let us notice *the kind* of stone that is to be understood, which Jehovah has laid before Joshua. It cannot mean an immense block of marble, granite, or of any other stone, cut from a quarry and designed for a building. This notion is totally incongruous with the general sense of the text and its connection. It means, as I consider, what we commonly call a jewel,—a small, sparkling stone, having light and beauty in itself without cutting or polishing. As the breastplate consisted of twelve jewels, so this STONE is a jewel, a precious jewel, a splendid jewel, a divine and glorious jewel; and it is designed to set forth the Person of our most glorious Christ, who, in his Person as their Mediator, is also their representative, and the way of access to God the Father, and he *ever abides* in the holy of holies.

That this view of the Stone laid before Joshua is more in harmony with the doctrine of Christ's Person and character than a block of stone cut out of a quarry, I would just observe one or two points: First, jewels are found by themselves as an entire whole, not in pieces broken from a mass, but perfect, without flaw; not chipped or cracked, for if so, they would be comparatively worthless. Large sizes are very rare, and are exceedingly valuable. So the Lord Jesus Christ, in his human nature and his mediatorial character, is a jewel, a gem, a precious stone, found entire, perfect in himself, sinless, without a stain. No one could convince him of sin.

> " His life was pure, without a stain,
> And all his nature clean."

Again. Jewels, or precious stones, are found in caves, mines, pits, tops of mountains, often encrusted with subsoil, as clay, gravel, and the like, but without detriment to their intrinsic value. To the common observer they have no appearance as gems, but the practised eye discovers them by the spark, the living light which they possess, notwithstanding the incrustation. So it may be said of Jesus, who, though he was found in the fashion of a man, in the form of a servant, in the likeness of sinful flesh, mean and abject as to his position in this world, yet without sin in himself. In his Person he is eternally divine, being God's only-begotten Son in whom he is well pleased; while to his church he is ever precious, their most precious stone; and they come to him as their choice precious gem or living stone. Every view they have of him creates intense delight. He is called a living stone because he has life and light in himself: " In him was life, and the life was the light of men." (John i. 4.) The peculiarity of precious stones, as diamonds, sapphires, rubies, &c., is this,—they possess sparkling light in themselves, not by reflection. A diamond, for instance, is a stone with light in itself, hence its name, " a heap of daylight;" hence also the celebrated Indian stone, Koh-i-nor, from its large size, is named " Mountain of light." Now Jesus, as his people's Head and Mediator, is their mountain of light; he is their daylight; he is their Koh-i-nor: " The Lord is my light and my salvation;" (Ps. xxvii. 1;) " The Lord shall be to thee an everlasting light;" (Isa. lx. 19;) " God is light, and in him is no darkness at all." (1 John i. v.) From Jesus, God's elect precious stone, his people derive all their light. Hence, when called by divine grace from the horrible pit of their unregeneracy, the pit of nature, the miry clay of sin that sticks fast to them, they are made " light in the Lord;" being united to him by faith, they also become "lively stones." God calls them his jewels; and though like the Jewish priests' breastplate of old, they are scattered and lost in the captivity and ruin by Satan, yet God knows where they are; he knows their number, not one shall be lost, for in his own good time he will make up his jewels and manifest them to be his. Jesus, however, is called emphatically *the stone*, both for its beauty and its size. With the Jews sapphires were in great esteem; with us they rank next the diamond. It is probable that the stone which Jehovah laid before Joshua was a sapphire of unequalled size and lustre. Brilliancy, colour, and glory in respect of the celestial state are likened to sapphire stone. The oriental sapphire is of a sky-blue colour, or a fine azure; whence it is the prophets describe the throne of God, as it were of the colour of a sapphire; that is, a celestial blue or azure. (Ex. xxiv. 10; Ezek. i. 26; x. i.) Now Jesus is a sapphire stone of divine rarity; none like him for beauty, none like him for light; none like him in value. He is a non-such, " yea, he is altogether lovely." He is altogether unique, unequalled, having none to be compared with him; he is beyond comparison. For in his Person as Mediator he is holy, harmless, separate from sinners. How heavenly in his origin, his dwelling, his dominion; how immaculate, how beautiful is he in respect of his human nature; and how wonderfully glorious is he in his complex Person as the God-man. The highest estimation we can have of the choicest stones admired amongst men fail to set forth the glories and perfections of Immanuel.

So far, then, our idea of Christ as a precious stone, a gem, a jewel, will not comport with the commonly received notion of a block of stone dislocated from a mass of rock in a quarry. Jesus is not a derived being, for though "born of a woman, made under the law, that he might redeem those who were under the law," yet that holy thing which was conceived in Mary was a distinct creation of the Holy Ghost. "A body hast thou prepared me." And observe, our Lord does not speak of himself as the foundation of his church, as a disintegrated portion of stone, but *a rock*, an integral part of the immovable earth itself, and mineralogically speaking, "a living stone." (Matt. xvi. 18.) Even the gospel is spoken of as "a stone cut out of the mountains without hands." (Dan. ii. 34.)

SECOND. We will proceed a little further. Our text says, "Upon one stone shall be seven eyes." Here again, we find in this fact a most glorious substitute for the lost twelve stones on which were engraved the twelve names of the twelve tribes of Israel, the Urim and Thummim, which names signified "*light and perfection.*" The most sensible opinion given on this subject is that these stones were called *Urim*, because they were *clear, lucid, and transparent;* and *Thummim,* because they were *perfect and complete*, having no blemish or defect in them. Now on this precious stone laid before Joshua, there was engraved, not the twelve names of the twelve tribes, but seven eyes; an engraved gem in which we have in a far superior and exalted manner all these ideas embodied more than in the original breastplate—the Urim and Thummim. The stone is light and beauty in itself, the eyes give a human life-giving light, such as a human eye only can give; the number seven denotes perfection, the perfection of light and whatever is represented by it. Here, then, we have light and perfection restored to the church of God in THE ONE STONE laid before Joshua. Here is, then, found in the Person of the Lord Jesus Christ, both the representative of his people and their living oracle. In the divinely engraved eyes we see what could not be seen in the Urim and Thummim—*Expression*. In the eye we see the expression of the soul; it is the window of the soul through which it looks. The hands have language; the lips have language; but oh the language of the human eye, the beaming eye of intelligence, of love, compassion, watchfulness, of power! How divinely superhuman are all those seven eyes intended to set forth him who is in himself light and perfection—the Urim and the Thummim of the church of God; the language of which is their oracle of life: "I will instruct thee and teach thee in the way which thou shalt go. I will guide thee with mine eye." (Ps. xxxii. 8.)

Sometimes we hear of this our text as if it read "upon one stone there shall be seven eyes," or seven persons, *looking at it*. And some good men have racked their inventive powers to find seven sorts of representative men, as Adam, Noah, Abraham, Moses, &c., or the eyes of God the Father, God the Holy Ghost, the eyes of angels, devils, &c., but these strange fancies must be passed by; they are void of idea, and contrary to the literal reading of the text. What we have before us is a vision, intending to convey much spiritual truth, having certain correspondencies as set forth in the stone itself, the eyes, the engraver, and the engraving.

By the seven eyes engraved on the one stone we may understand a seven-sided prism; *a sapphire stone with seven sides*, and in this stone we see the excellency and the glory of it, for no sapphires are found with more than *six* sides. On each side of this stone is engraved a human eye by Jehovah. Such a stone being transparent, and with seven eyes engraved would present to the view when looking through direct but one eye. Whichever side might be looked at, there would be but the one eye direct through, as if solid: "If thine eye be single, thy whole body shall be full of light," perfectly so. O, this is a wonderful stone, and a wonderful engraving, and what wonderful workmanship! The Person of Christ is truly wonderful. His name shall be called Wonderful. Do not suppose this is a visionary imagination as to the one solid appearance of the eye; we have photographs taken on this very principle in "crystal cubes" as they are called, in which the bust of the person appears solid.

The workmanship of this engraved stone is divine. The seven eyes engraved on this one stone are the work of God the Father. He is the heavenly engraver. It is a divine engraving on the most precious unique stone. Not sculptured, for that is not the word used, though our com-

mentators do, but it is most inappropriate. Engraving
and sculpture are two distinct arts for very different purposes. Chisels and mallets are used for the latter; but
small pin-like tools, called gravers, for the former. An
engraving is an embodiment of much idea in a little compass upon some fine substance, as a gem, or piece of metal.
A sculpture is invariably an enlarged view of the thing
represented, and generally on a material of sufficient size
and strength as to require heavy tools for working it. In
this divine engraving we see more than can be uttered.
The more this stone is studied the greater the wonder
becomes; turn it which side you will, you see fresh beauties; lights and perfection every way; a living, loving,
speaking, sympathetic eye. The eyes of the Lord, when we
are seeking to know his will, become our oracle. One look,
one word, makes darkness light before us, makes crooked
things straight, for in his light we see light. The eye of
love, the eye of sympathy, how beaming from the Saviour
to the poor cast-down soul.

> " One look from that dear Lord,
> Whose brow compassion wears,
> Will much of heavenly bliss afford,
> E'en in this vale of tears."

In the Person of Christ the Mediator is seen the work of
God the Father. It is his choicest piece of workmanship.
The stone in itself symbolises the divinity and eternity of
the Person of his only begotten son, full of grace and
truth. In *the engraving* the qualification of the Redeemer
is set forth as to his mediatorial character, he is of God
made unto the church " wisdom, righteousness, sanctification, and redemption;" and, in *the graving thereof,* is set
forth the sufferings he endured as the God-man from the
divine hand: " for it became him, for whom are all things,
and by whom are all things, in bringing many sons unto
glory, to make the captain of their salvation perfect
through sufferings." Here, in this stone setting forth the
eternal Son of God, is seen the divine workmanship of God
the Father. "He that hath seen the Son hath seen the
Father." The number seven while they set forth perfection, as the eyes set forth lights, may also set forth his attributes as the God-man Mediator, and are displayed in that
character to the view of the church of God by the engraving of God the Father on this one stone having seven
eyes. Here is, 1st, *He is Self-existent.* Here is his

divine Personality as the Son of God. "In him was life and the life was the light of men;" (John i. 4;) "Because I live ye shall live also;" (John xiv. 19;) "As the Father hath life in himself, so hath he given the Son to have life in himself." (John v. 26.) 2nd. *He is Light.* "I am the light of the world;" (John ix. 5;) "God is light;" (1 John i. 5;) "The Lamb is the light thereof," (of heaven.) (Rev. xxi. 23.) 3rd. *He is Power.* "All power is given unto me in heaven and in earth;" (Matt. xxviii. 18;) "Power belongeth unto God;" (Ps. lxii. 2;) "Christ the power of God." (1 Cor. i. 24.) 4th. *He is Love.* "God is love;" (1 John iv. 8;) "He is the God of love;" (2 Cor. xiii. 11;) "The love of Christ passeth knowledge;" (Eph. iii. 19.) 5th. *He is Goodness.* "Ye know the grace of our Lord Jesus Christ that, though he was rich, yet for our sakes he became poor, that ye, through his poverty might be made rich;" (2 Cor. viii. 9;) "The Lord God abundant in goodness and truth." (Ex. xxxiv. 6.) 6th. *He is Wisdom.* "He is of God, made unto us wisdom;" (1 Cor. i. 30;) "Jesus was filled with wisdom;" (Luke ii. 40;) "In whom are hid all the treasures of wisdom." (Col. ii. 3.) 7th. *He is Holiness.* "Who did no sin, neither was guile found in his mouth;" (1 Pet. ii. 22;) "Who is like unto thee, glorious in holiness;" (Ex. xv. ii;) "I am the Lord, the holy one of Israel, the Saviour;" (Isa. lx. 3;) "Be ye holy, for I am holy." (1 Pet. i. 16.)

In these seven attributes thus briefly sketched, you will perceive the first three belong essentially to his Godhead. The other four are displayed in his mediatorial work through his manhood. All these perfections, indeed, are conjoined in his complex Person as the God-man Christ Jesus, by which he is a most able and willing Saviour of all who come unto God the Father by him. Other perfections are also embodied in the Person of Christ, besides these now named, for it pleased the Father that in him should all fulness dwell; in him dwelleth all the fulness of Godhead bodily. He is of God made unto us wisdom, righteousness, sanctification, and redemption. Every need being supplied by God the Father from his riches in glory by Christ Jesus. Christ is the channel of every blessing to the church of God.

The human eye expresses the kind of spirit we are of, whether of love, compassion, watchfulness, delight, goodness, anger, or malice. So the expression, "the eyes of the Lord," are sometimes used to set forth the seven Spirits of God, as well also his plenitude of qualifications or perfections. In the 4th chap. of this prophecy, 10th verse, the seven eyes are explained to be "the eyes of the Lord which run to and fro the whole earth." Also, in 2 Chron. xvi. 9, "to show himself strong in behalf of those whose heart is perfect towards him." "The eyes of the Lord are in every place." (Prov. xv. 3.) "The eyes of the Lord are upon the righteous." (Ps. xxxiv. 15.) These passages set forth his providential care, supply, and government. In Rev. v. 6, we read: "In the midst of the throne stood a Lamb, having seven horns and seven eyes, which are the seven Spirits of God sent forth into all the earth." Here is the same Person, the Lord Jesus Christ, in one place described as a divinely engraved Stone with seven eyes, and in another place as a Lamb with seven eyes. In both similitudes, the Stone and the Lamb, the mediatorial work and character of Jesus Christ is designed to be set forth. The seven eyes of the Lamb of God, and the seven eyes upon the One Stone of Israel, represent the seven Spirits of God. And these seven Spirits of God are the same with the seven Spirits which are before the throne of God, spoken of in Rev. i. 4, iv. 5. Hence, therefore, Christ is, by this figure of seven eyes represented to us as possessing all the fulness of the Spirit. The fulness of the Godhead dwells bodily in him, and, therefore, to show the church of God this great treasury that there is in Christ, God the Father hath used similitudes which, under the teachings of his Spirit, convey to our understandings deep spiritual truths. In one place as the Son of man, in another place as a Stone, and in another as a Lamb. Thus Jesus is represented as having in himself the fulness of all divine perfections, as possessing the Spirit without measure. In Isa. xi. 1, 3, the sevenfold gifts are prominently pointed out by the prophet speaking of Christ's anointing with the Spirit, and his consequent authority as the Mediator. I will read the passage as it stands: "And there shall come forth a rod out of the stem of Jesse, and a branch shall grow out of his roots. And the spirit of the Lord shall rest upon him, the spirit of wisdom and understanding, the spirit of counsel and might, the spirit of knowledge and of the fear of the Lord; and shall make him of quick understanding in the fear of the Lord; and he shall not judge after the sight of his eyes, neither reprove after the hearing of his ears."

THIRD. We will now pass on to notice *the graving* of these seven eyes. "*Behold, I will engrave the graving thereof.*" Now, as these words are prefixed with a call to our admiration, we must not pass them by lightly, for when God calls us to behold, and this word in our text, you must observe, is repeated, we ought, therefore, to give the more earnest heed lest at any time we let them slip.

Here is an allusion to the engraver's art, which by means of skilfully chasing out particles of the substance from itself, leaves a figure in the substance itself representing the idea or mind of the engraver. It is an art, as you may suppose, which is very difficult, and requires great skill and care, or a precious stone might soon be spoiled and rendered worthless. To engrave a jewel is to pierce and cut it with an instrument called a graver. The intelligence of the engraver, and his whole attention, must be absorbed in directing the point of the graver, in regulating the motion of the fingers, and the momentum of the arm in using the instrument. For the time being, until the graving is finished, and the stone is polished by the lapidary, the stone, to all common observers, appears marred and out of condition, but under a skilful workman, when completed, its beauty and its value are greatly enhanced.

Now, in applying the language of our text to the Lord Jesus Christ, it may be truly said how he was pierced and cut : " It pleased the Lord to bruise him ; he hath put him to grief. Surely he hath borne our griefs and carried our sorrows. He was wounded for our transgressions ; he was bruised for our iniquities. The chastisement of our peace was upon him, and with his stripes we are healed." But not only did God the Father bruise him and pound him as in a mortar, how he endured the contradiction of sinners against himself! What cruel mockings and opposition from the malicious Jews! What subtle and sore temptations from Satan, all combined to make his visage more marred than any man. We have seen faces marked with grief and sorrow. " Is it nothing to you, all ye that pass by ? Behold, and see if there be any sorrow like unto my sorrow, which is done unto me, wherewith the Lord has afflicted me in the day of his fierce anger."

But O ! what piercing and cutting was there in the Garden of Gethsemane, when the holy, suffering Lamb of God lay prostrate, weltering in his bloody sweat. It was the graving of a divine hand; it was an engraving which was to set forth the loving eye of God the Father, the loving eye of God the Son, and the loving eye of God the Holy Ghost, all engaged in equal acts of love, grace, goodness, and mercy to every chosen vessel of mercy. If we want to trace the deep lines cut in the Saviour's soul we must look back to the Psalms and to the prophets for the things which were written concerning him. Read the 22nd Psalm, and see how, under the title, the Hind of the Morning, the persecuted, the hunted hind, the soul of the stricken Redeemer is set forth.   Here you see the bursting of his heart: "My God, my God, why hast thou forsaken me ?   Why art thou so far from helping me, and from the words of my roaring ?"   It was the withdrawal of his Father's countenance, though not his heart.   It was the Father's displeasure against sin, and sin being embodied in the Person of his Son, though personally innocent, yet substitutionally it was necessary he should endure the whole of wrath divine. His soul was made an offering for sin.   It was necessary that he should suffer before he entered into his glory.   He suffered as the Head of his body, the church.   All this was the divine engraving of his heavenly Father.   It was the graving of his righteous displeasure against sin in the holy, immaculate human nature of his dear Son.   While it was the chasing out of sin's demerit, we see, at the same time, the deeply engraved lines,—the law is honoured, justice is satisfied, sinners are pardoned and righteously saved with an everlasting salvation.

Now an engraving when finished is an embellishment of the thing engraved, as in seals, plate, &c.; it intensifies the thing engraved, it increases its value; it is for use, ornament, admiration, and enjoyment; it is the means of its identification, the engraving bespeaks its own individuality.   So the work of Christ, it is honourable and glorious. The piercing and cutting, the graving of the divine hand has produced an engraving which will command the admiration and praise of angels and millions of the lost race of Adam through all eternity.   His glory is great in our salvation.   The captain of our salvation is made perfect through suffering.   It was his own saying: "And I, if I be lifted up, will draw all men unto me." The richest display of his graces, those seven spirits proceeding from the throne, the dominion he exercises in the world over all flesh, the prerogative of judging the world in righteousness, and the praises he will inhabit through eternal ages, all result from his sufferings: "We see Jesus, who was made a little lower than the angels for the suffering of his death," the graving of his Father, "crowned with glory and honour." We see in the seven eyes engraved in this ONE STONE the heart of God the Father beaming in the gift of the Person of his well-beloved, his only begotten and eternal Son. In his sufferings we see the accomplishment of the Father's eternal purpose and the display of his own glory. Did not our Lord when communing with the two disciples on their way to Emmaus seem to look back with complacency and approbation upon his recent sufferings, and he puts the question: "Ought not Christ to have suffered these things and to enter into his glory." He justifies the conduct of his Father in their appointment as worthy of the divine character. His words imply that his sufferings were the effect of design, a part of the whole counsel of God, or, to speak in unison with the similitude employed in our text, the sufferings of Christ were the engravings of the Father in the Person of his Son. He had a baptism to be baptized with, and he was straitened until it was accomplished. It was accomplished. It began at his birth, when no human accommodations could be afforded him, and though he grew in wisdom and stature, and in favour with God and man, yet for thirty years his character was concealed in a life of privacy and manual labour. At the moment of his entrance into the public ministration of his Father's business, the Spirit drove him into the wilderness to be tempted of the devil. Throughout the period that he was with his disciples, what contradictions of sinners he endured against himself. He hungered, he was athirst, he was weary. He was grieved; he sighed, he wept. His soul was filled with sorrow in Gethsemane. He agonised on the cross; his Father hid his face from him. He died broken-hearted. All these sufferings, toils, pains, sorrows, and death, were the divine gravings of his Father's hand.

The engraving of the seven eyes on this one Stone is now complete, it is perfect. Here we see the beauty of the engraving now it is finished.   The Stone itself is precious, but now with the engraved eyes, the result of the divine workmanship, we see reflected in the perfect manhood of Christ every attribute of the Godhead.   In each and every eye is seen the glory of God the Father in the Person of Jesus Christ his Son.   It is laid before the whole church of God.   It has become the wonder of angels, and is the everlasting praise of all his saints.   Because he hath poured out his soul unto death, therefore God hath highly exalted him, and given him a name above every name.   In Jesus is the representation of every member of his militant church.   In Jesus they possess Urim and Thummim; light and perfection they ever possess in him.   He is their oracle in every age, and in every clime.   "The eyes of the Lord run to and fro through all the earth to show himself strong in behalf of all them whose heart is perfect towards him."   We come before the Lord in secret at the throne of grace; it may be, we are troubled on every side, yet not distressed; we are perplexed, but not in despair; persecuted but not forsaken; cast down but not destroyed; and why is it?   Because we see in this glorious Stone is divinely engraved this heavenly truth, "In all our affliction he was afflicted."   We see in that wondrous Stone, eyes of mercy, grace, love, sympathy, compassion, Jesus the Son of God who is passed into the heavens, is touched with the feelings of our infirmities: " For in that he himself hath suffered being tempted, he is able to succour them that are tempted."   These are the truths which are seen embodied in the life and experience of our Lord and Saviour Jesus Christ as the result of his sufferings on this earth: "Who in the days of his flesh, when he had offered up prayers and supplications with strong crying and tears unto him that was able to save him from death, and was heard in that he feared; though he was a son, yet learned he obedience by the things which he suffered, and being made perfect, he became the author of eternal salvation unto all who obey him." (Heb. v. 7, 8, 9.)   He is the precious Stone in which are engraved the seven eyes by the graving of Jehovah, the Lord of hosts.

Believer in the Lord Jesus.   Here is, in this beautiful similitude, something adapted for your comfort as you pass through the toils of the wilderness.   Have you never found something analagous in your own experience, as is here set forth by the divine engraving ?   How often God has pierced you, and cut you to the very quick! How have you been perplexed and discouraged because of the way. What deep lines God seems to have been engraving in you; what chasing out of your very substance. What losses, what crosses, what defacings, what spoiling of all "pleasant pictures!" Yes, truly, it has been so indeed. Yet all the crushings, destructions, humblings, crumblings, and heartrending sorrows, by the heavenly engraver, what have they done? Have they not produced an engraving in your soul that represents the loving eye, and evinces the skilful hand of God your heavenly Father? I think you must admit it. So in the work of divine grace in the heart. It is God the Father that engraves every grace of his Spirit there; every truth we know, we learn by his engraving it in our own experience. He engraves on the heart the image of Christ. He commences his divine engraving in us by creating godly sorrow for sin; a godly sorrow for sin that shows the heavenly workman's hand, that needeth not to be repented of; the love of sin is chased out, and the love of God engraved by this heavenly engraver. This heavenly engraving is carried on until the image of Christ is completely formed "in you the hope of glory." But oh, what pungent grief of mind, what woundings of soul, what a chasing out of self; cut, cut, cut, the cutting process goes on. Self-love lies deep. All love of self must be chased out, so that Christ may be engraved our ALL IN ALL. Pride must be chased out. Secret pride requires deep cutting, and till it is completely hollowed out by the heavenly engraver, the graving of humbleness of soul cannot appear. Again, oh, what sad woundings of soul from our brethren, so that God may engrave "cease ye from man." You who have prayed that you might bear more of his gracious image, you little thought how much of your very substance had to be chased out—the hidings of his face, his reproofs, smitings of conscience—all these are strokes of the divine engraver; and whether your conflicts and trials be sharp or long, they are the work of his divine art. "Our light afflictions which are but for a moment, worketh out for us a far more exceeding and eternal weight of glory." "No affliction for the present is joyous, but grievous; but afterwards it yieldeth the peaceable fruits of righteousness to them who are exercised thereby." My hearers, do you think you can trace the engraving of a divine hand in your own experience?

Dear brethren, we are his workmanship. His work in us may be sharp and cutting, but it will not suffer loss. Our present loss will be our eternal gain. "All things work together for good to them who love God, and are the called according to his purpose." The piercing and cutting, be it ever so deep, is to make an impression that will last for ever. His work will stand the fiercest fire of trial; he will prove it to yourself of what sort it is, and it shall eternally command your adoring wonder, gratitude, and praise. It may be that God is cutting you deep—hollowing out your very substance by sharp, bitter, long affliction; but it is to produce in you the likeness of himself. Your earthly cares are his heavenly engravings. Remember, God engraves only precious stones. Believers are his jewels; they are the jewels of his crown; and it is to make them resplendent with his glory. But suppose we are reckoning his engravings as chastisements? Be it so. Even then they furnish us with an evidence of our divine sonship. Perhaps you are being cut so deep, and so long, that you imagine that your sufferings are the only evidence of your sonship. Well, ye have need of patience, your God will come with a recompense.

"From all your afflictions his glory shall spring,
The deeper your sorrow the louder you'll sing."

AMEN.

THE TRUTH AS IT IS IN JESUS.

A SERMON,

BY CHARLES GORDELIER.

PREACHED AT THE THIRD ANNIVERSARY OF HIS MINISTRY AT HEPH-
ZIBAH CHAPEL, DARLING PLACE, NEAR MILE END GATE,

On Lord's Day Evening, 25th March, 1866.

"As the truth is in Jesus."—EPHESIANS iv. 21.

THE words which I have read as a text, though dis-
membered from its connection, may with propriety be
considered as a complete sentence in itself. I call it
"a divine sentence in the lips of a king," (Prov. xvi. 10,)
commanding both our attention and admiration; for it
possesses a glory, excellency, and fulness which is singularly beautiful. It is an expression nowhere else found
in Scripture. It conveys to the mind of the spiritual
believer in Christ that which is understood of Truth in
its life, light, power, and unction; and it embraces all
that can be known as God's revealed truth, doctrinal, experimental, and practical. It is, as you know, a favourite
expression with me, and hence I have adopted it as a
title to the little volume of Sermons now in course of
publication.

I shall look upon the words of our text by way of a
rallying point, desiring, if possible, to bring around it
some of the main features of gospel truth by which true
religion is distinguished from the false, and which, by
the Lord's help and blessing, I have been enabled to set
before you during the three years of my ministry in this
place.

Under the teachings of the Spirit of Truth I shall endeavour to consider, in the *first* place, that the knowledge
of the truth is two-fold; for our text evidently implies as
much, there being a condition expressed, "if so be," &c.;

No. 24.   G so that there is a knowledge of the truth, but not as it is in Jesus. In the *second* place, consider some of the experimental and practical effects which the knowledge of the Truth as it is in Jesus has upon the believer in his life before God and man. Then, in the *third* place, make some brief observations upon the development, progress, characteristics, and the ultimate triumph of the Truth as it is in Jesus; concluding, by glancing at the state of being into which the righteous shall enter on the death of the body, and also, at the grand consummation of all things.

FIRST. I am to consider, that the knowledge of the Truth *is two-fold*.

Our text expresses a condition supposed; and it is not to be understood as if it were put for argument sake, but it is designed to awaken a serious inquiry in the mind. In the 3rd ch. 2nd verse, the apostle uses the particle *if* by way of affirming, not of doubting; and so here, it would signify *inasmuch* as ye have heard the Truth as it is in Jesus; for he had just affirmed his opinion of the Ephesian believers in relation to the immoral courses of other Gentiles, "that *they* had not so learned Christ." Now, in so grave a subject as the right knowledge of divine truth, it is better not to take for granted what the best of men may think of us, and so deceive ourselves, but to examine ourselves and know whether we be in the faith. It is essential in a matter so intimately associated with our peace and happiness in this life, that our hopes for eternal life should be rightly placed and firmly fixed. It is not sufficient that we possess a general acquaintance with the doctrinal truths of the Bible, it is not sufficient that our deportment in life be that which is unreprovable, but there must be a knowledge of the Truth as it is in Jesus. But I say again, there is a two-fold, or two kinds of knowing the truth. There is an outer circle, and there is an inner circle in which the truth is known. Jesus is the centre in whom all the lines of the entire circle of divine truth meet; from him they all radiate. He is the Truth. To know the Truth is to know Him, whom to know is life eternal.

The outer circle of divine truth is that which may be known by *the outward ear*—the outward ear through which faith comes. It is a hearing about Jesus. It is an outward knowledge, a verbal knowledge of the truth, a knowledge of the letter of Scripture. In itself it may be quite sound and correct, and so far it is so good, for it has its uses; but mark you, a mere verbal knowledge, a bare understanding of the truth is insufficient to indicate that we have been taught by him as the truth is *in* Jesus.

The inner circle of divine truth is that which is revealed to the soul by Jesus Christ himself; it is that which is known by the *inner man* of the heart; it is that which is received by a faith which has been wrought by the operation of God the Holy Ghost.

The one is a natural knowledge, the other is a spiritual knowledge. *Natural knowledge* is that which may be known by men in their natural state by their natural understanding, and yet may not be made wise unto salvation. To hear of Jesus, to hear about Jesus, is good in itself; but natural knowledge of itself will leave the soul as it found it, dead, destitute of spiritual life. *Spiritual knowledge* is that which is derived by the teachings of Christ himself; to be " taught by him;" it is knowing the truth as it is *in* him. Being an inner knowledge, it is an inward work altogether; it is the work of God's Spirit upon the spiritual mind; for he is the Spirit of Truth, and takes of the things of Christ that he may reveal them to the believer; hence, the believer possesses a knowledge of Christ after *the inward* man, for he is taught the Truth as it is *in* Jesus. The difference between the Truth as it is *in* Jesus, and the truth as it is *out* of Jesus, is this,—the one is eternal life to all who know it, the other is eternal damnation to all who do not know it. There is no middle way. These are solemn facts. O may God fasten his truth upon your consciences.

Let us look at this matter a little closer. Truth so momentous as this must be looked at full in the face. What is this knowledge of the truth *out* of Jesus? Whatever it is, it comes *short* of being the truth *in* Jesus. The apostle in his first epistle to the Corinthians, 13th ch. 2nd verse, speaks of the possibility of having *all* knowledge, understanding *all* mysteries, or having *all* faith so that one could remove mountains, yet without the principle of the love of God in the heart, a faith that worketh by love, it avails nothing; it comes short of the gospel standard—the Truth as it is in Jesus. However much there may be understood of the doctrines of divine grace, the doctrine of the sacred Trinity, the true doctrine of the Person, work, and character of the Redeemer himself, yea, even to admiration, yet if it be only a bare, naked, speculative notion, such an one is only deceiving himself and deceiving others. What does their knowledge amount to? Nothing at all; it has no influence on their hearts before God, nor yet in their lives before men, for they remain as worldly minded as ever, and their ungodly practices show their true character.

But supposing *all* the form of truth to be perfectly understood, and the exterior life conformable to it, yet it is still not the Truth as it is in Jesus if the heart is unrenewed and the judgment unconvinced that something more is wanting. How can there be any spiritual living on the truth if there be no life derived from Christ? The soul is dead to God. There is no spiritual or quickened mind. There is no communion with Christ; no realising its union with him. There are thousands of religious professors of this description to be found everywhere. They know the truth by the outward ear only; *in* their hearts it never had any place. What they know of the Scriptures may be the truth so far as the letter of it is concerned; but it is a form of godliness without the power, not the Truth as it is in Jesus.

Perhaps we have said enough for the present upon the negative part of our subject. I have tried to put it in a variety of forms, hoping to make an impression upon some who may be contenting themselves with a name to live while they are dead. It is an awful fact that though there is so much profession of religion, there is so little that is genuine, of the right kind. I feel very strongly upon this matter; having been for many years unavoidably thrown in amongst the superficial and nominal Christians of the day, I have had ample opportunities of witnessing that which I am protesting against. Nearly twenty years since, the Lord suffered me, in the pride and folly of my heart, to leave my spiritual home and beloved friends in the gospel, for the sake of finding, as I then thought, in an intellectual ministry more food for the soul; but it was the greatest mistake I ever made, for in doing so I wandered out of my place and out of the way of understanding; and the Lord punished me by permitting me to remain in the congregation of the dead for sixteen years; my soul was there as in a prison-house,

starved and famished; and until the Lord thrust me into
his service, I had no means of getting out any more than
I could get out of my own skin. But this I can testify,
" He brought me up out of the horrible pit, out of the miry
clay, and set my feet upon a rock and established my
goings." Praise to his great and ever blessed name for
his delivering hand. I am now convinced that the true
knowledge of Jesus Christ is a divine revelation, and not
a human acquisition.

But passing this by, let us consider *affirmatively* what
it is to know the Truth as it is in Jesus; and in order to
show the distinction and difference of the points referred
to, I will recite a few passages from God's own word. In
the beginning of the gospel being preached we find a
believing *on;* afterwards a believing *in.* I take the believing *on,* to be that which is believed by the outward
ear; the believing *in,* to be that which is received by the
inward ear. " Faith cometh by hearing, and hearing by
the word of God." The first passage I shall quote you
will find in John i. 12: " As many as received him, to
them gave he power to become the sons of God, even to
them that believe *on* his name." John vi. 29: " This
is the work of God, that ye believe *on* him whom he
hath sent." John ix. 35: " Dost thou believe *on* the
Son of God." Here is the line of the outer circle defined;
that of the inner circle thus, " If thou believest with *all
thy heart* thou mayest," Acts viii. 37. Romans x. 10:
" For *with the heart* man believeth unto righteousness;"
9th v.: " If thou shalt believe *in thine heart* thou shalt
be saved." " We are not of them who draw back unto
perdition, but of them who believe to the saving of the
soul," Hebrews x. 39. Gal. i. 16: " And called me by
his grace to reveal his Son *in* me." 2 Cor. iv. 6: " God
who commandeth the light to shine out of darkness hath
shined *in* our hearts." 1 Cor. ii. 14: " The natural man
receiveth not the things of the Spirit of God, neither can
he know them, because they are spiritually discerned."
James i. 21: " Receive with meekness the engrafted
word which is able to save your souls." 2 Tim. iii.
15: " Thou hast known the Holy Scriptures, which are
able to make you wise unto salvation, *through faith,*
which is in Christ Jesus." Nor must we pass by that
important declaration of our Lord to Peter, when he
confessed his divine Sonship, Matt. xvi. 17: " Blessed

art thou Simon Barjona, for flesh and blood hath not revealed this unto thee, but my Father which is in heaven."
There are also other passages to the same purpose, but these
may suffice; you see, at least I hope you do, there is a
two-fold knowledge of the truth; one is known by the
ear only, and the other is received in the heart by faith.

To know the Truth as it is in Jesus, is to know it by
a sweet experimental proof of the indwelling of Christ in
the believer and the believer in Christ; for he dwells in
the heart by faith. It is to know and to feel that in
Christ is *all* truth; that he is *the* truth; that there is no
truth apart from him. It is to have it demonstrated to
the heart and conscience by the testimony of the Spirit
of Truth. It is to know Christ really and truly. It is to
have an inward sense of his love. To know him inwardly
is to know him by his own teaching, to know him by his
Spirit's quickening and influencing the entire person.
His words are spirit and life: "The entrance of thy
words giveth life." The love of Christ is the constraining
power; for faith worketh by love. It is the realising of
the mutual union existing between Christ and his church.
It is to prove that he dwells in the affections; that his
graces are planted there, that he dwells in the heart by
faith, that it is Christ in us the hope of glory. "All
his people shall be taught of God, and great shall be their
peace." (Isa. liv. 13.) "The knowledge of the Truth as it
is in Jesus," says Mr. Eyles Pierce, "is a real spiritual
idea of Christ begotten in the soul by the Holy Ghost."
He teaches the soul to know Christ, and as Christ reveals
himself so he is known, believed, and loved. The believer
in Jesus knows his voice as his teacher, and he knows
nothing effectually but as he is taught by him.

To know the Truth as it is in Jesus, is to know the love
of Christ which passeth knowledge, it is to know its height,
its depth, its length and breadth, yet not to comprehend
it. It is to feel his love, to love him supremely, to know
him in his word, to know something of his work, his grace,
both in its fulness and in its power. It is to feel the
vitalizing power of his truth through every faculty of the
soul; it is to know it as it is in him, communicated from
him, communicated by him; the knowledge that Christ
imparts to his people is of the same kind as is in himself.
He has many things to say unto them and it is revealed
unto them as they are able to bear it; there is nothing

that Christ keeps back from them, either for their wisdom, knowledge, understanding, joy, or comfort.

The knowledge of the Truth as it is in Jesus consists in knowing, or receiving, the doctrines of the gospel, the truth as contained in the whole book of divine revelation; to have a sweet experimental proof in the heart and conscience of their life, light, and power by the teaching of the Spirit; it is to prove that Christ and the soul are one in the covenant bond of union ordered in all things and sure; to feel that he is united to him by a true and living faith; to feel that he knows and is sure that Jesus Christ is the Eternal Son of God; to feel that he died for him, that he is his Mediator, his Surety and Substitute, his Prophet, Priest, and King, a Friend that loveth at all times, and a Brother born for adversity.

Thus, my dear friends, I have attempted in various forms of expression to give you some idea what it is to know the Truth as it is in Jesus. It is a spiritual perception of God's Truth revealed to the heart and conscience of the renewed soul by the Holy Ghost. It is a spiritual receiving the truth; it is a spiritual understanding the truth; it is a spiritual growth in the truth, a growing in grace, and in the knowledge of the Lord Jesus Christ; such a knowledge of his Person, his work, and the offices he sustains to the church of God which each believer feels, more or less, is adapted to his own condition and experience. And before I close this part of the subject, let me ask you, what know you of these things? Of what kind is your knowledge of Jesus? the outer circle, or the inner circle? is it the letter of truth merely, or is it the grace of God in truth? Head knowledge without it in the heart will leave all your hopes and your profession in a mass of ruins.

> " No big words of ready talkers,
>   No dry doctrine will suffice ;
> Broken hearts and humble walkers,
>   These are dear in Jesus' eyes.

> " Tinkling sounds of disputation,
>   Naked knowledge all are vain ;
> Every soul that gains salvation
>   Must and shall be born again."

SECOND. I pass on now to consider *some of the experimental and practical effects* which the knowledge of the Truth as it is in Jesus, has upon the believer in his life before God and man. This is a very important branch of our subject. True religion consists of doctrine, experience, and practice. In doctrine, however, we may be deceived, for knowledge in itself, as we have already shown, though sound in itself, may fall *short* of the Truth as it is in Jesus. Nor is a correct deportment in life to be always taken as evidence of God's work in the heart; habitual respect for religion and morality may be fixed as the result of early religious training, a good education, or a superior position in life; but in having an experimental acquaint-ance with the Truth as it is in Jesus there can be no mis-take here. As the hearts of all men are fashioned alike, so it is found the work of divine grace is in all cases the same, in rich or poor, learned or illiterate. The test of real religion is experience. Not what we know in the head, not the purity of the life, but what is felt in the heart! a feeling religion, arising out of the life of God in the soul, for a religion without feeling is a false religion. Now if the root of the matter is in us, if we are trees of the Lord's right hand planting, the life will be manifested through the trunk, the branches, the leaves, and the fruit; and this, let me tell you, will be found in some such evi-dences as the following: "If so be that ye have heard of him, have been taught by him, as the truth is in Jesus."

1. *It has taught us to know, that we who were by nature born in sin, dead to God, have been quickened into a new life by the regenerating power of the Holy Ghost.*

The work of divine grace in the heart produces a great change in the person and character of the believer in Christ. He has become a new creature. He is hence-forth not of the world. Old things have passed away, and all things have become new. His affections are set upon things above, and not on things of the earth. The fear of God is planted in his heart; sin is hated and for-saken. The word of God, the house of God, the people of God, and the ordinances of the gospel have become the subjects of his happy choice; and he deems it his pri-vilege, his duty, and his interest to be found in the exer-cise and in the enjoyment of those gifts and graces of the Spirit with which he has been blessed:

> " Our quicken'd souls awake and rise,
> From the long sleep of death;
> On heavenly things we fix our eyes,
> And praise employs our breath."

2. *It has taught us to throw up all dependence on any*

works of our own, and to trust alone to the rigteousness and atonement of Christ for our only acceptance with God the Father.

Almost in every case, as soon as a sinner is convinced of his estate before God, his inquiry is what he is to do that he may be saved: " Wherewith shall I come before the Lord, and bow myself before the high God?" (Micah vi. 6.) Being ignorant of Christ's righteousness, we have attempted to bring something of our own; but after vainly striving, on the footing of our own performances, to obtain peace and pardon, and made fully sensible how utterly worthless are all human efforts to obtain merit and acceptance with God, and reduced almost to despair, the good Spirit of all truth leads us to Christ, and teaches us to see that by his perfect righteousness being imputed to all, and which is upon all who believe *in* Jesus, they are brought to acknowledge the worthlessness of all creature merits and doings:

" Stripped of all our fancied meetness
To approach the dread I AM,
We are led to see all fitness
Centring in the worthy Lamb."

Thus it is we are taught to know, by the obedience, sufferings, death, and the resurrection of the Lord Jesus Christ, we are freely justified from all things, from which we could not be justified by the law of Moses.

3. *It has taught us to know the blessedness of being made poor in spirit, and to sit an humble scholar on the lowest form in the school of Christ.*

Here it is we learn to know ourselves,—one of the les. sons of the utmost importance; for until we know ourselves as *sinful creatures*, and that in our flesh dwelleth no good thing, we are apt to be vainly puffed up in our fleshly mind. We are also taught to know our own *help-lessness;* made to feel that without Christ we can do nothing. Here it is, too, we are made sensible of our *igno-rance.* Oh this knowledge of our sinfulness, helplessness, and ignorance will make us humbled in our own sight; and we shall take the language of Elihu, " That which I see not, do thou teach me." (Job xxxiv. 32.) And this is the blessedness, God's people shall all be taught of the Lord; and " who teacheth like him?" He is our Teacher in all good things, he is a most pains-taking Teacher, for we are dull scholars; our hearts are hard, our ears heavy,

and often unwilling to receive his lessons; but if once
admitted into the school of Christ, we shall continue in it
until his work is finished; the blessedness will be that
"we shall know the truth, and the truth shall make us
free." Every truth shall be indelibly impressed in the
heart, and nothing shall ever efface it, either in time or in
eternity.

4. *It has taught us to know that in Christ alone is the
source, the fountain of all real joy and happiness.*

We are taught to know Christ as the way of life and
salvation, to trace the streams of our seeking him to the
source of God's eternal choice of our persons in him before
the foundation of the world. We are taught to know the
suitableness of his righteousness as being adapted to our
wants; the completeness of his atonement, its all-sufficiency to remove all our sins; for he is of God made unto
us wisdom, righteousness, sanctification, and redemption.
Whatever may be the soul's need it is supplied from his
fulness and grace to help in every time of need. Having
been taught our own nothingness, we see in the Person
and work of the Lord Jesus Christ every blessing we can
possibly need or desire, for they are all treasured up in
him; he is our all, our all in all. From him we derive
all our peace now and all our hopes of glory. In this
time state his presence cheers the darkest scene, helps us
along the rugged and steep ways in the wilderness; for
he is "our God and will be our guide even unto death."

5. *It has taught us to know that the believer whilst in
the world is saved from its pollution.*

The believer is passing through this world; though
conscious he is not of it, yet often feels he is defiled with
it. The manners and customs of the world are always
hurtful to believers. It is this that constrains us to fear
and say in the language of David, "I shall one day perish
by the hand of Saul;" this or that evil influence seems
too much for us; and were it not that we are taught to
look to the strong for strength, it would be so. Fear and
doubt rush upon the spiritual traveller in the wilderness and cause him to stumble; but under the teachings
of the Spirit, his prayer is, "Hold thou me up and I shall
be safe." Every spiritual traveller is assured of his present well-being and of his ultimate safety. As David was
assured of the kingdom, though often harassed in the
wilderness, so are believers now: "Sin shall not have

dominion over them." Our Lord makes his people conquerors over all their sins, corruptions, and lusts. Being
redeemed from the slavery of the world, redeemed from
the hand of him who is stronger than them, they are
taught to know and to feel that grace reigns through
righteousness. And whether it be sin in the world, or
the raging of indwelling sin, they shall overcome in the
Redeemer's strength, and shall come off more than conquerors through him that loved them.

6. *It has taught us to know that we are not our own,
we are bought with a price; and therefore we aim to glorify God in our body and in our spirit, which are the Lord's.*
We make no pretensions to sinless perfection in the
flesh; but our desire is this, that in simplicity and godly
sincerity, not with fleshly wisdom, but by the grace of
God, to have our conversation in the world as becometh
the gospel of Christ: "For the grace of God that bringeth
salvation hath appeared unto all men, teaching us that
denying ungodliness and worldly lusts, we should live
soberly, righteously, and godly in this present world;
looking for that blessed hope, and the glorious appearing
of the great God and our Saviour Jesus Christ, who gave
himself for us that he might redeem us from all iniquity,
and purify unto himself a peculiar people, zealous of good
works." We are not to be scared from the Truth as it is
in Jesus because the hollow professors of religion stigma-
tise us as Antinomians. Our answer is, a tree is known
by its fruit.

7. *It has taught us to know that nothing in time, nothing
in nature, above or beneath, can ever separate the soul from
the eternal and everlasting love of God which is in Christ
Jesus our Lord.*
Nothing can be more incompatible with the glorious
liberty of the sons of God than for a believer to be in
continual doubt and despondency as to his standing in
Christ; for God hath not given us the spirit of fear, but
of power, and of love, and of a sound mind. The Spirit
itself beareth witness with our spirits that we are the
children of God; and because we are sons, we may call
God our Father, and that too in the most endearing
sense. As, therefore, the kingdom of God in the heart of
the believer is righteousness, joy, and peace in the Holy
Ghost, this is what he is to aim at and pray for until he
shall have come to the full assurance of faith. Now if the

believer is under the teaching of the Spirit, to this measure
of understanding, he will, sooner or later, be ultimately
brought.   This assurance of the soul's final perseverance, the everlasting love of God, the eternal security and safety of God's chosen is the result of being
taught the Truth as it is in Jesus.   Mark ye, I do not
mean that the soul has *always a joyous, a rapturous sense
of it;* there is no real need for that, and God does not
often give it, but he does in every variety of form and expression assure us of his unchanging, eternal, immutable
love.   The high tone of assurance of God's unalterable
love which the apostle Paul was favoured with is certainly
not the lot of all the Lord's people to possess ; but nevertheless it is certainly their privilege, and all may covet it,
and pray for it.   It is the sun of our day, it is the lamp
of our night ; and when it is otherwise, we may say with
the poet,

> " Assure my conscience of her part,
>   In the Redeemer's blood,
>   And bear thy witness in my heart,
>   That I am born of God."

Believer in Jesus, keep this prayer in constant use
until the Lord shall be pleased to lead you on so that
you can adopt the apostle's exulting language : " For I am
persuaded, that neither death, nor life, nor angels, nor
principalities, nor powers, nor things present, nor things
to come, nor height, nor depth, nor any other creature,
shall be able to separate us from the love of God, which
is in Christ Jesus our Lord."

Such are some of the experimental and practical effects
of the knowledge of the Truth as it is in Jesus.   Time
forbids enlarging upon this point of our subject as I had
intended.   As a general remark it may be said, that if the
believer has been *taught* the Truth as it is in Jesus, he
has also been taught to *hold* the Truth as it is in Jesus.
These are times when truth must be outspoken and contended for.   The faith of God's elect in respect of the
true and proper Sonship of our Lord Jesus Christ is a
foundation truth which must be held *firmly* and contended for *earnestly*.   The sword of the Spirit must be
grasped with a tight hand, and decided strokes must be
dealt wheresoever needs be.   The contention is not so
much with the avowed enemies of truth as it is with its
professed friends.   Consequently, we must on principle,

and for the sake of consistency, refrain from associating or co-operating with those who *oppose* the doctrine of Christ's eternal Sonship. The professed friends of truth seem to say to us, " Let us build with you, for we seek your God as ye do ;" but our answer must be, " Ye have nothing to do *with us* to build a house unto our God."

Where there is an essential difference on so vital a point as the eternity of our Lord's Sonship, it is manifest believers cannot worship together in the unity of the Spirit in the bond of peace. Where there is no unity of belief there can be no community of feeling. On the points of difference I shall not now speak, as my views are before the public and are well known. Far be it from me to unchristianise any who differ from me in this matter ; but this I say, we, who hold the true and proper Sonship of Christ, must say to our opposers, " *we our- selves together* will build unto the Lord God of Israel." We have no party interest to serve ; but I would ask, how can those who believe that Jesus Christ the Son of God is co-essential and co-eternal with God the Father, have fellowship with those who believe his Sonship to be coeval only with his manhood? Neither can we have fellow- ship with those who believe that the human soul of Christ was pre-existent before time. We may by some be charged with bigotry in all this ; but no, we disclaim any such spirit. If we hold a principle, let us act on principle. Truth must be, and is, consistent with itself. To have fellow- ship with those who hold views essentially different from our own on the Person of the Son of God, would subject us to the imputation that we attached no value to the truths we assert, while in others it would only tend to confirm wavering minds in their unsettledness.

THIRD. I proceed now to the third subject proposed —the development, progress, characteristics, and triumphs of the Truth as it is in Jesus. My remarks must neces- sarily be very brief and of a very general character, when we consider that the period of time which we intend glancing at extends over, at least, seven thousand years.

My first observation is, that *the progress* of the Truth as it is in Jesus, from its first dawn upon this dark world of sin and error to the position and influence it now occu- pies in the present dispensation, has been marked with a *divine certainty* too plain to be ever gainsayed or resisted by its adversaries. And, let me say too, that its glorious

triumph in the millennium state until the grand and
final consummation of all things in this earthly state will
be no less certain; for not one jot or tittle of God's revealed will shall fail until all has been faithfully fulfilled.
From the inspired record we perceive the light of divine
truth in respect of the great doctrine of the atonement
of the Lord Jesus Christ for sin was a gradual development, by different methods, perfectly distinct and intelligible in each, yet shining more and more as each
dispensation advanced. First, it was intimated to man
immediately after the fall, the provision of mercy being
made known under the promise that the seed of the
woman should defeat the designs of the serpent, and that
thenceforth God would deal with man, not according to
the rigour of a broken law, but on terms of mercy. Then
this grace, after it had been made known to Adam and
his successors who lived before the flood, was again
further disclosed to Abraham as to the substitutionary sacrifice of Christ, and also the precise spot of ground on
which the great atonement should be accomplished. To
Abraham, God made a promise that from his descendants
should arise the Redeemer of mankind; and he also set
apart Abraham and his posterity as a race specially
favoured and separated to his service. Then, in the time
of Moses, there was still a further display of the truth,
and the Jewish nation became its depository throughout
that dispensation, and devout Jews and others were led
by the sacrifices and other types in their ritual service
under the teachings of the divine Spirit into a fuller view
of the mediatorial and priestly work of Christ and the mysteries of redemption. In the prophetical age, the prophets
taught the worthlessness of mere ceremonial worship which
had then grown up, and they also foretold the spiritual nature of Christ's work and character. Then, when Christ
became incarnate, John the Baptist prepared the Jewish
mind and others for receiving a more expansive view of
the atonement; and in pointing out to them the Person
of Jesus as the Lamb of God, he showed them the Light
which lighteth every man that cometh into the world.
To the Jews our Lord taught more fully the spiritual
nature of religion and also the freeness of the gospel. To
the Gentiles he taught the spiritual nature of God the
Creator of all things. To his disciples he taught the
germs of all truth belonging to his Person, work, and

character, and also their mission as his disciples. After his resurrection, his teaching was exclusively to them; he then further opened their minds, so that they not only understood the Scriptures respecting himself, but were led into deeper, brighter, and richer views of divine truth, as most plainly appears in the several epistles of the apostles.

The present dispensation, the age in which we live, commencing from the time of the apostles, I regard as the last and closing dispensation of Christianity. It is peculiarly the ministration of the Spirit in the revelation of the knowledge of Jesus Christ, and also in the manifestation of his spiritual presence to believers. I believe that gospel truth and grace are to be more and more unfolded to the view of a fallen world; that this is to be effected by all Scriptural means within the compass of sincere, devout, and holy men, both by personal and combined efforts, until the whole earth shall be full of the knowledge and glory of the Lord, when all shall know him, from the least unto the greatest; that is to say, all men shall be, more or less, under the influence of religious principles, though it may be, not all, universally, possessing a saving knowledge of the Truth as it is in Jesus. Reason and Scripture favour such a supposition; besides, the nature of Christian truth is such as would lead us to suppose that all men must bow to the sceptre of King Jesus and crown him Lord of all; to say nothing of the unconquerableness of the law of progress and the purpose of God as revealed in the prophecies of holy writ. Look at *the grand comprehensive principle* of Christianity! it is not to be found in any of the multiform religions of ancient or modern times. Other religions, in which is classed every form of idolatry and superstition, possess peculiarities adapted only either to the age, people, or clime where they were instituted, and are mostly perpetuated, not by the power of its own elements, but by the policies of those whose interest it was to sustain and protect it. Nations have perished and with them their religion; but Christianity has an element possessing the character of universal applicability and perpetuity, as well as of its capability of imparting the knowledge of the one true God and Jesus Christ whom he hath sent, conditions which none other ever yet possessed, not excepting even the Jewish; for Judaism, though established under the divine appointment, was nevertheless unfitted to become the

religion of the entire human family: it is one so exclusively national as to repel all attempts to its diffusion;
and though it has long ceased to be local, yet its exclu-
siveness remains. Neither do Brahminism, Bhudhism,
or Mahommedanism possess features in entire harmony
with man's nature and circumstances; for each of those
systems, extensively as they prevail, are encumbered with
special observances, and embrace tenets attached only to
certain places, and consequently fitted only for peculiar
nations. But the gospel of Jesus Christ, with a marked
contrast, is supremely adapted for every part of the habi-
table globe, for it corresponds to the universal and spiritual wants of fallen humanity; it is confined to no
places, is restricted by no circumstances, but is to be
preached to every creature. He that believeth and is
baptized shall be saved; but he that believeth not shall
be damned. Thus the purpose of God in accomplishing
the salvation of his elect from every people is made manifest through all time.

And let me observe, too, that the religion of Jesus
Christ is characterised by the integrity of its nature.
That which is of the flesh is flesh, and that which is of
the Spirit is spirit. This is plainly to be seen in the fact
that, though under whatever denomination, with whatever
form, and however long, the Christian religion may have
been identified with human creeds, ceremonies, customs,
and corruptions, it has nevertheless maintained an un-
compromising inflexibility. God's truth is like himself,
eternally the same. Whatever ceremonies or particular
creeds have been associated with it, belong not to its
nature, but to those accidental circumstances which have
happened to it in the history of man; these are those
outer things by which its spiritual nature has been too
often concealed and lost sight of. The externals of religious profession are not to be confounded with spiritual
truth. The principles of Christianity and the pretensions of
its professors have ever been dissimilar; for while the latter
have been moulded and formed according to the common
usages, absurdities, or superstition of the times, the former
have ever preserved their own distinctive individuality-spi-
rituality. Truth is eternally consistent with itself. As it
did not spring from man, neither will it own for its offspring the product of man. It was never a deposit committed to the care of either a Greek, a Romish, or an

Anglican hierarchy. National establishments, denominational distinctions, sectarian theology, form no part of true religion; they are rather its antagonists; for as soon as the exterior of religion obtains the predominance over the interior, its spirituality, its vitality departs; this is abundantly proved by history, observation, and experience. But nevertheless, despite all these things, it shall be found that God's truth is an everlasting kingdom, it shall never be destroyed. God has evidently destined that his truth alone shall be the great panacea for all the evils which afflict the soul of man; and though it has long been despised and restricted by those who plead for human inventions, it has hitherto maintained its integrity and its individuality throughout the fiercest opposition, has survived the ruin of empires, and will eventually overturn and annihilate every system that leads man to seek salvation upon a false basis.

As to *the millennium state*, the thousand years personal reign of Christ upon this earth, now the popular theme of the day, I confess, I am not inclined to the common opinion that it will be effected by his corporeal presence. I admit there are parts of Scripture which seem to look that way, but I feel I must hesitate in adopting a particular theory which apparently lacks a consistency with the general tenor of truth. It appears to me that the personal presence of Christ is unnecessary for the accomplishment of this great event. If the reign of Christ on this earth be personal, it must be local, which I regard as contradictory to his own word. My belief is, that the millennium state will be brought about by his spiritual presence only; that is to say, there will be, whenever this happy change shall take place, a greater demonstration of the spirit and power of the Lord Jesus Christ in the hearts of his people than has ever yet been known. Then God's ancient people, the Jews, and all the Gentile nations will be under the influence of the Truth as it is in Jesus. There is good reason to believe, that this universal sway of Christian truth and principles will continue uninterrupted for a thousand years, there being during that time a complete subjugation of all evil and error. Trade and commerce, the arts and sciences, will still be carried on, but all in the Spirit of Christ; selfishness and jealousy will be unknown. War, slavery, Popery, and every other form of priestcraft will be held in chains.

After the period of a thousand years, the powers of Satan will be again permitted for a little season, probably, as I think, at first through a gradual decay of spiritual religion and a relapse into ecclesiastical formalism and mere ceremony, when superstition, error, and bigotry will revive, and the saints of the most high God will be persecuted by the enemies of truth and vital godliness.   Then God will again marvellously vindicate his truth and the cause of his people once more and for ever, and will triumph most gloriously over all the powers of Satan. Every superstition, every error, and all evil shall be effectually destroyed from off the face of the earth, and for EVER. All this will be accomplished in the hearts and minds of men by and through the Word of God alone, the Sword of the Spirit, which, while it will enter the hearts of the King's enemies, will, nevertheless, be received with increased clearness and power to the fullest extent by those who obey the gospel, the grandeur and magnificence of which will be in its universality and the consummate completeness of the triumph of the Truth as it is in Jesus. Then will be the glorious period of the new Jerusalem and the new earth, wherein dwelleth righteousness, the holy city, whose inhabitants will be holy, those whose names are written in the Lamb's book of life. And when the appointed time shall come that God will judge the world, then there will be an assembly of all mankind before his bar.   To this end there will be a general resurrection of the body and a reunion of the spirit, each individual possessing its original consciousness and identity ; the mortal part will become immortal; the Son of God will descend with great power and glory, and every eye shall see him.   He will separate the righteous from the wicked ; these will be condemned and sent into *everlasting punishment*, but the righteous will be called into life eternal.   Immediately after the judgment, the final consummation and end of all earthly things will then take place ; this world and the works therein will be destroyed and burnt up.

As to *the state of being into which the righteous are called on the death of the body*, I can only say, that it is described as one of eternal blessedness, felicity, and security.   It consists in dwelling for ever in the presence of the great and glorious God, as seen embodied in the Person of the Lord Jesus Christ, in whose presence there is

fulness of joy, and from whom flows perpetual and uninterrupted bliss. In heaven, the employment of the blessed
will consist in praising the wonders of the Incarnate
Jehovah's redeeming love, praising his matchless and
adorable perfections, celebrating his glorious triumphs
over Satan, sin, death, hell, and the grave. The ransomed of the Lord will be in the enjoyment of full communion with the society of the blessed, especially of
those who were known to each other in Christ on
earth. In heaven they will be able to trace the lines
of wisdom, love, and mercy drawn straight through all
the crooked, the dark, uneven, painfully mysterious, and
shifting scenes of human life on earth; and in adoring
wonder, gratitude, and praise, their song will be, "Just
and true are all thy ways, thou King of saints." They
will enjoy perfect life, holiness, glory, and happiness, both
in body and soul; their bodies being immortal, possessing
a brightness inconceivable, like unto the glorious body of
Christ, they will see him with their bodily eyes; they
will enjoy perfect communion with him to the uttermost
perfection of all their desires and capabilities. The perpetuity of this bliss is eternally secured to all the saints
by Christ's own will and gift, over and above and beyond
and apart from his mediatorial work or his atonement;
the design of the Lord Jesus being, that they should behold the glory he possessed with his Father before the
creation of the world, and that they should be with him
in that primeval state, and be in possession of the same
felicity as himself: "Father, I will that they also, whom
thou hast given me, be with me where I am; that they
may behold my glory, which thou hast given me;" "the
glory which I had with thee before the world was." O
the love of Christ! it passeth knowledge. Having taken
his church into union with himself, the bride, the Lamb's
wife, she is to be made a participator of the glory of God's
eternal Son! We are lost in the contemplation of so
delightful a theme! We must die to know it.

Yet one thought more, and that is, as to *the grand
consummation of all things.* If I know anything of the
Truth as it is in Jesus by the teaching of his Spirit and
his word, I would say, that I believe that after the resurrection and the final judgment, and the earth that now is
being burnt up, then the grand consummation of all
things *in heaven* will take place. All the ends of Christ's

mediatorial work, for which it was designed, being accomplished; the ransomed church of God being all brought home to their heavenly inheritance, and their everlasting felicity secured according to the covenant of grace made in eternity; Satan's power and of every enemy to God and his church being completely and for ever destroyed, the Son of God will then surrender to his Father his mediatorial kingdom, and all judicial authority and power, that God may be ALL in ALL. The glory of Jehovah, in his trinity of Persons, Father, Son, and Spirit, will then be displayed in all its inconceivable magnificence, shining forth in all its fulness of majesty, grandeur, and brightness throughout the countless ages of eternity. God the Father will then be seen, known, loved, and enjoyed by each and every individual member of the church of God, without the intervention of the mediatorial office. God the Son, in his glorified and eternal manhood, will be seen in his primeval glory, the glory which he had before the world was. His Person, work, and character will then be seen and known in its fullest perfection, and will be the subject of everlasting adoration, gratitude, and praise of all the redeemed family of God; while the whole universe of heavenly intelligences, angels, and spirits of just men made perfect will be everlastingly kept in their purity, uprightness, and bliss by the supercreative power of God the Holy Ghost. Even so; come, Lord Jesus. Amen.

Now may the grace of the Lord Jesus Christ, the love of God our heavenly Father, and the witness of the Holy Spirit that we are the children of God by faith in Christ Jesus rest upon our hearts and consciences from this time and evermore. Amen.

GRACE TRIUMPHANT.

A NARRATIVE

OF A

REMARKABLE AND TIMELY VISIT
BY CHARLES GORDELIER

TO AN

ELDERLY FEMALE

IN A STATE OF DEEP DESPAIR AND NEAR DEATH.

SOME years ago, while walking near the London Hospital, I was met by a dear Christian brother, now deceased, who asked me to visit a poor woman for him, who was on Little Alie Street Sick Fund, as she lived near to me, and he was suffering from sciatica,—urging principally that she was in that state of mind approaching madness, or, at least, fixed melancholy, or despair; and that she obstinately refused to hear a religious word from any one— would not allow the Bible to be read, but set up yelling and screaming; and, therefore, not being permitted to speak to her, or to read the word of God, he did not wish merely to carry the money. I consented, and went, not without earnest prayer for help; for indeed I felt deeply my insufficiency, and had not long, myself, been brought out of deep exercise of soul before God.

Her name was Munro; she was a widow, and lived in the Globe Road, Mile End, close by the railway arch. Passing through a passage under the house, and proceeding up the stairs, outside at the back, I knocked at the door, when two women came, and, ascertaining the nature of my call, forbade my seeing her; but they offered to take the money, which I declined to give, unless I could see the woman myself, personally. Their objection was, that if any one spoke to her on religion, it would send her raving mad. After some entreaty, I promised, that *unless she spoke to me I would say nothing.* On that condition, they opened the door, and I entered.

4th Edition, Revised.

The room merely contained two old chairs, a table, a chest of drawers, and a stump bedstead, on which lay a tall, large-framed Scotch woman, her feet overhanging the bedstead; she was lying on her right side, with her left arm on her side outside the bed, with her face towards the door; her eyes seemed to dart red flaming glances at me, her countenance was the expression of malice, the horrid glare of which induced me to take my seat on the other side, at her back. I took hold of her cold hand, held it for some time in mine. I did not speak, nor did she, but she groaned heavily and frequently; the language of which, however, was perfectly intelligible to me, and I could not refrain myself from echoing her groans by deep-fetched sighs. At length she broke silence; she turned her face, and fixing a piercing look at me, said in a slow, demanding, unearthly, and surly tone of voice, "What have you to say to me?"

Gently pressing her hand, and looking kindly at her, I replied, " Hope in God."

Instantly she snatched away her hand, sprang up, and became shockingly frantic, exclaiming most furiously, "THERE'S NO HOPE FOR ME! THERE'S NO HOPE FOR ME!"

She continued this for a long while, alternately shrieking, screaming, raving, and shouting, " There's no hope for me!" gnashing her teeth, and making a harsh, gutteral noise, expressive of rage; she flung her arms about with such force that neither myself nor the two women were able to keep her in the bed. This dreadful scene lasted nearly half an hour, till at length she became exhausted. We then succeeded in placing her down in the bed, and put the clothes straight. The women begged me to leave her, for, said they, "You have done more harm than good. We told you what it would come to." I replied, I could by no means leave her yet, and so I resumed my seat.

There I sat, and there she lay, on her right side as before, her face away from me; she groaned most hidiously, now and then giving me furtive glances. At length, finding I was immovable, she turned her face, and in the same gruff, surly voice, said, " You cruel man to come here and disturb me like this; my soul is in hell."

I answered, " Poor soul! I have been where you are!"

Raising her head, and looking at me with scornful steadfastness, she said, in the same surly tone as before,

"You have been where I am? How dare you say that?"

"Ah!" I said, "I have indeed! and so has David, and so has Peter, and so has the Lord Jesus Christ!"

On hearing this, she seemed to be going off into another paroxysm as before, but in the tone of grief and distress, crying, "Oh! oh! what blasphemy! Oh! what blasphemy! do pray go away; oh! what blasphemy, to say that Jesus Christ has been where I am! Jesus Christ never sinned, he never was where I am. Oh do pray go away; I cannot bear this!"

I succeeded in pacifying her a little, and assured her if she would listen to me I would explain what I meant. She replied, it was no use my talking to her, her soul was in hell, though her body was on the bed, and that she was at that moment suffering all the torment that could be felt by damned spirits.

"Soon," she continued, "my body will die, my breath will return to God who gave it, and my body be laid in the earth."

I said, "I know all you feel; I know where you are."

"Ah!" she replied, "you may know where I am, but you cannot know what I feel."

"Yes," said I, "I do."

"What!" she exclaimed, with an indignant and scornful look, "You know what I feel?—impossible! My soul, I tell you, is in hell; I have trampled under foot the blood of Christ,"—"and," said I "counted it an unholy thing?"

This was too much for her; she responded by an involuntary roar of grief and a flood of tears; again she urged me to leave her, saying "Go away, go away. · It is no use you talking to me; my soul is in hell. You have never been there; you are here; your soul is in your body, mine is not, that is in hell, though I am talking to you. It is no more use you trying to comfort any one in a place of torment, than the tip of one's finger dipped in water would quench the fire of hell. I have committed the unpardonable sin; I have trampled upon the blood of Christ; and then with a wild shriek she kept repeating, "THERE'S NO HOPE FOR ME,—THERE'S NO HOPE FOR ME."

I endeavoured to assure her there was hope for her; she had not trampled upon the blood of Christ as she supposed; for, that I could see her feeling was still tender on that point.

"Sir," said she, "I have sinned, and sinned, and sinned again."

I said, "So did David, Peter, and so have others; they did not lose their hope."

"No," she replied, "they never lost their hope; they sinned, they repented, and were saved. But I have sinned; I have never repented; I cannot repent; I wish I could repent; it is too late," and, shrieking out in wild agony, "I have trampled upon the blood of Christ. I tell you again there. is no hope for me; my soul is in hell, and I am there for a never-ending eternity;" and with a piercing yell, again she uttered, "There's no hope for me—there's no hope for me!"

At this sad and hopeless speech, I felt on the point of yielding the contest; but, raising myself, looking firmly at her, lifting up my hand, and, in an emphatic tone, I said, "My good woman; I know you feel as if you were in hell; I know you feel all the agonies of remorse; I know you feel that self-reproach has broken your heart, but it IS NOT YOUR SOUL THAT IS IN HELL—IT IS HELL THAT IS IN YOUR SOUL!" At that moment it was as if a veil had fallen from her face; light had broken in, the cloud was gone; her countenance immediately changed; its blackness went off, and her face radiated with surprise and attention. I saw what was done, and what was going on; HOPE had sprung in and brought relief to her fainting soul. I then began to talk to her of Christ's sufferings and griefs as borne for us. I recited several passages out of the Messianic Psalms, especially the 22nd and 69th; and also attempted to show how his sufferings qualified him for sympathising with the believer when under grief and self-reproach for sin; and that the believer did really find that it was Christ's sympathy which restored the fainting soul, and brought it back to God; that it was under such extreme distress of soul and sorrow for sin that Christ's sympathy was so especially needed and imparted. No human sympathy alone was sufficient; it must be divinely communicated, it must be by the Holy Spirit. Pointed to the experience of David, Peter, herself, and referred to my own; that it was all of the same kind, though different in degree, according to circumstances. To all this discourse she patiently listened with interest, and calmly argued the question of there being "no hope for her;" spoke of her long-continued course of backsliding and neglect of the worship of God, and which had originated in neglect of secret prayer, and in breaking the Sabbath day, by keeping open her shop on that day, and seeking out-door pleasure. She had been a member of an Independent congregation in the East of London. I exhorted and encouraged her to hope, appealing to David's own case; as in the 42nd Psalm; after which, I prayed with her, and bade her adieu. She entreated me to come again, which I promised to do. The two women who were there, expressed their astonishment, and thought the change most wonderful. Truly it was, but it was the most dreadful sight I ever saw; such a sight as I would rather not see again.

The following week I renewed my visit, and found her evidently in her right mind. She had been peaceful ever since; but she was weaker in body and evidently fast sinking. How differently was I received this time! Her eyes gleamed with delight on seeing me enter. I took my former seat; she turned herself towards me. She could scarcely speak, but pointed to the place where the Bible was laid. I understood her meaning, and read a portion of the 40th Psalm. I found her resting on Jesus, trusting to his blood as her only hope; and again in prayer I commended her to God and to the word of his grace. She pressed my hand very fervently, and blessed God for sending me as the means of bringing her out of the horrible pit, and setting her feet on a Rock.

I went again, but I found my work was done; for I was informed she had died, and died happily; and that even in her coffin she seemed to have a smile; so that it appeared while she was crossing the Jordan, " the enemy was still as a stone," and she, literally, as Dr. Watts expresses it,

> " —— with a smile upon her cheek,
> Passed the important hour of death!"

This incident in my visits among the sick is related without comment, dress, or finish; let the fact speak for itself. First, to the praise and glory of Jehovah Jesus, who never forsakes his people, though they forsake him. He will search and seek them out in the cloudy and dark day of unbelief, guilt, and despair; he will bring them back with weeping and supplication; and, it may be, with broken bones. The covenant of grace shall not be dishonoured and broken by the wilfulness and departure of any of the members of Christ's mystical body.

Again, how this fact speaks to *the wanderer*. You who have tasted that the Lord is gracious, look at this poor woman's case; look at it as a looking-glass in which you may see your own. You have left your first love, you have left your Father's house; where are you now? You know not to what a dread precipice you are hastening. When you leave the closet of communion with God, you enter upon a down-hill path; the further you proceed the faster will be your steps, and nothing but mercy can stop you! You may soon reach the place where this poor woman was found! O beware of neglecting the throne of grace in secret, and of grieving the Holy Spirit by the commission or indulgence of any wrong habits of thought, feeling, or action.

Finally, let this fact encourage *visitors of the sick,* and all who are desirous of serving God in his people. It may be that you have been brought into circumstances of deep trial and bitter experience. Many of the Lord's people are called to endure a hard fight of affliction of every shape and name, for the sake of others, as was the prophet Ezekiel; (xxiv. 15, 18;) or the apostle Paul; (2 Cor. i. 6;) but out of them all the Lord will not only deliver his tried ones, but he will make use of them as instruments to be of great use to others who may be brought into the like. These trials of your faith, your hope, and your patience, may be hard to bear, but they are good to bear, notwithstanding; this you will eventually prove, and you will find that this is the method the Lord is taking to answer your prayer for usefulness.

I trust that as the reading of this narrative has been made, under the Lord's blessing, exceedingly useful to several other persons who were in a similar state of mind as this poor woman, that this reprint may also, in the leadings of Providence, find its way to some others who are broken-hearted—God's broken-hearted ones, such whom God alone knows where to find and how to touch. For myself, I can say, if I were never to hear of any other case of God's blessing my feeble efforts in his cause, this testimony to the power of his grace will be a crown of abundant honour to the latest hour I live. May we not say, "Is not this a brand plucked out of the fire?"

A. GADSBY, STEAM MACHINE PRINTER, 10, CRANE COURT, FLEET ST.

BY THE SAME AUTHOR.

THE HEAVENLY STATE AND THE EVERLASTING HAPPINESS OF THE RIGHTEOUS.
THE ANGELS OF GOD, THEIR NATURE, ORDERS, AND MINISTRATION TO THE CHURCH ON EARTH.

Two Discourses, 8vo, 32 pp., stitched in a neat printed cover, price 4d. ; post free, 5d.

" We have *never* read anything *better* on these subjects, and *seldom* anything so good."—*Gilead.*

" Discourses full of Scripture truth, forcibly presented and adapted to general edification."—*Baptist Messenger.*

THE GREAT PLAGUE OF THE HEART.

The substance of Two Discourses, 8vo, price 2d; three copies post free.

SELECTIONS FROM " THE TRUTH AS IT IS IN JESUS."

Twelve Sermons, being Nos. 5 to 16, consecutively, price 2s. cloth. Also Parts, Nos. 2, 3, containing Four Sermons each, and No. 4, Three Sermons on " The Unsearchable Riches of Christ," may be had, 6d. each ; post free, 7d.

" Inasmuch as there is a time coming—yea, is even now come—when the Lord is fulfilling his word, ' I will send them famine, not a famine of bread or thirst for water, but of hearing the word of the Lord,' sermons by men of truth and deep experience, having Christ for their object and subject, will be increasingly estimated by the people of God. We commend these sermons to the attention of our readers."—*Gospel Magazine.*

" I have read your sermons with the greatest pleasure. I find them very precious. It is rare to find thoughts so deep and clear combined with such liveliness and unction."—*The Rev. P. Maclaren, of Brighton, to the Author.*

Sermon 13.
THE ETERNAL SONSHIP OF JESUS CHRIST ASSERTED AND DEFENDED.

Third Edition, price 3d. ; two copies, post free.

Sermon 24.
THE TRUTH AS IT IS IN JESUS.

Second Edition, price 2d. ; three copies, post free.

GRACE TRIUMPHANT.

Fifth Edition, price 1d. ; eight copies sent post free.

LONDON:
J. GADSBY, GEORGE YARD, BOUVERIE STREET, E.C.
And may be had of the Author, 13, Stepney Green, E.

www.ingramcontent.com/pod-product-compliance
Lightning Source LLC
Chambersburg PA
CBHW030821110726
47900CB00006B/1691